THE DYNAMICS OF
INFIDELITY

THE DYNAMICS OF INFIDELITY

Applying Relationship Science to Psychotherapy Practice

Lawrence Josephs

American Psychological Association • Washington, DC

Published by
American Psychological Association
750 First Street, NE
Washington, DC 20002
www.apa.org

To order
APA Order Department
P.O. Box 92984
Washington, DC 20090-2984
Tel: (800) 374-2721; Direct: (202) 336-5510
Fax: (202) 336-5502; TDD/TTY: (202) 336-6123
Online: www.apa.org/pubs/books
E-mail: order@apa.org

In the U.K., Europe, Africa, and the Middle East, copies may be ordered from
American Psychological Association
3 Henrietta Street
Covent Garden, London
WC2E 8LU England

Typeset in Goudy by Circle Graphics, Inc., Columbia, MD

Printer: Bang Printing, Brainerd, MN
Cover Designer: Nicci Falcone, Gaithersburg, MD

Library of Congress Cataloging-in-Publication Data

Names: Josephs, Lawrence, author.
Title: The dynamics of infidelity : applying relationship science to psychotherapy practice / Lawrence Josephs.
Description: Washington, DC : American Psychological Association, [2018] | Includes bibliographical references and index.
Identifiers: LCCN 2017009999 | ISBN 9781433827983 | ISBN 1433827980
Subjects: LCSH: Sex (Psychology) | Adultery—Psychological aspects. | Interpersonal relations. | Psychotherapy. | Couples therapy.
Classification: LCC BF692 .J67 2018 | DDC 158.2—dc23 LC record available at https://lccn.loc.gov/2017009999

British Library Cataloguing-in-Publication Data
A CIP record is available from the British Library.

Printed in the United States of America
First Edition

http://dx.doi.org/10.1037/0000053-000

In memory of Annette and Mike Josephs

CONTENTS

PREFACE

Psychotherapists who treat patients grappling with conflicts around infidelity are the audience for this book. This means virtually all psychotherapists because infidelity is not just an issue for couples therapists. Unfaithful partners whose affairs have yet to be detected often seek individual treatment to decide whether to end the affair, end the marriage, or learn how to better manage the dread of exposure until they decide. Betrayed partners may seek individual treatment when they have sneaking suspicions that their partners are being unfaithful but lying about it. Once their suspicions have been confirmed, they may then seek help to decide whether it's worth trying to save the marriage. Affair partners who are trying to decide whether to end an affair with a married person who is reluctant to leave his or her spouse may seek individual treatment. And affair partners may suffer heartbreak when their unfaithful partners break up with them in favor of recommitting to the betrayed partner.

This book provides an up-to-date review of the psychology of infidelity from the perspective of *relationship science*—research by social, personality, and evolutionary psychologists on the psychology of intimate relationships. It also provides an integrative treatment approach that, although grounded in basic psychodynamic principles, uses treatment techniques from mentalization-based therapy, transference-focused therapy, emotion-focused therapy, marital communication skills training, and mindfulness/acceptance. My aim is to promote empathy and understanding for all points of view in a love triangle so that all players can be treated with compassion and respect as well as helped to assume responsibility for their role in the unfolding drama despite their defensiveness.

I have come to appreciate that having a husband who has tried to become an expert on the psychology of infidelity puts the wife of such an expert in an awkward position: What's it like to be married to a husband who is an expert on infidelity? As a consequence, I owe my wife, Dr. Laura Josephs, a special debt of gratitude on multiple fronts: for graciously being the wife of an infidelity expert, for our marriage of more than 30 years, and for doing more than her fair share of the heavy lifting raising our three boys for all those years in which I was acquiring the knowledge to eventually be able to write a book on the psychology of infidelity. I also want to thank my three sons—Aaron, Matthew, and Sam—who have generously tolerated growing up with a father intellectually absorbed in the process of becoming an expert on infidelity. Now that they are young adults, each successful in his own right, I am happy to see that lessons I've learned about accepting people for who they are have paid off handsomely.

This book is about infidelity, but it is also very much about building bridges. It is about building bridges between clinicians who treat relational problems and researchers who examine such problems through more systematic empirical research. It is also about building bridges between more psychodynamic and more cognitive behavioral approaches to treating relational problems. To that end, I must thank Jacques Barber, the dean of the Derner Institute of Advanced Psychological Studies at Adelphi University, and Christopher Muran, the director of clinical training at Derner, for creating an atmosphere that supports these sorts of integrative efforts. I also thank George Stricker, a former dean of the Derner Institute, who originally hired me and is one of the founding fathers of the movement for the integration of psychotherapy.

Special thanks are in order for Dr. Orshi Hunyady, an experimental social psychologist who subsequently trained as a clinical psychologist; Dr. Hunyady first enabled me to see how bridges could be built between disciplines as disparate as Freudian psychoanalysis and the experimental social psychology of adult romantic relationships. Dr. Hunyady and her husband, Dr. John Jost, a professor of social psychology at New York University, coauthored my initial foray into bridge building when we published a paper together on using the experimental technique of mind-set priming to test an esoteric Freudian hypothesis about the oedipal conflict.

I also thank the students in my research workgroup who have been sounding boards for many of the ideas discussed in this book: Nina Katzander,

Jessica Shimberg, Annette Attolini-Fertuck, Kirby Weinberg, Laura Tittel, Olivia Medvedov, Aleksandra Goncharova, Jett Stone, Remi Coker, Taylor Liberta, Ben Warach, Patrick Mele, and Sara Shapiro-Halberstam. All have been conducting interesting relationships research that they will apply to clinical practice. I thank Derner colleagues Robert Bornstein, Joel Weinberger, Kate Szymanski, and Joy McClure for being good sounding boards, coauthors for integrative efforts, and good friends over years if not decades.

Finally, I must express a special debt of gratitude to my patients who have shared their personal struggles with infidelity as unfaithful partners, betrayed partners, affair partners, and children of parents who struggled with exposed infidelity. Hearing their stories over the decades has provided the clinical experience that has enabled me to learn more about infidelity than I could ever learn from simply reading the research literature on the topic. To share their stories, I provide numerous clinical illustrations in this book. To protect patients' confidentiality, those case examples are composite portraits drawn from multiple patients.

THE DYNAMICS OF INFIDELITY

INTRODUCTION

My first patient, whom I met in postdoctoral psychoanalytic training more than 30 years ago, was a single woman in her early 30s. She was conflicted about an affair she was having with a married man, with whom she was deeply in love. He had promised to leave his wife for her but just never got around to it. She couldn't decide whether to break up with him. In the years since then, I have worked with many married men and women living secret double lives for years or even decades, existing in a state of perpetual ambivalence about how to resolve the apparently permanent love triangles in which they find themselves. Some of these married men regularly have casual sex with work colleagues or sex workers but then are pressured to relinquish their preferred sexual outlet when their wives discover their extensive extramarital sex life. I've worked with many patients individually and in couples therapy trying to recover from the traumatic aftermath of exposed extramarital affairs. Perhaps surprisingly, many patients are those who were aware of their parents' extramarital affairs during their childhoods and are still troubled by it.

http://dx.doi.org/10.1037/0000053-001
The Dynamics of Infidelity: Applying Relationship Science to Psychotherapy Practice, by L. Josephs

This introduction provides an overview of the book so the reader will know in advance how all the pieces of the puzzle will be put together. Each chapter is a piece of the puzzle that looks at infidelity from a particular vantage point. The introduction provides the "big picture" so that the reader will foresee a glimpse of the destination.

A CLINICIAN'S PERSONAL JOURNEY INTO RELATIONSHIP SCIENCE

My psychoanalytic training offered little practical guidance about how to deal with the dynamics of infidelity. Freud (1910/1957b, 1922/1955, 1924/1961) had hypothesized that adult romantic love triangles are ubiquitous because childhood oedipal conflicts are ubiquitous. Per Freud, young children universally wish to have sex with the opposite-sex parent and kill off the same-sex rival parent during early childhood. Resolution of one's childhood oedipal conflict allows one to reconcile with monogamy, whereas irresolution of that conflict leads one to become embroiled in endless complicated love triangles as an adult. Right or wrong, Freud's formulation of the dynamics of infidelity didn't provide me with much practical assistance in dealing with my patients (see Josephs, 2015b, for a review of the empirical status of certain aspects of Freud's oedipal theory).

Meanwhile, my patients wanted to better understand their current predicament and receive some practical advice about what to do. I couldn't very well say that their love triangles would finally be resolved in a constructive way if we work through their underlying oedipal conflicts after years of psychoanalysis. For most patients, a constructive resolution means finding a way to have a stable long-term intimate relationship without deceit. Often that means making a sexually exclusive relationship work. Sometimes it means exploring other deceit-free options, such as open marriage or polyamory, to which sexual minorities may be more open.

I started reading the psychology literature to see what insight it might provide into the topic of infidelity. I discovered that there is a significant marital therapy literature for how couples can recover from infidelity that offers sound advice for couples therapists willing to take on this daunting clinical challenge (Baucom, Snyder, & Gordon, 2009; J. S. Gottman, 2004; Johnson, 2004; Weeks, Gambescia, & Jenkins, 2003). Yet this literature was of little help to my single patients who were romantically involved with married partners or for my married patients who were having affairs and didn't want to go for couples therapy or were already in couples therapy but still concealing their affairs. I also found that this literature did not have that much to say about the personality dynamics that determine why some individuals have affairs and some do not when grappling with similar marital stresses. The couples therapy literature doesn't like to implicitly blame individuals by highlighting the personality characteristics that make some individuals more prone to infidelity or more vulnerable to sexual betrayal. The systems emphasis on the couple or the family as the unit of analysis tends to overlook or downplay the individual personality dynamics of the perpetrators and victims of infidelity.

I discovered that evolutionary psychologists were very interested in the topic of infidelity because they are interested in understanding the sexual strategies that lead to reproductive success. From an evolutionary viewpoint, infidelity might be an adaptive, although socially unacceptable, reproductive strategy if it results in a reproductive advantage (Buss & Schmitt, 1993). Evolutionary psychology was illuminating as to why prevalence rates of infidelity are so high cross-culturally, yet humans also appear to have evolved to engage in romantic pair bonding for biparental care. Evolutionary psychology clarifies that both infidelity and monogamy have biological bases: Evolutionary psychologists believe that humans have evolved to be "strategic pluralists" (Buss & Schmitt, 1993) who can deploy various reproductive strategies as adaptations to different ecological conditions.

Contemporary evolutionary psychology argues that it is a false dichotomy to assume that either monogamy or promiscuity is "natural" while the other is "cultural." Both are natural, and both are responsive to current cultural conditions. Gangestad, Haselton, and Buss (2006) noted that cultural variation can be evoked by underlying ecological variables such as pathogen load, resource scarcity, or sex ratio. Cultural responses to those ecological conditions may then change the underlying ecology, as when human responses to resource scarcity creates environmental pollution or the extinction of other species. Restrictive sexual moralities may be evoked by increasing prevalence rates of sexually transmitted diseases (STDs), but then the decrease in STDs achieved by those restrictions may evoke more permissive sexual moralities as sex becomes safer (i.e., evoked culture). Ecology evokes culture, while culture creates ecologies.

For clinicians, however, many of the insights of evolutionary psychology were of limited practical application because evolutionary psychologists often focus on proving universal and innate gender differences in adult romantic behavior. Biologically based and universal sex differences are not always relevant, for instance, when working with unique individuals who often do not conform to the statistical norms for their gender. Such individuals usually need help relieving their shame sensitivity for their gender nonconformity.

Only recently has evolutionary psychology begun to explore the personality subtypes of men and women that begin to explain why particular individuals are more predisposed toward infidelity than others. The evolutionary psychology of individual differences (Buss & Hawley, 2011) does begin to illuminate the psychology of the unique individual with which clinicians must contend in daily practice. Particularly intriguing was new research on the Dark Triad of narcissism, Machiavellian intelligence, and psychopathy that is associated with an opportunistic and exploitative approach to adult romantic relationships (Jonason & Kavanagh, 2010).

FROM RELATIONSHIP SCIENCE TO EVIDENCE-BASED TREATMENT

The research I found had the most direct clinical applicability to infidelity was research on adult attachment styles as it related to styles of marital communication (Anders & Tucker, 2000; Domingue & Mollen, 2009; Feeney, 1994). It emerged that securely attached individuals have more constructive styles of marital communication and are less likely to be unfaithful. In contrast, insecurely attached individuals possess less constructive styles of marital communication and are more likely to engage in infidelity. New research also linked insecure attachment style to impaired reflective functioning, a limited ability to reflect on one's own and others' mental states (Fonagy, Gergely, Jurist, & Target, 2002). Insecurely attached individuals have a limited ability to understand their partners' mental states and therefore engage in styles of marital communication that exacerbate marital conflict and insecure attachment (Overall, Simpson, & Struthers, 2013). Those marriages are at greater risk for marital infidelity.

Treating infidelity might therefore mean facilitating secure attachment in ways recommended by Johnson (2004) in *The Practice of Emotionally Focused Couples Therapy* and increasing reflective functioning in ways recommended by Bateman and Fonagy (2004) in their work on mentalization-based treatment. A link can then be made between infidelity as a symptom of insecure attachment and low reflective functioning and evidence-based treatments for increasing attachment security and reflective functioning.

The emphasis in clinical psychology these days is on evidence-based treatment for specific disorders like depression and anxiety. This psychotherapy research literature is of limited usefulness for practitioners looking to help patients seeking assistance with their conflicts around fidelity and infidelity in their most intimate relationships. Patients are often depressed, anxious, and angry for specific, rather than generic, reasons. Psychotherapy treatment manuals do not provide the specialized understanding necessary to treat patients who are depressed, anxious, and angry because of their conflicts around fidelity and infidelity. The betrayal trauma (Lusterman, 2011) that betrayed partners suffer might not be amenable to an exposure therapy for posttraumatic stress disorder (PTSD) in which they imagine their partner having sex with a romantic rival until their hurt, humiliation, jealousy, and rage are extinguished. That kind of exposure might be retraumatizing: Recovery from infidelity appears to be better facilitated when the betrayed partner is spared the graphic details of the unfaithful partner's extramarital sex life (Baucom et al., 2009).

Both clinical psychology and psychotherapy research seem disconnected from the emerging science of intimate relationships that is being developed by social, personality, and evolutionary psychologists and is beginning to be referred to as *relationship science* (Gillath, Adams, & Kunkel, 2012). This is ironic because psychotherapists since Freud have routinely acknowledged that the anxiety, depression, and anger management problems they treat are often symptoms of an unhappy love life. Psychotherapists are often unaware that social, personality, and evolutionary psychologists have been developing an evidence-based science of intimate relationships that for the most part has yet to be applied to clinical practice.

Psychotherapy process and outcome research has discovered that an important predictor of outcome is the therapeutic alliance (Norcross & Wampold, 2011; Wampold, 2001). Therapist personality variables such as trustworthiness, empathy, and authenticity are associated with a good therapeutic relationship and a good therapeutic outcome (Wampold & Imel, 2015). Relationship science has discovered that those exact same personality variables—trust, empathy, and authenticity—are also associated with successful long-term relationships in which the infidelity risks would be relatively lower (Brunell et al., 2010; Neff & Suizzo, 2006; Shimberg, Josephs, & Tittel, 2016).

An evidence-based treatment for infidelity can therefore be derived from the kind of evidence-based relationships (i.e., therapeutic relationships associated with positive psychotherapy outcomes), intimate as well as therapeutic, that lead to good outcomes. Evidence-based treatment in the broadest and best sense of the term isn't entirely reducible to the evidence provided by randomized controlled trials (RCTs). Such trials only show that a manualized treatment is better than no treatment (e.g., a waitlist control) or bad treatment (e.g., a pseudotreatment missing essential ingredients). RCTs have yet to show that any manualized treatment is substantially better than a competing manualized treatment (see Wampold & Imel, 2015, "The Great Psychotherapy Debate"). According to Wampold and Imel (2015), the evidence convincingly shows that some therapy is better than no therapy. Yet for empirically validated treatments, the remission rate of patients getting well and staying well is only around 25% in treating simple cases of depression and anxiety in which complex cases with personality problems have been screened out (Shedler, 2015).

Treating infidelity means treating complex cases of patients who are simultaneously depressed, anxious, and angry and suffer underlying personality problems (i.e., the kind of patients excluded from most psychotherapy studies). Findings have indicated that couples who are dealing with infidelity showed greater marital instability, dishonesty, arguments about trust, narcissism, and time spent apart (Atkins, Yi, Baucom, & Christensen, 2005). Fortunately, couples therapy does appear to successfully help couples recover from infidelity (Atkins, Marín, Lo, Klann, & Hahlweg, 2010). Nevertheless, treating infidelity is only sometimes about helping couples recover from it. Infidelity treatment often involves individual treatments, with the unfaithful partner, the betrayed partner, and the affair partner each trying to figure out how to go forward with their lives despite being embroiled in a complicated love triangle that might have no foreseeable end in sight. Evidence-based treatment for infidelity therefore needs to be based on a science of intimate relationships as well as on evidence-based therapeutic techniques and relationships that can work with both complex and simple cases.

INFIDELITY BELIEFS AND DICHOTOMOUS THINKING

Over time, I discovered that many patients arrive in psychotherapy with certain "infidelity beliefs." Those beliefs often mirror ideas floating around in the popular culture. Infidelity beliefs reflect moral values as well as "implicit theories of relationships" (Knee, Patrick, & Lonsbary, 2003) that are culturally relative and individually variable and so are often a topic of polarized debate. Cognitive reappraisal, an evidence-based therapeutic technique that is central to cognitive behavioral approaches to treating depression, anxiety, and anger, has yet to be applied to cognitive restructuring of infidelity beliefs. But suffice to say that cognitive reappraisal of any belief is challenging when such a belief is held with a strong sense of conviction. It is not always clear to psychotherapists how to engage in cognitive reappraisal of those infidelity beliefs and theories without unwittingly slipping into a moralistic position that implicitly takes sides in a polarized conflict.

Infidelity beliefs often reflect either–or thinking—what cognitive psychologists call *dichotomous thinking* (Napolitano & McKay, 2007) and what psychoanalysts call *splitting* (Kernberg, 1996). Popular infidelity beliefs are also often reflected in the more sensational or polemical books on infidelity that are published for general audiences. Such books are either promonogamy, like how to "affair-proof" one's marriage (Staheli, 1998), or are antimonogamy, suggesting that humans aren't naturally monogamous and that monogamy is only an oppressive cultural institution (Ryan & Jetha, 2011). The promonogamy popular books suggest that it is easy to find sexual fulfillment in a monogamous arrangement if only couples follow the correct prescriptions for marital happiness. Such books assume that sexual ambivalence and frustration don't have to be a permanent feature of married life with which everyone must learn to constructively cope.

In contrast, the antimonogamy books knowingly assume that sexual ambivalence and frustration are permanent features of monogamous married life, and that is exactly why monogamy is an oppressive cultural institution that is not natural. The antimonogamy popular books imply that individuals could achieve greater happiness in an open marriage or polyamorous arrangement if only people overcome their culturally instilled irrational sexual jealousy and possessiveness. Such books assume that sexual jealousy and possessiveness aren't an inherent part of human nature and recommend unlearning culturally instilled sexual jealousy so one can happily share one's sexual partner with others. Yet a recent study suggested that the polyamorous may suffer from "polyagony" in attempting to overcome jealousy (Deri, 2015). Dichotomous thinking is evident whenever one arrangement is idealized and the other devalued, be it monogamy or nonmonogamy.

Patients often arrive in the consulting room with infidelity beliefs that rationalize their current marital predicament. Unfaithful men who enjoy a casual extramarital sex life often mistakenly assume that evolutionary psychology suggests it is not natural for men to be monogamous; therefore, their wives should become more accepting of their extramarital affairs. Such men don't appreciate that paternal care would not have evolved were it not for some innate tendency to engage in sexually exclusive pair bonding for biparental care. The evolution of paternal care requires the paternity certainty that monogamy facilitates (Gray & Anderson, 2010). Betrayed women who believe that monogamy is the natural state of affairs may mistakenly assume that their husbands' infidelities are only a symptom of a deep-seated fear of intimacy and commitment that should get fixed in psychotherapy. Betrayed women might not realize that a comprehensive review of the research literature suggests that men might have a stronger sex drive with a greater need for sexual variety than women, and thus they might be more frustrated by monogamous constraints than are women (Baumeister, Catanese, & Vohs, 2001).

Patients' conviction in their own infidelity beliefs and fear of being unfairly judged for those convictions may make them intolerant of those with opposing infidelity beliefs. They see their partners' infidelity beliefs as mistaken perceptions that need to be corrected. Patients then mistakenly think that a therapist's job is to validate the patient's correct infidelity belief while correcting the partner's mistaken one instead of learning to reframe their own infidelity beliefs in the terms of a larger metaperspective that can contain conflicting points of view.

It is difficult to accept that romantic partners are entitled to a mind of their own when their partners' seemingly misguided infidelity beliefs result in their own sexual frustration or betrayal. Patients can easily be shamed for their infidelity beliefs. As a consequence, therapists need to be able to validate the kernel of truth in patients' infidelity beliefs while respectfully helping patients assimilate an alternative but more complex viewpoint that can contain multiple and seemingly conflicting perspectives.

Infidelity beliefs are an expression of what developmental psychologists call *theory of mind* (Frith & Frith, 2003, 2006). Part of successful individual and couples psychotherapy is enabling patients to mentalize infidelity, that is, to look at infidelity through the prism of a more sophisticated theory of mind that can contain multiple and contrasting perspectives (Josephs, 2015a). Betrayed partners have difficulty mentalizing how a person they trust could possibly betray that trust through sexual infidelity. Unfaithful partners have difficulty mentalizing the traumatic impact of sexual betrayal on partners with whom they feel sexually frustrated. The ability to reflect on and empathize with a romantic partner's viewpoint deteriorates when feeling sexually frustrated and rejected by that partner. As hurt and anger intensify, reflective functioning diminishes (Josephs & McLeod, 2014).

Facilitating dialectical thinking (i.e., seeing both sides of a conflict) when it comes to infidelity beliefs is challenging because it may evoke strong, but hopefully transient, negative reactions toward the therapist. After all, patients are highly invested in their infidelity beliefs—in having them validated by their therapists and having opposing infidelity beliefs invalidated. That makes it difficult for a therapist to assume the role of a neutral third party who can see both sides of a conflict. The therapist may be perceived as criticizing and invalidating the patient's infidelity belief by suggesting it is only partially true. The therapist may seem to be abdicating the responsibility of empathizing with the patient's viewpoint by recognizing and empathizing with the kernel of truth in a romantic partner's opposing infidelity belief.

A therapist who notes the downside of infidelity may be seen as implicitly moralistic and imposing the therapist's sexually restrictive values on the patient. In contrast, a therapist who notes the upside of infidelity could be seen as perversely rationalizing deceit and betrayal in romantic relationships. The therapeutic alliance may be ruptured by such negative reactions to the therapist's attempts to facilitate the development of a metaperspective that sees both sides of a conflict. In this case, the therapeutic alliance will then require repair through acknowledgment of the therapist's own personal contribution to the relationship rupture (Safran & Muran, 2003). Clarification of the therapeutic rationale for approaching the patient's infidelity beliefs in a dialectical manner may enable the patient to see the value of searching for ways to transcend polarizing discourse on a sensitive issue.

Absolute conviction in one's own infidelity beliefs often coexists in a dissociated way with puzzlement, self-doubt, and confusion as to why people are unfaithful. Do people who are unfaithful possess a fear of marital intimacy?

Are humans meant to be monogamous? Does infidelity only occur when a couple has a poor sex life, and do people who are unfaithful not really love their partners? Betrayed spouses wonder why their partners were unfaithful. Were they not good in bed, are they fundamentally unlovable, or have they lost their youthful good looks with age and weight gain? Or perhaps they were in denial about the possibility that their husbands might be "lying pigs" or their wives "cheating sluts"?

Even unfaithful partners privately wonder what was the "real" reason they were unfaithful, especially after the affair is exposed and they realize the devastating consequences. Were they trying to get out of an unhappy marriage, to make their partners jealous as punishment for taking them for granted, to have a vacation from the stresses and responsibilities of family life, or to resolve a midlife crisis? People who have affairs with married people (i.e., "mate poachers" as evolutionary psychologists call them) often wonder why their married lovers are being unfaithful: are they just interested in casual sex, or is this an attempt to leave an unhappy marriage and live happily ever after with someone new?

Patients need help bridging a deep-seated contradiction within their personalities between absolute conviction in their own infidelity beliefs and another side that is totally confused. Infidelity as a hot-button issue can activate the kind of dichotomous thinking, emotional flooding, and emotional dysregulation most characteristic of individuals who suffer from borderline personality disorder (Brodsky & Stanley, 2013). Treating infidelity therefore requires helping patients mentalize the psychology of love triangles and sexual betrayal in the face of their own emotional dysregulation and defensive ways of coping with that dysregulation.

THE EVOLUTIONARY ROOTS OF HUMAN SEXUAL AMBIVALENCE

The evolutionary point of view begins to help us gain insight into why humans may live in a permanent state of sexual ambivalence. As noted earlier, evolutionary psychologists have suggested that humans are "strategic pluralists" (Buss & Schmitt, 1993) who can deploy either short-term or long-term reproductive strategies as ecological conditions warrant. As a consequence of possessing these opposing reproductive strategies, the central but often unseen sexual conflict in human nature may be between the desire to find happiness and emotional security in a long-term monogamous relationship and the desire to reexperience erotic excitement and romantic intimacy with other partners once the honeymoon phase of a relationship is over. That inner struggle may be experienced acutely whether one is male or female, gay or straight, young or old, single or married.

The human species appears to live in a state of perpetual sexual warfare but for the most part is only marginally aware of living in such a battle zone. There are no known cultures in which infidelity is absent. Yet there are also no known cultures in which individuals don't go a bit berserk as a result of sexual betrayal, sometimes to the point of homicide. Evolutionary anthropologists such as Helen Fisher (2004) and William Jankowiak (1995), as well as evolutionary psychologists like David Buss (2000), now believe that romantic love and romantic jealousy are cross-cultural universals.

It seems that in all historical periods and cultures, some people are trying to get away with infidelity, while other people are trying to catch and punish "cheaters." There appears to be never-ending guerilla warfare between those trying to get away with infidelity and those trying to prevent it. Psychotherapists are often drawn into the battle when unfaithful partners try to enlist their therapists to help them feel less guilt-ridden about their hidden infidelities or betrayed partners try to recruit their therapists in their efforts to punish and fix their unfaithful partners; affair partners too may try to recruit therapists to help them find a way to break up with their affair partner and finally move on with their lives or to convince their married lovers to leave their spouses for them.

Humans may have evolved to be eternally at war with themselves about whether to remain faithful and with each other in trying to prevent and punish their partners' infidelities while trying to successfully conceal their own (even if it's just hiding their adulterous fantasy life or innocent flirtations). This psychological warfare produces innumerable casualties: the couples trapped in joyless but monogamous marriages; unfaithful individuals living secret double lives praying that they don't get caught; the partners whose infidelities have been exposed and whose marriages and families have fallen apart; the single people in love with married partners who will not leave their spouses for them; the betrayed partners who feel scarred for life; and finally the children who witness parental conflict around exposed infidelity and draw their own conclusion about the nature of married life. These casualties of the infidelity wars often make their way into the offices of individual and couples psychotherapists.

Previti and Amato (2004) found that 21% of divorced individuals reported exposed infidelity as the reason for the breakup of the marriage. Yet what remains an unsolved mystery is the number of divorces precipitated by hidden infidelities that were never detected by the betrayed spouse. One clue that infidelity may be an even more common reason for divorce than is often realized is the speed with which many divorced men start new relationships (Duncombe & Marsden, 2004). These relationships may be a continuation of affairs previously concealed from their wives and children. Thus, hidden conflicts around infidelity may be a much more frequent cause of marital breakup than usually appreciated. Many will not leave an unhappy marriage until they have secretly lined up a suitable replacement.

Most people appreciate that infidelity puts a marriage at significant risk of dissolution, and that's why unfaithful partners take such pains to cover it up. What is rarely considered is the impact of infidelity on children, even when it doesn't result in divorce. In a study I conducted with one of my students among 300 undergraduates at Adelphi University where I teach, 25% reported awareness of parental infidelity (Hunyady, Josephs, & Jost, 2008). A child's reaction to exposed parental affairs appears to be quite similar to their reaction to parental divorce: It undermines the child's belief in the durability of stable lifelong relationships (Duncombe & Marsden, 2004). Thus, children become noncombatant casualties of their parents' sexual conflicts.

Infidelity is a common phenomenon: In a frequently cited study of prevalence rates, 23% of currently married men and 12% of currently married women admit to engaging in extramarital sex (Wiederman, 1997).[1] In any given year, it is estimated that 1.5% to 4% of individuals will engage in marital infidelity (Wiederman, 1997). The infidelity rates among unmarried individuals (e.g., college students in committed relationships) are even higher, and the phenomenon crosses gender lines (Feldman & Cauffman, 1999). The most recent research suggests that women under age 40, especially on college campuses, are quickly catching up to men in the infidelity rates in egalitarian countries in North America and Western Europe (Drigotas, Safstrom, & Gentilia, 1999; Glass & Wright, 1985; Wiederman, 1997).

The high prevalence rates of infidelity worldwide make it questionable to pathologize such a common sexual behavior. Yet it does seem that the more severe the psychopathology, the more likely it is a person will have unstable intimate relationships characterized by conflicts around infidelity. Perhaps the best way to think of it is that negotiating ambivalence about sexual fidelity is a common challenge of married life, like marital bickering or sexual boredom. More disturbed individuals will have greater difficulty negotiating this conflict than individuals more skilled in dealing with the many challenges and frustrations of long-term intimate relationships. For this reason, prevalence rates of infidelity are higher among individuals who are insecurely attached (Hazan, Campa, & Gur-Yaish, 2006) and high on narcissism (Buss & Shackelford, 1997). Infidelity can be an outgrowth of the underlying personality problems of all three members of the love triangle that give rise to maladaptive patterns of communication in intimate relationships. To change those patterns, it is often necessary to treat underlying personality issues, such

[1]These figures most likely underreport the issue because of the sensitivity of making this disclosure and the fact that the samples include many younger people who have not been married long.

as impaired reflective functioning, insecure attachment, defensive grandiosity, narcissistic entitlement, and dichotomous thinking.

Different cultures have different prevalence rates as well as different attitudes toward infidelity (Druckerman, 2007). Nevertheless, reactions to exposed infidelity appear to be a cross-cultural universal whether one is American, French, or a hunter–gatherer living a Stone Age lifestyle. Bruce Knauft (1991), who studied violence among hunter–gatherers, discovered that a leading cause of homicide was sexual jealousy. Kenneth Good (1997), who lived with the Yanomamo of South America, found that revenge for infidelity was sometimes delivered by a poison arrow to a mate poacher's back. Sexual betrayal by one's romantic partner evokes not only jealousy but humiliation and rage. Betrayed partners experience symptoms of PTSD, such as flashbacks of the philandering spouse having sex with the affair partner, because infidelity constitutes a serious attachment injury that prevents secure attachment (Johnson & Makinen, 2003).

Affairs create considerable emotional turmoil for everyone involved in the love triangle. The unfaithful partner may suffer intense shame and guilt upon exposure, as well as reputational damage. The unfaithful partner may feel overwhelmed by having to learn how to deal with the betrayed partner's PTSD. Affair partners may be precipitously rejected by unfaithful partners who decide to recommit to their betrayed partners. The casualties of conflicts surrounding infidelity may require considerable psychological rehabilitation to heal these wounds of war. Given the potential costs, few people are prepared to accept infidelity: Nearly 99% of married Americans expect their spouse to have sex exclusively within the marriage and assume that their partner expects the same of them. More than 90% think that it is "always" or "almost always" wrong for a married person to have extramarital sex (Treas & Giesen, 2000).

A ROAD MAP FOR THE SCIENCE OF INTIMATE RELATIONSHIPS

It is not widely appreciated that there is a considerable research literature on infidelity, widely scattered among the subdisciplines of psychology as well as evolutionary biology and evolutionary anthropology. Currently, these areas of infidelity research tend to exist in isolation. To fully understand all sides of the conflict between fidelity and infidelity, it is important to develop an integrative perspective covering many areas of research so that no important variables are overlooked.

I begin in Chapter 1 by discussing infidelity from the perspective evolutionary psychology and clarifying how humans became monogamously inclined cooperative breeders who often resort to uncooperative reproductive strategies. Chapter 2 looks at how infidelity may be a symptom of insecure attachment and diminished reflective functioning. Chapter 3 considers gender differences in motivation for infidelity and how those gender differences interact with attachment style. I discuss infidelity as an outgrowth of narcissistic ways of coping with insecure attachment in Chapter 4, while Chapter 5 looks at infidelity through the lens of what evolutionary psychologists call *mate value*—our sense of our relative desirability as a romantic partner. Chapter 6 discusses the psychology of romantic jealousy and how it can result in retaliatory infidelity, an often-overlooked motive for infidelity. In Chapter 7, I examine how the reasons for infidelity evolve across the lifespan, while Chapter 8 looks at the problems betrayed partners and affair partners face when unfaithful partners resist recommitting to monogamy. Chapter 9 considers the challenges of treating infidelity when it derives from sexual addiction. Chapter 10 looks at the communication styles associated with fidelity and infidelity. Finally, the Conclusion describes how high mentalization, authenticity, and generativity appear to be crucial ingredients of successful long-term relationships.

AN INTEGRATIVE APPROACH TO TREATING INFIDELITY

Treating infidelity, whether the patient is the unfaithful partner, the betrayed partner, or the affair partner, in either individual or couples therapy, is often a specialized instance of treating individuals who tend to be relatively high on insecure attachment, be it anxious or avoidant attachment style, and relatively high on narcissism, be it grandiose or vulnerable narcissism, regardless of their particular role in a complicated love triangle. Such individuals tend to be deficient when it comes to reflective functioning, empathy, authenticity, and communication skills. The treatment approach is therefore to remediate these relationship skills deficits regardless of the particular personality style and dynamics.

Fortunately, there are now evidence-based approaches to remediating these relationship skills deficits of which infidelity may be a symptomatic eruption. Mentalization-based therapy for borderline personality disorder is an effective approach to increasing reflective functioning (Bateman & Fonagy, 2004). Increasing the ability to reflect on the mental states of others improves empathy. Integrative couples therapy is an effective approach to improving communication skills (J. M. Gottman, 1999) and to mindful acceptance of romantic partners as they are despite their frustrating imperfections (Christensen & Jacobson, 1998).

The unreflective tendency is to want to "fix" a partner's "unhealthy" sexuality so one won't feel so frustrated, rejected, disgusted, and betrayed. It is difficult to extend the acceptance, understanding, and respect for a partner's sexuality that one would like to receive for one's own sexuality when a partner's sexuality seems problematic. *Mindfulness* in this context means learning how to look at the enduring personality traits, emotional problems, and sexuality of one's romantic partner with nonjudgmental acceptance rather than moralizing judgment. Integrative couples therapy facilitates learning to accept a partner's personality rather than trying to fix it (Christensen & Jacobson, 1998). That recommendation is challenging to implement when a partner possesses significant narcissistic or borderline traits and engages in sexual infidelity or responds to sexual betrayal in a vindictive way.

Only recently has mindfulness been used in couples therapy to increase empathy (Gambrel & Keeling, 2010). Empathizing with the viewpoint of an egocentric partner who has been unreasonably devaluing and blaming and who has betrayed one's trust is not easy. It is one thing to learn how to accept a partner's minor character flaws that have been blown out of proportion. It is another thing to learn how to patiently accept a partner who has been deceitful, abusive, or angrily withholding sex and affection as that partner gradually learns how to acknowledge and assume responsibility for curtailing the kind of unacceptable behaviors that result in serious attachment injury. Such partners are often at significant risk of relapse even when they have made reasonable incremental progress.

To restore trust and intimacy, romantic partners must relate to one another not only with accurate empathy and acceptance but also with authenticity, transparency, and honesty. Partners must learn to say what they mean and mean what they say. That is not so easy because such intimate risk taking may mean exposing irreconcilable differences of opinion and confronting painful truths. Why make oneself vulnerable to being misunderstood and criticized for sharing one's true self? Communication skills are required to openly but respectfully speak one's mind while demonstrating acceptance of a partner's right to have a mind of his or her own. Couples often avoid these moments of truth, fearing that the relationship won't survive the ugly scene that might erupt when everyone's hurt and anger is finally expressed with full force. Partners may need encouragement to confront rather than avoid such painful conflicts and require coaching about the most constructive ways to broach shame-sensitive topics without putting a partner on the defensive. Johnson (2004) noted that couples cannot feel securely attached to each other until they each feel it is safe to express, openly and nondefensively, the aspect of themselves that feels vulnerable to further attachment injury and can trust that their partners will respond with acceptance and empathy.

Treating infidelity, be it in individual or couples therapy, requires psychotherapy integration. That integration requires combining psychodynamic approaches to enhance reflective functioning, such as mentalization-based therapy (Bateman & Fonagy, 2004) and transference-focused therapy (Levy, Meehan, et al., 2006), with behavioral approaches to couples work that use mindful acceptance of a partner's frustrating limitations (Christensen & Jacobson, 1998), communication skills training (J. M. Gottman, 1999), and emotion-focused work to heal attachment injuries (Johnson, 2004). Owen and Hilsenroth (2014) found that therapists who implement treatment manuals flexibly obtain better results than therapists who implement treatment manuals rigidly or formulaically.

Wachtel (2010) noted that RCTs that study "pure" types of treatment for patients without dual diagnoses disadvantage psychotherapy integration. Psychotherapy integration mixes apples and oranges to make an original fruit salad by individually tailoring a treatment to a specific patient in a specific situation when the patient's problems don't exactly fit some singular diagnostic category. Stricker and Trierweiler (1995) recommended the "local clinical scientist" model in which clinicians keep abreast of the latest research but also feel free to draw on their unique clinical experiences and clinical judgment to utilize the best mix of approaches for a particular patient in a particular situation.

Therapist *cultural humility*, an attitude of respect for and lack of superiority toward people from a different cultural background, appears to be associated with a stronger therapeutic alliance (Hook, Davis, Owen, Worthington, & Utsey, 2013).Treating infidelity does not necessarily mean idealizing monogamy over various forms of consensual nonmonogamy such as open marriage or polyamory, toward which sexual minorities may have more favorable attitudes. It does mean recognizing that nonconsensual nonmonogamy (i.e., infidelity) is an unethical act that inflicts relational damage be one male or female, gay or straight. Trust and secure attachment are eroded anytime one is caught lying or breaking a promise.

An emerging approach to effectiveness research is not to compare pure types of treatment for patients with singular diagnoses but to look for common factors that cut across effective treatments to discover the evidence-based relationships (Norcross & Wampold, 2011) and evidence-based therapeutic processes (Castonguay & Hill, 2012) that make psychotherapy effective with even complex cases. An evidence-based therapeutic relationship and process may be facilitated whenever a therapist of any theoretical orientation role models the communication skills, reflective functioning, mindful acceptance, and secure attachment style that he or she hopes to promote.

The therapist must actively confront shame-sensitive issues in direct, straightforward language and in a way that is respectful when patients are avoidant (i.e., the therapist must use communication skills). The therapist must contain moralizing reactions in order to respond empathically to narcissistic and Machiavellian personality traits that betray the trust and diminish the self-respect of significant others (i.e., mindful acceptance). The therapist must demonstrate an ability to discover the integrative metaperspective through dialectical thought when lapsing into dichotomous thinking in emotionally trying circumstances that encourage polarization (i.e., high-level reflective functioning). Research suggests that attachment style is implicitly revealed in communication style (Mikulincer & Shaver, 2010): Secure attachment is revealed in verbal communication that is clear and coherent, whereas insecure attachment is revealed in language that is overly abstract and experience-distant or confused and confusing. Therapists must speak in clear and coherent but emotionally evocative language to break through the cognitive impenetrability of anxious patients who are responding defensively.

The therapist's ability to role model reflective thought, acceptance, and constructive communication is put to the test when patients respond negatively to attempts to approach the negotiation of conflicting infidelity beliefs in a dialectical manner. Can the therapist practice what he or she preaches when put to the test by being angrily or contemptuously accused of being moralistic (i.e., anti-infidelity) or perversely Machiavellian (proinfidelity) by a patient who feels implicitly judged and invalidated by the therapist's attempt to empathize with both sides of an inner conflict?

CONCLUSION

We begin our journey into infidelity research and its treatment in Chapter 1 as we delve into our evolutionary heritage. Why is it that sexual ambivalence appears to be built into human nature? And what ecological variables influence how different individuals learn to cope with that ambivalence? To rephrase Shakespeare: "To cheat or not to cheat? That is the question."

1

TO CHEAT OR NOT TO CHEAT? THE EVOLUTION OF FIDELITY AND INFIDELITY

Social scientists from cultural anthropologists to evolutionary biologists have debated the question of whether human nature is inherently monogamous, promiscuous, or polygynous and whether certain cultural arrangements are therefore antithetical to something fundamental in human nature (Barash & Lipton, 2001; Bullough, 1976; Chapais, 2008; Dixson, 2009; Frayser, 1985). These debates enter the clinical literature as practitioners note the implicitly monogamous ideal of most psychotherapeutic practice (Horney, 1928) and as consensual nonmonogamy has been proposed as a viable alternative to infidelity (nonmonogamy without consent of the betrayed partner) as well as monogamy (Mogilski, Memering, Welling, & Shackelford, 2017).

Does monogamy suppress our natural promiscuity, as the authors of *Sex at Dawn* (Ryan & Jetha, 2011) suggested, or does polygamy unfairly pressure women into sharing a husband when most would rather have exclusive possession of one husband (Al-Krenawi, 2001; Al-Krenawi, Graham, & Al-Krenawi, 1997)? Some cultural relativists have argued that, given the incredible diversity

http://dx.doi.org/10.1037/0000053-002
The Dynamics of Infidelity: Applying Relationship Science to Psychotherapy Practice, by L. Josephs

of human sexual arrangements across cultures and historical epochs, it may be that there is no fundamental human nature when it comes to sex (Montgomery, 2009). In contrast, primatologists like Dixson (2009) have argued that monogamy is the norm in all cultures. Although more cultures have been officially polygamous than monogamous, it is usually only a small percentage of high-status men who have multiple wives, while most men only have one at a time (H. E. Fisher, 2004).

Dixson (2009) argued that the reduced body dimorphism of male and female humans, as well as certain anatomical features of human genitalia (e.g., testes size), is consistent with anatomical changes that are associated with evolution in a more monogamous direction in other species. The attempt to form successful long-term monogamous relationships appears to be universal even if such relationships are frequently disrupted by infidelity, divorce, and attempts at consensual nonmonogamy. H. E. Fisher (2004) argued that the emotion of romantic love has evolved to motivate sexually exclusive pair bonding for biparental care, and Jankowiak (1995) maintained that romantic love is a universal emotion found in all cultures and all historical periods.

Conflicts around infidelity tend to evoke the kind of polarization that is characteristic of what cognitive therapists call *dichotomous thinking* (Napolitano & McKay, 2007; Oshio, 2009, 2012) and what psychoanalysts call *splitting* (Kernberg, 1996; Yeomans, Clarkin, & Kernberg, 2015; unfaithful partners are sluts or pigs, affair partners are home-wreckers, and betrayed partners are cuckolds). Clinicians engage in dichotomous thinking when they begin to think of behavior as either adaptive or maladaptive rather than as simultaneously possessing costs as well as benefits. They need tools to help patients, as well as themselves, overcome either–or thinking in relation to infidelity; the dialectical method is one such tool to manage extreme but antithetical affect states that may be overwhelming (Linehan, 1993). Contemporary evolutionary psychology may help clinicians see the adaptive import of both sides of the inner conflict in the context of infidelity, providing a metaperspective to help their patients overcome dichotomous thinking.

The dialectical method suggests that when two points of view are in conflict, it doesn't necessarily mean one is right and the other is wrong. Each point of view might be right in its own way, and each may contain a kernel of truth. Yet each point of view may also be subject to a certain degree of tunnel vision. Thesis and antithesis can result in an integrative synthesis when opposing viewpoints are seen as potentially complementary: Each viewpoint may compensate for the tunnel vision of the seemingly opposing and perhaps morally offensive viewpoint. From one point of view, infidelity seems like a solution to marital unhappiness, but from another, infidelity is the cause of marital unhappiness. Therapists can use the dialectical method to help overcome dichotomous thinking and promote acceptance in the marital context (Alberts, Thewissen, & Raes, 2012; Gambrel & Keeling, 2010; Linehan, 1993).

What kind of integrative synthesis can contain the dialectical tension that exists between construing infidelity as a solution versus as a problem? By providing a theory of human nature in which ambivalence about sexual fidelity is central, evolutionary psychology begins to explain why infidelity is simultaneously both. Every solution to that inner conflict has its costs and benefits. Self-acceptance can be facilitated when one's inner conflicts and solutions to those conflicts can be normalized as part and parcel of a universal human nature with which everyone grapples in some shape or form. Cognitive regulatory control processes can be facilitated by techniques such as *normalization* and *cost–benefit analysis* (Bowins, 2013), which evolutionary psychology can inform by providing a theory of the costs and benefits of adaptations for reproductive success.

Evolutionary psychology clarifies that although infidelity can be adaptive (i.e., it has benefits despite the costs), it is still an uncooperative and unethical reproductive strategy that undermines the trust necessary for cooperative relationships. We can look to evolutionary psychology to facilitate a better understanding of the origins of a "dark side" of human nature. Understanding this dark side doesn't rationalize or excuse it for the harm it causes others. However, nonjudgmental and empathic understanding of the dark side is an essential step in mastering it because one cannot master a strong human tendency that one doesn't understand but instead rationalizes or repudiates in fear of a partner's or a therapist's moralistic judgment. Likewise, evolutionary psychology helps therapists overcome their own moralizing tendencies when they see infidelity as "only" psychopathology to be treated when it can "also" be appreciated as an adaptive, although uncooperative, response to challenging ecological conditions.

THE DIALECTICS OF HUMAN MATING

Two questionable assumptions are that (a) if infidelity is natural, it must be good (see Buss, 2003, on the naturalistic fallacy) and (b) if monogamy is cultural, it must be arbitrary and oppressive of something that is inherently good and natural. Evolutionary psychologists David Buss and David Schmitt (1993) developed an inspired solution to these age-old debates about the fundamental nature of human sexual psychology, what they call *sexual strategies theory*. The basic idea is that all species possess a sexually selected species-specific reproductive or mating strategy through which they try to maximize their reproductive advantage (Dixson, 2009). Evolution is driven not so much by survival of the fittest as by reproductive success (Ash & Gallup, 2008).

Traits that result in reproductive success (i.e., siring offspring who survive to maturity and reproduce themselves) are traits that are selected to be passed down through the generations. From this perspective, fidelity and infidelity constitute competing strategies for reproductive advantage. From an evolutionary perspective all adaptations possess costs as well as benefits, and the cost–benefit ratio varies under different ecological conditions (Williams, 1992). Just because something is ultimately adaptive doesn't mean it's all good (the benefits come at a significant cost), and just because something is ultimately maladaptive doesn't mean it's all bad (there may still be substantial benefits even though the costs exceed the benefits).

Gorillas reproduce by forming harems headed by a silverback male (Dixson, 1998). The most reproductively successful male gorillas are the alpha males that can defend and maintain a harem. The most reproductively successful female gorillas mate with the alpha rather than a male lacking a harem. Chimpanzees, in contrast, maintain a more promiscuous arrangement in which the females mate with all the males (de Waal, 2007; Dixson, 1998). Nevertheless, male dominance does tend to correlate with reproductive success among promiscuous species, albeit not perfectly because of the influence of female choice as well as efforts by subordinate males to look for sexual opportunities when the alpha males are not looking (de Waal, 2007; Dixson, 1998).

Do humans have a recognizable reproductive strategy like our closest primate relatives? At first blush, it might seem that we do not because of the incredible diversity of human sexual behavior. Perhaps culture acts to suppress our primate legacy, in which a few dominant males monopolize all the women who choose to mate with the alphas (i.e., Darwin's, 1871, female choice) rather than be impregnated by a beta loser? Or perhaps human sexual nature is more egalitarian yet still essentially promiscuous, as the authors of *Sex at Dawn* argued (Ryan & Jetha, 2011).

Buss and Schmitt (1993) proposed that humans do indeed have an identifiable and uniquely human reproductive strategy. They claimed that humans are "strategic pluralists." *Strategic pluralism* means that humans are capable of multiple reproductive strategies that are sensitive to and activated by particular ecological conditions. Humans may be designed by evolution to implement the reproductive strategy most likely to optimize reproductive success under a particular ecological condition. The effect of sex ratio on sexual behavior is one instance of an ecological condition affecting reproductive strategy (Pedersen, 1991). When men are in short supply, there is a tendency for humans to mate more promiscuously. Women begin to cater to men's desire for sexual variety by dressing in ways that suggest sexual accessibility (Barber, 1999). Women also begin to choose "briefcase over baby" (Durante, Griskevicius, Simpson, Cantú, & Tybur, 2012). Yet when women are in short supply there is a tendency for humans to mate more monogamously. Men begin to cater to women's preference for more monogamous arrangements that women communicate by dressing in ways that suggest sexual inaccessibility (Barber, 1999).

Human reproductive strategies are not simply the assumption of whatever the culture arbitrarily programs us to do to gain social acceptance. Human reproductive strategies are indeed strategic decisions, usually formulated without conscious awareness, made to optimize reproductive success under particular ecological conditions. Sometimes implementing the optimal strategy may require conforming to cultural expectations, but often it may require subversively resisting cultural expectations if conforming to those expectations would diminish one's own reproductive advantage. Thus, teenagers and young adults have always eloped for romantic love despite cultural expectations to accommodate to arranged marriages (Jankowiak, 1995), and humans in all cultures engage in infidelity despite cultural expectations to remain faithful (Druckerman, 2007).

Monogamy tends to prevail under some ecological conditions, and nonmonogamy prevails in others, regardless of cultural attempts to constrain human sexual behavior. Humans everywhere are capable of expressing their sexuality surreptitiously if need be when cultural conditions are inhospitable to human reproductive self-interest. In fact, we may have evolved to express our sexuality secretively: Humans everywhere appear to possess a preference for having sex in private in contradistinction to other primate species (except for a few exhibitionists; D. Brown, 1991). Humans have invented cultural control of sexual behavior only to find creative ways to subvert it. Subordinate individuals or subgroups use subversive reproductive strategies to counter the reproductive advantages of dominant individuals or cultures (Cummins, 2005). The sexual morality that cultures attempt to instill is not arbitrary or unrelated to reproductive biology but rather reflects the implicit reproductive self-interests of those who attempt to instill their sexual morality in others.

THE EVOLUTION OF SEXUAL STRATEGIES: THE SEARCH FOR SEXUAL VARIETY VERSUS A SOUL MATE

Life history theorists have distinguished two overarching reproductive strategies: *quantity over quality* and *quality over quantity* (Charnov, 1993; Del Giudice, 2014; Kaplan & Gangestad, 2005; Levins, 1968). In quantity-over-quality reproductive strategies, the idea is to have as many offspring as possible with minimal parenting. So, for example, insects and fish may lay thousands of eggs, and the offspring are left to fend for themselves. The fittest offspring, those most able to survive and reproduce on their own without any help from their parents, are the ones that survive. In contrast, quality-over-quantity strategies involve having fewer offspring but then investing in parenting those offspring to increase the odds that each individual will survive to maturity and be reproductively successful. In sharp contrast to insects and fish, most primate females (e.g., monkeys, apes, humans) have only one offspring at a time and spend considerable time and effort caring for that offspring until it reaches sexual maturity. (Dogs and cats are somewhere in the middle in having a litter of puppies or kittens but also providing care for their young offspring.)

The relative time and energy put into mating versus parenting is a central component of any reproductive strategy. Monogamy arises when both males and females commit considerable time and effort to parenting to ensure that each offspring will have the best possible opportunity to survive to maturity and be reproductively successful. Initially, monogamy requires a high investment in mating to obtain a high-quality partner for biparental care. Subsequently, monogamy requires high investment in parenting at the expense of further mating.

Monogamy is common among birds but rare among mammals (Barash & Lipton, 2001). Eggs in a nest and helpless young birds that can't fly are extremely vulnerable to predation. A single mother can't simultaneously keep the eggs warm and protect the nest while foraging for food. A two-parent family solves that problem nicely: One parent can keep the eggs warm and protect the nest, while the other parent leaves the nest to bring home worms or fish that can be regurgitated. Monogamy can give rise to "gender benders," for example, when male emperor penguins keep the eggs warm and protected while the females go hunting for fish (Lormée, Jouventin, Chastel, & Mauget, 1999). Most mammals, in contrast to birds, can be excellent single mothers due to internal gestation followed by lactation.

Monogamy is perhaps the gold standard for quality over quantity because it is two parents rather than one making a major investment in parenting at the expense of further mating effort. In humans, a quality-over-quantity reproductive strategy becomes even more advanced with the evolution of grandparenting—that is, making a major commitment of time, effort, and resources into the children of one's children at a time of life when fertility and sex drive are diminished. Evolutionary anthropologists have suggested that the evolution of grandmothering may account for the long lifespan that humans enjoy (Hawkes, O'Connell, & Jones, 2003). Chimpanzees and gorillas tend to live about 45 years in the wild, and the females become infertile around 42 years old (Robson, van Shaik, & Hawkes, 2006). Human females also become infertile around 42 years old but can easily live another 30 or 40 years or more. Thus humans may be designed for grandparenting—to spend the last half of life taking care of children by taking care of grandchildren.

In the environment of evolutionary adaptedness, the way contemporary hunter–gatherers live, one starts having children in one's late teens or early 20s, not too far after the arrival of a late puberty, so one is likely to become a first-time grandparent by one's 40s, just when our closest genetic relatives are coming to the end of their lifespan (Robson et al., 2006). Paternal grandparenting as well as fathering could not evolve without monogamy because fathers and paternal grandparents would not know who their children and grandchildren were without the paternity certainty afforded by sexually exclusive arrangements (Chapais, 2008).

The current thinking of primatologists as to why humans evolved in a monogamous direction can be paraphrased by Jolly's (1999) review of the archaeological record: With the evolution of walking on two legs with *Australopithecus* around 4 million or 5 million years ago, the expandability of the female human birth canal became limited. Nevertheless, around 3 million years ago, brain size began to significantly increase as *Homo erectus* spread out across the planet and began to make and use simple tools, like a stone hand ax. By the time modern humans evolved around half a million years ago, the brain had grown quite large, with the early human toolkit and social organization showing vastly increased complexity, as shown by the emergence of group hunting for big game using a spear. At this point, however, the bipedal human female's birth canal was now too narrow to allow such a large-brained baby to squeeze through. As a consequence, human babies started to be born much less physically developed than the newborns of great apes like chimpanzees and gorillas.

Human females therefore needed help raising their helpless but brainy infants, who needed to be carried around all the time without leaving any hands free for hunting or gathering. As a consequence, men started sticking around to help raise their offspring, especially by sharing nutrient-rich hunted food, and grandma started helping out as well. In fact, the whole community soon started pitching in: Humans, unlike most other primates, will help raise children to whom they are not genetically related to the point of adopting unrelated children, as well as infants of other species (i.e., pets), and raising them like their own children. Sarah Hrdy (2009), a primatologist, proposed that humans are cooperative breeders because everybody pitches in to raise the children. Early humans that were more predisposed toward cooperative breeding could raise smarter, bigger brained, and therefore more reproductively successful children than those disinclined toward cooperative breeding.

Monogamy isn't a bad deal for the average man as is sometimes assumed, despite the presumption that men are the more promiscuous sex and more likely to benefit by spreading their seed as widely as possible. Among non-monogamous primate species, subordinate males are at significant risk of being shut out of the mating market as the alpha males attempt to monopolize mating opportunities at the peak of fertility—a winner-take-all reproductive strategy (Dixson, 1998). In monogamy, the majority of males are enabled to reproduce with at least one female. Human females benefit by being able to raise their big-brained but helpless infant with the help of the baby's father and their extended family, which can now include both paternal and maternal kin. Monogamy creates what Chapais (2008) referred to as *primal kinship*. Sexual exclusivity allowed for the creation of the extended human family because, as noted earlier, without monogamy, humans would not know who their father is, nor would they know any of their paternal grandparents, aunts, uncles, or cousins (Chapais, 2008).

Species that implement a quantity-over-quality strategy tend to live fast and die young. They possess what is called a *fast life history strategy* (Del Giudice, 2014; Kaplan & Gangestad, 2005). When the situation is quantity over quality, the winners are the ones that grow up quickest and thus get on with the business of producing as many offspring as possible. For males, this means attracting as many females as possible and inseminating as many eggs as possible with as many different females as possible. For females, this means generating as many eggs as possible and seducing the best males, usually the most dominant ones, to get the best genetic material for their offspring. The more effort that is put into mating, the less energy that is left for parenting. From an evolutionary perspective, one would expect children to object to parental infidelity simply out of their own self-interest because it means fewer parental resources are directed toward their own welfare.

Species that implement a quality-over-quantity strategy tend to grow up more slowly and live longer lives. They are not in such a rush to reproduce because they possess a *slow life history strategy* (Del Giudice, 2014; Kaplan & Gangestad, 2005). When the situation is quality over quantity, there will be more investment in parenting than mating. It is still important to attract high-quality mates to get the best genetic material for one's offspring, but it is also important to attract mates that possess good parenting skills, like male birds that know how to build a good nest. The survival and reproductive success of offspring is now a combination of the genetic quality of the offspring (nature) and the quality of the parenting (nurture). Life history strategy, as well as parenting skill, may be partially heritable traits that can be sexually selected (Figueredo, Vásquez, Brumbach, & Schneider, 2004), and thus evolution begins to be about survival of the best caretakers (e.g., the best nest builders)—those individuals that are the best parents and with sufficient longevity to become good grandparents as well.

So if monogamy is such a great reproductive strategy by virtue of high parental investment from both parents, why isn't everybody consistently monogamous? Shouldn't humans have evolved to be exclusively monogamous for life if it's such an inherently superior reproductive strategy for which humans have evolved? Why do various forms of nonmonogamy exist at such high prevalence rates cross-culturally? As it turns out, evolutionary biologists have discovered that cheating exists among other monogamous species, like birds, as well, and many monogamous birds are serial monogamists that find a new breeding partner every year (Barash & Lipton, 2001). Maybe humans, like birds, are evolved for serial monogamy. Yet given how long it takes for humans to mature, and given the evolution of grandparenting, there could be selection pressures in humans for lifelong monogamy that do not exist in monogamous species in which the young reach maturity in a year and there is no grandparenting.

Monogamy is not a myth as some authors have suggested, but neither is it absolute. Biparental care would never have evolved in any species without a significant degree of sexual exclusivity because males require certainty of their paternity, and the females need some assurance the males will stick around to help out. Monogamy may only be best for reproductive success under certain ecological conditions, as when resources are stable and plentiful so that a slow life history strategy is more likely to pay off. Under resource-poor conditions, it might be better to adopt a fast life history strategy and be nonmonogamous.

Belsky, Steinberg, and Draper (1991) discovered that African American girls who grow up without fathers in urban environments and possess insecure attachment style reach puberty early, start having sex early, and are more likely to become teenage mothers with different fathers. Their insecure attachment style might be an adaptation for being reproductively successful in a resource-poor environment (Belsky, 2000). Maybe it's better to start having children as a teenager when grandma is only 40 years old and can help out like hunter–gatherers do if the father isn't going to stick around.

On the other hand, what is the best reproductive strategy for a handsome and rich married middle-aged man (i.e., an alpha male) with three children, supporting an Ivy League–educated stay-at-home mother whom he met in college (Jokela, Rotkirch, Rickard, Pettay, & Lummaa, 2010; Skjærvø & Røskaft, 2015)? He notices that young, smart, and talented professional women are making themselves sexually available to him without his even having to flirt. Why *not* have exciting affairs with young, beautiful women? Why not divorce his now middle-aged wife of 25 years to start a new family? After all, he can afford it. He will be the envy of all his rich friends at the country club for marrying a younger woman even if some people, like his ex-wife and children, think he is a cad and blame him for ruining their lives.

Conventional morality may try to suppress out-of-wedlock teenage motherhood or rich men divorcing middle-aged wives for younger women, but the unconscious algorithm that determines human reproductive behavior may calculate that absorbing the social costs or suffering one's own guilt-ridden conscience is worth the reproductive benefit. Conscious decision-making can be significantly influenced by self-serving biases of which individuals remain unaware (Paulhus & Buckels, 2012). Nevertheless, monogamy may still be the gold standard for raising children, as the children of the monogamous have fewer psychological problems on average than the children of the non-monogamous, as suggested by research on children of divorce (Weaver & Schofield, 2015), children of single mothers (Amato, 2001), children who experience parental infidelity (Schmidt, Green, & Prouty, 2016), and children of the polygamous (Al-Krenawi et al., 1997).

Therapists will be called on to adjudicate patients' guilt-ridden inner conflicts about putting their investment in mating (one's more immediate romantic happiness or sexual fulfillment) above their investment in parenting (the long-term welfare of their children). How much should they sacrifice their more immediate sexual fulfillment or romantic happiness for the sake of their children's future welfare? Is their guilt rational or irrational? Cognitive approaches to problem-solving and decision-making encourage patients to make a list of pros and cons to consciously and systematically assess the cost–benefit equation (D'Zurilla & Nezu, 2007). Evolutionary psychology can inform such an analysis by understanding the potential reproductive costs and benefits of fidelity and infidelity.

A cost–benefit analysis is always an educated guesstimate that in retrospect may prove prophetic or regrettable. A cost–benefit analysis does provide an opportunity to reflect on how tendencies to catastrophize or engage in wishful thinking might cloud one's better judgment. To what extent is the cost of a course of action seen through the prism of one's worst fears that have been blown out of proportion? To what degree is the benefit of a course of action based on wishful thinking that is overly optimistic? And if a cost–benefit analysis cannot be conducted with certitude, what level of risk is one prepared to assume to reap a potential benefit given that one's risk assessment might be erroneous? Low-risk, low-reward strategists (i.e., slow life history) that would rather be safe than sorry are more likely to catastrophize by prioritizing cost avoidance over benefit acquisition. They tend to be plagued by ruminative worry and neurotic inhibition. High-risk, high-reward strategists (i.e., fast life history) are prone to wishful thinking because they prioritize benefit acquisition over cost avoidance. They are more prone toward grandiosity, manic denial, and impulsivity (Del Giudice, 2014).

Adaptations for reproductive success are probabilistic estimates of what has tended to lead to reproductive success over the course of evolutionary history (Barkow, Cosmides, & Tooby, 1992), but there is never a guarantee that what worked out most of the time on average in the evolutionary past will continue to work out in the future. Selection pressures change as ecological conditions change. Humans have evolved a capacity to make such reproductive decisions consciously and thoughtfully. Yet humans still retain a strong tendency to make reproductive decisions in ways that may be unconscious or emotion driven just as all other species successfully do. It is often when unreflective ways of conducting one's love life don't work out as hoped that people seek psychotherapy to learn how to approach their love lives more reflectively.

THE EVOLUTION OF INFIDELITY: TRYING TO GET THE BEST OF BOTH WORLDS

From the point of view of reproductive strategies, infidelity is an attempt to enjoy the benefits of both quantity-over-quality as well as quality-over-quantity strategies without paying the costs of either strategy (i.e., a high-risk/high-gain strategy). Both strategies come with significant trade-offs. The costs of quantity-over-quality strategies can be significant in a species such as humans in which high-quality parental care makes a significant difference in the quality of offspring. Having large numbers of offspring that suffer serious competitive disadvantages as adults for lack of sufficient parental investment can be a cost of quantity-over-quality strategies. The costs of quality-over-quantity strategies can also be significant. Parents cannot mold their children like a piece of clay; each child is a unique individual with a certain inborn temperament (Clark, 2005) and innate talents (Simonton, 2013). Maybe it's wiser to have as many children as possible and hope that at least one child is naturally exceptional and destined for greatness.

Male infidelity in search of casual sex gives men an opportunity to have as many babies with as many women as possible. This is what the despots of ancient times did. They had large harems and many concubines to have as many sexual partners and children with those partners as humanly possible (Betzig, 1986). Infidelity can also facilitate serial monogamy through marriage to an affair partner because infidelity increases the likelihood of divorce and remarriage (E. S. Allen & Atkins, 2012). The strategy here is this: Don't divorce an infertile middle-aged wife until a suitably fertile younger replacement has been lined up.

Female infidelity allows women to be impregnated by men who may possess better genes than their husbands. Recent research has suggested that when they are ovulating, women prefer more masculine-looking men with greater facial symmetry (Gangestad, Thornhill, & Garver-Apgar, 2010). Unfaithful women can marry a more passively accommodating man to support the family and raise the children but surreptitiously get inseminated by a more dominant man so that her children will inherit traits that will make them more socially successful. The percentage of men unknowingly raising children as their own that are products of infidelity can be significant (K. G. Anderson, 2006). Unfaithful women can also surreptitiously look for a replacement, an upgrade, if their current husbands are unsatisfactory (e.g., losers with a bad temper) to obtain a new husband who is nicer or more successful.

Infidelity will never be entirely suppressed as long as it constitutes the more adaptive reproductive strategy under certain ecological conditions. Individuals will simply absorb the costs of societal disapproval or the pangs of their own guilt-ridden consciences to reap the implicit reproductive benefits that are consciously registered as greater sexual fulfillment or romantic happiness. Individuals do not necessarily consciously contemplate what is best for their genetic legacy. Their sexual and romantic desires have been shaped by evolution to maximize reproductive success with or without conscious awareness of the adaptive function of those sometimes forbidden desires. If unfaithful individuals can elude exposure or at least minimize the negative consequences of exposed infidelity, they may have the possibility of reaping the benefits of infidelity without having to pay the costs.

Infidelity is a high-gain but high-risk reproductive strategy that is more frequently adopted by individuals who possess high risk tolerance (McDonald, Donnellan, & Navarrete, 2012). Monogamy tends to be a low-gain but low-risk reproductive strategy and so is more frequently adopted by individuals with low risk tolerance. The inner conflict between the desire to stay faithful and the temptation to be unfaithful implicitly reflects indecision about whether to implement a low-gain/low-risk or a high-gain/high-risk reproductive strategy.

Whatever the therapist's personal biases may be, framing inner conflicts in the light of evolutionary considerations (i.e., clarifying and normalizing implicit cost–benefit analyses) provides patients with a metaperspective that may help them transcend dichotomous thinking. Self-acceptance means accepting that socially uncooperative sexual desires are part of life and have a basis in human nature; mastering such desires first requires owning such desires. It is not necessarily a sign of immaturity or perversity to possess socially uncooperative and therefore socially unacceptable sexual desires. Self-acceptance also means accepting that moralistic reactions to socially uncooperative sexual behavior like sexual betrayal (anger, contempt, and disgust that motivate punitive and vindictive behavior) are also part of human nature and also has a basis in human evolution. Self-acceptance means coming to terms with both the sexually uncooperative (Freud's id) as well as the moralistic aspects (Freud's harsh superego) of human nature without rationalizing one side of human nature and disparaging the other.

What also has a basis in human evolution is a latent capacity for thoughtful and nonjudgmental reflection on our socially uncooperative sexual desires and moralistic reactions to the enactment of those desires. Humans have developed theories of mind (C. D. Frith & Frith, 2003; U. Frith & Frith, 2006) that can be used to analyze our inner conflicts. Psychotherapy can help individuals cultivate that latent capacity for thoughtful and nonjudgmental contemplation of our inner conflicts. Self-reflection may be a therapeutic process that is facilitated by all forms of psychotherapy (Castonguay & Hill, 2012), although self-reflection on inner conflict, especially unconscious sexual conflict, has been central to the Freudian approach since its inception (Brenner, 2002).

IS SEX ONLY ABOUT BREEDING? THE EVOLUTION OF NONPROCREATIVE SEXUALITY

A problem that some critics have with evolutionary explanations of human sexuality is that it may not seem to account for the high prevalence rates of nonprocreative sexuality (Frayser, 1989; Pavelka, 1995). Humans engage in a wide variety of forms of sexuality that do not result in impregnation, such as masturbation, oral sex, anal sex, homosexuality, phone sex, computer sex, sex intentionally outside of the time of ovulation, and sex with birth control. Humans seem determined to enjoy as much sexual pleasure as they possibly can without making babies.

Primatologists have noted that humans are not the only animals to engage in nonprocreative forms of sexuality (Dixson, 1998). In fact, bonobos (what used to be called pygmy chimpanzees), one of humans' closest genetic relatives, engage in quite a bit more nonprocreative sexuality than humans do. Bonobos promiscuously engage in mutual masturbation and oral sex with same-sex as well as opposite-sex partners at a high frequency. Bonobo females are able to dominate the males by forming alliances mediated by sexual relationships with each other (de Waal, 1990; de Waal & Lanting, 1997). Primatologists call nonprocreative sexuality among primates *sociosexuality* because sex serves social rather than reproductive functions (Dixson, 1998). Sociosexuality can reduce conflict over resources ("make love not war"), solidify social alliances (i.e., cement friendships), or instantiate dominance hierarchies (i.e., establish who is on top and who on the bottom of the social hierarchy; Dixson, 1998).

More superficial views of human sexuality view sexual desire as simply a biological need like hunger that must periodically be relieved to prevent the build up of tension. It doesn't mean anything because, after all, it's just sex. Yet if human nonprocreative sexuality serves adaptive social functions as it clearly does in other primates, sex is never just sex: It is always serving some underlying social function that cannot be reduced to an impersonal biological need that is nothing more than a source of impersonal tactile pleasure and tension relief. Nonprocreative sexuality serves diverse social functions, such as exchanging sex for resources, as in prostitution, or cementing a long-term social alliance, as in monogamy.

There is no sex act that doesn't make at least an implicit social statement. People can endlessly debate the underlying meaning or intent of a sexual relationship, as when couples trying to recover from infidelity debate whether the extramarital sex did or did not mean something, and, if it did mean something, what did it actually mean. Of course, we can be misreading the underlying meaning or intention of a sexual relationship, but few assume that sex is entirely meaningless in social terms. Individuals might not always be aware of the underlying social reasons for having sex (e.g., being unfaithful while drunk at an office party) because the underlying reason may be repudiated if it's socially unacceptable (e.g., to get revenge, to make a partner jealous, to get an ego boost that alleviates low self-esteem, to advance one's career).

Nonprocreative sexuality within a long-term, sexually exclusive relationship can be a way of establishing and cementing a special bond of solidarity and commitment. Sexual exclusivity of this kind therefore has significant symbolic value to humans. Sexual exclusivity could be construed as a sacrifice humans make to assert their level of commitment to a unique social alliance. The extent of the sacrifice depends on the strength of the desire for sexual variety, for a new and intoxicating infatuation, or for a more secure attachment to someone else. Sexual exclusivity represents a commitment to not only raising children together but also to feeding and protecting each other throughout the lifespan, in illness and in health. A spouse becomes an invaluable resource to the degree that he or she takes over many of same nurturing functions of a parent and will continue to take care of the romantic partner when his or her parents are long gone. Is sexual exclusivity too high a price to pay for a devoted and loving life partner who will take care of a spouse like a parent would and also help raise the children who are produced from their union? Is unwillingness to commit to sexual exclusivity a sign that the romantic partner is implicitly perceived as unworthy or undeserving of such a significant sacrifice?

Infidelity is a threat to this unique form of social alliance because infidelity means bestowing love and resources on someone outside the marriage. Romantic jealousy is simply registering the fact that a romantic partner is inclined to bestow love and sexual favors on a rival. This may mean relatively less love and devotion for oneself as well as one's children and grandchildren. It may be part of human nature to want to monopolize the sexuality of a romantic partner who has become a lifelong parental surrogate.

At first blush, it may appear that evolutionary psychology assumes heteronormativity because making a human baby requires heterosexual intercourse. Yet a deeper reading of contemporary evolutionary psychology suggests various means of facilitating reproductive success that do not require heterosexual intercourse. The theory of kin selection (Hamilton, 1964) suggests that regardless of sexual orientation, one can be reproductively successful without ever having a biological child of one's own if one facilitates the reproductive success of kin with whom one shares common genes—siblings, nieces, nephews, and cousins. One doesn't have to be a breeder to be reproductively successful; cooperative breeders such as bees take care of the numerous offspring of the queen bee that they didn't sire themselves but to whom they are genetically related. One can be reproductively successful despite being childless by being a socially cooperative and altruistic person who makes the world a better place in which one's extended family can be fruitful and multiply.

Everyone has to adapt to their unique ecological niche, so "different strokes for different folks" may be the norm when it comes to sexual strategies. It could be maladaptive to enact a rigid preset sex-linked mating strategy regardless of an ever-changing ecological context. It may be more adaptive for mating strategies to become individualized in flexibly creative ways (strategic pluralism). Some of that unique individuality may have a basis in heredity or prenatal sex hormones that influence in utero brain development while still retaining sufficient sexual fluidity to remain responsive to changing ecological conditions. An aspect of homophobia is assuming that homosexuality is not "natural," as though only heterosexuality could be a natural outgrowth of evolutionary biology. Yet the data suggest that both homosexuality and same-sex pair bonding are common in the animal kingdom (Bagemihl, 1999).

Lesbian, gay, bisexual, and transgender (LGBT) individuals may have their own unique ways of forming families and becoming parents to facilitate their own reproductive success. To the extent that LGBT individuals experience reproductive disadvantages, it is often because homophobic cultures try to suppress LGBT marriage and parenthood and prevent openly LGBT individuals from assuming parental caretaking roles, like teaching or adoption. Adults in species that are cooperative breeders, like dogs, tend to have friendly, if not nurturing, relations with the offspring of individuals from one's own social group. That's why dogs are generally good with human children.

The evolved psychology of love triangles may be as applicable to LGBT individuals as it is to heterosexual individuals given that humans may be monogamously inclined cooperative breeders who struggle with strong nonmonogamous tendencies regardless of sexual orientation or self-identified gender. There is then quite a bit of cross-cultural and individual variability in sexual morality as to how one "should" negotiate that inner conflict as various forms of consensual nonmonogamy arise as ethical alternatives to infidelity.

Miranda and Nancy came for couples therapy because they were engaged to be married. Because she wished to start married life without secrets and with a commitment to monogamy, Miranda had recently confessed to having been unfaithful. Trust needed to be rebuilt. Nancy, who had no desire for other lovers or for an open marriage, wanted reassurance that Miranda could sustain her commitment to monogamy. Nancy saw nothing wrong with consensual nonmonogamy but preferred sexual exclusivity. After several months of airing their issues, sufficient trust had been restored to go ahead with the marriage in the hope of raising a family together.

About 6 months later, Miranda came back to see me for individual psychotherapy. She was struggling with the impulse to be unfaithful once again but didn't want to succumb to temptation. Miranda was a vivacious and alluring person who enjoyed the ego inflation she experienced when getting an attractive woman to fall in love with her. Especially when she was feeling badly about herself, it provided a quick fix to her self-esteem to flirt and obtain affirmation of her romantic desirability. Miranda felt ashamed of this tendency not simply because she didn't want to be unfaithful again but also because she knew that she was just exploiting these women as an ego boost and would ultimately break their hearts when she returned to Nancy as her life partner. Therapy focused on helping Miranda overcome her dependency on the ego inflation of romantic conquest to boost her failing self-esteem.

Miranda terminated treatment when she moved to the suburbs with Nancy to start a family. Several years later, I learned that she was the mother of four children achieved through in vitro fertilization.

ARE CHEATERS BAD PEOPLE? SEXUAL MORALITY AS STRATEGIC INTERFERENCE

In the modern world, there is an appreciation that sexual morality can often be a self-serving prejudice, a tool through which minorities and enemies are seen as less than human because of their supposedly disgusting sexuality (Cortes, Demoulin, Rodriguez, Rodriguez, & Leyens, 2005). It is also appreciated that sexual morality is often hypocritical; for instance, the worst homophobes may be secretly homosexual (Adams, Wright, & Lohr, 1996). Anthropologists have revealed the tremendous cross-cultural variability of sexual value systems (Bullough, 1976). Does cultural variability in attitudes toward infidelity (Druckerman, 2007) mean that sexual morality is cultural but sex is biological? Or might sexual morality also have a basis in evolutionary biology?

Sexual morality may be reflective of human evolution in the direction of becoming monogamously inclined cooperative breeders. Sexual morality facilitates cooperative reproductive strategies by establishing sexual ground rules that individuals perceive as fair despite the self-sacrifice for the greater good. Sexual morality facilitates trust that individuals will play by those ground rules even when no one is watching. From an evolutionary perspective, infidelity is an uncooperative reproductive strategy because it involves breaking promises of sexual exclusivity and then lying about it. Yet not all adulterers believe they are doing something wrong and should have to wear a scarlet letter on their breast like Hawthorne's Hester Prynne as a lifelong punishment for adultery. The punishment does not seem to fit the crime. Sexual morality can sometimes seem more moralistic than genuinely moral.

Breaking promises and lying about it may be seen as more or less ethical depending on situational factors that might mitigate the inherent immorality of such uncooperative, untrustworthy behavior. Unfaithful partners and affair partners may feel that there are extenuating circumstances that might justify engaging in extramarital sexuality and lying about it in their particular situation. For example, the unfaithful partner may feel that lying about extramarital sex is justified because without it, a sexless marriage would be over, but the betrayed spouse would never agree to consensual partner sharing to save a sexless marriage. Breaking a promise and then lying about it seems to be the lesser of two evils. Or perhaps the unfaithful partner is planning to divorce the spouse to marry the affair partner. The postdivorce relationship with the ex-spouse might remain friendlier and so be better for the children if the affair is never exposed. Thus, there may be situations in which engaging in extramarital sexual behavior and lying about it might seem like the right thing to do. People might seem more moralistic than ethical if they have difficulty seeing that infidelity in a particular circumstance might be justified, even though the hurt it may cause others is regrettable.

Patients may be intolerant of moral ambiguity and moral relativism when it comes to infidelity. Betrayed partners would like to feel that their vindictive fury is entirely justified by the betrayal of trust. Unfaithful partners would like to feel that extenuating circumstances justify breaking a promise of sexual exclusivity and lying about it. Affair partners ("mate poachers") don't want to feel like "home-wreckers" because they don't perceive that there is anything wrong with helping someone find true love or sexual fulfillment if he or she can't find it in an unhappy marriage to an undeserving partner. Patients look to the therapist for validation of the moral legitimacy of the way they have conducted their love lives. They often assume that a presumably neutral therapist is privately judgmental but hiding the therapist's moral bias behind a fake professional facade (Kris, 1990). Perceiving the therapist as judgmental when the judgment goes against the patient may result in a rupture of the therapeutic alliance that then requires repair (Safran & Muran, 2003).

It is difficult to feel safe and secure with people like a betrayed spouse and a therapist who believe you're a bad person because you've violated their moral principles. No one likes to be the target of moral outrage. Moralistic critics may be construed as imposing an unreasonable moral value system to implicitly serve their own self-interest in a rationalized way. The therapist is therefore called on to adjudicate who is a genuinely moral person—a good person who does the right thing at the sacrifice of his or her own expense—and who is moralistic—a bad person who tries to control others by imposing moral values on others that implicitly serve that person's hidden self-interest.

Addressing dichotomous thinking generated by the dialectical tension between what is genuinely moral and what is hypocritically moralistic is quite challenging given the self-righteous indignation that individuals feel with great conviction when their moral values have been violated or when they are feeling falsely accused of immorality when they believe that they are completely innocent of wrongdoing. The social psychologist Jonathan Haidt (2012) believes that humans have evolved to possess a righteous mind with a strong penchant for moral outrage. Perhaps humans have evolved to be moralistic as well as moral when it comes to sex, so that it takes quite a bit of emotion work to replace moralistic reactions with more compassionate ones. Why is sexual morality so often used in an oppressive and hypocritical way if it has evolved to facilitate socially cooperative reproductive strategies?

Haidt (2012) suggested that morality is constituted by six universal moral intuitions. The six moral concerns are harm/suffering, fairness/injustice, liberty, loyalty, authority, and sanctity/purity. Advocates of fidelity may believe that being faithful avoids the harm that sexual betrayal inflicts, is fair because it involves mutual sacrifice for the greater good of the family, is a choice freely given at least in individualistic cultures that grant individuals the free choice of marital partners, asserts loyalty to a family member, shows respect for traditional arrangements that have withstood the test of time, and preserves the sanctity and purity of a couple's romantic bond. Advocates of nonmonogamy may believe that monogamy causes harm by unreasonably frustrating a natural and healthy desire for new sexual partners, is unfairly oppressive, unreasonably denies liberty because of the social stigma associated with nonmonogamy, interferes with developing a loyal relationship to a new romantic partner based on true love, and surrenders to a higher morality based on romantic love as a transcendent emotion. They may further contend that transcendent emotion purifies a relationship that may have been tarnished by its possibly unsavory origins. The deceit involved in infidelity might be regrettable for the harm it causes others, but the infidelity may seem fully or at least partially justified when nonmonogamy serves a higher moral purpose, as advocates of consensual nonmonogamy might argue (Rust, 2003).

Humans appear to have evolved to be a hypercooperative species that engages not only in cooperative child care but also cooperative hunting, food sharing, trading with other groups, group defense, and egalitarian power sharing through reverse dominance hierarchies in which the subordinate males join forces to suppress the alphas (Boehm, 2012). Moralistic individuals are implicitly immoral because they are exploiting the appearance of being a cooperative person who plays by the rules to hypocritically serve their own self-interest. Recent research suggests that moralistic and egoistic self-enhancement, as well as narcissism, self-deceptive styles, and power motives, are associated constructs (Paulhus & John, 1998; Vecchione & Alessandri, 2013).

The pangs of conscience appear to be governed by two groups of emotions: (a) dread of punishment and (b) empathy with the suffering of others and a desire to alleviate it (i.e., compassion). Individuals are considered most moral when compassion leads them to live by the Golden Rule of treating others the way one would like to be treated (Oth Vilaythong, Lindner, & Nosek, 2010). Because people generally prefer forgiveness over punishment when they have been exposed breaking the rules, the most genuinely moral people, those who most follow the Golden Rule, would be more compassionate and forgiving than punitive when confronting the relational transgressions of others. Hypocrisy is feeling that others should be punished harshly when caught breaking the rules but one deserves forgiveness when caught doing the same. Narcissism is associated with an unforgiving attitude toward others in the face of relational transgression yet a sense of entitlement to forgiveness when caught breaking the rules oneself (Exline, Baumeister, Bushman, Campbell, & Finkel, 2004).

Anger, contempt, and disgust are universal emotions that Ekman (1992) discovered have distinct facial expressions. Each of these emotions possesses its distinctive environmental trigger and adaptive function. Anger is triggered by perceived unfairness that threatens autonomy; anger functions to forcefully right a wrong through the threat of a punitive attack (Fischer & Roseman, 2007; Hutcherson & Gross, 2011). Contempt is triggered by an implicit threat to the established status hierarchy and puts others in their place by devaluing, shaming, and excluding them by asserting their inherent inferiority (Fischer & Roseman, 2007; Hutcherson & Gross, 2011). Disgust is triggered by threats to purity, be it moral or otherwise, and functions to avoid the disgusting object by eliminating it if need be (Hutcherson & Gross, 2011). These three emotions appear to inform morally punitive reactions (Hutcherson & Gross, 2011). Anger (Bushman & Baumeister, 1998) and contempt (Schriber, Chung, Sorensen, & Robins, 2013) appear to be heightened among more narcissistic individuals, whereas disgust is associated with the perfectionism and obsessive–compulsive traits of the so-called anal character (N. Haslam, 2011). Thus, the most egoistic, perfectionistic, and rule-bound individuals are prone to responding to relational transgression moralistically. When this trio of moralistic emotions is self-directed, it leads to guilt (self-directed anger) and shame (a combination of self-contempt and self-disgust). One's inner critic can therefore be more moralistic than moral.

Sexual selection is basically a competitive enterprise in which there are reproductive winners and losers (Darwin, 1871; Buss & Schmitt, 1993). One individual's reproductive success is often another individual's reproductive defeat. Even a highly socially cooperative reproductive strategy like monogamy that facilitates biparental care has winners and losers. Not everyone will win an equally desirable life partner. Dominant males who could reproduce with multiple partners more easily in a more polygamous or promiscuous mating system may have to settle for reproducing with just one partner in monogamous arrangements. Monogamy denies females the opportunity of sharing a resource-rich alpha male with other females and may require females to settle for reproducing with just one not-too-successful male toward the bottom of the pecking order. Individuals who feel disadvantaged by monogamous arrangements might search for a way to subvert the system and rationalize that subversion.

The individuals who most benefit by a monogamous arrangement will want to justify it and get everyone else to play by their rules (a self-serving bias), which would be to one's own benefit. The strategic interference theory (Haselton, Buss, Oubaid, & Angleitner, 2005) suggests that one way to increase one's own reproductive advantage is by doing things that interfere with the implementation of the reproductive strategies of others that conflict with and undermine one's own. For example, dominant male primates engage in what primatologists call *mate guarding* (Dixson, 1998). The females are guarded so that other males can't have sex with them and so that the females don't stray. The alpha males try to monopolize access to the fertile females, similar to when human despots created eunuchs (castrated men) to guard their harems (Betzig, 1986). Female chimpanzees sometimes mate surreptitiously with more subordinate males to elude the surveillance of the alphas (de Waal, 2007). Males of many species, from chimpanzees to lions, will kill the offspring of females with whom they have not had sexual relations (Hrdy, 1999, 2009).

Sexual morality facilitates cooperative behavior when it comes to mating because everyone agrees to play by the same rules. Yet those rules may advantage some individuals over others. Sexual morality may also be a form of strategic interference, inflicting costs on individuals who are disinclined to play by rules that appear to work to their disadvantage. Naturally, those advantaged by a monogamous mating strategy are not going to want mate poachers to think they can get away with stealing their mate without suffering reputational damage as a "home-wrecker." Faithful spouses aren't going to want unfaithful spouses to think that they will simply be forgiven without a lengthy period of probation, "living in the doghouse" until they regain the trust that they betrayed. Responding moralistically to infidelity is a form of strategic interference, perhaps motivated by fear that responding with empathy, compassion, and forgiveness might be akin to rewarding bad behavior, thus making it more likely to recur.

Individuals who feel disadvantaged by monogamous arrangements (e.g., those who feel trapped in unhappy marriage, single people who can't find desirable single partners) have ways of rationalizing their rule breaking to justify their behavior when following the rules is not to their advantage. These individuals would of course prefer compassion and forgiveness if caught, given the extenuating circumstances that appear to justify rule breaking in their particular situation. They feel that those who respond to their rule breaking with anger, contempt, and disgust, rather than compassion for the desperate circumstances that motivated them to break the rules, are acting moralistically. Such individuals may seek psychotherapy to obtain a less judgmental hearing.

Ironically, it is not uncommon to respond moralistically to the moralism of others without seeing the hidden hurt, fear, and vulnerability that moral outrage hides. The victims of relational transgressions may hide their vulnerability behind moral outrage because they don't want to appear weak, assuming that perpetrators will further exploit their weakness. There is implicit hypocrisy when unfaithful partners hope to be forgiven for their infidelities but then go on to judge their betrayed partners harshly (moralistically) for holding a grudge against them (e.g., betrayed partners who are morally outraged "should" be more like the French, who are presumably above responding moralistically to extramarital affairs because of their presumed sexual sophistication about affairs of the heart).

Traits often coevolve in mutually antagonistic ways (West-Eberhard, 2014). For example, predators evolve ever more intelligent forms of stealth and conning to catch their prey, while prey evolve ever more intelligent evasive strategies to elude capture. *Antagonistic coevolution* means that for cooperative strategies to evolve, adaptive ways must be found to deal with uncooperative individuals (see Cosmides & Tooby, 1992, on cognitive adaptations for detecting cheaters). Likewise, for uncooperative strategies to evolve, adaptive ways must be found to defeat strategies designed to detect and punish cheaters—that is, strategies of avoiding detection, such as camouflage, and of avoiding punishment, such as defending one's innocence, counter-complaints that turn the tables by blaming the victim, and, if all else fails, begging for forgiveness.

The therapist who works with infidelity becomes embroiled in the process of *sexually antagonistic coevolution* (West-Eberhard, 2014) by being drawn onto one side or the other. Ultimately, the therapeutic profession usually does take a side—the side of trying to cultivate a moral (honest and trustworthy) and cooperative approach to long-term relationships based on empathy and compassion for the suffering that uncooperative, dishonest, and untrustworthy behavior causes. Therapists are generally cautioned against endorsing a moralistic approach to long-term relationships that shames uncooperative, dishonest, or untrustworthy partners by treating them as objects of moral outrage, contempt, and disgust in the hope that they will fall in line with cultural expectations of morality. Therapists tend to assume that the best antidote to depression, anxiety, and anger is being in a stable, securely attached, long-term relationship that is based on intimacy, trust, and mutual respect and so use psychotherapy to facilitate this interpersonal capacity (Florsheim & McArthur, 2009).

Responding with anger, contempt, and disgust to relational transgression might inhibit empathy in the transgressor for the emotional damage caused by the transgression (Josephs & McLeod, 2014). The betrayed partner's hurt, vulnerability, and suffering may be hidden behind a self-righteous, moralizing facade. Emotion-focused and integrative couples therapists note that more difficult emotions such as anger may hide softer emotions like sadness, humiliation, or fear of abandonment (Chapman & Compton, 2003; Johnson, 2004). It is not easy to empathize with hurt or frightened feelings when they are hidden behind someone's moral outrage and one is the object of that outrage. One's own automatic feelings of fear and reactive anger in response to moralistic aggression motivate defensive behavior. Such defensive responses tend to override any latent capacity for empathy one might possess. Empathy fades when people feel threatened unless a way is found to promote empathic identification with the offender that helps curb defensive reactions (McGregor et al., 1998; Schimel, Wohl & Williams, 2006).

Evolution appears to have equipped humans with two emotional operating systems for regulating sexual morality. One is based on the universal emotions of anger, contempt, and disgust and is the basis for moralistic outrage against rule violators; when internalized, this becomes the basis for shame and guilt. The second system is based on the universal capacity for empathic identification with the harm one's behavior has inflicted and a desire to repair the damage done (this capacity may be latent in some individuals). The moralistic response is defensive and automatic when feeling threatened. A more compassionate response requires cultivating an ability to reflect on the impact of one's behavior on the mental states of others, even when feeling attacked.

Sexual morality is Janus-faced—that is, it is two-sided. The aspect based on empathy, compassion, and forgiveness facilitates cooperative behavior. The aspect based on anger, contempt, and disgust is a form of strategic interference that tries to impose one's own rules on others even when those rules are to one's own advantage at the other's expense. The therapeutic enterprise is based on the premise that it is beneficial to replace moralistic reactions with more accepting and compassionate ones. This can be facilitated as much by role modeling as by didactic methods. It's not simply what the therapist says but also how the therapist says it. The therapist tries to role model treating even self-serving and offensive viewpoints respectfully and with empathy.

The therapist also tries to respond respectfully and empathetically to patients who commit relational transgressions against the therapist (e.g., missing sessions without calling to cancel) or moralistically (e.g., harshly castigating the therapist for his or her failure to be a "good-enough" therapist when the patient's expectations are perfectionistic). Therapists must show that they can practice what they preach when put to the test to be a compelling role model. That may require periodically lapsing into moralistic rather than moral responses when feeling frustrated or attacked by the patient. It takes time for a therapist to earn patients' trust—time for patients to learn that the therapist is looking out for their best interest rather than trying to make them feel badly for not living up to presumed moral standards. Patients may believe their therapist implicitly imposes certain standards while pretending otherwise.

Carol got married in her late 30s hoping to have a baby before her biological clock ran out. Her boyfriend, Ted, wanted to marry Carol but didn't want to have children. Carol played hardball by threatening to break up with him unless he consented to have children, so Ted consented. But after a few months of marriage, Ted changed his mind. Carol was enraged with him because she felt he had betrayed her trust. Ted protested that she had manipulated him into saying he would have at least one child, although it was wrong to bring a child into the world that was unwanted by his or her father.

Carol then embarked on a series of extramarital affairs, having unprotected sex hoping to get pregnant, as Ted never had sex with her without using a condom. If she got pregnant, she would then decide what to do about her marriage. Yet Carol started getting suspicious that Ted might have been having an affair of his own when he became friendly with a younger graduate student with whom he was taking classes at night school. Carol was outraged; she felt her infidelity was entirely justified given Ted's broken promise, but Ted's infidelity would be totally unjustified. Yet Carol wasn't sure that Ted actually was having an affair, and she worried that she might just be "paranoid," but she indignantly asserted that if she ever found out for sure, she would divorce him on the spot.

Initially, when I tried to help Carol see the world from Ted's point of view in a mindful way—to just observe it for what it was without judging it—Carol responded with self-righteous outrage. She chastised me, asserting that my job as her therapist was to take her side, not her husband's. She stormed out of the session early, slamming the door. I became the object of Carol's scorn because my attempt to help her see the world from her husband's point of view was seen as implicitly excusing him for not having kept his word. My job was not to become an apologist for her husband's bad behavior. Empathy with her husband's perspective aroused guilt because it made her feel that her retaliatory infidelity was not justified if he had potentially valid reasons for having broken his promise to have children, especially if his promise had been given under duress. Carol felt that breaking the rule of sexual exclusivity and lying about it was justified if honoring that rule unreasonably doomed her to childlessness. She wasn't going to divorce her husband and make herself vulnerable to ending up all alone without either a husband or a child.

Over time, Carol was able to appreciate that Ted loved her and was devoted to her in his own way. It wasn't right for him to agree to marriage on her terms only to change his mind as her biological clock was running out, but it was understandable: He didn't want to live his life without her just as she didn't want to divorce him without having a replacement already lined up. It wasn't right for her to manipulate him into marrying her knowing he really didn't want to have children and might have been dooming their future child to being raised by a begrudgingly accommodating father who really didn't want to be a parent. Nevertheless, it was understandable that she wouldn't let her biological clock run out without trying to get pregnant one way or another. Acceptance of Ted's viewpoint enabled Carol to eventually forgive him for his betrayal and allowed her to begin to appreciate their marriage for what it was rather than resent it for what it wasn't. Carol gave up having extramarital affairs (an example of retaliatory infidelity) as she forgave Ted for refusing to have a child with her.

Carol's acceptance of Ted's viewpoint was facilitated by her gradual identification with my ability to empathize with the hurt behind her moral outrage at my being sympathetic to Ted's viewpoint. I tried to role model as best I could a moral rather than a moralistic response to what to me felt like her unfair criticism of my attempt to see the world from her husband's viewpoint. If I could respond nondefensively and with empathy despite feeling unfairly criticized by Carol, maybe she could learn to respond with understanding to her husband's betrayal and assume responsibility for the destructive elements of her retaliatory response to his broken promises.

Initially patients might feel judged and invalidated by a therapist who empathizes with both sides of a conflict. Patients often feel that points of view they reject do not warrant empathy but should be met with contempt or disgust, shaming and silencing the person who possesses a morally offensive viewpoint. Empathy with an opposing viewpoint, especially an offensive one, seems to undermine the legitimacy of one's own currently advocated viewpoint and so is threatening; it may evoke a moralistic response directed at the therapist for seeming to betray the patient's trust by siding with an adversary. Yet if the patient is ever to have a successful cooperative relationship, it would need to be based on a capacity to empathize with the suffering of a frustrated but frustrating romantic partner. This is challenging when it requires empathizing with the suffering of a romantic partner who has inflicted an attachment injury, be it a sexual betrayal or a harshly moralistic response to a perceived transgression.

Buddhists say that your enemy is your best teacher (Wallace, 2001). It's easy to have compassion for the suffering of someone who has always treated you well. Having compassion for someone who has treated you poorly is not so simple. Empathy for the suffering that uncooperative behavior inflicts on a romantic partner motivates individuals to keep their promises and to curb moralistic tendencies when partners don't honor their promises. Evolutionary psychology deepens that empathy by helping clinicians understand why uncooperative reproductive strategies remain part of human nature. It's not so much that patients need to be given explicit evolutionary explanations of their behavior as that therapists need to cultivate a metaperspective about human nature that helps them transcend their own moralistic reactions to patients' uncooperative reproductive strategies.

CONCLUSION

Evolutionary psychology tends to focus on a universal human nature, although there is also an evolutionary psychology of individual differences (Buss & Hawley, 2011). Future chapters focus on individual differences—on how differences in attachment style, self-reported gender, narcissism, mate value, jealousy, culturally instilled attitudes, developmental level, and communication style interact to shape how unique individuals negotiate the psychology of love triangles. It can be overwhelming to see how many variables significantly influence the psychology of love triangles and the complexity of the interactions among all of these variables. The challenge for therapists is to appreciate their patients as unique individuals. Reducing patients' psychology to a simplistic psychological formulation is an omnipresent danger any time an influential individual difference variable is overlooked.

2

TOO CLOSE FOR COMFORT: ATTACHMENT STYLE AND INFIDELITY

Strategic pluralism suggests that humans must make adaptations for reproductive success that are responsive to the unique ecological conditions in which they are born. Evolutionary developmental psychologists, such as Belsky (2000), have suggested that adult attachment style—how people form long-term romantic bonds with others—may provide a means of adjusting one's mating strategy to the unique environmental circumstances. Humans are born into certain ecological conditions that may be resource rich or resource poor. Perhaps the quality and quantity of early childhood parenting are environmental cues that alert the individual as to whether one was born into a world in which monogamy or nonmonogamy will pay off as a future reproductive strategy.

If childhood learning prepares individuals to function adaptively in the adult world, it is likely that children are learning something about adult romantic relationships and parenting simply through observational learning. For example, hunter–gatherer children sleep with their parents and may

http://dx.doi.org/10.1037/0000053-003
The Dynamics of Infidelity: Applying Relationship Science to Psychotherapy Practice, by L. Josephs

witness parental sexual intercourse from an early age (Konner, 2005). Hunter–gatherer children as young as 4 or 5 years old engage in sexual rehearsal play in the bushes with their peers (Konner, 2005). Children are likely to role model whatever they observe of adult romantic relationships and are capable of observational learning from as young as 9 months old (Tomasello, 1999).

Resource-rich environments may activate a more quality-over-quantity reproductive strategy and a slow life history strategy. Plentiful resources allow for considerable investment in each child for an extended period of time. Resource-poor environments may activate a more quantity-over-quality reproductive strategy because there are only minimal resources for each child. Reproductive success is then more about the survival of the fittest child in an inhospitable environment.

Not surprisingly, monogamous parents tend to raise children who grow up to be monogamous. In contrast, children of divorce are more likely to divorce (Glenn & Kramer, 1987), just as children of parents who are unfaithful are more likely to be unfaithful themselves (Hunyady, Josephs, & Jost, 2008). Father absence predicts a more promiscuous orientation in both sexes (Surbey, 1998). Stable parental investment from two parents may be a cue of growing up in a resource-rich environment, whereas high parental conflict, infidelity, divorce, and father absence may be cues of a more resource-poor environment (Belsky, 2000).

Parents who invest more in mating (i.e., searching for new, better, or more sexual partners) because they are unhappily married, divorced, or just want sexual variety may have less time, energy, and sometimes money to invest in parenting. Children may object to parental divorce or infidelity because at some unconscious level they appreciate that it means fewer resources—emotional as well as material—for them, as limited resources are directed away from themselves and toward their parents' lovers and the children of their parents' lovers. One divorced father told me he wouldn't remarry because he didn't want his hard-earned money going toward stepchildren rather than his own biological children, who had already suffered downward mobility as a result of the divorce.

Children may be monitoring their parents' love lives closely. They may be drawing conclusions, unconsciously as well as consciously, about how to conduct their own future love lives using their parents as role models. More than a century ago, Sigmund Freud (1912/1958) discovered that children's experiences with their parents can become a template for their own adult romantic relationships. Freud believed that men may unconsciously be looking to marry someone like their mothers, and women may be unconsciously looking to marry someone like their fathers. This is an aspect of Freud's (1905/1953, 1910/1957b, 1924/1961) controversial Oedipus complex: Little boys and little girls want to sleep with and marry their opposite-sex parent.

Freud believed that adults repeat with their lovers the same conflicts they had with their parents while growing up. So a girl who grows up with an alcoholic father ends up with an alcoholic husband, although she may have vowed never to marry an alcoholic. A boy with a domineering mother grows up to marry a bossy wife, although he was consciously searching for the opposite. From a psychoanalytic perspective, there is likely to be dissociation between conscious romantic preferences as stated in a self-report measure and implicit preferences that unconsciously guide actual mate choices. There is some empirical support for the idea that adults are more implicitly attracted to faces that possess a family resemblance, although that attraction is repudiated when they are reminded of the similarity (Fraley & Marks, 2010).

Freud based his theories on his therapeutic work with adults in psychoanalysis. Thus, he reconstructed his patients' childhood conflicts and traumas that formed their adult personalities and approaches to adult romantic relationships. As it turns out, there is quite a bit of empirical support for the idea that early childhood experiences might shape one's future love map (Money, 1986); this support comes from attachment theory (Mikulincer & Shaver, 2010). The quality of the child's earliest relationship with her or his parents does indeed influence the quality of adult romantic relationships (Mikulincer & Goodman, 2006).

ROMANTIC LOVE AS A BOND OF ATTACHMENT: LOOKING FOR A GOOD MOMMY OR DADDY

Attachment theory was developed by the psychiatrist and psychoanalyst John Bowlby (1969, 1973, 1980, 1988); it proposes that the nature of the infant's attachment relationship to its mother in the first year of life has long-lasting effects. Bowlby noted that all mammalian offspring develop attachment relationships with their mothers and all mammalian mothers are oriented toward meeting their offspring's need for attachment. Attachment facilitates infant survival by keeping the offspring within close proximity of a protective mother until the offspring is mature enough to fend for itself in the world.

In the 1940s, psychoanalysts began to observe infants' actual relationship with their mothers, noting the effect of lengthy separations of mother and child on childhood development. Early in World War II, the Nazis began bombing London. For safety, many children were separated from their parents and sent to live in the English countryside. The children left behind in London with their parents had to flee to bomb shelters, where they could hear the bombing and then see the devastation when they emerged from the shelter. To the surprise of researchers, the children who had remained in London, close to their parents, appeared better adjusted after the war than the children separated from their parents but kept safe in the English countryside (Burlingham & Freud, 1949). Bowlby (1944) noted that juvenile delinquents had often suffered earlier loss of or separation from their mothers and that hospitalized children separated from their mothers responded poorly (Bowlby, 1951).

Further research demonstrated that lengthy separation from the mother is experienced as abandonment (Bowlby, 1973). Early childhood loss is a risk factor for depression in adulthood (Patten, 1991; Stikkelbroek, Prinzie, de Graaf, ten Have, & Cuijpers, 2012). Bowlby (1973) discovered a three-phase response to prolonged separation. The infant's initial response is angry protest to try to bring the mother back. If angry protest fails, the infant feels abandoned and becomes sad and depressed. Over time, the infant simply becomes detached. Detachment shuts down the pain of loss and suppresses attachment needs in order to survive in a world where the infant is alone. Similar responses are observable among infants of other species when separated from their mothers (Gilmer & McKinney, 2003).

For most birds and mammals, attachment is just a stage of infant development to be outgrown. Birds learn to fly and leave the nest, never to return. More solitary animals, such as bears, wander off one day to fend for themselves; more social animals join a herd or a troop different from the one in which they were raised to avoid inbreeding with siblings. In contrast, monogamous animals go on to form adult attachments for biparental care. For many monogamous animals, it might be serial monogamy, teaming up for a breeding season to raise an offspring, then finding a new partner for the next season. Most monogamous animals do not mate for life, but given how long it takes for human children to reach maturity and become independent, and with the evolution of grandparenting, there could be selection pressure for lifelong monogamy. It would seem that, for humans, the monogamous relationships of the securely attached are more stable and more likely to last a lifetime than the monogamous relationships of the insecurely attached (Knoke, Burau, & Roehrle, 2010).

Monogamy appears to work by activating the mother–infant attachment process in the adult sexual relationship between the sexes. Humans leave the nest only to begin searching for a parental surrogate in their adult romantic relationships. Like Freud before him, Bowlby initially suggested that the infant's relationship with the mother becomes the prototype for an adult romantic relationship. In a famous quote, Freud (1905/1953) noted that

> no one who has seen a baby sinking back satiated from the breast and falling asleep with flushed cheeks and a blissful smile can escape the reflection that this picture persists as a prototype of the expression of sexual satisfaction in later life. (p. 182)

A seminal article, "Romantic Love Conceptualized as an Attachment Process," published in 1987 by the social psychologists Cindy Hazan and Philip

Shaver, initiated the systematic empirical study of adult romantic relationships as an attachment relationship. Hazan and Shaver noted that for every documented feature of adult romantic relationships, there is a plausible parallel in the infant's attachment relationship to its mother. Love in both infancy and adulthood involves eye contact, holding, kissing, touching, caressing, smiling, crying, and clinging; the desire to be comforted by the relationship partner when distressed; the experience of anxiety, anger, and sorrow after separation and loss; and the experience of happiness and joy upon reunion. A secure attachment to one's attachment partner causes the person to feel more confident, safe, and happy and relate to others in more outgoing and kinder ways. In addition, there are typical negative reactions in the infant's relationship to his or her mother as well as in adult romantic relationships when the attachment partner is not available or responsive to a person's bids for closeness. The person can become anxious, preoccupied, and hypersensitive to signs of rejection or become withdrawn and distant to avoid the hurt of rejection. Hazan and Shaver concluded that an infant's attachment to his or her mother and an adult's bond to his or her lover reflect variants of a single core process.

Psychotherapists see these adult attachment processes clearly in their consulting rooms. Young adults often seek psychotherapy after a painful relationship breakup in which they were rejected. They are depressed and seek reassurance that they are not some unlovable person who will always be a loser in love. It seems their lives are ruined, having lost the seemingly irreplaceable love of their life. Months of therapy go by with minimal improvement, trying to help these forlorn patients see that they are catastrophizing—viewing themselves as more unlovable and the partner as more irreplaceable than is actually the case. They appreciate the reassurance but secretly believe everything really is as bad as they think it is. Then these patients typically come in one day after having found a new lover, feeling happy and without a care in the world. The new love confirms without a doubt that they are indeed lovable, and the old partner appears to have been replaced by someone much better. The therapy is deemed a great success, and the patients are ready to graduate. No matter how irrational the feelings generated by romantic rejection may seem, at least to an outside observer, it becomes apparent that there is no suffering worse than the heartbreak of romantic rejection because it feels like being motherless or fatherless. And there is no joy like finding the love of one's life because it's like finding a mommy or daddy who will love you forever and ever.

Infidelity is an intriguing puzzle from the attachment perspective. If the greatest bliss in adulthood is finding a surrogate mother or father who offers permanent love and makes one feel safe, secure, confident, and lovable, why endanger the security of the relationship by engaging in infidelity? If there is empathy for a romantic partner's deep feelings of attachment, why make him jealous and insecure by bestowing sexual favors or love on a romantic rival? Adult attachment appears designed by evolution to facilitate the monogamous relationships that support biparental care. Why then does adult attachment fail to achieve, at such a high frequency, the sexual exclusivity it seems designed to facilitate?

CHEATING ON MOM AND DAD: OEDIPUS REVISITED FROM AN ATTACHMENT PERSPECTIVE

Ainsworth (1967; Ainsworth, Blehar, Waters, & Wall, 1978) documented that as early as 1 year old, children have developed discernible styles of attachment dependent on the quality of the early mother–infant relationship. Ainsworth and colleagues developed a novel research method for exploring the nature of the 1-year-old child's attachment bond to its mother called the *Strange Situation*. The mother and her 1-year-old toddler are brought to a playroom that has a one-way mirror for observing their interactions. Mother and toddler are allowed to use the playroom and its toys, and usually the toddler begins to play. At a certain point, the mother is instructed to leave the toddler alone in the room. Almost immediately, the toddler begins to cry in separation protest. The separation is kept mercifully brief; the point is not to traumatize the child but to study how the child handles separation from and then reuniting with the mother. After a brief but often upsetting separation, the mother returns.

It turns out that observing the reunion after a brief separation is highly instructive. It reveals that children have already acquired a discernible style of managing their attachment relationship to the mother. Adult attachment researchers tend to see four basic styles of attachment that emerge in the first year of life and that can potentially last throughout the lifespan: secure, anxious/preoccupied, avoidant/dismissive, and disorganized (see Mikulincer & Shaver, 2010, for a discussion of the different attachment style nosologies). Toddlers who are securely attached to their mothers deal with the Strange Situation by soliciting a big hug from their mothers, and after a little comforting, they are calm and return to exploratory play using their mothers as a secure home base. In contrast, anxiously attached toddlers turn to their mothers for comforting, but they seem inconsolable. They cling to their mothers, apparently out of fear of further separation, if not abandonment. Another group of infants appear indifferent to their mothers' return. Those mothers get the cold shoulder. Those infants are considered avoidantly attached because they appear to suppress their attachment needs on the assumption that the mother will be unresponsive or unreliable.

Not surprisingly, mothers who are rejecting, unresponsive, or unreliable in meeting their children's attachment needs are likely to raise insecurely attached children who will deal with their attachment insecurity in two predominant ways: They either become anxiously clingy or dismissively indifferent and avoidant. Some children oscillate between these two coping strategies and are considered to exhibit disorganized attachment because they don't have one consistent coping style (Main & Solomon, 1986). Disorganized attachment is more likely to arise from neglectful or abusive parenting (Milot et al., 2014).

Researchers have developed different methods of measuring attachment style throughout childhood and into adulthood. It turns out that attachment style as assessed in the Strange Situation at 1 year can predict attachment style at later points of development (Fraley, 2002). It is not that one's attachment style is set in stone by the end of the first year of life, but there does seem to be some consistency in attachment style throughout childhood. Most likely, this is in part because the parents' ways of relating to their children and the children's ways of relating to their parents remain fairly consistent. However, trauma in later childhood may turn a securely attached child into an insecurely attached child (Muller, Kraftcheck, & McLewin, 2004), whereas an insecurely attached infant or toddler could become more securely attached if the parents alter their ways of relating to the child because they have become less depressed, less anxious, less angry, or have learned to express their feelings in more appropriate ways. Attachment-based interventions in childhood try to help parents alter their behavior to enable their children to become more securely attached (Dozier & Roben, 2015).

Self-report measures of attachment style in adulthood appear to be significantly correlated with many aspects of adult romantic relationships (Mikulincer & Goodman, 2006). For example, the Experience of Close Relationship Questionnaire comprises two subscales: an anxious attachment subscale and an avoidant attachment subscale (Brennan, Clark, & Shaver, 1998). A low score on both scales indicates secure attachment. One can also be high on both scales and experience both anxious and avoidant attachment simultaneously.

Cooper et al. (2006) summarized the research suggesting that individuals with different attachment styles use sexual behavior to achieve their optimal levels of intimacy within their romantic relationships. According to Cooper et al., securely attached adults are comfortable with their own sexuality and motivated to have sex to achieve intimacy with their partner. These individuals are more likely to have sex within a committed relationship, less accepting of casual sex, and less likely than insecurely attached individuals to have extra-pair sex, one-night stands, or promiscuous sex partners (Hazan, Campa, & Gur-Yaish, 2006).

Anxious attachment expresses itself somewhat differently in men and women within the sexual domain. Men who are anxiously attached tend to have sex less frequently and have fewer sex partners. Conversely, anxiously attached women tend to have sex at a younger age, are less likely to be in a sexually exclusive relationship, and are more likely to have extra-pair sex (Hazan et al., 2006).

People with avoidant attachment styles tend to have more permissive attitudes about sex and are more likely to have sex outside of a committed relationship (Hazan et al., 2006). Feldman and Cauffman (1999) demonstrated that individuals with an avoidant attachment style were more accepting of infidelity. Avoidantly attached individuals are more likely to separate love from lust. They may prefer sex to be more casual or impersonal because sex associated with emotional intimacy may feel too smothering and suffocating.

Allen and Baucom (2004) found that individuals with a dismissive style reported reasons for cheating consistent with wanting autonomy from the primary relationship. Individuals with fearful and preoccupied styles of attachment were more likely to report feelings of neglect or rejection from the primary relationship and a desire for closeness as reasons to seek an extradyadic relationship. Research has demonstrated that men may be more likely to possess an avoidant (dismissive) style, whereas women are more likely to possess preoccupied or fearful attachment style (Del Giudice, 2011; Feeney, 1999; Levy, Kelly, & Jack, 2006). Although men are more likely than women to be distressed by sexual as opposed to emotional jealousy, that sex difference diminishes significantly when comparing men and women with similar attachment styles (Levy, Kelly, & Jack, 2006).

To the extent that infidelity may be a symptom of insecure attachment, the treatment for infidelity is to facilitate a capacity for secure attachment, be it through individual or couples therapy. Individuals will not relinquish their defensive intimacy avoidance or their anxiety-ridden but angrily demanding quest for reassurance as long as they feel insecurely attached. The underlying attachment insecurities must first be alleviated for individuals to give up the defensive ways of relating that generate marital problems. Anxiously attached individuals may be perceived as too needy or angrily demanding, while avoidantly attached individuals may be perceived as withdrawn in a hostile way (Domingue & Mollen, 2009). Yet such individuals cannot give up their defensive ways of relating because those defenses protect them from their underlying fears of suffering further attachment injury. The underlying vulnerability to attachment injury must be addressed before individuals will express their hurt and anger in more open and constructive ways that are less angrily demanding or avoidant.

LOVE THEM AND LEAVE THEM: INSECURE ATTACHMENT AS AN ADAPTATION FOR A SHORT-TERM REPRODUCTIVE STRATEGY

Insecure attachment appears to activate a more short-term reproductive strategy. It may be telling the growing brain that when ecological conditions are resource poor, it's better to grow up quickly, reproduce quickly, and go for quantity over quality (Belsky, Steinberg, & Draper, 1991). Children who suffer parental divorce, infidelity, and father absence—all childhood experiences that tend to generate attachment insecurity—are less likely to have stable monogamous relationships as adults (Glenn & Kramer, 1987; Hunyady et al., 2008; Surbey, 1998).

Certain gender differences in motivations for infidelity—that men are more likely to seek casual sex, whereas women are more likely to seek intimacy outside of marriage (Atkins, Baucom, & Jacobson, 2001)—might be in part a function of men tending toward a higher prevalence rate of avoidant attachment and women tending toward a higher prevalence rate of anxious attachment (Del Giudice, 2011). Avoidantly attached men may practice a "love them and leave them" reproductive strategy. They may separate sex from intimacy to allow for impersonal casual sex without forming a romantic attachment, and to gratify the desire for sexual variety and novelty. When bored, they move on to someone new and more exciting. Such avoidantly attached married men may be more likely to go to strip clubs or use prostitutes so that they can enjoy sex without intimacy.

In contrast, anxiously attached women may form intense romantic attachments but respond poorly to the first hint of rejection by looking for an affair partner to supply external validation. Anxiously attached women may end up implementing a short-term strategy not because they consciously seek it as do avoidantly attached men, but by default because their long-term relationships are unstable.

Avoidantly attached men and anxiously attached women may be drawn to one another like moths to a flame and can be a risk factor for intimate partner violence (Doumas, Pearson, Elgin, & McKinley, 2008). Anxiously attached women may be attracted to avoidantly attached men because they seem independent and self-sufficient, qualities they feel they lack. They don't want a man who seems to be as desperately needy as they are. Avoidantly attached men may be attracted to anxiously attached women because they think such women might offer casual sex without commitment more freely than more securely attached women. Yet anxiously attached women may become upset when a more committed relationship does not form. They then become angrily demanding in a manner that drives avoidantly attached men away (Domingue

& Mollen, 2009). At that point, avoidantly attached men may begin to look for an affair partner who is "lower maintenance" (i.e., less needy or less demanding), while anxiously attached women might look for an affair partner to make their partners jealous and get affirmation of their sexual desirability.

Does attachment theory imply that casual sex outside of a committed relationship is always a sign of insecure attachment? Not necessarily. Securely attached individuals may enjoy casual sex even though they are not as oriented toward casual sexual relationships as the insecurely attached (Brennan & Shaver, 1995). The securely attached generally have more positive sexual experiences than the insecurely attached (Brassard, Shaver, & Lussier, 2007). Securely attached individuals are more likely to be authentic in their romantic relationships (Lopez & Rice, 2006). Being authentic and securely attached means being more honest in one's self-presentation, viewing deception as unacceptable, and being more likely to risk being vulnerable in an intimate relationship to achieve intimacy (Gillath, Sesko, Shaver, & Chun, 2010; Leak & Cooney, 2001; Lopez & Rice, 2006). The quality of casual as well as long-term sexual relationships among the securely attached is likely to involve less game-playing than these relationships among the insecurely attached.

COMMUNICATION BREAKDOWN: ATTACHMENT STYLES AND MARITAL COMMUNICATION

Adult attachment researchers have discovered that adult attachment styles predict not only sexual behavior but also the quality of an individual's thought processes and ways of communicating with others. Researchers have developed a measure called the Adult Attachment Interview (AAI; George, Kaplan, & Main, 1984, 1985, 1996). The AAI asks research subjects a variety of questions about their intimate relationships with their parents and others. Attachment style is assessed not so much from the content of the AAI (e.g., whether the research subjects had a happy childhood) as from the narrative style, that is, how research subjects talk about their happy or unhappy childhood. Securely attached individuals discuss their childhood experiences in clear and coherent ways. They are able to discuss difficult childhood experiences in direct and cooperative ways, and their memories sound believably grounded in reality (Crowell, Fraley, & Shaver, 1999; George et al., 1984, 1985, 1996). The securely attached are considered free and autonomous in respect to attachment. In contrast, dismissively/avoidantly attached individuals are uncomfortable being interviewed about their childhood relationships. They deny the influence of their early attachment relationships on their current personality, have difficulty recalling specific events, and have a need to put a positive spin on apparently negative experiences. Memories of parental rejection are reported despite claims that the parents were loving. Individuals classified as preoccupied/anxious give long-winded answers marked by confusion and inconsistency. They often report having had intrusive parenting from parents who demanded to be taken care of themselves (Crowell et al., 1999; George et al., 1984, 1985, 1996).

Unsurprisingly, not only do attachment styles predict how individuals think about themselves and their relationships with others, they also predict how individuals express themselves in their intimate relationships (Feeney, Kelly, Gallois, Peterson, & Terry, 1999). Anxiously attached individuals persistently seek reassurance from others that they are lovable no matter how often that reassurance has already been provided (Evraire, Ludmer, & Dozois, 2014). Anxious individuals may have difficulty attending accurately and consistently to a partner's thoughts and feelings because of their self-focus and worries about being criticized or rejected. Anxious individuals try to suppress behavior that might be perceived as too needy or clingy. Ironically, they may mistakenly think they are healthfully asserting themselves when they make angry demands subsequent to feeling rejected. They don't recognize that they come across not as confidently assertive but as unreasonably entitled, self-righteous, and excessively needy. (For a review of the communication style of the anxiously attached, see Mikulincer & Shaver, 2010, pp. 297–299.)

Avoidant individuals are less interested than nonavoidant individuals in promoting warm and affectionate interactions and may have difficulty expressing their concerns and feelings, as well as responding sensitively to a partner's needs and comments. Avoidant individuals report high levels of emotional self-control and hiding feelings from partners. They don't engage in "sweet talk" or "baby talk" because it embarrasses them. Avoidant individuals tend to laugh less, touch less, make less eye contact, and smile less. Their general way of relating seems cool, distant, and disinterested. (For a review of the communication style of the avoidantly attached, see Mikulincer & Shaver, 2010, pp. 297–299.)

Insecurely attached individuals have maladaptive reactions to a partner's relational transgressions, including infidelity. Anxiously attached partners are more likely to respond to a relational transgression either by "exit" responses—attempts to hurt the partner by leaving or retaliating—or by "neglect" responses, such as ignoring the partner or refusing to discuss things. Anxious individuals ruminate obsessively about the betrayal in nonproductive ways. In contrast, more secure individuals will deal with a relational transgression with less "voice" (i.e., less pressure to agree with the betrayed partner's viewpoint to avoid a punitive response) to avoid further escalation of conflict and more patience or loyalty that views the partner's transgression as a temporary aberration, so it makes sense to wait for the partner to come around. Avoidant individuals distance themselves from the transgressing partner and minimize the importance of the threatening episode. Secure partners are more likely to forgive their transgressing partners if their partner is available, attentive, and supportive, whereas insecurely attached individuals tended to remain unforgiving. In general, securely attached individuals have better conflict resolution skills than do the insecurely attached. Ironically, not only are insecurely attached partners more likely to be unfaithful, they are also more likely to respond moralistically when they are the betrayed party. (For a review of how attachment style influences the response to relational transgression, see Mikulincer & Shaver, 2010, pp. 299–301.)

Securely attached individuals communicate in comfortable and open ways. They communicate effectively and are less frequently involved in destructive arguments. Their empathic accuracy is greater than more insecurely attached individuals. (For a review of how attachment style influences conflict management, see Mikulincer & Shaver, 2010, pp. 301–305.) Securely attached individuals are more exploratory and open to intimate communication in their sexual relationships (Davis et al., 2006; Hazan & Zeifman, 1994).

In sum, securely attached individuals appear to possess the communication skills that marital therapists like John Gottman (1999) believe individuals require to have successful long-term relationships and that behavioral marital therapists teach individuals who lack these skills. Behavioral marital therapists coach couples to communicate the way more securely attached individuals do, hoping to facilitate a more securely attached relationship. Securely attached individuals may be less inclined to be unfaithful because they are having more satisfying marital relationships, whereas the insecurely attached are more likely to be unfaithful because they are suffering communication breakdown in their most intimate relationships.

AN EMOTION-FOCUSED APPROACH TO INCREASING COUPLES' ATTACHMENT SECURITY

Susan Johnson (2004) developed an innovative approach to couples therapy based on attachment theory. Johnson believes that many couples therapists are treating the symptoms (e.g., poor marital communication skills) rather than the cause of marital dysfunction. Marital communications therapists tend to believe that teaching couples communication skills will alleviate marital discord. Johnson instead contends that addressing the problem of attachment insecurity directly is the best way to alleviate marital discord.

According to Johnson (2004), insecurely attached individuals have certain coping styles—self-protective defensive strategies that tend to alienate their partners. Partners often cannot see beyond these off-putting defense mechanisms to appreciate the emotional vulnerability hidden behind the defensive facade. As a consequence, insecurely attached individuals do not receive the empathy that they need and desire not simply because their partner lacks empathy but because of the hostile distancing or angrily demanding way in which they relate, out of fear of suffering an attachment injury, which pushes their partner away. Such self-protective interaction activates the partner's attachment insecurities and defenses. Dismissive treatment feels like being put down, distancing treatment can feel like abandonment, and demanding treatment can make one feel one just isn't good enough. If couples desire empathy, they need to learn to stop relating defensively in ways that are dismissive, distancing, and demanding.

Johnson's (2004) solution is to get couples to speak from a place of emotional vulnerability rather than defensiveness. Many people fear that if they expose their vulnerability, they are also exposing weakness, leaving them open to attack by an angrily rejecting partner. Johnson found that more often, it is the opposite: Letting down a self-protective wall and opening up honestly and authentically (exposing vulnerability rather than hiding it) tends to elicit empathy and compassion from one's partner. If a partner can see the hurt behind the defensiveness, she can respond to it sensitively. If all a partner sees is emotional withdrawal, contemptuous dismissal, or angry demand, she will feel rejected, controlled, and unsympathetic.

Allowing oneself to be openly vulnerable is not a risk-free strategy. It leaves one open to being shamed for his vulnerability if it is treated as weakness, immaturity, or irrationality. Being openly vulnerable with a partner creates a moment of truth. Will the partner offer heartfelt empathy for one's vulnerability and genuine regret for whatever he or she has done to pour salt in the wound, or will the partner respond with contempt and criticism, leaving the first partner to regret opening up to such an unsympathetic and insensitive partner? To assume that risk, most people need to feel confident that they won't be shattered by a disappointing result. Is one resilient enough to survive and move on with the sober realization that her partner is currently incapable of responding empathetically to her hurt and humiliation and assuming responsibility for his role in causing it?

Attachment security in a romantic relationship is facilitated when partners can expose their emotional vulnerabilities to one another and reliably obtain a sympathetic response. Open, clear, direct, and nondefensive communication is what emerges when romantic partners feel safe to express their vulnerabilities, confident in the knowledge that they will receive a sensitive response that does not shame them for their emotional vulnerabilities. From an attachment perspective, it is difficult to feel securely attached to someone who has been deceitful and betrayed one's trust, then blames the victim for the betrayal. That's why recovery from infidelity is so difficult: The trust on which secure attachment is based must be rebuilt. The betrayed partner will be reluctant to be openly vulnerable to a partner who has been deceitful because all reassurance now seems like false reassurance, which could in fact be a lie. Likewise, the unfaithful partner does not feel secure because it's unclear whether the betrayed partner will ever be able to forgive and forget. Couples therapy for infidelity requires that two vulnerable and mistrustful people find a way to feel securely attached to each other and safe to expose their vulnerabilities.

Bradley started a romantic affair with a work colleague and planned to end his marriage to live with his affair partner. Bradley felt that his wife, Maria, no longer loved him; they rarely had sex because she always seemed preoccupied with the welfare of their two young children. Maria was anxiously attached to her children; she was worried something horrible might happen to them if she didn't constantly give them her undivided and exclusive attention. It was difficult for her to relinquish her ruminative worrying about her children. As a consequence, she couldn't relax enough to enjoy sex. Although she missed having sex more frequently, it wasn't her highest priority. In contemplating leaving his wife for his affair partner, Bradley didn't think Maria would miss him—in fact, he wondered if perhaps she would even feel relieved of the burden of meeting his emotional and sexual needs. Maria was shocked when Bradley announced his plan to leave her for another woman. She had mistakenly assumed that everything was fine in the marriage because Bradley had never communicated his marital dissatisfaction to her (i.e., avoidant attachment style).

Maria felt hurt and angry and was tempted to retaliate by kicking him out of the house. Yet Maria didn't want to give up her marriage without a fight. She decided to risk being vulnerable with Bradley in a way that could leave her open to an even more humiliating rejection, adding insult to injury. Maria wrote Bradley a thoughtful and conciliatory letter saying that Bradley was the love of her life and she would be lost without him. She said she was sorry if she had been emotionally unavailable and wanted to work on making Bradley happy if he would give her a second chance. Bradley was deeply touched, broke off his affair without giving it a second thought, and recommitted himself to saving the marriage. Bradley's relationship with his affair partner was not particularly close or securely attached. The sex was rather impersonal, but his affair partner was available to him when he wanted attention, and Bradley equated attention on demand with love. It didn't occur to him that his affair partner was trying to win him by being exceptionally accommodating so that he would leave his wife for her. Of course, it was not clear how accommodating she might have been once she had won him and could take him for granted.

For him to remain in the marriage, Bradley needed to feel that Maria was really there, and her letter made him feel special again. He could not feel securely attached to Maria when he felt he would always take a back seat to her seemingly neurotic preoccupation with their children. Bradley could not see that his avoidant style and his long hours at the office made Maria feel that the burden of child care was entirely on her in a way that felt overwhelming. He also didn't see how his avoidant style exacerbated the anxious preoccupations that led him to feel neglected by his wife. As their vulnerabilities were shared in couples therapy, they were able to recover from infidelity.

YOU'RE DRIVING ME CRAZY: COMMUNICATION BREAKDOWN AND MENTALIZATION

Effective communication is not about what you say, but how you say it. Communication breakdown may derive from faulty assumptions about how to effectively enable a romantic partner to understand and empathize with one's point of view. Securely attached people know how to express their viewpoints in ways that are more likely to elicit sympathy and understanding. In contrast, the insecurely attached appear to express themselves in ways that provoke either escalating angry arguments or hostile withdrawal. The securely attached may have better communication skills because they possess a greater capacity for *mentalization*, the ability to be reflective about the mental states of self and others. The securely attached have a better appreciation of others' perspective and so can use their understanding of where others are coming from to adjust their communication accordingly.

Conflict-avoiding couples may become sex-avoidant as well, then give up on trying to make themselves understood because it seems like a frustrating exercise in futility; they may then simply pretend everything is fine (Charny & Asineli-Tal, 2004). Consider how effective parents intuitively appreciate how to talk to young children at a developmental level and with a tone of voice ("baby talk") their children can understand (Devine, 1991). Effective communication requires what developmental psychologists call an accurate *theory of the mind* of the people with whom one is trying to communicate—their developmental level, their unique perspectives, their values and biases, their wishes and fears, their defensive response tendencies when faced with threatening information. Communication breakdown is likely to occur if one has a faulty theory of a romantic partner's mind. Instead of receiving understanding, empathy, and validation, he or she may be met with hostility, defensiveness, misinterpretation, and seemingly unfair criticism.

Fonagy and colleagues (Fonagy et al., 2002; Fonagy, Target, Steele, & Steele, 1998) discovered that individuals high on what they call mentalization or *reflective functioning* tend to be securely attached. In contrast to other animals, humans possess a theory of mind, which starts to emerge fairly early in human development (Achim, Guitton, Jackson, Boutin, & Monetta, 2013; Green et al., 2008; Harrington, Siegert, & McClure, 2005). Humans tend to think about what is going on in the minds of others and are curious about what other people are thinking and feeling. Humans are also introspective and tend to contemplate what is going on in their own minds. Why did I do something? What do I really feel about something? How do things look when I step back from my feelings and put things in broader perspective? Does the world look different when I am relaxed than when I'm stressed out? How does the world look from someone else's point of view? How do other people see me? To answer such questions, one must possess a theory of mind, and the better the theory of mind one has, the more likely the inferred answers to such questions will be accurate.

Accurate mind reading allows for better assessment of the motives and intentions of others, which in turn allows better prediction of their future behavior. When it comes to survival and reproduction, the ability to accurately predict someone's future behavior is an adaptive capacity that should give one an advantage over competitors who are not as good at predicting the behavior of others. A sophisticated theory of mind is required to accurately predict who is likely to be unfaithful and in which circumstances, to foresee the long-term negative consequences of infidelity or a moralistic response to an unfaithful partner's infidelity, and to understand how one's own personality characteristics contributed to an unfaithful partner's motivations for infidelity or a betrayed partner's moralistic response to relational transgression.

Dogs appear to be very good at reading the facial expressions of humans (Merola, Prato-Previde, Lazzaroni, & Marshall-Pescini, 2014). A dog knows if its master is angry, sad, happy, or anxious—whether the master is approving or disapproving, eager to play, or prefers to be left alone. Dogs are sensitive to the feelings of humans and eager to be on friendly terms with them, hence why dogs are "man's best friend." Dogs do not appear to possess a theory of mind, however. They don't know *why* a human is happy or sad, anxious, or angry. Dogs might attentively study human facial expressions, but they don't contemplate the inner thoughts that might give rise to those outward displays of emotion. In contrast, a theory of mind begins to emerge in humans quite early in psychological development. Between 9 and 14 months of age, babies begin to engage in joint-attention behavior. They begin to track the gaze of adults, turn their heads to see what the adults are looking at (Okumura, Kanakogi, Kanda, Ishiguro, & Itakura, 2013), and point at things so that their mothers or other people will turn their heads to see what they are looking at (Behne, Liszkowski, Carpenter, & Tomasello, 2012). This is called *social referencing* (Slaughter & McConnell, 2003). By the end of the first year of life, babies are beginning to appreciate that others have a mind of their own with a separate perspective and that for people to see what others see, their gazes have to be coordinated to look at the same thing.

It is not until after the third year of life that children can begin to pass the *false belief* test (Perner, Leekam, & Wimmer, 1987). Before that time, children are fairly egocentric and mistakenly assume that others know what they know and see the world pretty much the same way they do. At about 3 years old, children begin to appreciate that other people may possess false beliefs by virtue of not having made the same observations the child made, which are necessary to possess a true belief.

Empathy is thought to develop throughout the second year of life, but certain aspects of empathy may begin to emerge even in the first year (Davidov, Zahn-Waxler, Roth-Hanania, & Knafo, 2013). As children develop empathy, they begin to care whether others are sad and try to offer comfort to make the sad person feel better. At an early age, children are also spontaneously cooperative and take pleasure in being helpful (Tomasello, 2014). Thus, humans have evolved to be a highly cooperative species with interest in and empathy for the minds of others from an early age. Theories of mind become progressively more sophisticated with psychological development. This allows us to appreciate that everybody has a mind of one's own with a unique perspective; that the way the world looks depends on how the person is feeling at any given time; that people with different personalities, cultural backgrounds, genders, or sexual orientations may view the world differently; that people of different ages view the world differently according to their developmental level; that people with different life experiences view the world differently; that they might not consciously know their own minds because people might not want to admit to their more socially unacceptable thoughts and feelings as Freud suggested (Fonagy et al., 1998).

It turns out that theory of mind can be measured through reflective functioning or mentalization—the capacity to understand the mental states of self and others (Fonagy et al., 1998). Some people possess more developmentally advanced theories of mind than others, but that capacity doesn't seem to be correlated with traditional measures of intelligence. It is an independent capacity that appears to be lacking in individuals with autism or Asperger syndrome. Such individuals can have a high IQ but are "mindblind"—they do not understand the mental states of others (Lombardo & Baron-Cohen, 2011). To have cooperative relationships with people, it helps to be able to accurately read the minds of others and understand where they are coming from. To develop a secure attachment to another person, one must understand how to earn his or her trust; to have a good sexual relationship with another, one must understand what turns that person on and off.

Main and Hesse (1990) discovered that parents' unresolved traumatic experiences are related to infant disorganized attachment status. Fonagy, Steele, and Steele (1991) conducted an ingenious study that demonstrated the relationship between reflective functioning and secure attachment. They gave pregnant women the Adult Attachment Interview and scored it for level of reflective functioning. Their children's attachment security in the Strange Situation was then assessed at 1 year old. As it turns out, the higher the mother's reflective functioning while pregnant, the more securely attached the child was at 1 year old. Even mothers with childhood histories of trauma were able to raise securely attached children if their reflective functioning was high. High reflective functioning contributes to secure attachment because reading people's minds accurately facilitates empathy, which in turn facilitates the kind of trustworthy emotional connections that enable people to feel deeply understood and loved. That sort of understanding facilitates emotional regulation so one isn't so overwhelmed by one's feelings (Fonagy et al., 2002). People who are egocentric and mistakenly assume that everybody thinks just like they do or who project their own issues onto others are likely to misread other people and suffer communication breakdowns in their relationships. Thus, their relationships will be more troubled, less trusting, and less stable because there is less mutual understanding.

Mentalization can be appreciated as both a personality trait that is stable over time and as a mental state that fluctuates depending on the level of emotional arousal (Liotti & Gilbert, 2011). Mentalization deteriorates when attachment injury generates insecure attachment (Allen, 2013). It is difficult to be reflective when feeling hurt, shamed, anxious, and angry and it seems as though no one is likely to be sympathetic to one's feelings. The ability to accurately understand and empathize with the mind of a romantic partner deteriorates when responding defensively to feelings of criticism, rejection, betrayal, or abandonment (Josephs & McLeod, 2014). That ability increases when feeling safe, secure, and understood within a romantic relationship. Yet mentalization is also a trait that is generally low in individuals with severe personality disorders even when their relationships are going reasonably well for the moment (Fonagy, Luyten, & Bateman, 2015).

Mikulincer (1997) discovered that the insecurely attached have certain cognitive deficits compared with securely attached people. The cognition of the insecurely attached tends to be associated with dogmatic thinking and low tolerance of ambiguity. Such individuals are threatened by new information that challenges their dogmatic beliefs because it makes them vulnerable to feeling emotionally overwhelmed. Communicating effectively with a dogmatic romantic partner with low tolerance of ambiguity and who responds defensively to information that challenges his or her rigidly held viewpoint requires a sophisticated theory of mind. It requires appreciating how the world looks from the partner's perspective without being unduly judgmental with what likely seems a highly prejudicial and biased view. A way must be found to introduce a discrepant viewpoint that doesn't evoke a reflexively antagonistic and defensive response.

Communicating effectively with a rigid and dogmatic person is easier said than done in romantic relationships because one must arrive at an accurate theory of the other's mind and communicate effectively at a moment of heightened conflict, while likely feeling frustrated by the partner's rigidity and dogmatism. For a couple to do this in the aftermath of exposed infidelity is nearly impossible (Josephs, 2015a). It is nearly impossible to mentalize how a trusted partner could betray that trust through infidelity without one's reflective functioning being distorted by hurt and humiliated fury. It is also nearly impossible for the unfaithful partner to mentalize the impact of infidelity on the betrayed partner without one's reflective functioning being distorted by defensive self-justification, driven by overwhelming shame, guilt, self-disgust, and dread of punitive retribution.

MENTALIZING HUMILIATED FURY

Angry states of mind triggered by threats to attachment security and to the security of one's social status may activate more primitive modes of apprehending reality, such as psychic equivalence, in which inner and outer realities are equated (i.e., intolerance of separate minds); the pretend mode, in which inner experience loses all relationship to external reality; and the teleologic stance, in which actions are understood only in terms of their physical as opposed to mental outcomes (Fonagy, Target, Gergely, Allen, & Bateman, 2003). Josephs and McLeod (2014, p. 70) described how romantic partners tend to think in the midst of a conflict that threatens attachment security as follows:

1. angrily arguing and insisting that their current interpretation of their own and the other's mental state is the only correct interpretation;
2. angrily denying the possibility of any defensive self-deception or self-serving bias implicit in their own viewpoint, while indignantly pointing out the self-deception and self-serving biases of others' viewpoints;
3. naively assuming that their own normative judgments are not relative but are timeless truths independent of life experience or developmental level;

4. naively assuming that their understanding of other's mental states is based on direct, objective perceptions of reality unfiltered by underlying assumptions that could lead to misattribution or projection;
5. assuming that when there are differences of opinion, only one perspective is right and all others must be wrong, as though different perspectives could not each be right in their own way;
6. angrily insisting that the way the world looks when they are feeling threatened and angered is the way the world actually is; anybody who denies this is being willfully obtuse or lying for self-serving reasons and so deserves to be punished;
7. angrily insisting that others surrender their own independent but fundamentally flawed viewpoints to see the world in exactly the same way that they do;
8. unquestioningly assuming that other angry individuals are trying to impose their own incorrect view of reality on them and so are authoritarian bullies to be defied, whereas their own indignant protest is bravely speaking truth to power; and
9. angrily insisting that what things appear to be is what they actually are.

Attempts to effectively communicate with a romantic partner when feeling insecure, hurt, and angry and one's reflective functioning is low are likely to result in a communication breakdown. As a consequence, treatment must address these mentalization deficits that give rise to poor communication skills and attachment insecurity. Treatment must try to facilitate better mentalization of the mind of a romantic partner and of how one's own ineffective ways of expressing oneself are bringing out the worst in the romantic partner, which in turn threatens the partner's attachment security and brings out a more close-minded and defensive response, rather than a more open-minded and empathetic one.

It is natural enough to wish we could dump all our frustrations on a romantic partner and be met with an understanding and sympathetic response. Yet if we flood our romantic partners with all our pent-up frustrations, for which we hold them partly to blame, we are probably only making them feel unloved, insecure, and bad about themselves. This activates their defense mechanisms against those aversive mental states. As a consequence, treating conflicts around infidelity requires addressing the impaired reflective functioning that conflicts around infidelity tend to activate. Betrayed partners must learn that punishing their philandering partners to "teach them a lesson they won't forget" will not make unfaithful partners more faithful. On the contrary, it often makes the unfaithful partner feel the infidelity was justified because the betrayed partner continues to be such an "angry asshole" or "castrating bitch." Unfaithful partners must learn that justifying their infidelities by blaming the betrayed partner will only make them seem unreliable and untrustworthy, resisting personal responsibility for immoral behavior. Affair partners must learn that angry demands designed to get unfaithful partners to leave a betrayed partner will only make them seem like unsuitable long-term partners who throw temper tantrums to get their way.

Some of these anger management issues may need to be worked through in the relationship with the therapist before they can be worked through in the patient's love life. Is it safe to be openly vulnerable with the therapist without being shamed for one's vulnerabilities? Is it safe to express a mind of one's own with the therapist if what is on one's mind might offend the therapist or hurt the therapist's feelings? Does the therapist respond defensively to angry accusation, contemptuous devaluation, or hostile withdrawal? The patient may need to test the therapist in such ways to confirm whether the therapist can actually practice what he or she preaches (see Weiss, 1998, on passing unconscious tests). If the therapist passes this test, it will allow the patient to feel sufficient trust and attachment security to expose vulnerability without fear of being shamed and to express potentially offensive and unflattering opinions without fear of being rejected for expressing those opinions.

Louis was 30 years old, married, and without children when he started an affair with a younger work colleague, Kathy, who admired his work. Louis was ambivalent about his wife, Barbara, whom he described as bossy and controlling and who was pressuring him to have children when he didn't feel ready. Louis came for therapy because he didn't know what to do.

Several months into our work together, Barbara received an anonymous e-mail exposing Louis's affair. She confronted Louis about the infidelity, so he admitted the truth but blamed Barbara for driving him to the affair by being bossy and controlling. A screaming match ensued, during which they started trading insults. Louis came to the session complaining that his wife was a "crazy bitch." I noted that blaming his wife for the affair might have brought out the worst rather than the best in her. Louis snapped back at me, "You can be a real prick; my marriage is falling apart, and you're not being sympathetic."

I acknowledged that it was difficult for me to be sympathetic when he seemed to be dealing with his guilt by blaming the victim. Louis said, "I know. Sometimes I feel like I'm some kind of monster." Nondefensively owning my unsympathetic response to his marital predicament despite Louis's accusing me of being "a prick" enabled him to be reflective about the impact of his scapegoating on my mental state and to own the possibility that blaming everyone else for his own problems could be perceived as "monstrous."

Shortly after the marital blowup, Barbara went to Louis's office to confront Kathy. They, too, had a screaming match. Barbara slapped Kathy in the face and stormed out. Kathy complained to Louis's boss about the incident. His boss told Louis that he better keep his personal problems out of the office or he would be fired. Barbara then made an ultimatum that he quit his job or she would leave him. Louis said he would keep his job. Barbara didn't see that asserting herself by being confrontational and making ultimatums to protect her interests was actually self-defeating and drove Louis away. Louis didn't see that expressing his hostility toward his wife indirectly by having an affair and then blaming her for it once exposed only provoked the demanding and confrontational side of her that he didn't like.

Louis started to see, as I pointed it out, that blaming the victim to manage his guilty conscience provoked the unsympathetic response he dreaded; in other words, this was an increase in his reflective functioning. His scapegoating hid his secret hope that his wife and therapist might have some empathetic understanding of his inner conflict, even though he was ashamed of the deceitful way he dealt with his conflicts about fidelity and fatherhood and regretted the hurt it inflicted on his wife.

MENTALIZING SEXUAL CHEMISTRY FROM AN ATTACHMENT PERSPECTIVE

Low reflective functioning may lead individuals to look at a romantic partner's sexuality through an egocentric lens, making it difficult to perceive and accept how a partner's sexual desires and needs could be significantly different from one's own. Negotiating that difference becomes a challenge in any long-term relationship. Being reflective about the impact of one's own sexual desires, needs, and morality on a partner's mental states, when one's own desires, needs, and morality are in opposition to a partner's, becomes essential to successfully negotiating sexual conflict.

From an attachment perspective, sex is never simply an impersonal biological function designed to provide sensual pleasure or make babies. Sexual relations always possess a relational meaning, even if that meaning is more implicit than explicit (Birnbaum, Reis, Mikulincer, Gillath, & Orpaz, 2006). The tendency to split love from lust and seek casual impersonal sex outside of a securely attached relationship may be a symptom of avoidant attachment. The avoidantly attached are likely to be dissatisfied with marital sexuality if it is associated with an implicit "demand" for intimacy that feels smothering and suffocating and threatens their avoidant defenses (Cooper et al., 2006; Hazan et al., 2006). The kind of casual sex that the avoidantly attached prefer may only be found outside of marriage if the spouse prefers more emotionally intimate sexuality. As a consequence, for the avoidantly attached, the best sex may sometimes be extramarital.

Conversely, the anxiously attached prefer more intimate sex that reassures them of their essential lovability (Cooper et al., 2006; Hazan et al., 2006). The anxiously attached won't be happy with marital sex if it is too impersonal, routine, or casual. They may also feel that the best sex is extramarital if the only way they can get sex with sufficient emotional intimacy and affirmation is through an extramarital affair that assures them of their lovability and self-worth. When an avoidantly attached person marries an anxiously attached person, it is quite possible that neither can obtain the kind of sex they prefer within the marriage. For one person, marital sexuality is too close for comfort; for the other, it's not close enough. Both avoidant and anxiously attached individuals have poor marital communication when it comes to sex (Davis et al., 2006).

What effect does it have on a couple's sex life if both partners feel sufficient trust and safety to be openly vulnerable with each other? It means feeling free to be open about one's sexual desires without being shamed for them. That's why research shows that the sexuality of securely attached couples is more experimental (Davis et al., 2006; Hazan & Zeifman, 1994). Secure attachment rests on making the relationship as sexually gratifying as possible without doing anything that would threaten attachment security by making the other partner feel unduly threatened, insecure, jealous, humiliated, or ashamed. It doesn't occur to patients that sexual chemistry is something that arises in part out of the way two people relate to each other (Chesney, Blakeney, Chan, & Cole, 1981; Chesney, Blakeney, Cole, & Chan, 1981) and therefore can be generated by changing the ways partners relate to each another.

Individuals who are sexually frustrated in their marriages and blame their partners for this may need to develop reflective functioning to perceive that the ways in which they manage or mismanage their partners' attachment insecurities are likely to affect the quality of their sex lives. Increasing a partner's attachment security is likely to improve a couple's sexual chemistry, whereas increasing attachment insecurity is likely to decrease that chemistry. Improving a couple's sexual chemistry requires insight into how the anxious or avoidant aspects of each partner's attachment style influences the mental states of the other partner. Being reflective means appreciating that making a romantic partner insecure in the relationship is likely to adversely affect that partner's sexual motivations.

CONCLUSION

Is attachment style the only salient central individual difference variable that predicts how individuals will conduct their love lives? What about gender? Do men and women conduct their love lives in significantly different ways? Much research demonstrates that there are in fact significant gender differences in prevalence rates and motivations for infidelity. Nevertheless, when attachment style is included as a moderating variable, it turns out that gender differences diminish among the securely attached and increase among the insecurely attached. The next chapter further explores the complex interaction between gender and attachment style in predicting how individuals negotiate love triangles.

3

THE WANDERING EYES OF MEN AND WOMEN: SEX DIFFERENCES IN MOTIVATIONS FOR INFIDELITY

Sex differences appear to be biologically grounded, whereas attachment style can be seen as environmental, if not cultural, to the degree that it is shaped by culture-bound parenting styles. After all, sex differences may be grounded in innate differences in fetal brain development, genital anatomy, and the secondary sexual characteristics that arise with puberty. This may be a false dichotomy, however. Adult romantic attachment as it facilitates biparental care may be as much a human adaptation for reproductive success as possessing a boneless penis rather than the baculum that most other male primates have or a vagina that lacks notable vaginal swellings during ovulation as occurs in many other female primates (Dixson, 1998). There is no reason to assume that innate sex differences in humans are somehow more biological or more determinative of human mating strategies than are differences in adult attachment styles. Sex differences in physical anatomy as well as mating strategies tend to diminish in monogamously inclined species (Dixson, 2009).

http://dx.doi.org/10.1037/0000053-004
The Dynamics of Infidelity: Applying Relationship Science to Psychotherapy Practice, by L. Josephs

The complicated empirical question is how innate sex differences interact with attachment style to predict human mating strategies. Secure attachment, the mating strategy of the more monogamously inclined, appears to diminish sex differences, whereas insecure attachment, the mating strategy of the less monogamously inclined, appears to exaggerate sex differences. The so-called war between the sexes may obscure the more subterranean warfare between more monogamously inclined individuals (the securely attached) and individuals inclined toward infidelity and promiscuity (the insecurely attached) regardless of self-identified gender.

Gender role stereotypes about infidelity may be changing in more egalitarian societies where women appear to be catching up to men in terms of prevalence rates of infidelity (Schmitt et al., 2004). Sex differences in infidelity rates diminish when we look at women younger than 40 years of age or when we use more inclusive definitions of infidelity (i.e., like kissing as well as sexual intercourse; Brand, Markey, Mills, & Hodges, 2007; Wiederman, 1997). There might be ecological conditions that cut across cultures in which infidelity might be to women's reproductive advantage (e.g., when husbands are cold, abusive, unfaithful, infertile, inadequate providers, sexually unsatisfying, or poor fathers).

On most individual difference variables, when there are significant differences between the sexes, those differences aren't that large (Costa, Terracciano, & McCrae, 2001). Gender differences in infidelity diminish when we compare men and women with equivalent levels of empathy (Shimberg, Josephs, & Tittel, 2016). Impulsive individuals appear to be more inclined to be unfaithful regardless of gender, whereas more conscientious individuals appear to be less inclined to be unfaithful regardless of gender (Schmitt, 2004). Individuals with greater executive control tend to be more faithful (Pronk, Karremans, & Wigboldus, 2011). Sex differences in prevalence rates of infidelity may be a function of sex differences in prevalence rates of different personality types within different cultures.

Gender role stereotypes might seem confirmed to clinicians who treat a disproportionate number of anxiously attached women who are not getting the emotional intimacy they need and avoidantly attached men not getting the sexual variety, novelty, and frequency they would like (Del Giudice, 2011). Anxiously attached women tend toward promiscuity and infidelity (i.e., high-risk reproductive strategies), whereas anxiously attached men tend toward sexual inhibition (i.e., low-risk reproductive strategies; Del Giudice, 2009). Avoidantly attached women and anxiously attached men seem to go against gender role stereotypes. Thus, attachment style may determine the degree to which men and women conform to gender role stereotypes.

Evolutionary psychologists have suggested that love, an attachment-based emotion, and lust possess two different evolutionary histories and different underlying neural circuitry and are regulated through different hormones (i.e., oxytocin vs. testosterone; L. M. Diamond, 2004; H. E. Fisher, 2004). Levels of oxytocin, which regulates the attachment system, are approximately 7 times higher in women than in men (Oatley, Keltner, & Jenkins, 2006), whereas levels of testosterone, which regulates the strength of the sex drive, are approximately 7 to 8 times higher in men than in women (Dabbs, 2000). High prenatal testosterone levels "masculinize" the brain, creating a brain that is relatively better at systematization than empathy, whereas low prenatal testosterone levels "feminize" the brain, creating a brain that is relatively better at empathy than at systematization (Baron-Cohen, 2003). "Gender benders" could therefore have a biological basis in women whose brains have been masculinized and men whose brains have been feminized by prenatal hormone levels.

H. E. Fisher (2004) proposed a third emotional operating system that influences human reproductive psychology and is regulated by serotonin. There may be a romantic love circuit in the brain that motivates individuals to look for a unique soul mate, with whom there will be a meeting of minds as well as bodies, that evolved to facilitate sexually exclusive pair bonding. According to Fisher, there do not appear to be significant sex differences when it comes to romantic love except that men are perhaps more inclined to fall in love at first sight, whereas women are more inclined to wait to get know the unique individual.

DO MEN THINK WITH THEIR PENISES?

Baumeister, Catanese, and Vohs (2001) published a controversial but comprehensive literature review titled "Is There a Gender Difference in Strength of Sex Drive?" There is no consensus in the field as to how best to measure a concept as elusive as sex drive. These authors looked for converging lines of evidence by summarizing research using multiple measures and multiple populations. They discovered that on all measures and in all populations, men possessed a stronger sex drive than women. They offered this summary of their literature review:

> Men think about sex more often, experience more frequent sexual arousal, have more frequent and varied fantasies, desire sex more often, desire more partners, masturbate more, want sex sooner, are less able or willing to live without sexual gratification, initiate more and refuse sex less, expend more resources and make more sacrifices for sex, desire and enjoy a broader variety of sexual practices, have more favorable and permissive attitudes toward most sexual activities, have fewer complaints about low sex drive in themselves (but more about their partners), and

> rate their sex drives as stronger than women. There were no measures that showed women having stronger drives than men. (p. 264)

Men's stronger sex drive leads to certain typical marital conflicts. A typical source of marital conflict is that men are more likely than women to want more sex, while women are more likely than men to want less sex (Johannes & Avis, 1997). One frequently self-reported reason for women engaging in sex is to placate men who are pestering them for sex (Meston & Buss, 2007). Wives tend to report being satisfied with the amount of sex in their marriages, whereas husbands on average would prefer a 50% increase (Ard, 1977). Men appear to initiate sex more frequently than women do (O'Sullivan & Byers, 1992), and women may be more likely to refuse sex than men (M. Brown & Auerback, 1981).

Baumeister and Bratslavsky (1999) suggested that there may be a brief honeymoon phase of romantic love during which intimacy and passion are rapidly increasing and the couple's sex drive may be perfectly matched. Women are happy to have sex at a high frequency, and men are happy to be emotionally intimate in their lovemaking. Unfortunately, as the honeymoon phase of romantic infatuation based on mutual idealization wanes, men return to wanting sex that is more casual than intimate but at a frequency that remains as high as the honeymoon phase. They begin to feel smothered by and resentful of the expectation to engage in a high level of intimate relatedness every time they have sex. It strikes them as excessively needy. Meanwhile, women begin to prefer a lower frequency of sex that preserves the high level of emotional intimacy of the honeymoon phase. They resent pressure to have casual sex without intimacy at the frequency men would prefer. They begin to feel that their needs for emotional intimacy are being rejected and that they are being shamed for being too needy and believe their husbands are frightened of intimacy. This can be the beginning of communication breakdown in a marriage.

The honeymoon phase gives both genders false expectations of the kind of sex life that might be reasonable to expect from a long-term monogamous relationship. There is some disappointment and resentment that marriage has not lived up to its advance billing. Disillusioned men then become more inclined to be unfaithful because they are seeking the sexual frequency, variety, and novelty lacking in their marriage; disillusioned women become more inclined to be unfaithful because they are seeking the emotional intimacy and acceptance lacking in their marriage. As a consequence of these sex differences, unfaithful men are much more likely to have multiple extramarital partners than are women, who are more likely to have only one (Spanier & Margolis, 1983).

One of the largest sex differences to emerge in the study of individual differences between men and women is the frequency of masturbation

(Oliver & Hyde, 1993). Males begin masturbating at an earlier age than females, even though females enter puberty earlier than do males (Asayama, 1975). Even past age 60, men are still masturbating more frequently than women (Bergström-Walan & Nielsen, 1990). When men lose one source of sexual gratification, they are more likely than women to seek out a new one as soon as possible (Leiblum & Rosen, 1988). Men seem to maintain a certain level of orgasmic constancy from week to week, whereas women are more likely to do without the sexual release of orgasm until they find their preferred sexual outlet in an emotionally intimate sexual encounter (Kinsey, Pomeroy, & Martin, 1948; Kinsey, Pomeroy, Martin, & Gebhard, 1953).

As consequence of men's attempts to maintain a certain level of orgasmic constancy, they are more likely to turn to private masturbation, pornography use, or infidelity when feeling sexually frustrated in the marriage rather than learn to make do without as women are more inclined to do. Women low on reflective functioning who are happy with the frequency of sex or make do without if they aren't may egocentrically assume that men are not seeking sexual outlets in between infrequent marital sexual episodes. They may be shocked by exposure of their partners' frequency of masturbation and pornography consumption and experience the exposure of their partners' private sexual activity as implicit infidelity (Paul, 2005).

Robert Trivers (1972) developed *parental investment theory* to explain the differences in sexual behavior between males and females in humans and other animals. This theory suggests that the sex that invests less in offspring, usually but not always the male, is more competitive with rivals over gaining reproductive access to the opposite sex and is less discriminating in choice of partner. The lesser investing parent chooses a quantity-over-quality reproductive strategy. The greater investing parent, usually but not always the female, is more choosey in selecting a mate because a quality-over-quantity reproductive strategy is being pursued. Men have the greater sex drive because they are, on average, the lesser investing parent. On average, men are more disposed toward a quantity-over-quality reproductive strategy.

The theory also implies that the most paternal men (i.e., securely attached with more feminized brains) would be least likely to be unfaithful, whereas the least maternal women (i.e., avoidantly attached with more masculinized brains) would be most likely to be unfaithful. The most paternal men will be more inclined to invest in parenting the children they have than invest in pursuing new mates to have more children. The least maternal women might invest more in further mating than parenting the children they already have to acquire more resources or have more children with better genetic quality. Gender benders may be an adaptive variation in reproductive strategy given the human strategic pluralism that generates individual variability within each sex.

The sex drive is designed by evolution to facilitate reproductive success. Thus, in individuals pursuing a quantity-over-quality reproductive strategy, sex drive is activated by variety and novelty (Buss, 2003). For heterosexual males, gratifying the desire for sexual variety facilitates reproducing with as many females as possible. Yet the sex drive in humans as well as other animals also searches for what evolutionary biologists call *sexually selected indicators of fitness* (Andersson, 1994). Men who are primarily attracted to infertile women (e.g., postmenopausal women, prepubertal females, sickly women) would not be as reproductively successful as men attracted to the healthiest and most fertile women. The most reproductively successful men will be attracted to the women most likely to give birth to healthy babies and to those with the mothering skills to raise those children successfully to maturity. As a consequence, men on average will be most attracted to women with youthful good looks and nurturing personality characteristics. Gay men, like straight men, prefer youthful good looks so are attracted to the secondary sexual characteristics to which women are most drawn (Bergling, 2007).

Women will also be motivated to have sex with partners who possess sexually selected indicators of fitness. Women will be more reproductively successful if their children inherit genes that would predispose them to be healthy, good-looking, athletic, dominant, popular, smart, and creative individuals. Such attractions express what Miller (2008) called *mating intelligence* (i.e., adaptations for reproductive success). There is increasing evidence that during ovulation, heterosexual women appear to be more attracted to men who possess higher testosterone levels, greater facial symmetry (i.e., an indicator of good health), and facial masculinity (Gangestad, Garver-Apgar, Cousins, & Thornhill, 2014). With the advent of genetic testing, there is better appreciation that a certain percentage of men are unknowingly raising children as their own who in reality are the result of extramarital affairs that were never detected (Cerda-Flores, Barton, Marty-Gonzalez, Rivas, & Chakraborty, 1999). Lesbian women, like heterosexual women, display mating intelligence when they are drawn to women who are healthy, good-looking, athletic, popular, smart, creative, and sensitive.

Heterosexual women report being attracted to "nice guys" (i.e., Dads) for long-term relationships but being attracted to "bad boys" or womanizers (i.e., Cads) for short-term relationships (Kruger & Fisher, 2005). The attraction to Cads appears to be stronger among women who are anxiously attached and tend to pair with more avoidant men (Doumas, Pearson, Elgin, & McKinley, 2008), the men most likely to split love from lust and be more oriented toward casual sex, sexual variety, and infidelity.

Therapists can convey empathy for the frustrated lust that motivates infidelity even though they are usually sympathetic to the sentiment that "honesty is the best policy" given the research-based presumption that the healthiest relationships are based on trust, honesty, and authenticity (Wickham, Reed, & Williamson, 2015). Individual psychotherapy with patients who have unsatisfactory marital sex lives is often about treating ruminative thinking. What if the sexual aspect of the relationship is beyond fixing, yet the patient still craves peak sexual experiences? Patients often don't like any of their choices (divorce, continue to have affairs and just live with the guilt and dread of exposure, try an open arrangement, develop better frustration tolerance and resistance to extramarital enticements), so they torture themselves, obsessing about what the "right" choice is in their predicament. Patients may procrastinate in coming to terms with a final decision because the downside of whatever decision they make is significant, so they keep postponing a definitive course of action, hoping a better solution will eventually come along. There is an implicit expectation that the therapist will come up with an ideal solution that doesn't carry significant risk or cost. Psychotherapy can seem like a waste of time if it means spinning one's wheels about the same old things week after week with a sympathetic therapist who points out the pros and cons of different courses of action but leaves the ultimate decision-making to the patient.

The therapist's patience and nonjudgmental attitude help patients who are conflicted about their undetected infidelity come to terms with their unfortunate situation without undue self-blame and eventually reconcile to a future course of action with all its anxiety-ridden risks and depressing costs. In the end, the therapist can't save patients from the negative consequences of their choices, but they can only help them find a way to make the best of a bad situation. Such a situation lends itself to a mindfully accepting approach to therapy (Johns, Allen, & Gordon, 2015; Pierson & Hayes, 2007) in which patients learn to tolerate the anxiety-ridden risks and depressing costs that inevitably arise.

Chris, a good-looking and somewhat successful actor, came for psychotherapy because he felt guilt-ridden and confused about his history of cheating on his girlfriends to have casual sexual affairs that were easy to arrange given his celebrity. He was often caught, and this was usually the beginning of the end of the relationship. Chris felt that he couldn't commit to monogamy and didn't know what to do. I asked Chris if he felt that open arrangements might be an option. Chris reported that he didn't think his current girlfriend, Lucy, could handle it, although he felt he wouldn't be jealous if Lucy had sex with other people. No longer wanting to live a lie, Chris did propose an open arrangement to Lucy, and as predicted, she broke up with him. Chris felt relieved and decided that for the time being, he would just be a single guy enjoying a casual sex life. He terminated treatment, thanking me for my help in clarifying his inner conflicts and learning to approach intimate relationships more honestly.

A year later Chris returned for further treatment. He was having a casual sexual relationship with an overburdened divorced mother, Beverly, who was comfortable having an open relationship, although she had no need for other lovers. Chris had begun to develop deeper feelings for Beverly and had proposed a more committed relationship. Beverly felt that a deeper commitment would require monogamy, so Chris was once again back in the same boat and didn't know what to do. He didn't feel he could commit to monogamy, yet he also didn't want to lose Beverly or lie about casual sex outside of the relationship. Once again Chris was ruminating on this issue and couldn't make up his mind about what to do. He still wasn't prepared to sacrifice sexual variety for a long-term committed relationship or sacrifice a long-term committed relationship for the sake of sexual variety.

ARE WOMEN "NEEDIER" THAN MEN?

There are two species of prairie voles. One is promiscuous, and the other is monogamous. The monogamous prairie vole possesses more oxytocin receptors in its brain, which makes sense because, as noted earlier, human women, who tend to be more monogamous, have 7 times the circulating oxytocin levels as men (Oatley et al., 2006). The monogamous prairie vole becomes promiscuous if given a drug that blocks oxytocin reception. In contrast, the promiscuous prairie vole becomes monogamous if given oxytocin (Carter, DeVries, & Getz, 1995). Love driven by lust is regulated by testosterone, but it seems that love driven by the need for attachment is regulated by oxytocin, which inclines humans as well as other animals toward monogamy. The lust circuit in the brain regulated by testosterone is basically promiscuous; it seeks novelty, variety, and cues of fitness. In contrast, the attachment circuit regulated by oxytocin facilitates monogamy by motivating the development of a strong attachment bond to a specific nurturing caretaker that is not easily replaceable.

The attachment circuit is looking for a secure long-term bond to a specific nurturing caretaker that will provide a secure home base, a sense of home and family. Secure attachment means finding a partner who is warm, loyal, devoted, trustworthy, open, and honest, and these are preferred traits in a long-term partner (Buss, 1989). Emotional security comes from knowing that our partner has "got our back" and will make sacrifices on our behalf. A partner who is emotionally unavailable, selfish, unsupportive, distant, critical, condescending, or philandering doesn't meet the need for secure attachment.

The concept of neediness implies the possession of some unhealthy level of dependency or need for reassurance that should be outgrown. From the perspective of adult attachment, neediness is what any mature adult would naturally feel when healthy and mature needs for secure attachment remain unmet (Besser & Priel, 2008). Neediness is the experience of insecure and anxious attachment. Individuals with anxious attachment tend to express their neediness openly and may seem openly clingy, insecure, and unreasonably demanding when fearing rejection and abandonment because their attachment system is defensively hyperactivated. Individuals with avoidant attachment are no less needy (i.e., no less insecurely attached), but they hide their neediness beneath a pretense of self-sufficiency because their attachment system is defensively deactivated (Shaver & Mikulincer, 2006).

There are also significant individual differences among women and men in oxytocin levels, although as discussed earlier, they are generally higher in women than men (Bartz et al., 2015). Thus, some individuals may just be more oriented toward monogamy than others because their oxytocin-driven attachment needs are stronger, just as some individuals have stronger sex drives than others. Gratification of a strong need for attachment is not a bad thing, just as gratification of a strong sex drive is not necessarily a bad thing. In fact, gratification of the need for secure attachment has some remarkably beneficial effects. Secure attachment in adults results in not only greater emotional security but greater self-confidence and more fearless exploratory behavior (Wu & Yang, 2012). There is nothing needy or immature about getting needs for secure attachment gratified; such gratification appears to be quite ego enhancing.

There do appear to be some associations between attachment style and hormonal levels. High testosterone levels in men are associated with attachment avoidance (Turan, Guo, Boggiano, & Bedgood, 2014). Relatively high oxytocin levels were associated with attachment anxiety in women but not men (Weisman, Zagoory-Sharon, Schneiderman, Gordon, & Feldman, 2013). Looking at sexual desire and attachment as separate drives for which there are significant individual differences in strength allows for a clinical stance in which there is respect for those individual differences. Pathologizing what seems to be an unduly strong or weak sex drive or need for attachment or a gender atypical sex drive or need for attachment as something that "should" be fixed tends to exacerbate marital conflict and make people feel bad about who they are. If these are enduring personality traits, they are unlikely to get fixed, at least not quickly. Romantic partners who believe that incremental behavior change through hard work is possible may conclude that a failed change attempt indicates that the person attempting to change simply did not try hard enough and feel somewhat distrustful toward him or her. Partners who view personality as more of a fixed entity are less optimistic about change in the first place but are also less distrustful after failed attempts to change (Kammrath & Peetz, 2012).

Marital adjustment is facilitated by learning to accept and commit to a partner who seems excessively needy despite one's relative self-sufficiency or to a partner who has a strong need for frequent casual sex despite one's preference for sex with intimacy (Christensen & Jacobson, 1998). This doesn't mean learning to live with a partner who expresses neediness in abusively demanding ways or a partner who gratifies a strong sex drive through ongoing infidelity; we all have limits on what we can learn to live with. How much frustration and disappointment someone can accept in a relationship is a difficult thing to estimate. That's why people would generally prefer it if their partner can be "fixed" so that they don't have to come to terms with the limits on how much a partner can change.

Continually critiquing and complaining about the strength or weakness of a partner's sex drive or need for attachment in the hope that it will lead to positive behavior change only shames partners for being who they are and breeds feelings of resentment for being made to feel "not good enough." Couples' sex drives and need for attachment are rarely perfectly matched after the honeymoon phase. Couples, be they gay or straight, must learn how to negotiate the frustration inherent in dealing with someone whose sex drive and need for attachment is different from, and therefore conflicting with, one's own.

In long-term extramarital affairs, an attachment bond may be formed. The affair partner becomes a source of emotional security and comfort for the unfaithful partner, perhaps like a family member—a second wife or husband. The affair may be as much about the affection and the mutual support that is shared as it is about the sex, especially as the honeymoon phase of the affair wanes. Human children have evolved to form multiple attachments to multiple caretakers as humans evolved to be cooperative breeders, although the primary caretaker, usually the mother, still tends to be the object of primary attachment (Meehan & Hawks, 2014). The capacity to form multiple attachments to multiple parental surrogates may underlie polyamorous desires in humans. Infidelity is more likely to lead to divorce and remarriage when the affair partner becomes the primary object of attachment so that the relationship with the affair partner becomes a more securely attached relationship than that with the betrayed spouse.

Vincent, a middle-aged man, came for therapy conflicted about a 15-year-long affair with a divorced mother who was his colleague. He felt sexually frustrated in his marriage because he and his wife only had sex once every 6 weeks. Sex was becoming increasingly difficult because his wife, Alice, had put on so much weight that he found it difficult for his penis to reach her vagina, and he would begin to lose his erection. Vincent wouldn't have minded having oral sex instead, but his wife wasn't interested in providing oral sex and tended to gag on his penis. His affair partner, Emily, was up for anything. Vincent was often worried that his wife might catch him one day. Sometimes she had dreams about him cheating on her, as though her unconscious mind knew of the affair but her conscious mind denied her intuition. Nonetheless, Alice reassured herself that he was too busy at work to have time for an affair.

Emily would have liked Vincent to leave his wife for her but didn't put any pressure on him to do so. She had dated quite a bit and didn't like what was out there. She felt it was better to have a long-term affair with someone she loved than to have no one at all. Although Vincent felt guilty, he appreciated that implicitly both of the women in his life would allow him to live his secret double life indefinitely without ever forcing him to pick one over the other. With his wife, it was "don't ask, don't tell." After 15 years, the affair with Emily was as much about the emotional intimacy as the sex. They often spent time discussing issues at work in which Alice had little interest, as well as issues with their children.

Vincent came for therapy feeling that after 15 years, he should finally make up his mind and either leave his wife for Emily or end it with Emily and recommit to his marriage. Living a secret double life was driving him crazy. Vincent tortured himself with obsessive rumination about what he should do to resolve this inner conflict because no potential solution seemed satisfactory. What eventually emerged was a plan so secret that he didn't even admit it to himself: to retire to Arizona in another 5 to 10 years. At that point, he would end the affair with Emily and recommit to a monogamous marriage because he assumed that by that time, his sex drive would be so low it wouldn't be frustrating to live in a sexless marriage. He didn't like to admit that this had been his intention all along because it felt like a selfish, opportunistic, and exploitative way to conduct his love life.

Vincent confessed that he felt ashamed admitting this to me because he assumed I treated women better than he did and that I would look down on him like he was "the scum of the earth." I admitted that it did make me feel good about myself to treat women well and that I was not beyond indulging in fantasies of moral superiority to my patients. Nevertheless, I appreciated that it was my job to rise above indulging such ego-driven fantasies and have compassion for the moral compromises that may be required to make the best of a bad situation. I acknowledged that I was lucky my life was such that I didn't need to make the sort of moral compromises he felt compelled to make. Vincent expressed appreciation for my honest and heartfelt response. His ruminative worry subsided as he developed greater tolerance for living with an unsatisfactory status quo with self-compassion rather than self-blame when there seemed to be no preferable alternative.

Patients need to learn to mourn the loss of the more ideal love life for which they have always longed when reality appears to require them to settle for a compromise that seems barely good enough. It means mourning the loss of a more morally ideal self-conception as the kind of person who doesn't have affairs when in fact one is the kind of "selfish" person who does because of an unwillingness to sacrifice sexual or romantic happiness to honor a commitment to monogamy.

Betrayed partners often receive conflicting messages about how they "should" cope with infidelity. Betrayed partners are often judged as "masochistic" if they choose to look the other way and remain loyal and faithful to a philandering partner who "should" be either divorced or reformed. The assumption is that a self-respecting individual should not remain loyal to an unrepentant and unreformed serial philander that refuses to recommit to monogamy. Yet there can be an opposite judgment—that it is moralistic for betrayed partners to judge unfaithful partners harshly because no one is perfect and humans may not be meant to be monogamous. Americans "should" be more like the French and just take infidelity as a common part of married life. Infidelity, according to this view, should not be a cause for breaking up a marriage or a family but perhaps an inspiration to go out and have an affair oneself because, after all, you only live once. From a therapeutic viewpoint, what is often most helpful is being freed from the presumption that there is one "right" way for betrayed partners to cope with exposed infidelity.

THE YEARNING FOR A SOUL MATE

Psychologists have long discussed the distinction between love and lust and noted that love comes in many varieties. There is the love one has for one's parents, one's children, one's friends, and one's lover, for example. All varieties of love appear to activate the human capacity for developing strong bonds of attachment. Yet only recently has there been appreciation that romantic love, independent of sexual desire, can be separated into two separate components, attachment as previously discussed and a more purely romantic emotion. Patients in psychotherapy may regretfully say, "I love my partner, but I'm not *in* love with my partner." What they seem to mean is that they care deeply about their partner as a person, are concerned for their partner's welfare, and would like to stay connected to them forever, like a brother or a sister (i.e., attachment), but they are no longer infatuated with this person, and the sex is no longer quite as passionate as it once was. They might say that objectively they appreciate that their partners remain physically attractive individuals with winning personalities. Yet some special quality is sadly missing.

What is missing is that blissful feeling of romantic infatuation based on mutual idealization. Some patients report that they once had those blissful feelings during a honeymoon phase of the relationship that eventually ended. Other patients report that they may never have had those blissful feelings with their current partner. Either way, the yearning for romantic bliss may motivate infidelity as they seek to reexperience or experience for the first time the experience of romantic ecstasy that is painfully lacking from the current relationship.

Helen Fisher (2004), the evolutionary anthropologist, has done groundbreaking work on the psychology and neurophysiology of romantic love. Fisher believes that romantic love is a basic human motivation, a fundamental mating drive, like sex or attachment. It motivates individuals to search for a unique and special person with whom to mate. The scientific study of this basic human motivation, she says, was obscured by a belief that romantic love is a social construct invented by the troubadours of medieval France. In contrast, William Jankowiak (1995) accumulated anthropological evidence that romantic love exists in all cultures during all historical periods. Romantic love appears to be a cross-cultural universal that has motivated humans to form sexually exclusive relationships and appears to be an aspect of our evolved reproductive psychology. Institutions such as arranged marriage may suppress this universal desire by pressuring children to marry partners chosen by their parents. Yet like Shakespeare's Romeo and Juliet, some teenagers and young adults will try to escape arranged marriages to marry someone with whom they have fallen deeply, madly, and passionately in love.

Humans can lust after multiple partners simultaneously and also be attached to multiple partners simultaneously. But it seems that most humans can only be madly and passionately in love with one romantic partner at a time. Romantic love may initially involve an obsessive focus on a unique individual whom someone can't get out of one's mind (Acevedo & Aron, 2009). The love-possessed person focuses all attention exclusively on the beloved to the detriment of everything and everyone else to the point of intrusive thinking about that person (H. E. Fisher, 2004). Idealization makes the beloved seem like the most desirable person in the world. Winning the heart of the beloved is the greatest bliss, and losing it is the greatest tragedy imaginable, so that romantic love can result in major mood swings.

Anxiously attached individuals appear to be more predisposed to falling passionately in love, whereas avoidantly attached individuals are less likely to do so (Cruces, Hawrylak, & Delegido, 2015). Practically speaking, romantic love becomes problematic when an anxiously attached person falls in love with an avoidantly attached person who doesn't reciprocate, so the anxious person's love is unrequited (Sprecher & Fehr, 2011). The avoidant individual predisposed to infidelity feels that the relationship with the betrayed partner is smothering, suffocating, and stifling if it seems accompanied by angry demands that seem to unreasonably limit one's freedom and independence. In contrast, the affair partner may seem to provide an opportunity for "free" love that comes without strings attached and is based purely on a meeting of minds and bodies without ulterior motives.

Helen Fisher (2004) discovered that romantic love has a shelf life: The honeymoon phase doesn't last for more than 18 months. Nevertheless, romantic love without the obsessive aspect can survive in long-term relationships and is associated with marital satisfaction, well-being, and high self-esteem (Acevedo & Aron, 2009). Romantic love appears to involve the activation of certain areas of the brain regulated by serotonin and the dopamine-rich basal ganglia system and overlaps with regions of the brain associated with maternal attachment (Acevedo, Aron, Fisher, & Brown, 2012; Aron et al., 2005).

H. E. Fisher (2004) proposed that romantic love serves an adaptive biological function. It facilitates monogamy by bringing two people together in an extremely intense passionate relationship in which there will be a high frequency of sexual relations and the probability of impregnation would be high without the use of birth control. By the time the honeymoon (i.e., obsessive) phase wanes, it is likely that a strong attachment bond has been formed and a child is either on the way or has already been born. It probably takes about 6 months for a strong bond of adult attachment to form, just as it takes about 6 months for an infant to form a strong bond of attachment to the mother.

Secure attachment requires developing a sense that a person is reliably present to meet one's emotional needs, and that takes time. Romantic passion provides the glue that brings two people together long enough for a bond of attachment to form. Romantic passion motivates intense involvement with someone who is meeting, in a consistent and reliable way, not only one's sexual needs but also one's need for affection and mutual understanding. These are the right ingredients to facilitate the formation of a strong bond of attachment. Romantic love appears to have the same effect on homosexual as heterosexual individuals. It facilitates the formation of lasting bonds of attachment that might inspire a couple to want to raise a family together.

By the time the mutual admiration society of the honeymoon period wanes and people begin to see their partners for who they really are, warts and all, it is not so easy to leave the relationship. The partners have become too attached. It is no longer possible to end the relationship without experiencing considerable separation anxiety and painful feelings of loss. There is now dependency on the romantic partner to meet one's attachment needs, so it is not easy to wean oneself from that dependency if it seems in retrospect to have been an error of judgment to have fallen in love with this particular person. Grand romantic affairs of the heart can end badly when it becomes apparent that the object of romantic passion is not the person he or she seemed to be in a state of romantic intoxication.

From an evolutionary perspective, the honeymoon period should be short-lived. It would not be adaptive to be obsessively focused on a romantic partner once a newborn has arrived. The infant now needs to be the focus of exclusive obsessive attention—what the psychoanalyst D. W. Winnicott (1956) called *primary maternal preoccupation*. Unfortunately, the limited shelf life of obsessive romantic passion creates a risk factor for infidelity if the resulting attachment relationship is not a secure one after the mutual idealization dissipates. For those predisposed to dichotomous thinking, there is a risk that idealization will turn into devaluation (see Kernberg, 1984, on sudden swings between idealization and devaluation in the face of narcissistic deflation among those with borderline ego organization). The relationship becomes unstable when mutual idealization turns into mutual devaluation.

The residual feelings of romantic love that remain as the obsessive aspects fade and the secure attachment that has evolved provide an incentive to work at learning to live with a partner's frustrating imperfections. This is easier for those who have transcended dichotomous thinking and understand that nobody is perfect. In addition, securely attached individuals are likely to possess the reflective functioning and communication skills to negotiate the perpetual conflicts that inevitably arise. The ability to accept each other "as is" and constructively negotiate conflict strengthens the bond of attachment.

Romantic love conceived as an emotional operating system with its unique triggers, neural circuitry, and evolved function may function as a serial monogamist that looks for a new object of romantic infatuation once the honeymoon phase fades. The need to always be in love, sometimes as an antidepressant, may create a compulsion to replace a fading love with a new and exciting love that qualifies as a "love addiction" (i.e., needing to live one's life in a constant state of romantic ecstasy; H. E. Fisher, 2014). During the obsessive phase of romantic infatuation, sexual exclusivity is easy. Obsessions are quite successful at focusing the mind on one thing and that thing alone—it's almost impossible to focus on anything else. During the obsessive phase of romantic love, nobody else seems nearly as desirable. Once this phase ends, it becomes possible to notice other desirable individuals again and to begin to make comparisons. The comparisons are not always fair because one is comparing a long-term romantic partner whose imperfections are well-known, who has been seen at both their best and worst, with new romantic prospects whom one has seen only at their best and can be idealized.

It is human nature to wish to reexperience the obsessive phase of romantic love with someone new and to repeat what can be a once-in-a-lifetime peak experience (i.e., the vulnerability to the high of love addiction). This creates a situation in which one may wish to maintain the attachment bond to the current partner while experiencing romantic bliss with someone new. As such, there is a split not so much between love and lust but between attachment and romantic love. The relationship with the attachment partner remains a somewhat asexual one with a parental surrogate, whereas the affair partner meets the need for a passionate romance with someone with whom one does not share familial responsibilities. Such arrangements may fall apart if a betrayed partner doesn't want to be treated as only an asexual parental surrogate or if the unfaithful partner ultimately prefers to end the asexual relationship with the parental surrogate and commit to a monogamous arrangement with the affair partner with whom there is more romantic passion.

The romantic love circuit may reflect a paradox. On the one hand, romantic love motivates serial monogamy—looking for a new object of romantic passion as the honeymoon phase fades—because it is human nature to want to reexperience peak experiences to the point of making us vulnerable to love addictions. On the other hand, romantic love may be inherently possessive because it craves validation of being in an absolutely unique and special relationship that could not be replicated with anyone else. That feeling of absolute uniqueness may be an illusion, but it may be a necessary illusion to sustain the residual feelings of romantic love once the obsessive phase is over.

Human vanity may demand the affirmation of being at least one special person's favorite lover. Sexual exclusivity says to the world that a couple feels they are each other's favorite lover and so will forgo others to be together exclusively. Partners may maintain a feeling that they are each other's favorite lover by derogating attractive alternatives (Lydon, Meana, Sepinwall, Richards, & Mayman, 1999). The stronger the identification with the relationship and with being a member of a couple, the more likely that responses to relational threat will be prorelational (e.g., ignoring attractive alternatives; Linardatos & Lydon, 2011). Of course, monogamy becomes a prison if it feels as though one is trapped having sex with a least favorite lover for the rest of one's life. For that reason, the loss of romantic connection is a risk factor for infidelity.

Sexual exclusivity may be required to preserve a partner's need to feel that he or she is a unique, special, and irreplaceable person who is respected and admired even if no longer an object of obsessive adoration or infatuation. Romantic love gratifies human narcissism, the sense of having won an intense sexual competition for an extremely desirable partner because one is an exceptionally desirable romantic partner oneself. Narcissistic pathology appears to be associated with an increased vulnerability to love addiction as a means of reflating deflated grandiose fantasies (Dubrow-Eichel, 1993). Pathological narcissism appears to mediate the influence of insecure attachment on compulsive behaviors such as bulimia (Dakanalis, Clerici, & Carrà, 2016). Infidelity may be a way the insecurely attached restore self-worth by resorting to a narcissistic solution to the problem of insecure attachment.

Unfortunately, although infidelity may be one partner's narcissistic solution, it is the betrayed partner's narcissistic trauma. Infidelity, especially for romantic love, bursts the narcissistic illusions that romantic love supports. Infidelity may signify that one is no longer thought sufficiently desirable to be worth the sacrifice of sexual exclusivity so that infidelity constitutes a major blow to feelings of self-worth. Exactly how much narcissistic disappointment and deflation a person can tolerate and still remain committed to a romantic partner will be variable from one individual to another and from one marital situation to another.

SEXUAL MIND READING AND SEXUAL MORALITY

Not surprisingly, research suggests that men possess more favorable attitudes than women toward sexual behaviors such as infidelity, pornography, and casual sex (Laumann, Gagnon, Michael, & Michaels, 1994). Women possess more favorable attitudes toward monogamy and long-term commitment than men do (Laumann et al., 1994). Thus, each sex tends to disapprove of the sexual tendencies that the other prefers more strongly. As a consequence, men, especially those who are avoidantly attached, tend to lack empathy for women's desires for intimacy and commitment. That lack is only exacerbated by the angrily demanding and controlling way that anxiously attached women tend to express those frustrated desires. Such men tend to see women's desire for emotional intimacy and commitment as reflecting a shameful neediness. Avoidant men then tend to withdraw from suffocating and smothering women that seem to infringe too much on their freedom and independence. Avoidant men tend to lose their tempers when anxiously attached women who feel rejected attempt to block their hostile withdrawal and can become physically abusive (Genest & Mathieu, 2014).

Women, especially anxiously attached women, may lack empathy for men's sexual frustration, especially when intimacy-avoidant men are feeling frustrated about not getting enough casual sex or sexual variety. Anxiously attached women take it as personal rejection that diminishes their feelings of sexual desirability. They may be disgusted by aspects of male sexuality that seem too impersonal, cold, perverse, sexually objectifying, and demeaning to women. Anxious attachment appears to be associated with greater disgust sensitivity, whereas avoidant attachment is associated with weaker moral concerns (Koleva, Selterman, Iyer, Ditto, & Graham, 2014). Anxious women may send men to psychotherapists to "fix" their fears of emotional intimacy as well as their "disgusting" sexual tendencies. Those men may think women are the ones who need to see a psychotherapist to "fix" their excessive neediness and sexual prudery. The lack of mutual understanding then results in power struggles, with both partners trying to fix each other to make the other more like themself. It's a no-win situation.

Gender benders may occur when it is the women who are avoidant and the men who are anxiously attached. Avoidantly attached women who can separate love and lust and enjoy casual sex "like a man" may be perceived as unfeminine or "slutty." Anxiously attached men who are extremely rejection-sensitive, shy, passive, or needy of reassurance may seem "nice" but not virile or masculine. Partners can judge and shame each other both for not fitting the gender role stereotype and for fitting it. Either way, it results in communication breakdown. Although sex differences may remain between gay men and lesbian women in strength of sex drive (see Baumeister et al., 2001), differences in attachment style may generate the same relational conflicts in same-sex relationships as they do in opposite-sex relationships. It can be problematic to generalize about the sexuality of all gay and lesbian individuals because their sexuality may be shaped as much by their attachment style as their sexual orientation.

The tendency to judge a partner whose sexuality is different from one's own reflects a failure of cross-attachment style as much as cross-sex or cross-sexual orientation mind reading, the inability to accurately understand and empathize with a person's attachment vulnerabilities and the sexual predispositions that attempt to compensate for those attachment vulnerabilities. *Error management theory* suggests that there may be an adaptive basis for biases of cross-sex mind reading (Haselton & Buss, 2000). Heterosexual women may tend toward commitment skepticism because they assume men are more oriented toward short-term mating, whereas heterosexual men may oversexualize relationships in the hope of finding women who aren't biased against casual sex as they might presume most women would be (Geher, 2009). The discovery that men aren't as commitment oriented or that women aren't as oriented toward casual sex as they initially seemed to be is experienced as deception and provokes moral outrage. Such gender differences may be moderated by differences in attachment style if avoidantly attached individuals pretend to be more emotionally available than they really are, whereas anxiously attached individuals pretend to be more independent.

Janice and Jason were lawyers in their late 20s with demanding careers. They came for couples therapy because they hadn't had sex in months. Arguing about who was at fault never led anywhere. Janice said that she didn't miss sex with Jason that much because when she was angry with him, she wasn't in the mood for sex—and she was angry with him all the time. Jason faulted Janice for this, noting that he was always in the mood for sex whether he was angry or not and he would not punish her as she punished him by withholding sex when angry. Janice felt criticized for being too avoidant of sexual intimacy, while Jason felt faulted for being too needy for sexual intimacy.

I asked each of them how often they would want to have sex in an ideal world in which they weren't overburdened with work. Janice said that once a week on weekends would be fine; Jason said daily would be his preference. They both looked shocked and in disbelief that the other needed sex as little or as much as she or he did. They looked to me to tell them whose sex drive was normal and whose was too high or too low and perhaps needed to be adjusted to a healthy level. I said that sex drive is variable from person to person so that there was no point debating whose sex drive was normal or pathological, sexually repressed or sexually liberated. There was no point making the other feel bad about his or her sexuality because they each seemed fine with the strength of their own sex drives. The question, then, is how couples whose sex drives are mismatched can find a constructive way to negotiate that difference.

Janice and Jason both agreed that they could meet somewhere in the middle and try to have sex two or three times a week, but Janice added the caveat that it would only be possible for her to have sex at that frequency if they were getting along reasonably well. Fortunately, Janice and Jason were able to openly address the frustrating difference in their sexual psychologies early in their relationship before it became a significant risk factor for infidelity. Jason was considering accepting a temporary appointment working for a prestigious judge in another city, and Janice wondered whether she could trust Jason to remain faithful in a long-distance relationship if they were no longer having a sexual relationship. Janice knew that remaining faithful would be easy for her because she didn't miss sex all that much when she was busy with work but was uncertain whether Jason's frustration tolerance was up to the job given the strength of his sex drive. Jason reassured her that he could refrain from infidelity even if they weren't having sex that frequently but that he didn't want to commit to a sexless marriage for the rest of his life.

What motivated Jason and Janice to resolve their differences? Their sexual conflict threatened their attachment security so that they were motivated to seek couples therapy to avoid a breakup. I helped them reflect on the impact of their sexual preferences on each other's sense of attachment security. Janice couldn't feel secure if feeling pressured into having sex when angry. Coercive pressure only made her feel smothered, so she responded avoidantly. Jason couldn't feel secure experiencing Janice as emotionally unavailable for sexual intimacy. Sexual rejection increased Jason's anxious attachment, so he felt even needier and became more sexually demanding. Treatment helped them realize that they had to meet somewhere in the middle if they were ever to feel securely attached to each another.

When frustrated, there is a tendency to judge and pathologize a romantic partner's sexual and romantic predispositions for not being more like, and therefore more compatible with, one's own. Overcoming egocentrism is challenging when feeling sexually rejected and frustrated or worried about sexual betrayal. Nevertheless, securely attached individuals are more likely to possess the reflective functioning and communication skills to constructively negotiate conflicts about differences in sex drive, attachment needs, and romantic yearnings.

CONCLUSION

Mentalizing the perspective of someone whose sexuality or attachment style is different from one's own requires overcoming egocentrism. Are there individuals who find it particularly difficult to overcome their egocentrism to empathize with the perspective of others who are different? As it turns out, individuals high in narcissism, a personality trait associated with insecure attachment, find it particularly difficult to overcome their own egocentrism to empathize with others. Narcissists are also more inclined to be unfaithful. The psychology of infidelity cannot be fully understood without understanding the psychology of narcissism as a strategy for coping with underlying attachment insecurities (i.e., don't put all your eggs in one basket). Narcissism is one of the key personality traits that form what is known as the "Dark Triad"—the subject of our next chapter.

4

FATAL ATTRACTIONS: THE DARK TRIAD AND INFIDELITY

Do unfaithful partners tend to possess a certain personality organization, a certain way of coping with insecure attachment? And are certain personality types that are also insecurely attached unconsciously attracted to those who might be predisposed to being unfaithful? Single patients, especially if they have suffered sexual betrayal in the past, wonder how they could know if they are dating someone who might turn out to be a philanderer. Such patients no longer trust their own judgment in picking a romantic partner and are hoping the therapist might be a better judge of character than they are. Infidelity can be experienced as an assault on truth (Elise, 2012). Noticing a declining sex life and a partner who increasingly works late at the office, married patients might wonder if they are married to the sort of person who might be unfaithful. They want to know what the therapist thinks and to determine whether they are just being unduly paranoid. Patients wonder what it might say about them if it turns out they are unconsciously attracted to philandering types, like their philandering father, without consciously knowing it.

http://dx.doi.org/10.1037/0000053-005
The Dynamics of Infidelity: Applying Relationship Science to Psychotherapy Practice, by L. Josephs

Research by personality psychologists (Baughman, Jonason, Lyons, & Vernon, 2014) has revealed that there is indeed a personality organization predisposed toward infidelity, and it's not always hard to detect who they are. These individuals tend to score high on the "Dark Triad" of narcissism, Machiavellian intelligence, and psychopathy, and they also score low on guilt and empathy (Giammarco & Vernon, 2014; Jonason & Krause, 2013; Jonason, Lyons, Bethell, & Ross, 2013). Although everyone, even individuals low on these personality characteristics, is capable of infidelity in certain circumstances, individuals high on these characteristics are more likely to be unfaithful. Opportunities to be unfaithful might indeed activate a more narcissistic mind-set in individuals who are otherwise generally low on narcissism. Emotions like lust and infatuation, as opposed to mature love and caring, may activate a more egocentric, opportunistic, and implicitly self-serving mind-set. Individuals who feel swept away by romantic passion are less likely to consider the long-term consequences for themselves or others of gratifying immediate desires for sexual or romantic pleasure (Ariely & Loewenstein, 2006).

It is not that individuals possessing other personality characteristics are incapable of infidelity—be they obsessive, paranoid, or hysteric. There is a tendency to think of personality in categorical ways, as though personality types are mutually exclusive and one is either one type or another. A dimensional way of thinking suggests that one could simultaneously be highly obsessive, moderately paranoid, and low on hysteria. Infidelity appears to be more closely associated with an elevation in the narcissistic dimension of personality functioning than other dimensions of personality functioning such as being depressive or masochistic. When patients who are predominantly obsessive, paranoid, hysteric, schizoid, or depressive engage in infidelity, clinicians would be prudent to look for latent narcissistic characteristics that may have been overlooked.

Ironically, many individuals with narcissistic personality traits possess a seemingly irresistible social charisma that increases their allure and that may blind their admirers to their potentially "cheating hearts," despite their admirers' better judgment. An intriguing study by Back, Schmukle, and Egloff (2010) found that high narcissists are indeed found to be more charming on first sight than low narcissists, although that initial charm wears off the better one gets to know them. So it seems that the very personality type most likely to be unfaithful is also capable of inspiring "fatal attractions" that makes certain individuals vulnerable to exploitation by their sexual opportunism. Detecting a predisposition toward infidelity can be challenging when wishful thinking and denial inspired by romantic love may cloud one's better judgment. Therapists frequently must help patients understand the sexual psychology of their potentially unfaithful, narcissistic partners, with whom they are becoming progressively disillusioned and frustrated.

Do opposites attract, or do birds of a feather flock together? In general, researchers have discovered that *assortative mating* in personality style (Rammstedt & Schupp, 2008) appears to guide mate choice for agreeableness, conscientiousness, and openness; in other words, birds of a feather flock together. Campbell, Foster, and Finkel (2002) discovered that narcissistic game-playing types tend to attract each another. It is ironic that high narcissists are not only predisposed toward infidelity, they also seem to be implicitly attracted to the sort of person most likely to be unfaithful. As a consequence, narcissistic individuals may not be quite as savvy about how to play the mating game because they usually believe they are actually living their grandiose romantic fantasies.

Treating infidelity often raises the same clinical challenges as treating narcissism: How does the therapist address the defensive grandiosity, the entitlement to be above the rules, the sense of victimhood and self-righteous indignation when others frustrate the patient's sense of entitlement? How does the therapist treat the egocentrism and lack of empathy that make it difficult for others to tolerate being in a long-term relationship with these patients without complaint or trying to "fix" them? Both the betrayed and the unfaithful partner may be relatively high on narcissism, so treating the narcissistic couple recovering from infidelity means treating two individuals who angrily experience themselves as an innocent victim of the other. The countertransference challenge for the therapist is containing both frustration with narcissistic patients' impenetrability and moralistic reactions to their self-justification for deceit, betrayal, condescension, and revenge.

According to Kernberg (1984), narcissistic pathology reflects an underlying borderline ego organization so that narcissists are also predisposed to splitting (i.e., dichotomous thinking). From an evolutionary viewpoint, the Dark Triad appears to predispose individuals to more short-term high-risk/high-gain reproductive strategies (Jonason, Li, Webster, & Schmitt, 2009) and may be heritable (Onley, Veselka, Schermer, & Vernon, 2013). Defensive grandiosity appears to rationalize this high-risk strategy: These individuals believe that because of their inherent superiority, they will be one of the winners who will reap the benefits of a high-risk approach without paying the costs. At the same time, high narcissists believe that individuals lacking their superior characteristics will be among the many pathetic losers. Dichotomous thinking is revealed in viewing individuals as either enviable winners or shameful losers. It is difficult for narcissistic people to appreciate their realistic strengths without feeling smugly superior or their own limitations without feeling ashamed. Likewise, it is difficult for them to appreciate the realistic strengths of others without feeling envious and inadequate or the limitations of others without feeling contempt or disgust. Their capacity for accepting self and others as they are, warts and all, is limited.

Such individuals seek psychotherapy when the costs of their high-risk strategy become too much to bear (i.e., they feel more like a pathetic loser than a proud winner). Their initial hope is that psychotherapy will help them implement their high-risk mating strategy more successfully. However, these patients are inclined to criticize and devalue the bearer of bad news if the therapist suggests that making them a winner on their terms is an improbable long shot. More narcissistic patients recoil from the thought of cutting their losses by recalibrating to a lower risk mating strategy and using therapy to acquire the reflective functioning, empathy, and communication skills necessary to successfully implement an alternative mating strategy. Narcissistic pathology may be a symptom of underlying attachment insecurity (Fossati, Feeney, Pincus, Borroni, & Maffei, 2015). Facilitating the skills necessary for forming secure attachments may help such patients switch to a lower risk mating strategy if they can learn to accept the modest benefits that fall short of their grandiose compensatory fantasies of impressive romantic triumph.

NARCISSISM: HOW TO HAVE YOUR CAKE AND EAT IT TOO!

Freud (1957a) was the first to define narcissism as a personality trait; he believed that narcissists suffered from excessive self-love, like Narcissus of Greek myth who fell in love with his own reflection. Freud was not particularly optimistic about the treatment of narcissistic pathology, but the groundbreaking work of psychoanalysts such as Heinz Kohut (1971) and Otto Kernberg (1984, 2009) has shown that narcissistic individuals are amenable to psychotherapeutic treatment, although controversy remains as to the optimal therapeutic approach. D. Diamond and Meehan (2013) successfully used transference-focused therapy, an evidence-based treatment for severe personality disorders, in the treatment of narcissistic personality disorder.

Personality psychologists have developed measures of narcissism to empirically investigate this psychoanalytic construct. The assumption is that narcissistic traits exist on a continuum from low to high in the general population. The average prevalence rate from a variety of different studies of narcissistic personality disorder is only 1.06% of the general population with a range of findings from 0% to 6.2% (Dhawan, Kunik, Oldham, & Coverdale, 2010). A diagnosable narcissistic personality disorder is rare; however, with the development of a quantitative measure of narcissism, the Narcissistic Personality Inventory, by Raskin and Hall (1979, 1981), it became possible to systematically explore the differences in the adult romantic relationships of those relatively high versus relatively low on narcissism among individuals who do not possess a diagnosable personality disorder.

Personality psychologists explore what might be called the "garden-variety narcissism" of everyday life rather than the malignant narcissism of that small percentage of the population that possesses a diagnosable narcissistic personality disorder. Psychiatry tends to look at personality disorders in categorical ways. You have either have one or you don't according to some arbitrary cutoff suggested by a diagnostic manual. In contrast, personality psychologists think of personality in dimensional ways—as traits one can possess a little of or a lot. Most individuals who are unfaithful or who have been betrayed do not possess a diagnosable narcissistic personality disorder. Nevertheless, individuals who are unfaithful are likely to be significantly higher on narcissism than individuals who remain faithful (Buss & Shackelford, 1997; McNulty & Widman, 2014).

The narcissistic dimension of anyone's personality contributes to the propensity to be unfaithful. The narcissistic dimension may be unconsciously activated by strong temptations to be unfaithful. Lust as an emotion contributes to an objectifying state of mind in which others are construed more as objects than as subjects. Lust can therefore activate a narcissistic mind-set in individuals who might otherwise be generally low on narcissism. Sexual arousal activates an imperious need to experience immediate sexual bliss unimpeded by concern about other people's feelings or the long-term consequences of one's actions (Ariely & Loewenstein, 2006). Thus, narcissism can be a trait, an enduring personality characteristic, and a transient state of mind elicited by particular circumstances.

According to the fifth edition of the *Diagnostic and Statistical Manual of Mental Disorders* (*DSM–5*; American Psychiatric Association, 2013), narcissistic people consider themselves unique and superior to others. They maintain their grandiose self-concept by fantasizing about fame, power, or love and by defending the self against even the slightest criticism, affiliating with high-status others, and seeking admiration. Indeed, narcissists tend to be exhibitionistic and may be quite charming in the pursuit of attention and adoration. In pursuit of meeting their narcissistic needs, such individuals tend to act in entitled and exploitative ways, lacking in empathy while being envious of others' achievements and abilities (both the *DSM–5* and the *International Classification of Diseases*, 10th revision [World Health Organization, 1992] criteria include all of these features). When it comes to adult romantic relationships, high narcissists are more likely to be unfaithful in committed relationships, and this unfaithfulness is associated with sexual entitlement, sexual grandiosity, and lack of empathy (McNulty & Widman, 2014). Campbell et al. (2002) found that the narcissistic approach to adult romantic relationships is "game-playing" and that game-playing narcissistic individuals tend to be attracted to one another.

Baumeister, Smart, and Boden (1996) challenged the conventional wisdom that narcissists suffer low self-esteem and that their overestimation of themselves is only a defense against underlying feelings of inferiority. Narcissists might actually have quite high self-esteem, which they aggressively defend whenever their inflated egotism is threatened (Bushman & Baumeister, 1998). They feel entitled to extramarital sex because they feel they are exceptional—the rules that apply to ordinary people do not apply to them. Because narcissists are egocentric and low on empathy, they don't think too deeply about what the consequences might be for their betrayed spouses or their own marriage if they are caught cheating. When narcissists engage in infidelity, it is not only a symptom of their hidden inferiority complex or dread of intimacy, as both psychodynamically oriented clinicians and betrayed partners often assume, but also of their sense of entitlement and low empathy—personality traits that tend to be treatment-resistant and for which patients rarely seek treatment voluntarily.

Betrayed partners, often in cahoots with therapists they have recruited, hope to fix what they presume to be unfaithful partners' fear of commitment and intimacy so that they will be able to fully commit to monogamy. A clinical focus on the unfaithful partner's hidden fears of commitment and intimacy can sometimes be a strategic error if it overlooks the egocentrism and low empathy that facilitates rationalization of the infidelity to reduce guilt. The unfaithful partner may think, "I am committed because I don't want to leave my spouse. I only want to have meaningless casual sex on the side; that shouldn't be perceived as a threat to the marriage" or "I am capable of great sex and emotional intimacy with my affair partner, so it's my spouse's problem if we don't have great sex or emotional intimacy." Either way, the high narcissist is skeptical that the underlying problem is their own repudiated fear of commitment and intimacy. For treatment to move forward, the therapist must find a way to facilitate cognitive reappraisal of self-serving infidelity beliefs.

In individual therapy, highly narcissistic patients who have been unfaithful might have to concede the necessity of learning to better contend with being "unfairly" perceived as someone avoidant of commitment and intimacy by their romantic partner and perhaps the therapist. Highly narcissistic patients may find themselves in arguments with romantic partners about just how narcissistic they actually are. Of course, because their partners may also be high on narcissism, it is easy enough for high narcissists to engage in what J. M. Gottman (1999) called countercomplaint by accusing the accuser of being even higher in narcissism than they are. They may argue that if they are avoidant of commitment and intimacy, it's because their partners' own unacknowledged narcissism shuts them out and pushes them away.

Couples therapists may have to learn how to help couples deal with each other's unflattering perceptions of the other's problematic character traits, especially viewing the partner as a selfish, self-centered, egotistical, and unreachable (i.e., a narcissistic) person. It is difficult to learn how to listen to what seems like unfair character assassination without taking it personally but with tolerance and acceptance. It is challenging to simply notice and contain one's own reflexive tendency to respond with defensive self-justification and countercomplaint that only escalates conflict. It is difficult to learn how to empathize with the hurt and vulnerability hidden behind harsh and unfairly accusatory complaints when feeling personally attacked. And it is especially hard to empathize with the hurt and vulnerability behind derisive countercomplaint when there is a sneaking suspicion that the person making the complaint might actually be a cold-hearted person through and through (a psychopath who is beyond ever feeling genuine remorse but only capable of faking it).

Communication skills training advises partners not to engage in global character assassination because of the hurt and defensiveness it evokes (Gottman, 1999). Yet patients still need help learning not to take the harsh critique so personally. Partners may learn to bite their lip and refrain from verbalizing the harsh critique of a partner's personality characteristics, but when frustrated, the expression on their faces still communicates what they think. It is difficult for narcissistic people to accept that everybody is entitled to their own opinion. You can't control what other people think, so you can't stop them from thinking poorly of you. You have to learn to live with other people's unflattering and offensive perceptions of your personality without taking it personally.

Narcissistic infidelity beliefs often reflect a hypocritical double standard: It's acceptable for the narcissist to be unfaithful, but unacceptable for their partners. Exline and colleagues (2004) found that those high in narcissistic entitlement were particularly unforgiving in the face of relational transgression. So it seems that those most likely to be unfaithful and rationalize it are also those most likely to be unforgiving when they are sexually betrayed themselves. The underlying logic is that their own infidelity is entirely justified by the insufferable personality deficits of their partners—the wife is a "cold bitch" or the husband is an "abusive asshole." Seeing themselves as an innocent victim of a horrible spouse deactivates whatever latent guilt they might feel about being unfaithful. They feel their infidelity is entirely justified by their unhappy marital situation. In contrast, they can't imagine that their partners could have any valid reason to be unfaithful to them, so their partners' infidelity would constitute a grievous moral offense to be harshly punished.

Addressing the double standard is challenging for the clinician because the patient is likely to feel that the therapist is unsympathetic and unreasonably critical to call attention to the implicit hypocrisy of the patient's double standard. These patients feel that a supportive therapist would reinforce their sense of entitlement to be unfaithful given their marital unhappiness and their spouses' insufferable personality problems, rather than judge them in a way they perceive as moralistic. Yet if the therapist validates the patient's infidelity beliefs, the patient remains ill-equipped to appreciate the point of view of others, including their betrayed partners, that will be offended by their rationalization of deceit and betrayal. Unfaithful narcissistic patients must learn how to contend with being perceived, fairly or unfairly, as an untrustworthy, hypocritical, and possibly psychopathic individual who is rationalizing sexual betrayal to avoid assuming responsibility for its negative consequences and to do so without getting angry. The point is not whether that unflattering assessment is valid. The point is that one cannot stop others, including the therapist, from privately making an unflattering assessment even if they can be stopped from openly voicing their opinions.

Ironically, highly narcissistic individuals may not only be more likely to be perpetrators of infidelity; they might also be more likely to be victims of it, given their attraction to people like themselves. Highly narcissistic individuals are shocked when they become victims of infidelity because it is inconceivable they could have done anything that would warrant such mistreatment. Because of their egocentrism, they can't imagine that their own personality difficulties may be contributing to any of the relational messes in which they find themselves. They have difficulty appreciating their impact on others because of their low reflective functioning; they cannot see that it might not be easy for their spouses to live with their narcissistic traits (e.g., being controlling, always being right, being unreachable).

Without a therapist pointing out their interpersonal impact on others, narcissistic patients are unlikely to recognize it. Such patients can spend years in insight-oriented psychotherapy and gain great insight into their own inner conflicts or dichotomous thinking, yet remain relatively clueless as to their emotional impact on others. Their relationships remain highly conflictual despite their introspective self-understanding because they never learn to adjust their narcissistic behavior so that others don't feel devalued and diminished by them. In fact, they may implicitly brag about the years spent in analysis and the deep insights they have accrued to make others feel inadequate for their lack of in-depth introspective self-understanding.

Recovery from infidelity is particularly difficult for betrayed partners if the posttraumatic stress disorder after the betrayal is combined with a preexisting narcissistic disturbance. Such patients often feel the therapist is blaming the victim when he or she tries to help them assume responsibility for their role in the marital difficulties, which their unfaithful partners point out to rationalize the infidelity. It is difficult for such patients to see that their self-righteous indignation has become an impediment to recovery from infidelity because their partners are reluctant to recommit to monogamy if they dread never getting out of the "doghouse" because their betrayed, narcissistic partners will forever hold a grudge against them.

To some extent, self-justification is part of human nature. Social psychologists call this way of thinking the *fundamental attribution error*: When we do something wrong, it is because of extenuating circumstances, but when others do something wrong it is because of something unsavory in their personalities (Haney & Zimbardo, 2009). It would appear that narcissistic individuals think this way much more than others. Treatment must include cognitive reappraisal of the fundamental attribution error in the face of the narcissistic individual's skepticism. Narcissistic patients need to alter their attributional style to empathize with the extenuating circumstances that affect their partners' behavior (i.e., the impact of their own narcissism on their partners') while appreciating how their own enduring personality tendencies (i.e., their narcissism) makes them partially responsible for their relationship outcomes.

Narcissism has been associated with an increased self-serving bias (McAllister et al., 2002). The self-serving bias is to attribute success to internal causes but failure to external causes. The self-serving bias occurs in relationships when what's good about a relationship is attributed to oneself and what's bad about a relationship is attributed to a partner. Such dichotomous thinking contributes to unfaithful partners feeling justified in their infidelity and to betrayed partners feeling justified in their vindictive fury. Cognitive reappraisal of the self-serving bias is challenging because it requires acknowledging one's own biases and also that others might have a good point despite their biases.

Narcissism may also be associated with the *just world fallacy*, the belief that if the world is a just place, one should be treated fairly (Lerner, 1980). It doesn't seem fair when marriage proves to be sexually frustrating and one has buyer's remorse, when all the good romantic partners seem to be taken, leaving one with only the undesirable leftovers from which to choose, or when one's partner has been unfaithful despite the fact that one has been a good spouse. As a consequence, being unfaithful, initiating an affair with a married individual, or getting revenge on an unfaithful spouse may seem justified as forms of compensation for the unfairness and injustices of one's adult romantic relationships. One may suffer posttraumatic embitterment disorder, a traumatic reaction to the injustices and humiliations that may be an unavoidable part of life (Linden, Baumann, Lieberei, Lorenz, & Rotter, 2011), in response to the unfairness that may be inherent in adult romantic relationships. Reality falls short of our sexual and romantic fantasies despite our best efforts to fulfill those longings and desires. Because high narcissists feel more entitled to privileged treatment than most people, they may be more vulnerable to traumatic embitterment when experiencing what Shakespeare called "the slings and arrows of outrageous fortune."

Twenge, Konrath, Foster, Campbell, and Bushman (2008) found that when the Narcissistic Personality Inventory was first developed back in the

1980s, men always scored higher on narcissism than women. But just as women appear to have caught up to the men in infidelity rates, they also appear to have caught up to the men in narcissism. Grijalva and colleagues (2015) found small or no gender differences on the various subscales of narcissism and cautioned against overapplying small effect sizes (small but statistically significant differences) to perpetuate gender role stereotypes. So the data at this point appear to suggest that women have achieved gender equality when it comes to narcissistic propensities. Twenge et al. (2008) also found that there appears to be a significant increase in narcissism in more recent generations, so it would not be surprising if infidelity rates begin to increase as well.

Charlie and Ginger came for couples therapy because Charlie discovered that Ginger had been having an affair with one of her colleagues at work. To get even, Charlie went out and slept with one of his work colleagues and told Ginger about it. They wanted to see if therapy might help them recover from infidelity and save the marriage. Ginger reported that Charlie had been disinterested in sex with her for quite a while. As a consequence, she was feeling sexually unattractive and needed the validation that indeed she was a sexually desirable woman. Men had always treated Ginger as a sexy woman, so she felt entitled to that validation. Ginger felt that Charlie should have felt privileged to have won her, and she was indignant that he didn't appreciate how lucky he was. She angrily decided that she would show him that if he didn't appreciate her, many other men would. She felt that the punitive way he had gotten even was not called for because the punishment didn't fit the crime.

Charlie was not comfortable with sexual intimacy, although he found Ginger quite attractive. He was used to having casual sex without intimacy. Charlie didn't think he had a fear of intimacy but rather that Ginger was too needy, and that was a turnoff. When Ginger became angrily demanding in response to sexual rejection, he just withdrew. We analyzed together that neither was aware that the ways in which they expressed their feelings (Ginger made angry demands while Charlie withdrew in anger) only served to drive the other partner away. We decided to make a contract. If Ginger stopped angrily demanding sexual intimacy, Charlie would take the initiative in their sexual relationship. Ginger would respect Charlie's need for space and freedom from behavioral control if Charlie would be sensitive to her need for sexual validation.

Ginger appeared to be anxiously attached, while Charlie appeared to be avoidantly attached, yet they each used narcissistic defenses to cope with their attachment insecurities. When Ginger received validation of her grandiose fantasy that she was an irresistibly sexy woman whom men couldn't live without, it helped mask her fear of abandonment. To meet his underlying dependency needs, Charlie craved validation of his grandiose fantasy that he was a completely independent, self-sufficient man who could win a highly desirable woman whom he didn't really need. Narcissism may therefore be a defensive solution to unacknowledged attachment insecurities. Defensive grandiosity allows the individual to ignore his or her attachment insecurity.

To address their egocentrism, I needed to explicitly point out and encourage Ginger and Charlie to mentalize the emotional impact of the counterproductive ways that they expressed their hurt and anger. The underlying complaint might be legitimate, but their way of expressing it might be counterproductive if it put the other partner on the defensive. In a case such as this, the therapist might also need to suggest a constructive alternative because egocentric patients are unlikely to arrive at one on their own, even if they can see the self-defeating nature of the way they express themselves once the therapist points it out. Self-preoccupation only increases when one is feeling blamed by a romantic partner and put on the defensive (Josephs & McLeod, 2014).

The next week, Ginger and Charlie reported getting along quite well; however, although Ginger gave Charlie space, he didn't initiate sex. Charlie reported that he just wasn't in the mood. I noted that for trust to be restored, they must both keep their promises. I also noted that marriage may require a certain amount of sex work, of being willing to have sex when one isn't in the mood so the other partner won't feel unduly frustrated. I added that one often gets in the mood once things get started. I noted that in traditional marriages, women were expected to service their husbands when they weren't in the mood for sex. I suggested that in an egalitarian marriage, they both had responsibilities to meet each other's sexual needs even if they weren't in the mood to do a certain amount of sex work. The next week, they came in beaming. Charlie initiated sex and, to his surprise, had a great time. Ginger proclaimed that I was a miracle worker and had saved their marriage (this reflects the narcissistic tendency to adore the therapist when gratified but narcissists also have the disposition to despise the therapist when frustrated).

MACHIAVELLIAN INTELLIGENCE: BEING TOO CLEVER FOR YOUR OWN GOOD

Infidelity requires more than the activation of a narcissistic mind-set; it also requires a certain type of strategic intelligence. How does one successfully deceive someone in a long-term, sexually exclusive relationship? How does one explain all the evenings and weekends away from home, the declining interest in sexual intimacy, and the subtle emotional detachment that could be signs of infidelity? How does one cover up the smoking guns revealed by e-mails, text messages, unusual smells, lipstick smudges, bite marks, being observed by friends and acquaintances in public in overly intimate circumstances, not being at the office when claiming to be, and so on? Successful deception does require some relinquishment of an entirely egocentric perspective. To successfully deceive someone, the world must be imagined from the other's point of view to create a false reality that will be mistaken for the truth.

Personality psychologists have coined the term *Machiavellian intelligence* to capture the ability to successfully manipulate others for personal gain, often against their self-interest. Some people are more willing and able to be manipulative than others. Niccolo Machiavelli (1469–1527) wrote in *The Prince* that "men are so simple and so much creatures of circumstance that the deceiver will always find someone ready to be deceived" (Machiavelli, 1999, p. 57). In 1970, Christie and Geis (1970) developed a measure of Machiavellian intelligence that asks for levels of agreement with statements such as "Never tell anyone the real reason you did something unless it is useful to do so." Machiavelli noted that some individuals may be highly suggestible because their wishful thinking leads them to be more easily deceived. Taking advantage of that gullibility is one of the key skills a person with Machiavellian intelligence possesses. Brewer and Abell (2015) discovered that Machiavellian intelligence is associated with predispositions towards sexual deception and infidelity. McHoskey (2001) found that Machiavellians will feign love to have sex.

The fact that many individuals in monogamous relationships naively trust their partners and have a strong vested interest in believing that their partners are faithful individuals who would never cheat predisposes them to ignore and rationalize subtle clues of potential infidelity. Individuals high on Machiavellian intelligence would see that gullibility as an opportunity: A partner's naiveté makes it easier to get away with infidelity. Confident in their own cleverness and cunning, the Machiavellian person assumes that what the betrayed spouse doesn't know won't hurt them, and that the chances of exposure are sufficiently low that it is worth taking the risk of getting caught, given the significant sexual and emotional gratification that an affair may offer. A calculation may be made that the costs of exposure can be significantly reduced to a manageable level if one can successfully use one's cleverness and cunning for damage control if the need arises.

PSYCHOPATHY: WHAT'S SO BAD ABOUT A LITTLE WHITE LIE?

Infidelity requires one other character trait that goes beyond the simple activation of a transient, if not more enduring, grandiose fantasy of oneself as someone entitled to break the rules and possessing the strategic intelligence to get away with the deception. Infidelity requires a willingness to break the rules and lie about it despite knowing full well that it is an unethical and hurtful thing to do. It's one thing to fantasize about infidelity and another to actually do it. It is this element of dishonesty that makes most people consider infidelity unethical. Most people recognize that the mating game is a competition often won by the most confident and savvy people and that one shouldn't be a sore loser if you gave the game your best shot but lost the competition. But it is generally assumed that there are certain rules by which the game is played. One doesn't cheat on romantic partners or try to steal someone else's. Most individuals play the game by these rules (at least in the United States, where the prevalence rate of infidelity is below 50%) despite strong temptations to the contrary, so most people don't take kindly to those who break the rules and lie about it.

Robert Trivers (1971), an evolutionary biologist, suggested that reciprocal altruism (i.e., shared sacrifice for the good of a social alliance) can only develop if we have mechanisms for punishing cheaters who take advantage of our cooperative natures. Human moral sentiments urge us to demand that cheaters be punished and to insist that it's not a just world if cheaters can get away with their deception. Acceptance of human nature requires learning how to contain this instinctive reaction by learning to look at the dark side of human nature objectively and with compassion for the inherent self-destructiveness of those who ruthlessly exploit the trust and vulnerability of others. Acceptance doesn't mean masochistically tolerating exploitative treatment but, rather, assertively setting limits on such mistreatment without punitively shaming the exploiter, just as one might try to calmly manage a child's manipulative temper tantrums without losing one's own temper.

Psychopathy is the character trait that appears to characterize individuals who feel they are free to break the rules without remorse, no matter who it hurts. From an evolutionary perspective, psychopaths are "free riders" who reap the benefits of the sacrifices that others make without making any of their own. These are the individuals who don't see anything wrong with lying to get what they want. Psychopathy predicts infidelity in women as well as men (Jones & Weiser, 2014) and sexually predatory and coercive behavior in men (Marcus & Norris, 2014).

Infidelity requires a certain kind of cold-heartedness that is most characteristic of the psychopathic personality, an indifference to the suffering infidelity may cause to individuals psychopaths might claim to love—their spouses, their children, their parents, their in-laws, their affair partners, or their best friends whose spouses they stole. It may seem harsh to characterize infidelity as a psychopathic act, but indeed it is, even if one is perfectly decent in all other areas of one's life. Patients who enter psychotherapy that feel remorse after the fact of infidelity might wonder how they could have been so heartless to thoughtlessly hurt the ones they love. It's difficult to admit to oneself that one might possess a ruthlessly self-serving aspect of one's personality and that one might thoughtlessly and recklessly engage in behavior one might later regret. Acceptance of the human capacity for sexual treachery is not easy when the initial shock of exposed infidelity evokes understandable feelings of homicidal rage.

In *The Mask of Sanity*, Hervey Cleckley (1941/2015) described the psychopathic personality: It is characterized by glibness and superficial charm, grandiosity, pathological lying, conning and manipulative tendencies, the lack of remorse or guilt, a superficial affect, an emotional life that is callous and lacking of empathy, and a failure to accept responsibility. These are the exact traits required to be a successful philanderer: One needs to be charming to seduce someone into a sexual liaison with a married person. One has to be comfortable lying repeatedly to hide the affair. One has to be comfortable conning and manipulating someone one claims to love without the interference of guilt or remorse to execute a successful cover-up. One must refrain from having empathy for the betrayal trauma being inflicted on one's partner; otherwise one wouldn't do it in the first place.

And if one gets caught, one must deny responsibility. First, one must indignantly protest one's essential innocence by claiming one's partner is being falsely accusatory and unduly paranoid. Second, once the truth is told, one must argue that it's all the partner's fault, that one was driven to infidelity by the partner's emotional neglect or mistreatment as though one did not possess free will but was only reacting to events beyond one's control. The deceit was only to protect the partner from the painful truth of the situation and so was in fact an act of caring.

Personality psychologists have discovered that narcissism, Machiavellian intelligence, and psychopathy are overlapping personality traits that are moderately correlated with one another. It has been found that if one creates a supermeasure combining all three variables, it is possible to obtain a strong predictor of exploitative and opportunistic behavior in adult romantic relationships. Paulhus and Williams first referred to this trio of personality traits in 2002 as the Dark Triad. Individuals high on the Dark Triad are prone to promiscuity and infidelity. Jonason et al. (2009) proposed that people high on the Dark Triad possess an opportunistic mating strategy that is game-playing, promiscuous, philandering, and more likely to replace one partner for another. There appears to be some degree of assortative mating among both men and women high on the Dark Triad for both short-term and long-term relationships (Jonason, Lyons, & Blanchard, 2015). Nevertheless, such short-term strategies may have significant long-term costs despite the more immediate benefits (Jonason, Li, & Buss, 2010).

ADDRESSING THE SELF-SERVING BIAS OF EGOCENTRIC TRANSGRESSORS

The art of psychotherapy is helping patients see that the problem with being a certain way (i.e., possessing Dark Triad traits) is not simply that it's "bad" and they are a "bad" person for acting that way but that they are engaged in a high-risk strategy that is likely to be self-defeating in the long-term. A patient's Machiavellian approach to love relations may reap rewards in the short term but is likely to backfire tragically in the long term, so it may be in the patient's enlightened self-interest to adopt a more honest, trustworthy, and authentic approach to love relations. Patients' egocentrism and low reflective functioning may make it difficult for them to accurately assess the dangers to which they expose themselves and others. Patients who get caught in a lie are no longer trusted even when saying something truthful.

Confrontation of self-defeating patterns inevitably threatens a patient's defensive grandiosity. Patients may rapidly switch from defensive grandiosity to self-loathing as their grandiose illusions are shattered, so it seems as though the therapist is "making" the patient feel badly about themselves. Confrontation feels like less of a personal attack when a patient can trust that the therapist is genuinely watching out for the patient's enlightened self-interest when the latter is in denial and having difficulty hearing the truth. It can be frustrating for therapists when they see the self-defeating nature of a pattern of behavior that the patient rationalizes and bring it to his or her attention, but the patient experiences this as a moralizing personal attack. Unfortunately, when the therapist's frustration is implicitly communicated in a confrontation that sounds unnecessarily harsh and judgmental, the patient will be quick to point out that the therapist is being unfairly critical or even taking a sadistic pleasure in bursting the patient's bubble.

The patient lacks recognition of how the therapist's frustration is in part a product of the patient's own narcissistic impenetrability and rationalized violations of moral norms of honesty and loyalty to which the therapist subscribes. Learning to be patiently accepting in treating a patient's narcissistic impenetrability is one of the more emotionally challenging demands of clinical work because patients embroiled in complicated love triangles lack the reflective functioning to see the metaperspective that a seasoned therapist has. Narcissistic patients will likely confront their therapists about inadvertent leaks of moralistic feelings (e.g., microexpressions of anger, contempt, and disgust), and it is important for therapists to respond nondefensively by acknowledging not always living up to the therapeutic ideal of responding without judgment.

THE ROMANTIC PSYCHOLOGY OF GAME-PLAYING NARCISSISTIC COUPLES

Infidelity cannot be fully understood as solely the expression of the personality of the unfaithful individual, but must be understood also as an expression of a particular dynamic that arises in the relationship between two people, each of whom possesses a particular constellation of personality traits. How is it that people in love often overlook the potential for sexual misbehavior of individuals who are relatively high on narcissism, Machiavellian intelligence, and psychopathy? When looking at these personality traits objectively, it's not a pretty picture, and it is not easy to respond without some degree of moral disgust. Who wants to admit that this is the sort of person with whom they have fallen in love? It's embarrassing to acknowledge one's poor judgment in choice of romantic partners. Nevertheless, many individuals in love routinely overlook these traits in their romantic partners despite their better judgment.

C. Haslam and Montrose (2015) found that women were more attracted to narcissistic men because of the men's higher status and greater capacity for resource provision despite the fact that they tend to be manipulative, game-laying, lack commitment, and are unfaithful. In addition, individuals who are high on narcissism tend to be more attracted to partners who are admiring and flatter their egos than those who are caring and have a capacity for intimacy (Campbell, 1999). There is a contradictory tendency to oscillate between making excuses for the negative traits of a narcissistic partner to maintain the romantic idealization and responding with moral contempt and disgust that is shaming when eventually disillusioned (i.e., a symptom of dichotomous thinking).

The field of psychology known as *person perception*, pioneered by David Funder (1995) at the University of California, examines how long it takes to make an objective assessment of someone's personality. As it turns out, sometimes only a rather thin slice of someone's behavior is needed to make an objective evaluation of their enduring personality traits. Movie directors have long known that character can be revealed in an instant through subtle forms of nonverbal communication, such as a fleeting facial expression that the camera can zoom in on. Gordon and Platek (2009) discovered differential neural responses to faces that vary in the expression of Dark Triad personality characteristics and trustworthiness.

The field of person perception suggests that it shouldn't be hard to detect a potential cheater on the basis of their nonverbal communication and even their facial characteristics. In fact, the evolutionary psychologists Cosmides and Tooby (1992) discovered that humans possess "cheater-detector mechanisms" as protection from being taken advantage of by free riders in cooperative relationships. Romantic pair bonding for biparental care probably requires the highest level of cooperation and mutual trust of the different types of cooperative relationships in which humans engage. The emotion of romantic jealousy may have evolved as a cheater detection mechanism because it is activated by a perception of having to compete for a partner's love with a romantic rival. Jealousy in an attachment relationship is observable as early as 6 months of age (S. Hart & Carrington, 2002).

Somehow, objective person perception using sophisticated cheater detection mechanisms motivated by jealousy can be overridden when it comes to prescreening the sort of untrustworthy person who might ultimately break one's heart. Due to assortative mating, narcissistic game-playing individuals appear to be most attracted to others like themselves. The narcissism of betrayed partners is not as obvious as the narcissism of unfaithful partners. Dichotomous thinking may make it seem as though the only narcissist in the room is the unfaithful partner while the betrayed partner is the maturely loving, faithful, and self-sacrificing partner for the sake of the relationship. It seems as though the betrayed partner has a right to self-construal as an all-good, innocent victim of an all-bad, lying "slut" or "pig." Yet the betrayed partner initially chose the sort of person who possessed an undetected latent capacity to be unfaithful. Betrayed partners with low reflective functioning do not see how their attempts to fix the narcissism of their unfaithful partners constitute a risk factor for infidelity as the unfaithful partner seeks an uncritically accepting affair partner.

A new measure of narcissism may provide deeper insight into this phenomenon. The Pathological Narcissism Inventory looks at narcissism in a multidimensional way (Pincus et al., 2009) and distinguishes two facets of narcissism: the grandiose and the vulnerable aspects. The grandiose side feels successful, giving rise to an inflated ego. Yet it may coexist with a more vulnerable side that feels unsuccessful in living up to the grandiose ambitions it has for itself. The vulnerable side can become bitter and depressed because it hasn't lived up to its unrealistically high standards for itself.

Pathological narcissism, grandiose as well as vulnerable, is associated with insecure attachment (Fossati et al., 2015). It may function as a maladaptive coping strategy for managing insecure attachment by treating others in controlling and condescending ways to try to make them more reliable and dependable. Pathological narcissism tries to ensure that romantic partners remain a secure home base by forcefully keeping them in a subservient and overly accommodating role. This approach backfires because treating romantic partners in contemptuous, condescending, controlling, and emotionally distancing ways makes them insecure and defensive. An insecure and defensive romantic partner is not going to make for a trustworthy home base for secure attachment. This creates what Wachtel (2014) referred to as a self-defeating vicious cycle.

Couples must learn to recognize the impact of their own narcissistic traits on their partners' mental states, that they activate insecure attachment in their partners and defenses against further attachment injury. It then becomes apparent that much of what narcissistic individuals don't like about their partners' personalities is something they have significantly exacerbated through their own personality issues, of which they have limited self-awareness. Couples must learn more constructive ways of managing each other's character pathology so that they learn how to bring out the best rather than the worst in each other in order to have a more securely attached relationship to one another.

Vulnerable narcissism might not seem like narcissism because it is associated with low self-esteem, if not self-contempt, rather than smug self-assurance. What makes vulnerable narcissism narcissistic is the obsessive self-involvement with living up to grandiose ambitions, the sense of entitlement to a privileged existence, egocentrism, and the lack of empathy. Vulnerable narcissists are implicitly failed narcissists, full of envy and walking around with a chip on their shoulder whether or not they openly acknowledge it. One of the best antidotes to deflated narcissism may be an ego-inflating sexual or romantic conquest of a highly desirable partner who appears hard to get. Jonason et al. (2009) discovered that those high in narcissism and Machiavellian intelligence are more likely to play hard to get.

The more vulnerable these narcissists feel, the more predisposed they might be to falling prey to someone who flatters their ego in the way they have always desired. Their need to maintain the appearance of being in a successful relationship may be so powerful that they are even more inclined than most to let wishful thinking override their better judgment. Vulnerable narcissism appears to be associated with socially prescribed perfectionism (Stoeber, Sherry, & Nealis, 2015)—a belief that others expect perfection and will be highly critical of failure to meet expectations. Narcissistic vulnerability leaves the individual susceptible to falling in love with grandiose narcissists who are potential philanderers, defenseless against the false pretenses philandering types maintain despite his or her sneaking suspicions. Although wishful thinking is part of human nature, the narcissistically needy may be even more predisposed to it than others, although they might be too proud to admit it.

Women with anxious attachment style appear to be more attracted to the look of men with contemptuous facial expressions than are more securely attached women and more attracted to men displaying contempt than men displaying pride (Stone & Josephs, 2015). Such insecure women may be prone to "fatal attractions" to the sorts of men who are most predisposed to betray them. Other research has found that partners who were equally high in grandiose narcissism tended to date each other (Lamkin, Campbell, vanDellen, & Miller, 2015).

Because grandiose and vulnerable narcissism are associated traits that are not mutually exclusive and can be high within the same individual, it is important not to think of these two dimensions in mutually exclusive ways, as though a person is either one way or the other. Both traits can exist within the same individual, with different situations bringing out either a more grandiose or a more vulnerable side (Ronningstam, 2009). In addition, psychoanalysts have long understood that grandiosity can defend against underlying vulnerability, while overstated vulnerability can defend against acknowledging secret grandiose fantasies (Kernberg, 1984).

During the honeymoon phase of mutual idealization, both partners enjoy the ego inflation of believing they have won the love of a perfect partner. Once the mutual idealization dissipates, both partners tend to suffer the narcissistic vulnerability of fearing that they have lost the love and respect of a perfect partner because of their own unacceptable imperfections or the narcissistic deflation of "buyer's remorse"—worrying that the partner isn't so perfect after all. The question is then how individuals relatively high on either or both dimensions of narcissism cope with their narcissistic disillusionment when mutual idealization turns into mutual devaluation and recrimination in the face of the frustrating realities of long-term relationships.

Shirley Glass (2002), an infidelity researcher, discovered that people in love are often fully aware of the faults and character flaws of their beloved (i.e., a diamond in the rough). The problem, though, is not lack of awareness but a naive, wishful belief that love will triumph over these flaws, that they will be fixed one way or another. Awareness of a beloved's flaws does not seem to deflate the romantic idealization, which may often be associated with an overestimation of one's own ability to change another person, to mold them like a piece of clay into the desired image, like Pygmalion who fell in love with one of his own sculptures (Plant, 2014). Narcissistic individuals may require the self-inflation that derives from feeling like they possess a perfect partner and are therefore intolerant of their spouses' imperfections once they're exposed. More narcissistic individuals must fix their partners to turn them into the perfect spouse that is demanded by their perfectionism. They then become harshly judgmental and devaluing when their partners appear to stubbornly resist being "fixed" for their own good.

Christensen and Jacobson (1998) suggested that truly accepting a partner "as is" means accepting that the person's core personality characteristics might not change. These marital therapists noted that trying to change a romantic partner's fundamental personality usually results in endless power struggles that prove to be no more than exercises in futility, leading to frustration and ugly scenes. Romantic partners must be accepted "warts and all," but that may be difficult to put into practice with a narcissistic partner who lacks empathy, is controlling and devaluing, and might be unfaithful. Acceptance is difficult because it is only human to judge untrustworthy individuals who might be deceitful and disloyal.

The justification for an affair may be the emotional fallout of the never-ending power struggle that arises when couples try to fix each other. If frustrated with trying to fix a recalcitrant partner, a potential philanderer's implicit infidelity belief might be: "I'm fed up and exhausted trying to fix my impossibly difficult partner. Why not start an affair with somebody it's easier to get along with?" If tired of being treated as a "fixer-upper" who is never quite good enough, a potential philanderer's implicit infidelity belief might be: "Why don't I start an affair with someone who thinks I'm great just as I am?"

Betrayed partners often seek psychotherapy not only for healing from the betrayal trauma but also to figure out how to "fix" their unfaithful spouse to facilitate recovery from infidelity. Betrayed partners are in an extremely shame-sensitive place, and the therapist doesn't want to end up in the role of implicitly blaming the victim. Nevertheless, the betrayed spouse may need to learn that the unfaithful partner can't be "fixed" and that trying to do so may have inadvertently brought out the worst in that partner, rather than the best. Now the betrayed spouse has to figure out how to make the best of a bad situation, when dragging the unfaithful partner into couples or individual therapy does not appear to be solving anything.

Gertrude had a successful corporate career when she met Claude, an extremely handsome, intelligent, and charming man who had not yet figured out what he wanted to do with the rest of his life. Claude had recently emigrated from France and aspired to have a successful corporate career, as Gertrude did. They had a whirlwind romance and then married. Implicitly, Gertrude saw Claude as a diamond in the rough whom she would polish by supporting his professional aspirations. To that end, Gertrude agreed to support him through graduate school, even if that meant living apart when Claude was accepted to a prestigious Ivy League graduate program in another city.

Gertrude trusted that Claude would ultimately reciprocate the sacrifices she was making on his behalf. As a consequence, she overlooked the presence of Dark Triad traits when he acted as though doing what was best for him was always what was best for both of them. For example, Claude could have gone to a slightly less prestigious program to continue living together and save quite a bit of money. Whenever Gertrude expressed any reservations about their plan of action, Claude mocked her for her ridiculous worries and provided glib reassurance that everything would turn out great if she simply trusted him. Claude made Gertrude feel like a fool for not trusting him, as though she might miss out on the opportunity of a lifetime.

Gertrude came to see me because their relationship had become increasingly distant. They used to talk on the phone all the time, and Claude visited her every weekend. But then he claimed school was just too busy to find the time to regularly call and visit. Gertrude wasn't going to visit him and sleep in his dorm room with his roommate. They hadn't had sex in ages. Their relationship had become contentious as Claude had started treating Gertrude as though she had become an unreasonably demanding and controlling woman who wouldn't give him the space he needed to be successful. On the one hand, Gertrude was furious with Claude because he seemed unappreciative of the sacrifices she made on his behalf. On the other hand, she felt guilt-ridden because she felt it was her job to support him in whatever way he needed to live up to his potential, and she should be secure enough to give him the space he needed.

Gertrude wondered out loud why they had grown so distant. I asked if it had ever crossed her mind that he might be having an affair. Gertrude looked shocked and offended by my comment but sheepishly admitted that it had crossed her mind. The one time she visited him at school and met some of his friends, she noticed that there were a number of exceptionally attractive women who appeared to appreciate Claude's charms. After that, Gertrude decided she would confront Claude because she didn't want to be played for a fool. Upon confrontation, Claude burst into tears and confessed that he had been having an affair and felt horrible about it. He said that he was confused and didn't know what he wanted to do because he still loved her. He said he hoped she would be patient and give him some time to figure things out. Once again, he campaigned for what was best for him rather than what was best for Gertrude.

Sometimes betrayed partners seek psychotherapy when they secretly suspect their unfaithful partners are having affairs but are still in denial. Unconsciously, they have been noticing the clues, but they resist putting the pieces of the puzzle together because it is just too painful to acknowledge the betrayal. They seek psychotherapy hoping there is some alternative explanation but dread that there may not be. The therapist might have to be the bearer of bad news, the one who points out that when all the pieces of the puzzle come together, it seems to point to infidelity as the most likely explanation. Patients are often initially shocked and disbelieving as their denial breaks down and may try to prove the therapist's hypothesis wrong, saying that the therapist is reading too much into things that can have a much more innocent interpretation. Until the patient discovers the truth, the therapist may just have to tolerate being perceived as a typical "shrink" who reads hidden meanings and malevolent intentions into things that should just be taken at face value.

In subsequent sessions, we clarified the nature of Claude's narcissistic personality. I pointed out his sense of entitlement to being supported by her without having to reciprocate or make any sacrifices until some distant future date, the way he instilled doubt by mocking her when she questioned his judgment, his lack of empathy for her insecurities, and his lack of gratitude or appreciation for the sacrifices she made. Gertrude found it difficult to listen to my recap of his narcissistic traits because it made her feel foolish to think that she had overlooked what now seemed obvious in retrospect. How could she ever trust her judgment in men again if she was so misguided in her current choice?

Gertrude decided that she was done trying to help Claude live up to his potential and that Claude was beyond fixing. And she no longer wished to try, even if he was fixable. He was just too much work, and all the work she had already put in had not paid off. Now it was time to cut her losses. Gertrude decided she wanted out of the marriage; she was still under 30 and felt she had time to find someone better. Sometimes when the truth finally comes out, the patient can feel ashamed that the therapist knew all along while the patient could not see in retrospect what now seems obvious. Sometimes the betrayed partner is among the last to discover a partner's infidelity when many others in the patient's social circle have known for some time. Shame is alleviated in learning to appreciate that it is only human nature to tune out the obvious when acknowledging a painful reality requires figuring out how to move forward in life despite one's shattered dreams.

Facilitating mentalization of the impact of one's own behavior on a romantic partner's mental states and accepting the fact that a romantic partner's core personality traits can't be fixed (at least not quickly) may help grandiose as well as vulnerable narcissists eventually work through the rage and deflation that prevents them from managing their marital predicament more constructively. Gertrude was able to appreciate in retrospect that adopting such a supportive and self-sacrificing role actually reinforced Claude's narcissistic sense of entitlement to be taken care of by an overly accommodating people-pleaser because he was so special. Gertrude was determined that her future relationships would be based on greater reciprocity from the beginning.

Cognitive reappraisal of narcissists' infidelity beliefs is challenging when those beliefs are implicitly motivated by defensive grandiosity that hides narcissistic vulnerability and attachment injury. The therapist may sometimes have to be the bearer of the bad news and try to nondefensively absorb the patient's attempt to "kill the messenger." For example, Gertrude initially complained that therapy was making her "paranoid" by increasing her awareness of how devious married men could be, even though she already harbored sneaking suspicions of her own that had motivated her to seek psychotherapy in the first place. It was challenging to help Gertrude see that I was not trying to make her paranoid but trying to make her less vulnerable to deception by high Dark Triad men in the hope that she would eventually be able to better discern potentially problematic personality traits. Moving forward, betrayed partners have to learn how to regain trust in their own judgment and intuition if these have proven untrustworthy in the relationship with an unfaithful partner.

Therapists may sometimes be reticent to try such an approach, fearing the patient is too fragile to tolerate it or that the therapist is too fragile to tolerate the patient's angry countercomplaint when confronting the defensive nature of infidelity beliefs. Can a therapeutic couple survive the mutual confrontation of the severe character flaws that they each perceive in the other and the disturbing possibility that perhaps they are each projecting their worst traits onto the other and then complaining about their own projections? Ultimately, therapists must trust their own clinical judgment as to the most tactful way of addressing these extremely shame-sensitive issues. They must learn to manage contradictory countertransferential tendencies. On the one hand, therapists must contain the tendency to be overly avoidant of shame-sensitive issues out of fear of injuring the fragile self-regard of patients perceived as too thin-skinned. On the other hand, they must contain tendencies to harshly confront patients who seem too thick-skinned and might make the therapist feel both frustrated and offended. Such a recommendation is easier said than done, given that narcissistic patients can possess vulnerable and grandiose aspects simultaneously (Ronningstam, 2009). Therapists may have to learn how to tolerate being "damned if they do and damned if they don't" when addressing the underlying narcissistic personality traits in both betrayed and unfaithful partners.

CONCLUSION

The psychology of Dark Triad traits is not restricted to simply the psychology of those who score higher on measures of those traits. There are narcissistic issues, for instance, issues of our own sense of being a unique and special individual compared with others, with which everyone grapples whether or not they are high on narcissism as a personality trait. One of those issues is what evolutionary psychologists call *mate value*. How desirable are we as a romantic partner? Are we special? Are we average? Are we below average? These and similar questions are the subject of the next chapter.

5

AM I SEXUALLY DESIRABLE? FIDELITY AND INFIDELITY AS PROOF OF MATE VALUE

A long-term relationship meets needs for self-esteem as well as for attachment. One of the most important sources of self-esteem is the sense being desirable as a romantic partner (Brase & Guy, 2004). People assume that someone must be a good catch if he or she possesses a desirable romantic partner who is committed to a long-term, sexually exclusive relationship and appears happy in the relationship. It is not exactly a ringing endorsement if one is only seen as a desirable partner for casual sex but is not perceived as serious material for a long-term commitment. It wounds our pride to be rejected in favor of someone else because it implies we aren't good enough to win and hold on to the enduring commitment of a desirable partner. Similarly, infidelity wounds our pride even if the unfaithful partner remains committed to a long-term relationship. Infidelity for casual sex implies that the sexual aspect of the relationship is unsatisfactory so the unfaithful partner requires extramarital outlets to tolerate remaining in the marriage. In sum, inspiring a sexually exclusive, long-term

http://dx.doi.org/10.1037/0000053-006
The Dynamics of Infidelity: Applying Relationship Science to Psychotherapy Practice, by L. Josephs

commitment appears to reflect well on a person, whereas failing to inspire such a commitment appears to reflect poorly.

For many people, self-esteem may require finding a desirable person who will make a long-term, sexually exclusive commitment to them, and it may be difficult to feel good about themselves without this. Of course, successful playboys and playgirls don't actually have to get married to obtain that affirmation; for them, the mating game is a popularity contest. Individuals with high mate value can get their self-worth affirmed by the high number of desirable suitors who are trying to win them as a long-term partner. It's difficult to have self-esteem as a single person if one is not desired as a long-term partner by anyone or by only the least desirable individuals. Relationship satisfaction is associated with the desirability of the romantic partner one is able to win and retain (Hromatko, Bajoghli, Rebernjak, Joshaghani, & Tadinac, 2015). People high in narcissism may be particularly sensitive to social comparisons that threaten their self-perceived mate value because such individuals generally have maladaptive responses to self-enhancement failures (Pincus, 2013).

People can learn to have self-esteem without being in a successful long-term relationship with a desirable partner, but they have to do quite a bit of self-acceptance "work" and need social support to achieve it. Self-esteem comes effortlessly if one successfully wins a desirable partner who remains loyal and devoted. Donald Symons (1979, 1987) coined the term *mate value* to explain why some individuals seem more desirable as romantic partners than others. Symons suggested that from an evolutionary perspective, attractiveness and youth in women as a measure of health and fertility determine women's mate value. Social status and dominance should determine men's mate value. The concept has been expanded to include other traits, such as intelligence, creativity, humor, emotional stability, warmth, and loyalty, that humans also find desirable in a long-term romantic partner for biparental care (Fletcher, Tither, O'Loughlin, Friesen, & Overall, 2004; Miller, 2000). Individuals who possess higher self-perceived mate value also report higher self-esteem and higher standards in what they seek in a romantic partner (Regan, 1998).

Self-perceived mate value may possess objective aspects that reflect cross-cultural universals (M. Fisher, Cox, Bennett, & Gavric, 2008). There appears to be a fair amount of consensus among raters as to how desirable a person is considered on the basis of first impressions (Asendorpf, Penke, & Back, 2011). Kirkpatrick and Ellis (2001) suggested that much of self-esteem is based on an inner mating sociometer that assesses to what degree one is a target of the romantic interest of others and the desirability of the kinds of people who show romantic interest. The self-esteem of more narcissistic individuals who make better first impressions (Back, Schmukle, & Egloff, 2010) and so win more popularity contests may have an objective basis in more frequently being the target of the romantic interest of desirable others.

Their sense of superiority, of superior mate value, is validated. Traits such as good looks, social status, and charisma can be easily assessed on the basis of superficial appearances. In contrast, personality traits such as intelligence, empathy, loyalty, emotional stability, and reliability that are attractive in a long-term partner may not be as easy to accurately assess without getting to know someone. More narcissistic individuals can sometimes fake being smarter, nicer, or more successful, or possessing greater youthful beauty than is actually the case (such as with plastic surgery to remove wrinkles, hair coloring to hide grey hair, makeup to hide blemishes, or clothes to hide weight gain). Over time, however, people like narcissists less the better they get to know them because the lack of empathy, loyalty, and respect are eventually perceived despite the superficial allure. Narcissists often do objectively possess the traits most desired in a short-term partner (e.g., attractiveness, vitality, status, resources) while hiding their deficiencies in traits desired in a long-term partner (e.g., warmth, trustworthiness; see Fletcher et al., 2004, on trait clusters desired for short and long-term mating).

Mate value is not reducible to youthful good looks and social status alone as Symons (1979) originally believed, although good looks and social status are no doubt important dimensions of mate value, especially for short-term mating. Mate value is also determined by the personality traits most desired in a long-term partner. Traits such as intelligence, empathy, loyalty, devotion, warmth, emotional stability, reliability, authenticity, and humor are highly valued in a long-term partner (Fletcher et al., 2004; Miller, 2000). They are "sexy" as well as admirable personality traits. So individuals are judged not only for looks and social status but also for the content of their characters. Mate value based on youthful beauty inevitably declines with age, despite efforts to look good for one's age or to simulate youthful beauty. Aspects of mate value related to social status and personality can potentially increase with age as professional careers advance and personalities mature. Infidelity can be motivated by desires to be with a partner of superior mate value to one's current partner—be it someone more physically attractive, of higher social status, or with a better personality.

It is difficult not to take infidelity personally. Sexual betrayal implies that one's looks, social status, or personality is just not good enough to inspire continued sexually exclusive commitment. Personality, more so than one's physical body, appears to be the essence of who one is as a unique individual. Infidelity motivated by the desire to be with a person with a more appealing personality implies the rejection of one's essence as a unique individual in favor of a romantic rival whose essence is more desirable. Of course, being sexually betrayed for "superficial" reasons like physical unattractiveness or social failure implies that one's winning personality was not sufficient to compensate for deficiencies in looks and social status.

Threats to mate value inevitably threaten attachment security. It is difficult to feel securely attached to someone who is inclined to have sexual or emotionally intimate relationships with romantic rivals because those rivals possess superior mate value on certain dimensions. Sexual betrayal is traumatic because infidelity is simultaneously an attachment injury that undermines secure attachment and an injury to one's sense of self that undermines self-esteem. It is difficult to feel securely attached and maintain self-esteem when one may lose the loyalty of a desirable partner to a romantic rival who appears to possess qualities one lacks.

AM I A GOOD CATCH? THE COMPONENTS OF SELF-PERCEIVED MATE VALUE

What makes someone a good catch? Evolutionary biologists have suggested that evolution is most essentially about reproductive success. Survival ability only contributes to evolution to the extent that it facilitates reproductive success. According to evolutionary biologists Ash and Gallup (2008):

> Contrary to what many people have been taught, evolution has nothing to do with the survival of the fittest. It is not a question of whether you live or die. The key to evolution is reproduction. Whereas all organisms eventually die, not all organisms reproduce. . . . Organisms do not compete among themselves for scarce resources or survival. Rather, they compete for genetic representation in subsequent generations. . . . As a consequence, what is or is not adaptive has to be measured in terms of its impact on reproduction. An adaptive trait is one that confers a reproductive advantage. (p. 313)

Among cooperative breeders such as humans, even individuals such as Buddhist monks who practice sexual abstinence could be reproductively successful if their altruistic and self-sacrificing lifestyles enable their kin and close allies (i.e., their communities) to be more reproductively successful. Alpha males with harems and concubines may be the most reproductively successful humans (Betzig, 1986). Yet most humans using a more cooperative reproductive strategy based on equitable sharing of resources for the greater good will strive to achieve a more modest level of reproductive success. Such cooperative breeders may use mating strategies that involve various forms of birth control and planned parenthood (sexual abstinence, nonprocreative sexuality, pregnancy prevention, abortion, delay parenthood until resources are more plentiful, forgoing parenthood to help raise other people's children).

A quality-over-quantity reproductive strategy can mean cultivating a community of caring and compassionate individuals who invest highly in a limited number of offspring for which resources will be sufficient. Not every community member has to sire his or her own biological child to achieve modest reproductive success in such a communal childrearing arrangement. Sexual conflict among humans may not be primarily between men and women, straight and gay, parents and the voluntarily childless, although superficially it often seems that way, but between cooperative and uncooperative breeders, regardless of gender, sexual orientation, or parental status.

Darwin (1871) identified two causal processes through which sexual selection could occur. *Intrasexual competition* is when members of one sex compete with one another and the victor gains preferential access to the most desirable members of the opposite sex. Sexual selection would then favor an increase in the qualities that lead to success in competitive contests. *Intersexual selection* occurs when members of one sex display some consensus about the qualities that they desire in the opposite sex. Those possessing the desired qualities have a mating advantage. Thus, individual differences in the qualities that ensure successful intrasexual competition and intersexual selection determine reproductive success. Mate value reflects an implicit assessment of those individual differences that make some individuals more successful at intra- and intersexual competition than others.

David Newlin (2007) hypothesized that a part of the mind tracks a person's self-perceived survival and reproductive fitness (SPFit). SPFit represents an internalized self-perceived model of survival and reproductive functioning.

> SPFit is embodied in such basic psychological characteristics as feelings of personal power, control, and omnipotence—all related to survival ability—and to feelings of personal sexiness (i.e., that relevant others find them sexually attractive), physical and behavioral attractiveness, and social desirability—all related to reproductive fitness. (Newlin, 2007, p. 286)

SPFit motivates goal-directed behavior by generating feelings of high self-esteem, elation, and triumph in anticipation of gratifying fantasies of successful survival and reproduction. Newlin (2007) suggested that SPFit is primarily nonverbal, especially in Western societies that do not explicitly endorse such thinking. It's offensive to suggest that not everyone is equal in mate value in Western societies that endorse egalitarian values and in which everyone is considered equal in human dignity. It's considered poor taste to openly gloat about one's competitive superiority to others—being more powerful or higher in status, more sexually attractive, more sexually gratified, having a more desirable long-term partner, having more children and grandchildren, and having those children and grandchildren be more attractive and successful than other people's. These fantasies of reproductive superiority are considered offensively narcissistic and so tend to be hidden from others, and even from oneself. Yet such fantasies may supply the implicit standard through which self-esteem is evaluated.

Shamelessly exhibiting one's reproductive superiority (i.e., acting narcissistically) seems insensitive and morally wrong if it makes people feel badly about themselves for their low mate value by comparison. The ideal romantic partner is smart, funny, beautiful, and successful but has genuine rather than faked empathy for the less fortunate. Without empathy, that person would be just one more privileged narcissist, exactly the sort of person likely to feel most entitled to be unfaithful in a long-term relationship, who feigns being a more caring person than he or she really is.

Animals attract mates by displaying indices of mate quality known as *sexually selected fitness indicators*, like a peacock's bright plumage (Andersson, 1994). Sexually selected fitness indicators are "honest signals" (Sugiyama, 2005) that individuals are fertile, healthy, or would make good parents (e.g., male birds that attract females by nest building) and would be capable of generating and raising fit and healthy offspring that will survive to maturity and be reproductively successful themselves. Sexually selected fitness indicators are the physical and psychological traits found by one sex to be attractive in the opposite sex and are therefore the basis of what could be called *sexual chemistry* when the feelings are mutual. Mate value is unconsciously and automatically assessed according to the degree to which these sexually selected fitness indicators are present or absent. Same-sex attractions, like opposite sex attractions, seem to derive from the same fitness indicators.

Deficiencies in sexually selected fitness indicators (e.g., an "hourglass" shape in women [Singh, 2002], a broad-shouldered upper body torso that looks like an inverted triangle in men [Sugiyama, 2005]) tend to be the personal characteristics around which one experiences the most self-consciousness. Pride is evoked when one's indicators of fitness are highly desired, and shame is evoked when they aren't. This is why self-esteem is so closely tied to assessments of mate value. Evolutionary psychology does not deny the role that culture plays in terms of which sexually selected fitness indicators are emphasized or minimized. Yet it is highly unlikely that a culture might consider an indicator of unfitness such as leprosy sexy or an indicator of fitness such as athleticism ugly.

Assortative mating suggests that "birds of a feather flock together" rather than "opposites attract," and it is reflected in many traits (Hill & Reeve, 2004). Most people appear to end up with partners fairly similar to themselves according to the principle of *optimal similarity* (Eagle, 2007). Assortative mating for mate value has been found in cross-cultural research (Figueredo et al., 2015). One is most likely to end up with someone of roughly equivalent mate value despite the yearning for a more ideal partner who possesses significantly superior mate value to oneself (someone "out of one's league") and the dread of settling for someone with inferior mate value. The mate value of one's partner is therefore a relatively accurate barometer of one's own mate value. Mate preferences may only weakly predict actual mate choice because individuals do not necessarily possess the mate value to win the partners they most prefer. People with high mate value can leverage that value into securing partners with the most desirable traits (Conroy-Beam & Buss, 2016).

Social exchange theory, which is used in social psychology to understand romantic relationships, suggests that social relationships grow, develop, deteriorate, and dissolve as a consequence of social exchange processes in which partners barter costs and benefits (Cameron, Oskamp, & Sparks, 1977; Huston & Burgess, 1979). As long as the benefits of staying in a relationship equals or exceeds the costs, individuals are likely to remain in the relationship. How the relationship compares with available alternatives is a significant determinant of the level of commitment (Thibaut & Kelley, 1959). Individuals can stay in an unhappy relationship if they believe the alternatives are even worse (i.e., ending up with an even less desirable partner or being alone). Judgments of the costs and benefits of staying in a relationship or leaving it are made by comparing self-perceived mate value, a partner's perceived mate value, and a viable alternative's perceived mate value.

Patients in psychotherapy can spend innumerable sessions ruminating about what their mate value actually is and what they can realistically obtain in the mating marketplace given their estimated mate value. Could they do better but lack the confidence? Do they have unrealistic expectations and so should be more appreciative of what they have? Bredow (2015) discovered that individuals with unrealistically high standards for a marital partner tend to delay or forgo marriage and have greater difficulty establishing higher quality romantic relationships. Patients, especially narcissistic patients, may not want to hear that their expectations are unrealistic when they are worried that in fact they may be predisposed to settle for someone beneath them. Assortative mating for mate value may be difficult to accept if it means accepting that an unsatisfactory partner is the best one can do given one's own relatively low mate value.

Ruminative patients implicitly put pressure on the therapist to be the objective assessor of their actual mate value so that they can judge whether they are overestimating or underestimating their own mate value. Whatever a therapist's level of expertise in personality assessment, they tend to be reticent to share their assessment of the patient's desirability as a romantic partner—their strengths and weaknesses in terms of looks, social status, and personality. Therapists generally prefer to be an affirmative presence in their patients' lives that bolsters feelings of self-worth rather than a shaming presence that might instill an inferiority complex. Nevertheless, it may be an extremely challenging part of a therapist's job to assess the extent to which patients possess grandiose narcissism and thus overestimate their mate value, are self-critical perfectionists who underestimate their mate value, or have borderline personality characteristics and thus oscillate between overestimating and underestimating their mate value without developing a more stable, balanced, and realistic evaluation of their own desirability as a romantic partner.

What complicates the ability to address this shame-sensitive issue is that patients often think of dimensions of mate value in dichotomous ways: One is either good looking or ugly, smart or stupid, caring or cold, a winner or a loser, a great success or a pathetic failure, strong or weak, proudly independent or shamefully dependent. Being only average or even above average is a disgrace from a dichotomous perspective. And if one is an outlier on some negative dimension of mate value (e.g., being a starving artist despite creatively thinking outside the box, a short man with a small penis but a great personality), the assumption is that one "should" be ashamed of oneself and hide in disgrace. There may be no self-compassion for one's realistic limitations when it comes to low self-perceived mate value if it dooms one to having to settle for a partner of low mate value or none at all. As Groucho Marx said, "I don't care to belong to any club that will have me as a member."

Low mate value is associated with depression (Kirsner, Figueredo, & Jacobs, 2003). Individuals with high self-perceived mate value respond to infidelity with indignation, whereas individuals with low self-perceived mate value respond with anxious insecurity (Philips, 2007). Thus, struggles with depression, anger, and anxiety that bring patients to psychotherapy may be associated with threats to mate value to which patients are responding defensively.

Matt was a successful divorced middle-aged businessman and father of three boys. He had gone through an ugly divorce and felt exploited by the settlement his ex-wife was able to achieve. What added insult to injury was that he had caught his wife having an extramarital affair, and she eventually married her affair partner, who was wealthier than Matt. Matt felt victimized by the divorce settlement—the result of no-fault divorce laws in his state—and vowed never to remarry.

Matt wondered why his postdivorce love life was going so poorly; women didn't seem to want to go on more than a few dates with him. It didn't occur to him that he was walking around with a chip on his shoulder. Women didn't want to get involved with someone who was not open to the idea of remarrying and who harbored unresolved hostility toward women in general for the way his ex-wife mistreated him. Matt thought that maybe he needed to lose weight to be more attractive to women, rather than address the defensive hostility that hid his underlying rejection sensitivity.

The mating sociometer reflects an assessment of how people "imagine" they come across to others. Self-perceived mate value therefore combines realistic perceptions of one's romantic desirability in the local mating market with some degree of egocentrism and projection. Those obsessed with appearances, as high narcissists often are (Vazire, Naumann, Rentfrow, & Gosling, 2008), often assume that, deep down, everyone is as appearance oriented as they are. Those who perceive themselves as innocent and blameless victims in love might not see how their own reactive hostility and self-protective walls might bring out the worst in romantic partners. These are shame-sensitive issues that therapists must raise with considerable tact. Yet if therapists avoid raising such issues, patients will remain unable to appreciate their strengths as a romantic partner without despising themselves for their deficiencies.

Unfaithful patients who believe in monogamy feel guilt-ridden and ashamed that they may have been so desperate for sexual or romantic affirmation that they betrayed their partner, as well as their own deeply held moral convictions. Individual psychotherapy then helps patients come to terms with the deep-seated narcissistic vulnerability that might lead them to act out their need for validation of their mate value in a way they later regret. Therapists must help patients see that there is no point in despising themselves for weakness in the face of sexual temptation. Moving forward, the task is to become more accepting of one's relative mate value so that one becomes less desperate for validation in the future.

There is nothing inherently wrong with wanting affirmation of one's romantic desirability by winning a desirable partner. It's one of the greatest pleasures of life and makes us feel good about ourselves, so it is difficult to take a pass on such a self-affirming experience. But if doing so betrays the trust of those to whom we have made serious commitments, it ultimately makes us feel worse about ourselves because loyalty, devotion, commitment, and capacity to let go of personal ego are attractive personality traits, whereas dishonesty, untrustworthiness, and excessive vanity are not, especially in a long-term partner.

HOT BODS OR GREAT PERSONALITIES? MATE VALUE AND ROMANTIC CHEMISTRY

Reducing long-term relationships to a social exchange of mate value might seem like a very cynical way of discussing love relations, mirroring the objectifying and calculating way that individuals high in Machiavellian intelligence might construe love relations—as simply a game won by the cleverest strategists. Is evolution simply about the survival of the prettiest women and the most dominant men, as it may have seemed when Symons (1979, 1987) first introduced the concept of mate value? No doubt the lust circuit of the brain can be activated by youthful beauty and social status as the most fertile females and most dominant males are often the most reproductively successful throughout the animal kingdom. Nevertheless, the evolution of romantic pair bonding for biparental care changes all that. Among humans, on average, it may be the individuals able to form the best long-term cooperative partnerships for biparental care who are the most reproductively successful. Personality is a significant source of mate value because the best parents and the best spouses are often those with the best personalities. Who would one want as a long-term partner, someone who is smart, caring, loyal, emotionally stable, and sensitive with a sense of humor or someone dumb, cold, unfaithful, emotionally unstable, insensitive, and humorless but beautiful or rich? In an ideal world, humans would prefer someone with a great personality who is also good-looking and high status. Buss and Shackelford (2008) found that women of high mate value as assessed by observer-rated physical attractiveness want it all: good genes, economic investment, parenting proclivities, and emotional commitment.

When individuals are asked to prioritize their mate preferences for a long-term partner, the personal qualities that make someone a good spouse and parent top the list. Overall, men's and women's preferences in a long-term partner prioritize finding a kind, understanding, and reliable mate, the kind who seems unlikely to be unfaithful or desert a partner (Buss, 1989). In addition, individuals have what they consider to be "deal-breakers" in choosing and staying with a romantic partner, and individuals with higher mate value possess more deal-breakers (Jonason, Garcia, Webster, Li, & Fisher, 2015). The top deal-breakers in long-term relationships were anger management problems, seeking multiple partners, already being in a long-term relationship, untrustworthy, health problems, uncaring, dismissive, alcohol and drug problems, poor hygiene, and smelling bad. Ironically, many of these deal-breakers are traits possessed by those high on narcissism (i.e., anger management, untrustworthy, unwilling to be sexually exclusive, dismissive) and traits one would not want in a parent of one's children.

As discussed in Chapter 3, the attachment circuit in the brain is looking for a romantic partner who has parental qualities, someone who is nurturing, caring, sensitive, loyal, and devoted. The romantic love circuit in the brain wants someone who is smart, creative, funny, and capable of deep empathic understanding of another human being. Beautiful but superficial or brawny but brutish doesn't sound like the kind of person anyone would want to be the caretaker of one's children, even if someone like that might be desired as a casual sexual partner. Fletcher and colleagues (Fletcher, Simpson, Thomas, & Giles, 1999; Fletcher et al., 2004) discovered through a statistical method called *factor analysis* that humans tend to use three general trait clusters to evaluate romantic desirability: (a) warmth/trustworthiness, (b) attractiveness/vitality, and (c) status/resources. They found that in choosing short-term sexual partners, both sexes put a premium on attractiveness and vitality over warmth and trustworthiness, but for long-term relationships, warmth and trustworthiness are high priorities. No one wants a long-term partner who will be cold, abusive, or unfaithful.

Li and Kenrick (2006) found that in long-term relationships, although both sexes prefer a well-rounded partner, women prioritize obtaining some sufficiency of status and resources, whereas men prioritize obtaining some sufficiency of attractiveness and vitality. Again, overall, men and women's preferences in a long-term partner are more similar than different. Yes, men care about looks and women care about how well a man can provide, but more importantly, both care most about having a warm and trustworthy partner when it comes to a long-term relationship.

Attractiveness and vitality tend to decrease with age. People lose youthful beauty, slow down, and get set in their ways. Of course, one can work out, diet, cultivate a good sense of humor, and maintain a love of learning new things to maintain or improve one's attractiveness and vitality despite advancing age. One can even have plastic surgery. But in the end, it's a losing battle because the human body and mind inevitably deteriorate with age. Status and resources can also increase with age as individuals become more established in their careers and accrue resources. Warmth and trustworthiness can certainly increase with emotional maturity facilitated by psychotherapy. Thus, many aspects of mate value can actually increase with advancing age and compensate for the loss of youthful beauty and vitality.

Li and colleagues (2002) discovered that mate choices appear to be guided by "budget allocations" in that there is a determination of which mate preferences are "necessities" and which are "luxuries." Men on a lower budget put a larger proportion of their budget into physical attractiveness, whereas women on a lower budget allocate a larger proportion of their budget to resources. As the budget increases, greater proportions go toward luxuries such as kindness, creativity, and liveliness. In an ideal world, everyone would prefer a well-rounded partner. In the real world, people on a limited budget, given the current exchange rate for their own mate value in the local mating market, try to hold out for some minimum standard on the necessities and may have to economize on the luxuries. It would seem that individuals have some minimum standards of looks and resources that their romantic interests must meet before moving on to consider personality variables.

Budget allocations may generate a risk of infidelity. When individuals feel they must compromise on personality requirements to meet the minimum standards of looks and social status, they become vulnerable to settling for a person with undesirable personality characteristics (e.g., being insecurely attached or high on the Dark Triad). The better looking and higher their social status, the more likely individuals with undesirable personality traits are to get a pass. The more personality variables are treated as luxuries rather than necessities in choosing a long-term partner, the higher the risk of infidelity.

High narcissistic individuals as "perfectionists" (Pincus, Cain, & Wright, 2014) are attracted to perfect individuals who are physically attractive, confident, and ambitious, if not caring, and devalue individuals who are less than perfect. As a consequence, they have higher minimum standards for looks and social status for a long-term relationship than those low on narcissism. High narcissistic individuals on a budget will therefore be more likely to compromise in the personality department than others and thus become more likely to end up with the romantic partners most likely to be unfaithful.

Less narcissistic individuals, being less perfectionistic, will have lower minimum standards for looks and social status for a long-term relationship and place more value on personality. Individuals who place more value on personality will take more time to get to know someone, and the sexual chemistry will eventually be there if that individual "grows on them" over time. The sexual chemistry derived from attractiveness and vitality is immediate. The romantic chemistry that derives from warmth and trustworthiness is something that develops incrementally over time from getting to know someone well as a bond of attachment begins to form. Thus, less narcissistic individuals are more likely to end up with faithful spouses because their choices are more determined by accurate assessments of a potential romantic partner's warmth and trustworthiness made over time.

Regina was an attractive 35-year-old artist who lived a bohemian lifestyle. She was hoping to get married and start a family before her biological clock ran out. She dated many investment bankers and real estate developers who were quite successful and with whom she experienced considerable sexual chemistry, but somehow those relationships didn't last long. Her boyfriends weren't ready to settle down, and sometimes she discovered that they were still dating and sleeping with other women. Technically it wasn't infidelity because they had never explicitly agreed to be in a sexually exclusive relationship, but Regina always stopped dating and sleeping with other men as soon as she began to date someone on a regular basis. She mistakenly assumed her partners did likewise. She felt hurt and betrayed to discover otherwise. She had assumed and hoped that her sexual partners were faithful to her, but she began to realize that was a mistaken assumption because these men were clearly keeping their options open and were not prepared to make a sexually exclusive commitment.

What was particularly galling was that the sex wasn't even that good. They were attractive, physically fit, and good flirts, but they were selfish lovers who weren't really that good in bed and often left her unsatisfied. Regina said that her mating strategy was entirely based on sexual chemistry, and she felt that if a long-term relationship was meant to be, it would just evolve over time if she took it one day at a time. It started occurring to her that this strategy was not working out as planned.

I suggested that the reason her strategy wasn't working was because the men to whom she was attracted didn't seem oriented toward committed relationships or at least not toward committed relationships with someone like her because she might not be their type if they were materialistic and status oriented and she wasn't. I noted that Regina never seemed to date the kind of man who was like herself, a more bohemian type, and that was clearly looking to start a family sooner rather than later. In other words, I was suggesting that she might consider looking for her male equivalent on the principle of assortative mating. Regina wasn't offended but was in fact intrigued by my theory of searching for her male equivalent and thanked me for thinking outside the box because it would never have occurred to her on her own.

Regina did wonder how she could change sexual chemistry when she just didn't seem to be that attracted to "nice guys." She suggested that part of her didn't want her male equivalent because she wouldn't like in him what she didn't like in herself: an inability to turn creative inspiration into commercial success (i.e., a loser). Yet in beginning to see the sexual psychology of narcissistic men more accurately, she began to be less attracted to them and to actually start finding them progressively more disgusting for their "piggy" behavior. Incrementally, the warmth and trustworthiness of "nice guys" began to seem more appealing. The sense that she might be able to trust such men, let down her guard and be herself with such men, and not have to play games with such men began to feel liberating.

Regina decided that she needed to look for a "daddy type" if she was to ever get married and have children. Finally, she found David, a divorced father of a young girl; he was a creative type like herself who didn't make that much money. David wasn't the most confident man, but in seeing him with his daughter, Regina appreciated that he was extremely high in warmth and trustworthiness. David liked being a father and was open to having another child despite the financial responsibilities that he could not easily afford. As it turned out, Regina had the best sex of her life with David. He was a patient and sensitive lover with whom she had more powerful and more frequent orgasms than with any other lover and without having to smoke marijuana in advance to get in the mood. Regina felt she had finally found her soul mate.

What if the patient's problem is not so much being attracted to the "wrong" type but being the "wrong" type (e.g., high on the Dark Triad) for having a successful long-term relationship? What if despite good looks and social status, someone has an unattractive personality—one that turns people off the better they get to know one's true personality? What if the sexual chemistry begins to fizzle once a partner recognizes narcissistic or insecurely attached personality traits? The arrogance and egocentrism of narcissism, the game-playing of the Machiavellian, the deceitfulness of psychopaths, the needy and emotionally demanding behavior of the anxiously attached, and the intimacy avoidance and uncommunicativeness of the avoidantly attached can be unattractive traits that ultimately push romantic partners away. Nobody likes to think that they have an unappealing personality that turns off or even disgusts potential or current romantic partners.

Psychoanalysts have long noted that personality traits are often ego syntonic (Josephs, 1994). One's own character traits seem to be a normal, reasonable, rational, and adaptive way to be. Treating personality disorders can be difficult for this reason. Individuals with personality disorders can't see anything wrong with the way they are. They feel unfairly criticized when others complain about their personality problems. To acknowledge a personality problem is like acknowledging that one might be unlovable in some fundamental and potentially unchangeable way. It is a bitter pill to swallow, so it's easier to blame the bearer of bad news than accept an unflattering character assessment and see whether something can be done to improve one's personality.

It's easier to hate oneself for personality problems that lessen one's desirability as a romantic partner than accept with self-compassion that one might possess some off-putting personality traits that might be challenging to change. Part of therapy, then, is helping patients recognize, accept, and change their personality problems to the extent that those problems are adversely affecting their love lives, implicitly pushing partners away rather than bringing them closer and bringing out the worst rather than the best in their partners.

Personality is an important dimension of mate value. Patients cannot fully understand their romantic desirability or undesirability without appreciating the impact of their personalities on the sexual and romantic attractions of others. To what extent is one's personality "sexy" and "lovable"? This is a shame-sensitive issue because no one wants to feel that they possess an unattractive and unlovable personality. This is an especially touchy issue during recovery from infidelity. The personality of the unfaithful partner may become an object of extreme disgust as that person becomes a "lying, cheating slut" or a "stupid asshole." There may be no recovery from infidelity if the betrayed partner no longer respects or is attracted to the unfaithful partner now that his or true colors have been shown. Recovery from infidelity is one type of challenge if it means restoring trust; it is another thing if it means restoring sexual attraction to a partner whose personality after exposed infidelity arouses revulsion. Unfaithful partners often seek psychotherapy to feel that infidelity hasn't turned them into outcasts who should be shamed and shunned for their treachery.

Additionally, it is extremely difficult for a betrayed partner to "own" the personality problems that may have contributed to the marital problems from which the unfaithful partner sought escape and relief through an affair. The betrayed partner needs help overcoming the irrational self-hatred derived from a sense of having caused one's own betrayal—that somehow one deserved to be betrayed for being a horrible person who became sexually undesirable. Betrayal trauma exacerbates irrational self-blame, and the unfaithful partner may reinforce this by blaming the victim to relieve his or her own guilt-ridden conscience.

Richard and Karen came to couples therapy for recovery from infidelity. Karen had discovered that Richard, a salesman, regularly had casual affairs while out of town on business. Richard was willing to recommit to monogamy, had apologized repeatedly, and was willing to do anything to save the marriage. Karen was undecided about remaining in the marriage because she didn't know if she could ever trust Richard again and she couldn't be sure Richard was now telling the truth. She described Richard as an uncommunicative person who was never particularly open or forthcoming. Maybe, she thought, he was just telling her what she wanted to hear so he could revert to his old philandering ways and go back to taking her for granted.

Richard protested that he was uncommunicative because Karen was intolerant of his expressing an opinion that was different from hers. She became argumentative and would eventually start screaming in a verbally abusive way if he didn't agree with her. Richard stated that he had learned to keep his thoughts and feelings to himself to keep the peace. He lost interest in having sex with Karen because he saw her as a temperamental person with whom he couldn't be himself. In addition, Karen wasn't interested in sex when she was in an irritable mood—and she was always in an irritable mood. Karen countered that she was always in a bad mood because Richard was an unreachable person and that trying to get through to him was as frustrating and futile as banging one's ahead against a brick wall.

Through couples therapy, Karen learned that although frustration with Richard's stonewalling was understandable, the way she expressed anger drove him away. Although she hoped to get through to him by breaking through the wall he had put up, he only withdrew further when feeling attacked. Richard had to learn that avoiding conflict by shutting Karen out only made her feel more hurt and angry. Richard and Karen both had to learn that their own personality problems exacerbated the personality problems of the other. Richard felt emasculated by the strident, sometimes verbally abusive way Karen expressed anger and sought affirmation from more agreeable and less demanding women who expected less of him. Richard's stonewalling and loss of interest in sex made Karen feel that she was no longer sexually desirable and was just an "unlovable bitch" who perhaps deserved sexual betrayal.

It was difficult to get Richard and Karen to see how their marital communication styles affected the other. Karen authoritatively asserted that Richard had "mommy issues" and that the therapy I was doing was superficial if it didn't get at the root of his infidelity, which she believed was in his troubled relationship with his mother. I noted that her assessment might be correct, but Richard's "mommy issues" might take years of psychoanalysis to work through; in the meantime, it was important that they both learn how to bring out the best, rather than the worst, in each other. When I noted Richard's stonewalling, he felt that withdrawing when Karen was being provocative was a mature way to stop a disagreement from turning into an ugly blow-up. I noted that he was right but that his lack of openness to having sex with his wife or dialogue with her even when she was in a good mood was counterproductive because he was failing to reward his wife for good behavior. She then felt that the only way she could get his attention was by expressing anger.

It becomes easier to accept one's own off-putting personality traits without self-hatred when those traits are understood as defensive responses to feeling rejected and humiliated. Such defenses hide one's hurt and vulnerability from a partner who seems to relish pouring salt in the wound, making it no longer safe to be openly vulnerable with that partner. Such defensive responses are self-protective but unfortunately push partners away rather than draw them closer. The hope is that as trust is restored, partners will be able to let go of their defensive responses. It is the defensive side of ourselves that isn't particularly attractive, sexy, or lovable—it is the side that withdraws in anger or that is critical and demanding without empathy. In contrast, it is the more open, good-humored, caring, sensitive, and sometimes vulnerable sides of us that create an emotional intimacy that keeps sexual desire alive in a long-term relationship once the novelty of a new sexual conquest of a highly desirable sexual partner has passed.

REPLACEABLE OR IRREPLACEABLE? SEXUAL EXCLUSIVITY AS AN EXPRESSION OF IRREPLACEABILITY

From the perspective of mate value, infidelity is not simply about sexual pleasure, love, or intimacy but also about self-worth as a unique individual. Individuals will be less likely to be unfaithful in a relationship in which their mate value is affirmed. Being treated as a sexually desirable person by someone who is sexually desirable affirms one's mate value. This is why taking one's partner for granted can increase the risk of infidelity. There is often a need for reassurance that one is retaining one's mate value in a long-term relationship, especially if the frequency of sex and of romantic intimacy is decreasing in the face of the demands of work, family, and declining sex drive with age.

Research by Eastwick and Hunt (2014) indicated that in addition to *objective mate value*, there is also a *relational mate value* that develops in a long-term relationship. Objective mate value refers to fact that there appears to be a fair amount of cross-cultural consensus on how physically attractive a particular individual is (Asendorpf et al., 2011; M. Fisher et al., 2008). At least some aspects of mate value appear to be objective—beauty isn't solely in the eye of the beholder. Yet beauty is in many respects a subjective assessment that is indeed in the eye of the beholder. A romantic partner becomes progressively more irreplaceable as a couple develops a shared history and raises a family together with some degree of success as a well-functioning team. Couples that are well suited to each other develop relational mate value as opposed to objective mate value based on superficial first impressions.

Relational mate value is a sense that the couple has built something together that is special and unique so that a partner could not easily be replaced without the loss of what has been built together as a team. People with low objective mate value could still come to possess high relational mate value in a long-term relationship with someone with whom they are highly compatible and to whom they have become indispensable. Conversely, many individuals with high objective mate value (i.e., physically attractive individuals with high social status) are in miserable long-term relationships in which they feel undervalued because they do not have relational mate value.

Partners with high relational mate value didn't necessarily start out with "great" personalities, but somehow they were able to work through their personality problems within the relationship. Eventually, partners see each other at their worst because partners' personality problems eventually bring out the worst in each other. Some couples learn a constructive way of dealing with each other at their worst, and others don't. Couples that learn how to successfully deal with each other at their worst have achieved something extremely special that is not easily replaceable; for this reason, such partners acquire high relational mate value for each other. This is an aspect of mate value that can keep increasing with age. A partner who can accept and manage you at your worst is the kind of partner you want to grow old with and to be there for you when you become frail and infirm.

Dealing with a partner at his or her worst sometimes means dealing with a partner who hates you and blames you just for being yourself because yourself is just not good enough—the partner feels he or she deserves better. Your very existence is a reminder that your partner couldn't do better, so you become a reflection of your partner's failure to live up to his or her romantic aspirations. Of course, it's not really fair to blame someone and make someone feel badly about himself or herself because one couldn't do better in the mating game.

Why are some women attracted to emotionally unavailable men or some men to "bitchy" women, only to incessantly complain about those personality traits once in a long-term relationship with them? It's not so much that those traits are attractive in themselves. What appears to incite romantic desire is the fantasy of turning an emotionally unavailable partner into an available partner, an angry partner into a loving partner, or an unsuccessful partner into a successful partner. The Pygmalion fantasy of fixing an imperfect partner with character flaws and turning that person into the perfect partner can inspire romantic passion (Plant, 2014). Yet that passion turns into frustration and disappointment when one's partner resists being perfected despite one's best efforts.

Freud (1912/1958) believed that adult romantic partners are unconscious surrogates for one's parents. As a consequence, one implicitly looks to one's partner to be the good parent one never had, thereby transferring the conflicts one had with one's parents onto one's romantic partners. Freud (1920/1955) called this phenomenon the *repetition compulsion* through which conflicts with parents are unconsciously played out repetitively in one's adult love life, making it difficult to learn from one's mistakes. Recent research suggests that transference does indeed have an empirical basis (Andersen & Przybylinski, 2012). Luborsky and Crits-Christoph (1998) developed a measure of transference, the Core Conflict Relationship Theme method, to assess transference in transcripts of psychotherapy sessions by looking for repetitive relational patterns.

As noted earlier, partners acquire high relational mate value when they see each other at their worst but still accept and love each other. Partners implicitly test each other's love and devotion by being difficult in one way or another. Passing such a test is challenging when someone incessantly complains about their partner's unappealing personality traits, tries to fix them, and then gets infuriated or withdraws when the partner doesn't change. Such a test might be impossible to pass if it requires learning to forgive, love, and respect a partner who has betrayed one's trust. Both partners bring Freud's repetition compulsion into their adult romantic relationships. The repetition compulsion is in part motivated by a narcissistic fantasy of finding a perfect and enduring love that will compensate not only for all the traumatic disappointments of childhood but also for all the disappointments of one's adolescent and adult love life.

Individuals don't give up on such compensatory fantasies without a good fight, but sometimes that fight can destroy a relationship when partners can't accept that ultimately it is a losing battle. Therapists must then help patients learn to accept the narcissistic deflation of romantic defeat without hating themselves and to better appreciate what they have instead of bemoaning what they don't. This is challenging when patients hope psychotherapy will magically turn them into romantic winners whose compensatory fantasies will be fully actualized thereby healing their narcissistic wounds.

CONCLUSION

Concerns about comparative mate value relative to a partner's relationship alternatives may leave people vulnerable to feelings of jealousy triggered by the fear of losing a partner to a rival with higher mate value. Those who suffer anxious attachment and vulnerable narcissism may be particularly sensitive to threats to their self-perceived mate value and therefore become particularly jealous when confronted with the possibility of having to share a partner or lose a partner to a rival with superior mate value. The next chapter explores how partner sharing, be it consensual or nonconsensual, may threaten attachment security and self-perceived mate value, thereby evoking jealousy.

6

SEXUAL POSSESSIVENESS AND JEALOUSY: THE PSYCHOLOGY OF RETALIATORY INFIDELITY

The emotional operating system for lust is essentially promiscuous and craves variety and novelty. The emotional operating system for romantic love, in contrast, is serial monogamy—readiness to fall in love anew once the obsessive phase of romantic infatuation subsides. And finally, the emotional operating system for adult attachment is polygamy: People do want a primary lifelong partner but wouldn't mind having a harem of spouses, all devoted to their welfare and sexual pleasure. Why would anybody remain monogamous if it were not for cultural pressure, given that none of the emotional operating systems that regulate adult sexual and romantic relationships appears to be inclined toward lifelong monogamy with one person? Prevalence rates of polygamy, promiscuity, divorce, and infidelity are quite variable because cultural pressure to remain monogamous is itself quite variable.

Many people are monogamous not because they want to be but because they have to be. After all, who wouldn't want to spend one's life experiencing sexual variety, reexperiencing romantic bliss with new lovers, or having multiple

http://dx.doi.org/10.1037/0000053-007
The Dynamics of Infidelity: Applying Relationship Science to Psychotherapy Practice, by L. Josephs

spouses? A patient once came to me for treatment to help him learn how to tolerate being in a polyamorous relationship. Jim had been married for more than a decade when his wife, Molly, decided that she wanted to be polyamorous. She had begun an affair with a married man and no longer wished to be secretive about it. Molly would remain married to Jim if he could tolerate sharing her with other men and he was allowed to do similarly if he wished. Molly asserted that she would seek a divorce if Jim refused.

Jim felt stuck. He really didn't want to share his wife with other men, but he felt he couldn't live without her. Jim had never been particularly successful with women and felt lucky to have Molly. In theory, he imagined that he might enjoy polyamory, but he didn't think he would be any more successful with women as a polyamorous married man than he had been as a single man. Yet to hold on to Molly, he felt he had no choice but to give polyamory a try. Individuals with high mate value who can attract a plentitude of desirable partners might benefit from nonmonogamous arrangements more so than individuals with low mate value, who might feel lucky to attract and hold on to a single partner in fear of living a socially isolated life deprived of sex and companionship.

Jim insisted that I read a book called *The Ethical Slut* (Easton & Hardy, 2009), which he described as the how-to bible for making polyamorous arrangements work. There was a chapter in the book on learning how to master dealing with sexual jealousy, a skill that clearly is essential to a successful polyamorous lifestyle. The basic point of the chapter is that sexual jealousy is learned, so it can be unlearned. The idea is that certain cultures teach that a romantic partner is a possession like one's home is a possession. Once it is appreciated that a romantic partner isn't a personal possession, it may be possible to share one's partner with others and even be happy for the sexual pleasure and emotional intimacy they experience with other people. A sexually confident and emotionally secure person shouldn't be threatened by the sexual pleasure and emotional intimacy that their partner experiences with someone else. After all, securely attached individuals are less jealous than insecurely attached individuals (Selterman & Maier, 2013).

From the polyamorous viewpoint, the cure for romantic jealousy is to talk about it with one's romantic partners until its irrationality is perceived and it can be overcome. After all, humans can take voyeuristic pleasure from watching other people have sex, so why not free oneself from jealousy to the point that one could experience such pleasure in watching one's partner have sex and emotional intimacy with other people and obtain vicarious pleasure in their happiness? It's not clear exactly how much talking about sexual jealousy it takes to successfully overcome it. Is it like short-term psychotherapy in which 3 months of cognitive reframing will enable one to see the irrationality of sexual jealousy and overcome it? Or is it more like intensive long-term psychotherapy, five times a week on the couch for a decade of talking about the origins of romantic jealousy in one's childhood oedipal conflict and early patriarchal indoctrination? What if one can spend one's entire life discussing the irrationality of sexual possessiveness and jealousy and never overcome it because the surrounding culture is still pedaling its oppressive promonogamy pedagogy. Perhaps hidden cultural biases are disguised by books that assume jealousy, as well as monogamy, originates in evolutionary biology?

One has a difficult choice to make regardless of whether one believes that cultural conditioning brainwashes us (Marx's false consciousness) or that evolutionary biology unconsciously drives us (Freud's id): Choose monogamy and spend the rest of one's life managing the sexual and emotional frustrations of a sexually exclusive relationship, or choose polyamory or open marriage and spend the rest of one's life managing pangs of jealousy when one's partner experiences sexual pleasure and romantic intimacy with others.

For some people, the sexual frustrations of monogamy are not that severe. Individuals with low sex drive or low need for variety, as well as individuals who feel that their monogamous sex life is more than good enough, may not feel that deprived. Similarly, it's not clear exactly what percentage of individuals experience polyamory as "polyagony" (Deri, 2015) due to the difficulty of transcending romantic jealousy. Curiously, recent research suggests that relationship satisfaction (Mogilski, Memering, Welling, & Shackelford, 2017) and attachment security (King, 2015) are equivalent for monogamists and polyamorists. Maybe monogamy and polyamory do not need to be thought of in dichotomous terms by idealizing one as a better and natural arrangement while devaluing the other as inferior and unnatural. Perhaps it's just different strokes for different folks.

It is quite possible that monogamous people struggle with sexual jealousy, worrying about whether their partners will be unfaithful or divorce them in favor of alluring rivals. The polyamorous may still struggle with sexual frustration despite open access to multiple partners, just as many single people do when they have sex with multiple partners but find that the sex isn't that great or emotionally satisfying because they can't attract the type of partners to whom they are most attracted. Quite possibly, the kind of personality conflicts or low mate value that prevent individuals from finding sexual satisfaction and emotional security in monogamous relationships might also prevent them from finding sexual satisfaction and emotional security in polyamorous relationships.

Jealousy may be a difficult emotion to transcend whether one is in a monogamous or a polyamorous relationship. Why is that? Is sexual jealousy so difficult to overcome because it is entrenched within a patriarchal culture that requires "compulsory monogamy" (Ritchie & Barker, 2006) or perhaps because it is an innate emotional tendency forged in human evolution (Buss, 2000)? What if jealousy is a personality disposition that is relatively fixed regardless of its origin in nature or nurture? Jealousy as a relatively fixed personality trait may exist in the general population on a bell-shaped curve so that only a minority of individuals might ever be sufficiently low on jealousy to freely share their partners with others.

Recent research in developmental psychology, evolutionary psychology, and evolutionary anthropology is beginning to suggest that jealousy may possess innate and cross-cultural aspects despite attempts to suppress it in certain cultures (e.g., wives should look the other way if men cheat if they are good fathers and providers). Monogamy might not be so much something that is culturally imposed as something that arises out of an innate human tendency toward sexual possessiveness and jealousy that may be culturally reinforced or suppressed but that may not be socially constructed in its entirety. It may not so much be that people "want" to remain faithful to just one partner for a lifetime. It may be that people remain monogamous primarily because they don't want to make their sexually possessive partner jealous and then suffer the fallout of that partner's hostile retaliation for making them feel jealous and insecure.

What may be universal to human nature is a natural desire to avoid the retaliation of jealous romantic partners. The only way to avoid such retaliation may be to remain monogamous, to surrender to being a lover's exclusive sexual possession that he or she can monopolize so that the jealous and insecure partner can feel more securely attached. What may also be a part of human nature, more developed in some than others, is to experience empathy for a partner's sexual jealousy and willingly refrain from any behavior that would make one's partner suffer the anguished pangs of jealousy. Empathy leads us to experience the suffering of others as if it were our own, so the desire for multiple partners is sacrificed as an altruistic act to spare the partner from feeling jealous and insecure. Of course, one would not need to make that sacrifice if one's partner were capable of freely sharing a romantic partner without feeling jealous or insecure. That's why the polyamorous have developed workbooks to overcome sexual jealousy (Labriola, 2013). Jealousy work requires owning one's jealousy, confronting the underlying insecurities without shaming oneself for those insecurities, and then trying to work through those insecurities through open communication with one's romantic partners.

Monogamy may be a cooperative endeavor in which a couple implicitly contracts to avoid doing anything that would make each other jealous by violating the expectation of sexual as well as emotionally intimate exclusivity. Open arrangements like polyamory can also be construed as cooperative endeavors in which the contract is to engage in consensual partner sharing but find ways to overcome jealousy to the degree possible and, if jealous, not to act out that jealousy in destructive ways but to contain it. All cooperative romantic arrangements appear to require some agreed-on way of managing the threat of jealousy to the viability of the cooperative arrangement. Infidelity in the sense of sexual betrayal can occur in any romantic arrangement if one breaks a promise to manage sexual jealousy in an agreed-on way and lies about it.

Sexual exclusivity may be the price humans pay for being prone to jealousy and not wanting to have to work at overcoming it. Those willing to do jealousy work may not have to pay that price (Easton & Hardy, 2009; Labriola, 2013). Is it possible to feel securely attached to a partner who has been made jealous and insecure by one's own flirtations and affairs with romantic rivals? A jealous partner is not a trustworthy partner because a jealous partner is hurt and angry and may want to retaliate in kind. It is only human nature to want to hurt others the way one has been hurt in order to give the other person a taste of their own medicine. In this case, the medicine is to inflict the same sort of injury to secure attachment and mate value so that the unfaithful partner can see what it feels like.

One risk factor for a partner's infidelity is one's own infidelity. People who discover a secret infidelity are more likely to express their hurt and anger by going out and being unfaithful themselves in retaliation for the relational transgression (Tafoya & Spitzberg, 2007). Not only are sexual possessiveness and jealousy parts of human nature but so is being vindictive and vengeful in the face of sexual betrayal. Interestingly, a study on sexual infidelity among male college athletes discovered that the infidelity rate was quite high, but none of these athletes wanted their girlfriends having sex with "another dude" (E. Anderson, 2012). Sometimes those most desirous of multiple partners are the least willing to share the partners they have.

OEDIPUS REVISITED: ARE BABIES JEALOUS?

Research in developmental psychology suggests that jealousy may come on line at 6 months of age. Hart and Carrington (2002) conducted an ingenious experiment to show that 6-month-old infants experience jealousy. The study builds on a previous study by Tronick, Als, Adamson, Wise, and Brazelton (1978) that used the "still-face" methodology. Six-month-old babies delight in making eye contact with their mothers and engaging in proto-conversations, in smiley "goo-goo gah-gah" dialogues. Babies connect to their mothers in this way. It makes them feel securely attached by feeling recognized as unique and special individuals in whom their mothers take delight. Here are the origins of that feeling of emotionally intimate bliss in the mother–infant relationship that Freud (1905/1953) and Bowlby (1969) recognized. Tronick et al. (1978)

wanted to see how infants would react when deprived of their mothers' lively responsiveness.

The still-face experiment has the mother face her 6-month-old infant sitting up and engage together in their usual playful back-and-forth interaction. Then the mother is instructed to be unresponsive by just looking at the infant with a blank face and stare. Initially, the baby tries to do all the usual tricks to seduce the mother into responding playfully. The infant gets upset if none of these overtures proves successful. Eventually, the infant gives up and turns away. This pattern exemplifies Bowlby's (1973) sequence of angry separation protest followed by eventual detachment when attachment needs are frustrated.

Hart and Carrington (2002) used the same research methodology to determine whether infants experience jealousy. They had the mother face her 6-month-old sitting up and engage in their usual playful back-and-forth interaction, as in the still-face experiment. Instead of having the mothers stare at the infant with blank faces, they had them read a newspaper without responding to their infants' overtures to engage them. As in the still-face experiment, the infants became upset. Hart and Carrington then tried a different experimental manipulation designed to evoke jealousy. They had the mothers start playing with a baby doll and engage in playful proto-conversations while being unresponsive to their babies' overtures. Not only were the infants understandably distressed, they were significantly more distressed than when their mothers were reading the newspaper. The infants appeared to understand that their mothers were paying attention to another baby, a rival for mother's attention, rather than just an inanimate object like a newspaper. Six-month-old babies get particularly upset and angry when their mothers are paying attention to another person while being unresponsive to them. Jealousy appears to be activated by a particular type of threat to the attachment relationship to the mother: losing the mother's love and attention to another person.

Infants appear to get angrier when exposed to the jealousy induction than to the still-face situation (Hart, Carrington, Tronick, & Carroll, 2004), and insecurely attached infants respond more jealously than securely attached infants (Hart & Behrens, 2013). Insecurely attached children respond more jealously to parental interactions with infant siblings (Volling et al., 2014). Insecure attachment exacerbates jealousy, but secure attachment does not seem to offer immunity to jealous reactions, and this may be why it takes work to overcome jealous reactions to romantic partner sharing, be it consensual (i.e., polyamory) or nonconsensual (i.e., infidelity). Recently, the same methodology was used to determine whether dogs experience something akin to jealousy (Harris & Prouvost, 2014). Indeed, dogs try to get in on the action when their owners pay attention to rivals, but not so much if the owners are paying attention to some inanimate object.

Something that begins to look much more like romantic jealousy emerges in the second year of life. Human infants as young as 10 months exhibit angry behavior in response to viewing affectionate interchanges among family members that evoke pushing behavior in the attempt to either interrupt or gain entry into the affectionate interchange (Cummings, Zahn-Waxler, & Radke-Yarrow, 1981). Toddlers don't seem to like watching their parents hug and will often try to come between them. Franz de Waal (2007), the author of *Chimpanzee Politics*, reported that chimpanzee children are fascinated by adult sexual relations and sexually harass the copulating couple by trying to push them apart and wriggle in between. It seems that even chimpanzee juveniles display behavior that looks like sexual jealousy. It becomes difficult to maintain that jealousy is learned when infants in the first year of life and highly social animals like dogs and chimpanzees also appear to experience it.

Evan and Judy were a 20-something couple who were living together when they came for couples therapy. Judy wanted to have an open arrangement. She reported that she had self-esteem and body image issues and needed more validation of her romantic desirability than she felt she could obtain from Evan alone. Evan expressed his frustration that his validation was insufficient to make Judy feel good about herself. Evan said that he didn't have any problem being monogamous and wished Judy felt similarly. Judy felt guilt-ridden that she couldn't give Evan what he wanted but made it clear that if he couldn't accept her as she was, she would break up with him. Evan begrudgingly said he would give an open arrangement a try because he thought it would be fun to have sex with other women, although for him it was not a necessity. Evan was good-looking and personable and didn't have any insecurity about being able to pick up women. Judy appreciated that fact and was worried about whether she could handle sharing him with other women.

Judy confessed that what she really wanted was for Evan to give her the freedom to play the field while he remained faithful. She realized that wasn't fair and ambivalently offered him the same sexual freedom she desired for herself. Evan took her up on the offer because she had indicated it was the only way to maintain their relationship. Yet Judy found it intolerable the first time Evan didn't come home at night because he was sleeping with another woman. She broke up with Evan in hurt and anger the next day and moved out. Evan felt it was unfair that he was being harshly punished for something he hadn't really wanted to do in the first place, but he wasn't willing to be faithful while giving Judy permission to play the field. The couples therapy ended with a strong recommendation for Judy to seek individual psychotherapy for herself because it might be difficult to find a desirable partner who was capable of happily sharing her with other men while remaining faithful himself.

Many patients, like Judy, have strong desires to be given the freedom to have sex or love relations with different partners while their primary attachment partner remains exclusively devoted to them. Patients appreciate that a healthy relationship requires reciprocity so that both partners agree either to sexual exclusivity or to a more open arrangement. Infidelity often reflects an attempt to gratify the desire to exercise a sexual freedom one is unwilling to grant one's romantic partner due to one's own jealous reactions. As a consequence, there is much shame and guilt associated with the desire for one-sided sexual indulgence and an assumption that the therapist will be judgmental if that forbidden desire is exposed.

The therapist can clarify that the desire to "have one's cake and eat it too" is part of human nature and that there is nothing inherently wrong with wanting to have forbidden desires happily indulged without returning the favor. The problem is that indulging a partner's forbidden sexual desires when the favor is not returned evokes resentment about the lack of reciprocity. Parents indulge their children in unreciprocated ways, but it is assumed that mature adult love relations are based on reciprocity and are not a one-way street. Reciprocity appears to be associated with relationship satisfaction and even oxytocin levels among couples (Schneiderman, Zagoory-Sharon, Leckman, & Feldman, 2012).

Consensual nonmonogamy can be a viable alternative for some couples who feel jealousy is more manageable than the sexual frustrations of monogamy. Peter came for psychotherapy because he was guilt-ridden about having been unfaithful to Joel, his partner for more than 2 decades. Peter had a regular extradyadic casual sex life that he didn't want to give up, but he didn't like living a lie. Peter felt that his sex life with Joel was beyond reviving because Joel wasn't really his physical type. Yet Peter felt deeply attached to Joel as his life partner with whom he could not live without.

I asked Peter if he ever considered raising the possibility of an open marriage with Joel because it didn't seem like there was a viable way of integrating love and lust in his relationship with Joel. Peter worried that Joel might feel deeply hurt and betrayed if he requested a renegotiation of the sexual ground rules of their relationship. After months of discussion Peter finally decided to raise the possibility of an open marriage with Joel despite the risks. To his pleasant surprise, Joel was quite agreeable, and they embarked on an open relationship. Relieved of the guilt, Peter terminated treatment feeling that our work had been successful.

Two years later, Peter returned for treatment struggling with feelings of jealousy. He had assumed that they had agreed to casual sex with others, but without emotional intimacy. Yet it emerged that Joel was only interested in sex with partners if there was mutual infatuation and emotional intimacy; he wasn't interested in casual sex. These infatuations usually dissipated in about 6 to 9 months, after which Joel began to look for a new partner with whom to become infatuated. Peter struggled with jealousy of the romantic intimacy that Joel shared with his lovers, even though Peter was quite confident that Joel would never leave him for a new life partner. Peter wasn't so sure that open marriage was such a good idea if he had to learn to live with the torments of chronic romantic jealousy.

I noted that Joel's sexual preferences (sex in a state of mutual infatuation) would have to be accepted for the open relationship to work if Joel had no desire for casual impersonal sex as Peter did. As an openly gay man, Peter accepted the idea that sexual preferences should be respected and accepted rather than judged and fixed. Peter reconciled himself to accepting Joel's sexual preferences despite the jealousy that Joel's mutual infatuations evoked. It didn't seem viable to try to recommit to a monogamous arrangement he would not be able to honor, and it didn't seem fair to now expect Joel to sacrifice his pleasure in mutual infatuation while still gratifying his own pleasure in casual sexual variety with his favored physical type.

JEALOUS CAVEMEN: JEALOUSY AMONG HUNTER–GATHERERS

The authors of *Sex at Dawn* (Ryan & Jetha, 2011) suggested that humans are naturally promiscuous and looked to both the primatology and the anthropology literature on hunter–gatherers to support this contention. These authors appear to believe that early humans happily shared their sexual partners with one another. Do the primatology and anthropology literatures actually support their contention? As it turns out, something like sexual jealousy appears to be endemic within the animal kingdom. Primatologists call it *mate guarding* (Dixson, 1998). The males guard access to ovulating females. Species like gorillas that maintain a harem don't allow other males to have sex with females in their harem, and males that try to are asking for a fight. Yet even promiscuous species like bonobos that have what are essentially orgies engage in mate guarding when the females are ovulating (de Waal & Lanting, 1997). Males fighting over access to ovulating females appears to be the norm.

All cultures have prostitution, in which men are willing to share certain females for sex with innumerable men (Bullough & Bullough, 1978). Thus, men who use prostitutes don't appear to be too disturbed about sharing casual sexual partners with other men. Yet the widespread presence of sexual partner sharing cross-culturally is not necessarily evidence that humans share their partners happily and without jealousy. Evolutionary anthropologists tend to look at contemporary hunter–gatherers to get a sense of what human relations may have looked like in what Bowlby (1969) called the *environment of evolutionary adaptedness*. I scoured the anthropology literature to see what I could find about jealousy among hunter–gathers in their adult romantic relationships; the following summarizes what I discovered (Josephs, 2012, pp. 262–267).

Infidelity rates appear to be high in many Amazonian tribal Indian cultures (Beckerman & Valentine, 2002)—as high as 75% among the Ese Eja, for instance (Peluso & Boster, 2002). These cultures tolerate extramarital affairs as long as they are done discreetly. For example, among the Panoan Matis of Amazonia, there is a high frequency of infidelity that occurs in the secrecy of the forest on a bed of leaves off of forest paths. Although the typical passerby discreetly walks the other way, the very young children do not, and their conversations and playful imitation of copulation as early as age 4 or 5 suggests how knowledgeable they are (P. Erikson, 2002, p. 129). Because these extramarital affairs often involve an exchange of resources, like food for sex, such affairs can sometimes benefit infant survival (Beckerman, Lizarraide, & Lizarraide, 2002).

Among the !Kung, women believe that

> to succeed at and to benefit from extra-marital affairs, one must accept that one's feelings for one's husband—"the important one," "the one from inside the hut"—and for one's lover—"the little one," "the one from the bush"—are necessarily different. One is rich, warm and secure. The other is passionate and exciting, although often fleeting and undependable. Some !Kung women (and men) think it ideal to have both. . . . One man can give you very little. One man gives you only one kind of food to eat. But when you have lovers, one brings you something and another brings you something else. One comes at night with meat, another with money, another with beads. (Shostak, 1981, p. 271)

Official partner sharing has been ritualized in some of these small tribal societies. For example, the Canela have a ritual in which adolescent girls are required to have sequential sex with multiple partners in public and are called stingy by their female relatives if they don't (Crocker, 2002; Montgomery, 2009). Among the Kulina, there is a ceremony in which the married women encourage the men to hunt for meat and reward individual hunters, who are not their husbands, with sex for bringing home the meat (Pollock, 2002). Some Eskimo tribes will let visiting men sleep with their wives as an act of hospitality (Balicki, 1970).

Despite these tolerant attitudes toward sexual partner sharing, husbands may still become jealous, sometimes violently so, if secret affairs become public. Husbands become less invested in children who they do not think are "mostly" or "purely" their child in a culture such as the Ese Eja despite the fact that spouses who display jealousy rather than indifference are shamed for being "stingy" (Peluso & Boster, 2002). Crocker (2002) noted that although many cultural anthropologists assume sexual jealousy is culturally determined, that idea is contraindicated by cultures like the Canela in which extramarital sex is not only condoned but required in certain situations, yet sexual jealousy still exists and had to be suppressed before and independent of any outside Western influences. The main source of potentially homicidal conflict among hunter–gatherers appears to be male sexual jealousy over women (Knauft, 1991).

The punitive consequences of affairs may be severe if the participants are caught. For example, among the !Kung, "Once she spent a few nights in the mongongo nut groves with her lover while her husband was away. Someone saw them leave and told her husband, who later beat her until 'I was almost dead'" (Shostak, 1981, p. 19) A !Kung mother confronted her son-in-law's female lover saying: "Horny, that's what you are! . . . if you ever have sex with him again, I'll crack your face open. You horny woman! You'd screw your own father!" (Shostak, 1981, p. 136). Lethal violence among !Kung men might be avoided by wife-swapping with the wives' consent: "If you want to sleep with someone's wife, you get him to sleep with yours, then neither of you goes after the other with poisoned arrows" (Marshall, 1998, pp. 359–360). Male–female relations are not egalitarian because men exercise their physical power to assert dominance (Shostak, 1976), so women are more likely to deal with their jealousy and humiliated fury through verbal reproach, retaliatory infidelity, or leaving the marriage than through violence.

Paternity certainty, until the advent of genetic testing, has never been absolute but always probabilistic so that men have been willing to invest in marriage and fatherhood despite possessing varying degrees of uncertainty about their wives' fidelity and their children's paternity. In Amazonian cultures that believe in "partible paternity," it is assumed that it requires multiple inseminations to make a baby, so a baby can have multiple fathers if the mother has had multiple lovers (Beckerman & Valentine, 2002). Fathers therefore will invest in children they think are "mostly" theirs. Fathers may throw a baby in the river if they think it's "mostly" someone else's child.

The anthropological literature suggests that humans everywhere would like to have multiple sexual and romantic partners but become jealous, sometime violently so, when required to share their own. Some cultures try to suppress sexual jealousy to promote greater tolerance of sexual partner sharing. Other cultures try to suppress the desire for multiple partners or at least acting on those desires so the kind of family drama and instability created by jealous rages and vendettas is minimized. To some extent, cultures and individuals must choose their poison—to learn to live with either the sexual and emotional deprivations of monogamous commitments or the pangs of jealousy of sharing one's primary romantic partner with others. Either way, it's a considerable amount of emotional work with which even hunter–gatherers had to contend, and without the help of psychotherapy.

Paradoxically, those high in avoidant attachment who have only been in monogamous relationships have more permissive attitudes toward consensual nonmonogamy but are less likely to actually try it out (Moors, Conley, Edelstein, & Chopik, 2015). The avoidantly attached may enact what may be the ambivalent attitude toward romantic partner sharing that is part of human nature: We desire multiple partners, but we don't want to have to deal with the jealousy and attachment insecurity of sharing our own.

Margarita was raised on a Caribbean island where she reported that all men have affairs, but women's mothers encourage them to look the other way if their husbands are good providers and husbands. Growing up, Margarita believed that her own father was one of the rare exceptions. She assumed she would find a monogamous husband like her own father. During high school, Margarita discovered that not only had her father been unfaithful but that he had another family on another part of the island and she had half-siblings she had never met. After the shock of discovering her father's infidelity, Margarita became extremely jealous and suspicious of all her boyfriends. Her boyfriends would plead their innocence and tell her that she was "paranoid" and "crazy." Margarita didn't know what to do.

Margarita came for psychotherapy after immigrating to the United States. She didn't know whether she should encourage her boyfriend, Antonio, to immigrate because she didn't know if she could trust him because he had too many platonic female friends. Was she "crazy" as her boyfriend suggested or was he just trying to make her feel that she was crazy? Margarita felt that if all men cheat, perhaps they should be treated as guilty until proven innocent. She believed that the only way to keep men in line and prevent their infidelity was to be constantly suspicious—to make them feel that she was onto their tricks so they would think they could never get away with undetected infidelity. Margarita hoped to make Antonio feel that he was under constant surveillance and that if she ever caught him cheating on her, the punishment would be so swift and harsh that he would regret it for the rest of his life.

In psychotherapy, we explored the possibility that her defensive strategy might backfire. I suggested that Margarita's strategy might make her boyfriend more rather than less likely to cheat because he would feel emasculated by the excessive control; perhaps he might even feel that she deserved to be cheated on as punishment for emasculating him. Her strategy made it less likely that Antonio would feel empathy for the betrayal trauma he would be inflicting on her. As a consequence, he would be less likely to inhibit his impulse toward infidelity. Perhaps sharing the adolescent trauma of discovering her father's infidelity and second family would enable him to appreciate that it would retraumatize her if he betrayed her trust as her father had.

Margarita's initial response to my advice was skeptical, and even suspicious. She felt that Antonio might take advantage of her admission of the possibility that she might be displacing her father issues onto him. Patients often feel they hide their vulnerabilities for good reasons. They fear that if they expose them, their vulnerabilities might be treated as shameful weaknesses to be exploited. Therefore, from a game-playing perspective, it is a strategic error to expose weakness to someone with whom you are in conflict. The trust that exposed vulnerabilities will be met with a consistently empathetic response was simply not there, given Margarita's relationship history. Patients have to be helped to understand that they will never feel securely attached to their romantic partners until they have the experience of being openly vulnerable with their partners and receiving an empathetic response. Why not take the risk of exposing vulnerability and finally clarify whether it is indeed safe to be oneself with a partner? It will certainly be disappointing if one's partner treats this exposed vulnerability as shameful weakness to be exploited, but at least one will know the partner's realistic empathetic limitations.

Margarita decided to try giving up controlling Antonio to see whether the relationship could be less combative. She instead tried to evoke compassion for her vulnerability. Margarita had to enable her boyfriend to see that, given her personal history and their shared cultural background that supported the sexual double standard, her suspicions might be more justified than he was willing to give her credit for, even if he was ultimately a loyal person whose friendships with women remained strictly platonic.

Margarita did bring Antonio to a couples session so I could "check him out," do my own assessment of his trustworthiness, and determine if she was "nuts" to trust him. Antonio made it clear that he appreciated her "father issues" but didn't feel she should take them out on him when he was a "good guy." I noted the frustration he must feel that no matter how many hoops he jumped through and no matter how many tests of his trustworthiness he passed, it did not seem to be enough. I suggested that if he wanted a long-term relationship with Margarita, he would have to gradually earn her trust by being patient with her endless tests and try not to take the testing so personally. If that was too much for him and he wanted out, it would be understandable, but he was unlikely to earn her trust by calling her paranoid and crazy. Antonio said that he knew what I was saying was true, but it was hard to hear because he was hoping that by seeing me he would be able to convince me that Margarita was crazy for not trusting him and I would then use the therapy to get Margarita to trust him.

I told Margarita in front of Antonio that I could judge no better than her whether he was being truthful or just conning her and that she could only wait and see if his patience, loyalty, and devotion stood the test of time. I noted that there was no point trying to keep him under 24-hour surveillance because that was impossible, and he could always find an opportunity to cheat if he really wanted to. Antonio looked happy that I was advising Margarita to be less controlling even though I wasn't willing to give him a character reference.

Not infrequently a betrayed partner is accused of being overly suspicious to the point of paranoia. It only adds insult to injury to have one's sanity questioned when it seems one's suspicions are justified. This is especially the case in exposed infidelity that was initially denied until definitive proof was discovered. It then becomes difficult to believe professions of recommitment to monogamy. The partner accused of being a liar must tolerate the possibly unfair character assassination of being called a liar when he or she is finally telling the truth. The betrayed partner must learn to tolerate being seen as unduly paranoid to the point of insanity. The unfaithful partner might be using such accusations manipulatively to conceal lies, but such accusations may contain a kernel of truth if lack of trust has driven the betrayed partner to begin reading something malevolent into almost everything the unfaithful partner says or does.

From the point of view of marital communication, the couple must learn that calling each other "liar" or "paranoid" is provocative even if it's true. Being accusatory through character assassination may seem like asserting oneself by telling it like it is, but it is an insulting and incendiary way of expressing oneself that will only evoke defensive self-justification, rebuttal, and counter-complaint. Unfaithful partners worry that they will never be trusted no matter what they try to do to regain the betrayed partner's trust. Betrayed partners worry that they will naively trust a deceitful person and be betrayed once again. Neither partner feels comfortable expressing their vulnerability openly in a way that might elicit empathy. Instead, they hide their vulnerability behind hostile character assassination that may possess a kernel of truth, so it particularly stings. Couples also have to learn that even if one partner stops calling the other a liar or paranoid, they can't be stopped from having such thoughts and expressing them indirectly through facial expressions.

Each partner has to work at not taking the character assassination so personally because they are unlikely to get the other partner to honestly concede that she or he has been lying all along or have been unduly paranoid. Naturally, partners want validation of their honesty and sanity from each other. It's difficult to tolerate the fact that it won't be freely or sincerely given because each partner has a mind of his or her own and genuinely thinks the other is lying or paranoid. Validation given under duress or begrudgingly out of fear of rejection isn't real validation but false-self compliance. As a consequence of these relational dynamics, taking personally a partner's assessment of one's character, be it validating or invalidating, may be to make one's sense of self overly dependent on the self-serving biases that implicitly influence one's partner's view of oneself.

Similarly, the therapist isn't in a position to validate either partner's viewpoint because therapists aren't in a position to know for sure who is telling the truth or who is overly suspicious despite having intuitive impressions that may often be accurate. This can be frustrating for patients who expect a therapist to adjudicate these conflicting points of view and decide who is right or wrong. All a therapist can do is express understanding that betrayed partners have good reasons for their suspicions, be they right or wrong, and that partners accused of lying may appear to be telling the truth, but that doesn't mean they are.

In general, therapists prefer to help patients by providing validation and affirmation, but sometimes they have to help patients cope with the inevitable hurt, anger, and self-doubt when they can't get the validation they feel that they need from either their partners or their therapists. Sometimes it has to be enough to know that one is sane or honest even if no one else knows for sure, including the therapist. The lack of validation becomes easier to bear if the therapist expresses empathy for their understandable hurt and frustration at not being affirmed as an honest or sane person, no matter how hard they try to prove to their partners and therapists that they are honest and sane.

To the extent that there is a kernel of truth in an unflattering character assessment, it is difficult to acknowledge that one hasn't been entirely truthful and doesn't recognize it because one has been lying to oneself as well. It is difficult to acknowledge that perhaps one's reality testing is impaired and that one is inflicting damage by making false accusations and unreasonably doubting honest statements. It then becomes the therapist's job to help patients acknowledge and accept their own dishonesty and paranoia without self-hatred for possessing destructive personality traits that hurt their partners. Therapists can help patients see that their destructive actions are defensive ways of protecting their own vulnerabilities and are self-defeating actions that hurt themselves as much as their partners. Of course, it's hard to live with the guilt and find ways to make amends for the hurt one's own dishonesty and false accusations have inflicted on a romantic partner with whom one is hoping to reconcile.

GETTING EVEN: THE PSYCHOLOGY OF RETALIATORY INFIDELITY

"Dark Side" researchers in social psychology have discovered that one frequent self-reported motivation for infidelity is revenge: to punish a partner for a relational transgression (Tafoya & Spitzberg, 2007). Sexually jealous individuals are inclined to engage in retaliatory infidelity to get revenge on their philandering partners. It is not just adultery that might provoke retaliatory infidelity. It may be provoked by any kind of perceived relational transgression. For example, the humiliation of chronic sexual rejection in a long-term relationship increases the probability of infidelity as a way of punishing a sexually rejecting partner.

Bernie and Jessica were engaged to be married. Bernie came back drunk from his bachelor party and confessed that a prostitute hired by his friends had given him oral sex and he had been too drunk to resist, although he felt guilty and was therefore confessing to the transgression. Jessica felt betrayed and went out and slept with Bernie's best friend to get even. At first, Jessica was not going to tell him, but she could not resist blurting it out during their next big fight. Bernie was stunned. Retaliatory infidelity can be conceived as an anger management problem—a destructive way of expressing one's anger that is counterproductive. Sometimes the retaliatory infidelity is hidden so that the unfaithful partner has just the private satisfaction of getting even. But as in Jessica's case, at a moment of hurt and anger, sometimes the infidelity is confessed. The confession is not an attempt to seek forgiveness and reconciliation but to wound and humiliate the partner in revenge for one's own hurt and humiliation. In the moment, it seems like the right thing to do to restore a sense of justice and fairness in the relationship.

Retaliatory infidelity is counterproductive if it leads to a vicious and escalating cycle of revenge. Victims of retaliatory infidelity are unlikely to feel that they had it coming and good-naturedly accept their punishment for their own relational transgressions: The punishment doesn't seem to fit the crime. The victim of retaliatory infidelity privately thinks, "My relational transgression wasn't so bad. I cheated out of sexual frustration (or in search of intimacy). You cheated just to hurt me because you're a mean-spirited person, so why should I feel guilty about what I did? You deserved it." Perpetrators of retaliatory infidelity lose the moral high ground because their punitive response to relational transgression makes them seem like an unforgiving and vindictive person who no longer warrants sympathy for the original relational transgression that they suffered. Bernie no longer regretted his drunken infidelity, for which he had felt genuine remorse, because his punishment seemed excessive. Secretly, Bernie began to feel glad he had had oral sex with a prostitute; in his mind it punished Jessica in advance for having sex with his best friend.

The evolutionary biologist Robert Trivers (1971) argued that the human penchant for revenge is actually a product of the human tendency toward altruism. Altruism has always been a puzzle for evolutionary biologists. Richard Dawkins (1976) recognized that genes are selfish. All genes care about is replicating themselves, and they use organisms, like human bodies, as transport vehicles to transfer genetic copies of material from one organism to another. Genes shed the bodies that house them, just like a snake sheds its skin. William Hamilton (1964) was the first to figure out that kin altruism makes a kind of evolutionary sense. Close genetic relatives carry copies of one's own genes so that a relative's reproductive success is equivalent to one's own to the degree that the relative is facilitating the transfer of genes that are shared in common. The sacrifice individuals make for their children, grandchildren, siblings, nieces, nephews, and cousins makes evolutionary sense because they all share copies of the same genes to varying degrees.

The question then arises as to why humans would make sacrifices for individuals with whom they share no common genes. Trivers (1971) solved that problem with his theory of reciprocal altruism. The basic idea is "if you scratch my back, I'll scratch yours." The payback for kin altruism is the relative's reproductive success. The relative does not necessarily have to return the favor if he or she puts the favor to good use by generating more copies of the genes one shares in common with that relative. In contrast, a nonrelative is expected to return the favor someday. It pays to be nice to friends and even strangers of at least one's own tribe so that someday they might be nice in return.

For reciprocal altruism to evolve, there has to be some sort of accounting system. A free rider could simply accept a favor that is never returned. Reciprocal altruism is based on trust that the favor will someday be reciprocated. Altruism toward unrelated individuals becomes maladaptive when that trust is betrayed. The evolutionary psychologists Cosmides and Tooby (1992) reasoned that humans would have to possess "cheater detection mechanisms" that were sensitive to discerning free riders who try to reap the benefits of others' sacrifices without paying the costs by eventually returning the favor. Detecting and punishing cheaters then becomes a way of dissuading free riders from taking advantage of the generosity of others.

Monogamy is a form of reciprocal altruism. The deal is, "I won't make you jealous if you won't make me jealous." Infidelity is "cheating" because the adulterer is a free rider trying to reap the advantages of monogamy without paying the price. Monogamy, despite the privations of giving up one's sexual freedom, comes with a number of impressive benefits. First, individuals willing to make a monogamous commitment can usually win more desirable partners than those unwilling to do so. Women of high mate value appear to hold out for men of high mate value who are willing to make a monogamous commitment (Buss & Shackelford, 2008), and high-status men who have harems expect their wives to remain faithful (Betzig, 1986). The most desirable partners often demand a monogamous commitment as the price of having a relationship with them. Advertising openly that one is not interested in monogamy severely limits the number of partners who will take a second look at such an openly nonmonogamous person. People who openly practice consensual nonmonogamy become stigmatized sexual minorities (Ritchie & Barker, 2006).

Second, partners who commit to monogamy are usually committing to putting more investment into parenting then further mating effort. Managing multiple relationships with multiple partners and the attendant jealousies aroused takes time and effort. And third, for men, monogamy fosters paternity certainty; for women, it guarantees a husband who won't be directing precious resources toward other women and their children. Infidelity diminishes the reproductive advantages of monogamous arrangements.

From an evolutionary perspective, romantic jealousy, even to the point of paranoia, is a specialized kind of cheater detection mechanism (Schlager, 1995). Romantic jealousy is the emotion that is evoked when there is a sneaking suspicion that a partner may be surreptitiously getting romantically involved with a rival. Sexual jealousy may be culturally reinforced or suppressed depending on whether the culture is for or against sexual partner sharing. Yet it would seem that all humans come factory-equipped with a specialized cheater detection mechanism that is sensitive to the clues of losing the affections of a romantic partner to a rival. There may be gender differences in the operation of those mechanisms, as women seem to be more sensitive to the presence of rivals, whereas men seem more focused on women's intentions (Ein-Dor, Perry-Paldi, Hirschberger, Birnbaum, & Deutsch, 2015).

"TO ERR IS HUMAN; TO FORGIVE, DIVINE"—ALEXANDER POPE

Rose came for treatment because she had caught her husband having an extramarital affair. The problem, however, was that Rose had originally caught her husband having had an affair 10 years ago. They went to couples therapy for a year, and she believed he had recommitted to monogamy. Rose concluded that she had been a fool to believe him and that he was a compulsive liar. Having caught him a second time, she didn't know what to do. They were a dual-income family with two children, 8 and 10 years old. Rose didn't feel she could afford to divorce him because they would all suffer downward mobility.

Her husband, Enrico, went out to a bar every Friday night with his friends to decompress after the workweek. Enrico claimed it was all innocent, but Rose discovered that Enrico went out to flirt with and pick up women. This time when Rose confronted him, he simply refused to give up his extramarital outlet and said Rose could do the same if she wished. So Rose went out and found herself a boyfriend to make Enrico jealous. Enrico was miffed but willing to begrudgingly tolerate it. Rose eventually broke up with her boyfriend when she saw that the relationship was never going to go anywhere and she really didn't need the extramarital sex. She still preferred having sex with her husband.

Rose resented having to resign herself to a marriage to an unrepentant philanderer, but she didn't see any other realistic option. Coming from a Latin American background, she remembered her mother's advice that all men cheat and she should just look the other way if he is a good father and provider. That's what her mother did, but Rose had vowed to herself that she would not follow in her mother's footsteps in this regard. Yet here she was, a middle-aged woman and mother of two coping with infidelity in exactly the same way her mother had. Rose hoped that her daughter would do better.

Supposedly revenge is sweet, as the saying goes. Revenge does feel good in the moment because it feels powerful (Strelan, Weick, & Vasiljevic, 2014) and gratifies the need for justice by punishing the perpetrator of a relational transgression (Gerber & Jackson, 2013), and, at least in fantasy, it seems to teach unfaithful partners a lesson they will never forget. But revenge can have negative long-term consequences. Individuals imagine that revenge will provide a hedonic reward by punishing an offender, but research suggests that people who punish an offender tend to ruminate about the offender, whereas those who move on do not (Carlsmith, Wilson, & Gilbert, 2008). In the case of infidelity, trying to damage an unfaithful partner's mate value through reputational damage doesn't necessarily do much to restore one's own damaged mate value. Bitterness, holding a grudge, and vindictiveness are not particularly attractive character traits. Recovery from infidelity eventually requires forgiveness as well as apology (Fife, Weeks, & Stellberg-Filbert, 2013).

It may be difficult to give up revenge motivation because it feels like being shamefully weak, powerless, and impotent. Letting go can feel less like acceptance and forgiveness than like resigning oneself to a humiliating defeat. Nevertheless, exercising forgiveness and letting go of revenge motivation appear to free oneself from endlessly ruminating about the relational transgression (McCullough, Bono, & Root, 2007). Conciliatory gestures facilitate forgiveness and reduce anger by modifying victims' perceptions of their transgressors' value as relationship partners and the likelihood of recidivism (McCullough, Pedersen, Tabak, & Carter, 2014).

Nonjudgmental acceptance may be a tough sell for the therapist in these circumstances and may be met with skepticism and scorn. Patients may feel that it is easy for therapists to "preach" nonjudgmental acceptance because they have never walked in the patient's shoes and been humiliated in the way the patient has. Johns, Allen, and Gordon (2015) suggested that mindfulness can facilitate forgiveness in response to infidelity by reducing overidentification with anger. Forgiveness is also facilitated by humility (Fife et al., 2013) in recognition that being punitive doesn't make one invulnerable to future betrayal. Therapists could note that "eating humble pie" is sometimes just a part of life with which even therapists must contend. Nobody likes it, but the challenge is learning how to live with oneself after the fact to keep a job or a spouse that one can't make do without. Some betrayed spouses even experience "posttraumatic growth" in the process of forgiving an unfaithful partner (Heintzelman, Murdock, Krycak, & Seay, 2014). Humility may be empowering, although betrayed partners may fear it will only weaken them.

How does a therapist enable a betrayed patient to rise above revenge motivation without seeming like some preachy authority figure who is making the patient feel guilty for a desire to restore self-respect in the face of sexual betrayal? Therapists can begin by helping patients see that revenge is a natural human response to relational transgression that has been shaped by human evolution (McCullough, Kurzban, & Tabak, 2011), and they can acknowledge that in some cultures revenge is seen as a constructive way of restoring one's honor (Rodriguez Mosquera, Manstead, & Fischer, 2000). Nevertheless, therapists can advise patients that reconciliation also has a basis in human evolution and is something that even chimpanzees are good at after a violent altercation (de Waal, 2007). The challenging therapeutic task is to facilitate reconciliation in a way that doesn't shame the patient for their vindictive tendencies. Yet in alleviating shame sensitivity the therapist must try to avoid falling into the trap of inadvertently rationalizing and normalizing such destructive tendencies.

Patients can feel that they are only being self-respecting and assertive when they express their revenge motivation even when it's expressed through a dramatic temper tantrum designed to instill the fear of God into their unfaithful partner. Yet in retrospect, patients can feel ashamed at their loss of control, especially if it's in front of children, family, and friends and designed to publicly humiliate the unfaithful partner. Such outbursts feed the narrative of the unfaithful partner that the betrayed partner is "crazy" and has serious anger management problems.

Evolutionary psychology helps us see that revenge motivation derives from a breakdown of reciprocal altruism. That means that deep down, every vindictive person is a reciprocal altruist at heart groping for some way forward to restore trust in a relationship based on reciprocated sacrifice for the sake of the team. Revenge fantasies defend against the shame and humiliation of having foolishly trusted and made sacrifices for someone who went on to betray that trust. The failure of reciprocal altruism in certain situations can make it seem in retrospect as though there was something wrong with being a trusting and self-sacrificing person if it only makes one vulnerable to betrayal. Dignity is restored when betrayed patients are reminded that the mature, responsible, trusting, and self-sacrificing side of themselves warrants respect even if no one else appreciates it and that getting even isn't living up to one's better nature.

Rose ultimately decided to remain committed to her marriage even if her husband didn't recommit to monogamy. She would treat him civilly and politely as the father of her children even if she no longer respected or admired him. Maybe it wasn't so bad to be like her mother, who, after all, kept the family together in difficult circumstances. It was regrettable that for women in Rose's situation, the options are limited; but there was no shame in remaining committed to a marriage to an unrepentant philanderer, at least for now, if that is what seemed best for her children. Rose appreciated that retaliatory infidelity had not given her any lasting satisfaction, and she no longer wanted to sink to her husband's level.

Interestingly, recent research has found that observers prefer (i.e., are more sympathetic to) victims of sexual betrayal who leave their unfaithful partners rather than remain with them (H. J. Smith, Goode, Balzarini, Ryan, & Georges, 2014). Betrayed partners can feel "damned if they do" leave their unfaithful partners if it goes against the expectations of more patriarchal cultures that expect women to look the other way and "damned if they don't" leave their unfaithful partners who violate the expectations of more individualistic cultures in which a self-respecting person wouldn't remain committed to an unrepentant philanderer for the sake of the family. Self-acceptance is accepting that all choices have costs as well as benefits. It is for patients to figure out how to live by their core values and to commit to a course of actions based on those values to be true to themselves regardless of what others think (see Pierson & Hayes, 2007, on empowerment by using the principles of acceptance and commitment therapy).

CONCLUSION

Possessiveness and jealousy may be universal emotions, and there is certainly much discussion of cross-cultural differences in attitudes toward infidelity. What is rarely considered, however, is how attitudes about infidelity evolve across the lifespan. Do teenagers, young adults, middle-aged adults, and older adults have different motivations for and attitudes about infidelity? Attitudes might change across the lifespan if sex drive, need for attachment, or propensity to fall in love change over time. This and similar issues are the subject of the next chapter.

7

WHEN THE BEST SEX IS EXTRAMARITAL: INFIDELITY THROUGHOUT THE LIFESPAN

Most people think of infidelity as a potential hazard of married life. However, individuals may start breaking promises of sexual exclusivity and lying about it as soon as they begin to form sexually exclusive relationships during adolescence. "Going steady" during adolescence may last only a few weeks or a few months, yet sexually exclusive dating relationships can still be shattered by the same feelings of hurt, humiliation, anger, and betrayal that arise when infidelity is exposed in a decades-old marriage with children (Roscoe, Cavanaugh, & Kennedy, 1988). In fact, infidelity rates appear to be higher in dating relationships during late adolescence and young adulthood than among older married adults (Feldman & Cauffman, 1999; Negash, Cui, Fincham, & Pasley, 2014; Vail-Smith, Whetstone, & Knox, 2010). During adolescence and young adulthood, the sex drive is high, and commitment levels to the current romantic partner are often low, increasing the temptation to be unfaithful. Infidelity is associated with relationship dissolution in college students (Hall & Fincham, 2006; Negash et al., 2014).

http://dx.doi.org/10.1037/0000053-008
The Dynamics of Infidelity: Applying Relationship Science to Psychotherapy Practice, by L. Josephs

Overall, infidelity rates go down with age as sex drive diminishes and commitment to a life partner and family increases. Likewise, marital sex incrementally decreases with advancing age (Call, Sprecher, & Schwartz, 1995). Older individuals often have more to lose and less to gain through infidelity than do younger individuals. Nevertheless, the risk of infidelity remains significant throughout the lifespan. Relationship dissatisfaction, sexual boredom, desire for sexual variety, and the wish for revenge can motivate infidelity at all life stages. Yet certain reasons for infidelity become more salient during different phases of the life cycle. Ambivalence about monogamy may last a lifetime as each phase of the life cycle presents challenges for which infidelity may seem like the solution.

PROVING YOUR SEXUAL PROWESS: WHY TEENAGERS CHEAT

Generalizing about why adolescents are unfaithful can be problematic because there may be both gender and personality differences in motivations for infidelity at any age. In addition, adolescents come of age in cultures that may have very different attitudes toward adolescent and premarital sexuality: Some cultures have restrictive attitudes toward adolescent sexuality (i.e., no premarital sex), and others have permissive attitudes that allow sexual experimentation and exploration. In addition, variability among adolescent attitudes about infidelity is likely associated with variability among their parental role models. Some adolescents have grown up with parents who appear to have a reasonably satisfying, sexually exclusive relationship with each other and may also role model good communication and conflict resolution skills. Others have grown up with awareness of parental infidelity (Schmidt, Green, & Prouty, 2016) or have divorced parents who have yet to find marital happiness with a succession of dating partners (Rhoades, Stanley, Markman, & Ragan, 2012). These factors can adversely affect adult relationship adjustment and ethics.

The sex lives of adolescent hunter–gatherers might give some sense from an evolutionary perspective of what adolescent sexuality was like in the environment of evolutionary adaptedness (see Chapter 6). Hunter–gatherer children enter puberty later than do children in modern societies because their nutrition isn't as plentiful or as good as what modern children enjoy. As a consequence, the females are usually not fertile until late adolescence. Growing up in a sexually permissive environment with late fertility means that hunter–gatherer teenagers can enjoy sexual experimentation with multiple partners for a number of years without worry of pregnancy. Yet by late adolescence, most females do become pregnant and have their first baby due to the lack of birth control (Konner, 2005, 2010).

Among hunter–gatherers, marriage and parenthood are common by late adolescence for females and in the early 20s for males. Most marriages are monogamous, and polygynous marriages rarely involve more than two wives (Marlowe, 2005). Parent–offspring conflict in regard to arranged marriage appears ubiquitous; romantic love is clearly in evidence among hunter–gatherer adolescents, who may pair off and elope (Konner, 2010). Divorce is also common among hunter–gatherers, with a divorce rate between 25% and 40% (Blurton Jones, Marlowe, Hawkes, & O'Connell, 2000). Howell (1979) noted that among the !Kung, married people are always "in the market" for new spouses, not unlike most unmarried people, because the rates of divorce and remarriage are high.

What the literature on the adolescent sexuality of hunter–gatherers suggests is that humans are most likely predisposed for a phase of sexual experimentation and exploration with frequent partner-switching before forming a longer term, sexually exclusive romantic pair bond for biparental care. A significant percentage of those early pair bonds will be challenged by infidelity and will end in relational dissolution, but some percentage will last even in a culture that has a generally permissive attitude toward infidelity and divorce. Hunter–gatherers live in resource-poor environments and become parents early in life as part of a faster life history strategy. In contrast, contemporary college-educated, middle-class professionals live in relatively resource-rich environments that may evoke a slower life history strategy characterized by an extended adolescence and young adulthood of sexual experimentation, frequent partner-switching, and delayed parenthood.

Marriages during young adulthood appear more likely to end in divorce than later marriages (Lowenstein, 2005). It may take a certain amount of relationship experience and emotional maturity (i.e., sufficiently high reflective functioning and communication skills) to be able to form a securely attached long-term sexually exclusive relationship that stands the test of time. Psychotherapy may help teenagers and young adults develop the relationship skills that engender stable long-term relationships in preparation for later life when resources will be sufficient to start a family.

The romantic fantasy that inspires a desire to find one's lifelong soul mate may arise early in life (during the oedipal phase for Freud but at least by puberty for non-Freudians). Yet the psychological capacities necessary to successfully actualize that romantic fantasy may not be in place until much later in life, and as a consequence, initial attempts to form long-term sexually exclusive relationships are likely to fail. Individuals need to learn from their mistakes to exercise good judgment in the choice of a partner, and then they must acquire the adaptive mate-retention skills (Buss & Shackelford, 1997) necessary to make that relationship last.

It may be human nature to keep trying to form long-term sexually exclusive relationships until one finally gets it right. Unfortunately, some never do and will spend their lives trying and failing; others will stop trying because they encounter too much frustration, hurt, and disappointment. A few might get it right on the first try, and others might eventually succeed after a number of failed attempts with the help of a psychotherapist. Adolescent and young adult partner-switching may be frequent because the likelihood that a first sexual partner would be someone who is well matched for a lifelong partnership is relatively low, and even if the couple is relatively well matched, the partners may not yet possess the skills necessary to make the relationship work. Having multiple short-term sexual partners is not always about the desire to have casual sex and gratify a need for sexual variety; it may in fact be a result of repeated failed attempts to form more lasting sexually exclusive relationships.

Adolescence and young adulthood can be a time of sexual exploration and experimentation that can be conducive to personal growth. The contemporary version of frequent partner-switching for casual sex has been referred to as "hooking up" (Manning, Longmore, & Giordano, 2005; Stinson, 2010). Adolescence is also a time during which peer group popularity is prioritized (Burt & Donnellan, 2015), even though being popular may be associated with increased risk-taking and antisocial behaviors (van den Broek, Deutz, Marike, Schoneveld, Burk, & Cillessen, 2016) and being unpopular with depression (Litwack, Aikins, & Cillessen, 2012). Both hunter–gatherer adolescents and contemporary teenagers seem to engage in popularity contests in which they are discovering their relative mate value in the local mating marketplace. They are discovering their place in what sociologists call the *erotic rank order* (Illouz, 2012; Zetterberg, 1966). Individuals pursuing a slow life history strategy may be using casual sex to obtain the sexual experience and confidence they feel they need to eventually win the most desirable long-term partner possible at the point in their lives when they are finally ready to settle down to a long-term committed relationship and start a family.

The best explanation thus far for the high prevalence rates of teenage and young adult infidelity in their sexually exclusive dating relationships is the *commitment calibration hypothesis* (Rusbult, 1983), which suggests that partners who have the most to lose are the ones most likely to engage in activities that protect and maintain the relationship. Teenagers and young adults appreciate that infidelity is wrong, and they might have some appreciation for the emotional trauma that sexual betrayal causes (Regnerus & Uecker, 2011). Yet because their commitment level to their current dating partners is relatively low and their empathy limited by their egocentrism, they are more inclined to be unfaithful than married adults with children, who are more committed and have a better sense of the costs of exposed infidelity. Adolescents and young adults are less inclined to make the sacrifice of sexual exclusivity to protect and maintain the relationship (i.e., to avoid making their partners feel jealous and insecure) because they are not as committed to it as they imagine they will be to a "real" relationship at some later point when they are ready for the responsibilities of marriage and family. Wilkins and Dalessandro (2013) called this "monogamy lite" among college students. Nevertheless, attitudes toward infidelity are significantly more permissive among college students who are high in narcissism and attachment insecurity, and that association is mediated by low empathy (Shimberg, Josephs, & Tittel, 2016).

The commitment calibration hypothesis helps to explain the occurrence of infidelity among young adults who are engaged to be married or newlyweds without children. Young adults or even 30-somethings ready for the responsibilities of marriage and family life recognize that the arrival of children requires a higher level of commitment. The potential costs of infidelity and divorce are much higher once children are born and one must factor in the effects exposed infidelity may have on their psychological development and standard of living. As a consequence, there is a window of time in a committed relationship when one can surreptitiously find a preferable long-term partner with whom to have a family without inflicting costs on the children one hopes to raise in the not too distant future. Those with a slow life history strategy may be motivated to "trade up" for a partner of higher mate value until the costs of so doing become excessively prohibitive (like running out the biological clock). At that point, commitment to the current partner solidifies, and attractive alternatives are devalued (Lydon, Meana, Sepinwall, Richards, & Mayman, 1999) instead of being idealized so temptation can be resisted.

MARRIED WITH CHILDREN: INFIDELITY AS VACATION FROM FAMILY LIFE

Commitment appears to be highest among married couples with children. Of course, this is in comparison with young adult dating relationships and with childless marriages, for which divorce rates are higher (Kinnunen & Pulkkinen, 2003; Miner & Shackelford, 2010). Despite this higher level of commitment, infidelity of which children become aware remains common (Schmidt et al., 2016). Among a college sample almost 25% were aware of parental infidelity (Hunyady, Josephs, & Jost, 2008). One of the highest risk factors for behavioral problems for children is to witness high parental conflict (Cummings & Davies, 2011). Exposed infidelity constitutes a significant source of high parental conflict; it may even trigger homicidal rage in the betrayed partner (Daly, Wilson, & Weghorst, 1982; Knauft, 1991). Children who discover their parents' infidelities may become "parentified" (Jurkovic,

1997) in having to manage the posttraumatic stress disorder that the betrayed parent suffers. Betrayed partners may use their children as sounding boards for their hurt and anger, hoping to elicit their children's sympathy and support even though they would rather not get caught up in their parents' conflicts.

What motivates infidelity when the potential costs of exposure are so high? Raising children appears to be highly stressful for married couples so much so that marital satisfaction increases once relieved of that burden. Marital satisfaction increases once children move out of the house (Gorchoff, John, & Helson, 2008). The "empty nest" has a silver lining as couples are relieved of the responsibilities, burdens, and the stresses of raising children, all of which can lead to a deteriorating sense of personal well-being (Nelson, Kushlev, & Lyubomirsky, 2014). Naturally, parents might want a vacation from the stresses and strains of married life that might restore a sense of well-being. Extramarital affairs may provide just such an escape.

Having an affair while married with children is a calculated risk if the aim is to marry the affair partner for a happier second marriage. There is always the possibility that the affair partner as a stepparent will not be as invested in his or her stepchildren as biological parents are in their own biological children. The chance of a child being murdered by a stepparent, compared with a biological parent, is substantially higher (Daly & Wilson, 1999). Perhaps when a marriage begins to fall apart consequent to the strain of raising children, there is an implicit calculation that the marriage isn't working, might not last, and the children will inevitably suffer, so why not have an affair, as there might not be that much to lose? Commitment may be low because there is a sense that the damage is already done and won't be made any worse than it already is by exposure of an affair or divorce.

MISUSING PSYCHOTHERAPY AS AN ESCAPIST SOLUTION

Patients entering psychotherapy in a state of emotional crisis precipitated by infidelity may feel that the purpose of therapy is to vent their feelings to a sympathetic audience. It seems that if their feelings are legitimate, they should be allowed to vent them until they get all their pent-up feelings out of their system. Patients are likely to react angrily if the therapist points out that although the feelings may be legitimate and warrant an empathetic response, the point of therapy is also to learn how to cope with overwhelming feelings through cognitive reappraisal.

Freud (1912/1958) discovered that catharsis without analysis provided symptom relief but not lasting change and may constitute a serious impediment to self-reflection. Recent research has confirmed Freud's discovery. Catharsis—venting anger in an attempt to release pent-up frustration—may actually have the opposite effect and exacerbate and dysregulate angry feelings (Bushman, Baumeister, & Stack, 1999; Lohr, Olatunji, Baumeister, & Bushman, 2007). Emotion-focused therapists (Pascual-Leone, Gilles, Singh, & Andreescu, 2013) note that what they call *secondary emotions* can defend against awareness of primary emotional responses. Harder emotions like anger may defend against awareness of softer emotions like shame or sadness. Venting a secondary emotion may simply reinforce a defense against awareness of the emotion associated with a greater sense of personal vulnerability. Focusing on the underlying emotional vulnerability may prove more therapeutic than encouraging further expression of the more defensive emotion.

Max had affairs to escape dealing with his wife, Denise, whom he perceived as maddeningly impenetrable. He felt that talking to Denise was like talking to a brick wall. She did whatever she wanted to do with the children and the finances without any regard for his feelings or opinions. Max finally separated from Denise after she discovered his affairs. He decided he wanted out of the marriage, although Denise wanted to go to couples therapy to recover from the infidelity. Max and his wife went for couples therapy but they ended up divorcing. Max came for therapy when he discovered that his embittered and vindictive ex-wife was now trying to alienate him from the children and was being more unrealistic than ever about money. Max fumed in the session how unbelievable it was that Denise couldn't see that what was best for everyone was to have a more civil and friendly postdivorce relationship for the sake of the children.

Max used his therapy sessions to vent his moral outrage, to which I was initially sympathetic. But I noticed that the more I was sympathetic to his self-righteous indignation, the more he indulged it and the more agitated he became, pouring out endless examples of his wife's insufferable irrationality. I felt I needed to interrupt his using therapy only to "dump" his feelings on to me without trying to put them in perspective through cognitive reappraisal.

I noted that it was unrealistic for him to think Denise would be any easier to communicate with after feeling emotionally shattered by sexual betrayal and divorce. The fear of losing him had probably kept some of her frustrating tendencies in check, but now there was no incentive for her to try to meet him halfway. I suggested that Denise probably felt free to treat his feelings and perspective with utter disregard given the way she felt mistreated by him. Max responded defensively, "But there are two sides to every story. Why doesn't she see it?" I responded, "Well, I guess that's why you divorced her—because she didn't seem able to see your side of the story. You felt invalidated, misunderstood, and alone in the marriage (i.e., focusing on the underlying emotional vulnerability). I don't know why you'd think it would be any different now that you're divorced, but I guess you would like the validation you never got and to be forgiven by your ex-wife for cheating on and divorcing her."

Max calmed down and looked thoughtful, as though for the first time he was able to contemplate the obvious: the emotional impact that sexual betrayal followed by divorce would most likely have on the mental state of an egocentric person like his ex-wife. Retaliatory infidelity, being punitive for invalidating him, and looking for intimacy outside of the marriage could be understood in retrospect as defenses against fully experiencing the loneliness he felt within the marriage and his dread of being shamed by his wife if he were to express his vulnerability more openly in the hope of obtaining an empathetic response. It was difficult for Max to accept his wife's emotional limitations and to forgive her for the hurt and anger her limitations caused him.

We looked at how Max and Denise always got into power struggles. Max felt that Denise lived in her own reality, and no matter how intelligently or forcefully he debated her, he never succeeded in getting her to see things his way. Max didn't see that he lived as much in his own egocentric reality as Denise did in hers and that they were equally intolerant of each other's expressing an independent viewpoint.

I noted that divorce hadn't alleviated their power struggles; it had, in fact, exacerbated them in a way that was now beginning to interfere with his relationship with his children, who were caught in the middle. I suggested that he could deescalate the conflict by learning to respectfully tolerate Denise's view of reality rather than relentlessly challenging it, which only antagonized her. Max finally took my words to heart and started coming in with a progress report of how "Zen" he was starting to become in dealing with his wife. Denise still did whatever she wanted, without regard for his feelings, but at least they no longer argued in front of their teenage children, who complained about having to endure "immature" parents that drove them crazy with their endless bickering.

Max started discussing feeling guilt-ridden (a more vulnerable emotion—his disappointment in himself) that he had taken a permanent vacation from the stresses and strains of family life because it had gotten to be too much for him. It started to dawn on him that the children were most likely suffering the consequences of his absence. He had left them behind with an emotionally unstable mother who used her children as a sounding board for her angry complaints about their father, who she felt had ruined their lives. Nevertheless, he found it a relief to be out of the house, and he couldn't see himself going back even if his wife were open to reconciliation.

YOU ONLY LIVE ONCE: WHY THE MIDDLE-AGED AND ELDERLY CHEAT

The frequency of marital sex decreases with age due to biological aging, diminished health, and habituation to sex (Call, Sprecher, & Schwartz, 1995). Do people become more or less inclined to be unfaithful as their sex drive and sexual functioning diminish? Advancing age is one of the best predictors of declining sex drive in both men and women (DeLamater & Sill, 2005). Might increasing sexual boredom due to habituation in decades-long monogamous relationships trump declining sex drive in tipping the tables toward infidelity? Many individuals remain sexual well into old age despite the challenges of diminished sex drive and functioning (Trudel, Turgeon, & Piché, 2010).

A problem arises if one partner is ready to incrementally phase out the couple's sexual relationship while the other partner would like to remain sexually active at a certain frequency. Sex drive and functioning may decline at different rates and for different reasons (i.e., loss of interest in sex with anybody vs. loss of interest in sex with one's particular partner) in each member of the couple. This mismatch is a risk factor for infidelity that may increase over the course of the marriage. It can begin early in a marriage if habituation and sexual boredom set in with the birth of children, with work stress, or as men begin to lose erectile potency and women suffer vaginal pain for lack of sufficient lubrication during intercourse. Dissatisfaction with frequency of sex is closely associated with relationship dissatisfaction (McNulty, Wenner, & Fisher, 2016). There may be "fixes" for all of these issues through couples and sex therapy, presuming that both members of the couple are willing to discuss and work on the problem. Unfortunately, the same factors that contribute to declining sex drive and functioning may also contribute to lower motivation to address them.

Some individuals would prefer to be in a sexless marriage. They may resent the coercive pressure (i.e., implicit threats of infidelity or divorce) to have to fix a situation that in fact is to their liking. There is increasing recognition that some people are asexual or become asexual and may self-identify as such (Robbins, Low, & Query, 2016; Yule, Brotto, & Gorzalka, 2015). What happens when one partner comes out as a self-identified asexual person and the other still prefers and expects a sexually exclusive commitment? It may reflect ageism to assume that individuals necessarily become asexual with advancing age, but it may also contain a kernel of truth: Prevalence rates of asexuality do increase with advancing age. Just as there should not be shame associated with remaining a highly sexual person with advancing age, neither should there be shame with becoming a progressively asexual person. Sexuality and asexuality do not need to be conceptualized in dichotomous good or bad ways but as dimensions on a continuum in which there is no one right way to be.

The problem is what to do when a relatively sexual person finds that his or her life partner is becoming progressively asexual with advancing age—and is content with becoming progressively asexual. In some ways, sexual desire is an aching need that is never completely fulfilled no matter how great the sexual experience. For some individuals, it's a relief to be relieved of a pressing need that can turn a person into an "ecstasy junky." What if the more sexually motivated person is also experiencing diminished sex drive and functioning but feels that he or she needs extra sexual stimulation (e.g., more foreplay, more sensitive and patient sexual touching, new sexual positions) to compensate for the increased difficulty getting and staying aroused, while an increasingly asexual partner is becoming progressively less motivated to provide added sexual stimulation because it makes sex seem like even more of a burdensome chore than it has already become?

The progressively asexual person may still desire a sexually exclusive commitment given that sexual exclusivity remains symbolic of the couple's romantic connection. Just because one has lost interest in sex doesn't mean that he or she would not experience jealousy and attachment insecurity if the partner wanted to have sex and romance with other people. Betrayed but asexual partners may still feel surprised, deeply hurt, and humiliated by the discovery of sexual betrayal even if they haven't had sex with their partners in years.

Asexual partners may egocentrically assume that their partners feel the same way they do if their partners seem to accept a diminishing sex life without complaint. For the progressively asexual person, the value of the relationship may be in growing old together in a warm, mutually supportive, and emotionally intimate relationship in which the sexual part is no longer important.

It may not occur to progressively asexual individuals that their partners may have lost interest in sex with them only because they have become sexually unresponsive. The more sexual partner may give up trying to seduce the more asexual partner if there is an expectation of being sexually rejected. Or maybe it's just too much work to get an asexual partner in the mood, so why even try? It can be humiliating when one's best efforts to be seductive, romantic, and sexually arousing are having marginal impact.

Unfortunately, it's not only sexual functioning and youthful good looks that may decline with age. Personalities can also become less sexy. People who lose their youthful vitality and sense of humor and turn into grumpy old men or women who seem to worry or complain about everything can lose their sex appeal. One may lose interest in maintaining one's sex appeal as one loses interest in sex. Why work at maintaining the qualities to attract a sexual partner when sex has become something that is no longer needed or desired? It's not that psychotherapy can't result in personality change in older adults (see Josephs, Sanders, & Gorman, 2014, on treatment of older personality-disordered adults) but that such individuals may not be motivated to go for treatment to work on their personality issues. They feel that at their advanced age, they should be accepted as they are without being pressured to change.

Progressively asexual partners may feel that if a partner genuinely cares about the other partner's feelings, the commitment to monogamy remains a reasonable expectation regardless of the quality of the marital sex life. The value of the relationship is in growing old together and being there for one another in sickness and health. Of course, the ongoing commitment to sexual exclusivity is easy for a partner who has little or no sexual desire. Monogamy is only a sacrifice for individuals who crave sexual variety (more often men; Schmookler & Bursik, 2007) but is not much of a sacrifice for those with little need for sexual variety or little or no sexual needs at all.

Potentially unfaithful individuals may make a different assumption: that monogamy is based on maintaining a reasonably satisfying sex life throughout a marriage. A partner who really loves you is a partner who is committed to ensuring your sexual happiness one way or another, whether or not he or she is in the mood. A declining sex life is taken personally because it is an indication that a partner no longer loves you enough to care about your sexual happiness. It doesn't seem fair to remain committed to sexual exclusivity with a partner who seems to have become indifferent to one's sexual happiness. In such a situation, infidelity seems justified if it offers a way of making a sexless marriage work with a person to whom one is attached rather than seek a divorce just to have a better sex life.

Some individuals have an increasing desire to reexperience intense sexual excitement and romantic passion as they age, before they are "over the hill." The best antidote for the depressing realities of aging and mortality may be the vital feeling of being alive that is generated by romantic ecstasy. Thus, unhappily monogamous individuals may become more prone to infidelity or divorce as their children become independent because it seems like they might have less to lose by breaking up the family. After all, you only live once. Nevertheless, the benefits of grandparenting might be greater for parents in a stable relationship than those in an unstable relationship marred by infidelity or divorce.

Harriet and Harold, a couple in their early 60s, had been married for more than 30 years and had raised a family together. They had always had a rather volatile and contentious relationship, but somehow they stuck together despite their bitter disagreements. They hadn't had sex in several years because Harold had lost sexual interest in Harriet after surgery for a nonmalignant brain tumor and was taking a wide variety of medications. Harriet knew that Harold still secretly masturbated with pornography on occasion and so did not believe his loss of interest in sex with her reflected only his medical condition. Harriet felt humiliated that Harold would rather masturbate than have sex with her, so she went out and found an affair partner. She felt she was too young, too attractive for her age, and equipped with too strong a sex drive to stop having sex for the rest of her life with only masturbation for sexual relief. Yet she didn't really enjoy the extramarital sex because she felt used for impersonal casual sex by a man she knew didn't really care about her as a person.

Harriet knew her husband genuinely loved her even if he was no longer "in lust" with her and that he was a loyal person who wouldn't deal with his sexual frustration by being unfaithful. Nevertheless, Harriet felt that her infidelity was justified. Even if his sex drive and functioning were diminished by his medical condition, Harriet felt that he should turn to her for sexual gratification on those occasions when he felt he needed sexual relief. Thus, she felt that Harold was being unreasonably sexually rejecting, and her feelings were hurt.

Unfortunately, Harold died unexpectedly during another brain surgery for an enlarging nonmalignant brain tumor. Harriet was devastated by the loss of her husband and felt wracked with guilt. She felt that Harold's untimely death was a punishment from God for her adultery. Perhaps Harold had intuited her infidelity, become depressed, and lost the will to live while she was out having fun. In retrospect, she regretted having been unfaithful. At this point, she had totally lost interest in sex and in men. Harriet said relationships with men were just too much work and too much of a headache. She said she was done with men and would just live for her children and grandchildren. Harriet said her girlfriends provided better companionship than men did. She felt that all younger men wanted from women was sex, and once they were over the hill sexually, all they wanted was a nursemaid to take care of them in their old age. Psychotherapy centered on helping Harriet overcome her irrational self-blame for Harold's death and learn to forgive herself for her infidelity.

Harriet seemed quite accepting, even relieved, to live the rest of her life without male companionship, so that did not seem like a problem that needed fixing. From her early to her late 60s, Harriet seemed to have evolved from a very sexual person who desperately needed affirmation of her sexual desirability to an asexual person who became indifferent to such matters. It wasn't clear to what degree her sex drive had suddenly plummeted with advancing age so that her affair was her "last hurrah," to what degree it was a function of irrational guilt in response to her husband's untimely death, and to what degree it was a function of her inability to have stable, emotionally intimate relationships with men.

Harriet had some appreciation that she could be perceived as a difficult person. Her guilt was based on a sneaking suspicion that Harold could tolerate her and still enjoy sex with her while he was young and healthy but that as he became old and ill, Harriet had become too much for him. As a consequence, he withdrew to insulate himself from what were now her excessive needs and demands given his weakening physical condition. Implicitly,

Harriet felt abandoned and responded as anxiously attached individuals with borderline personality characteristics frequently do.

Overcoming irrational self-blame is challenging because patients may feel that the therapist is only providing false reassurance and that their self-blame is indeed rational and reasonable. Patients may cynically feel that it is the therapist's job to make them feel good about themselves and that no therapist is going to say, "You should blame yourself because you were a terrible wife who betrayed your poor husband for no good reason but to flatter your own ego." Sometimes that therapist has to recognize that what seems moralistic to the therapist seems highly moral to the patient. Sometimes forgiving oneself for a relational transgression seems like making a self-justifying excuse rather than accepting the proper punishment, which might mean suffering years if not decades of self-flagellation. Leniency feels unearned and undeserved.

Ruminative worry may arise because unfaithful partners have mixed motives for infidelity, and the long-term consequences of infidelity are sometimes difficult to assess. Harriet felt guilt-ridden about being unfaithful because at some level she felt she should have remained loyal in a sexless marriage to a devoted but seriously ill husband, especially at her age, and that retaliatory infidelity for her husband's sexual withdrawal seemed like a harsh punishment for wounding her pride in her sexual desirability.

Harriet recognized that it was irrational to blame herself for her husband's untimely death. Yet, in retrospect, she was ashamed of her lack of self-control and self-respect in betraying her husband only to have an affair with a narcissistic womanizer who did not care about her as a person. It was difficult to forgive herself for what in retrospect seemed like her emotional immaturity in the face of a devoted husband's serious health problems. Furthermore, she could no longer do anything to make it up to him. Harriet admitted with great shame that during one argument several months before Harold died, she had called him a "worthless piece of shit."

The therapeutic task is to help patients look at their inner conflicts, and the ruminative worries they generate, through a prism that is less moralistic, more mindful, and more accepting (Keng, Smoski, & Robins, 2016). Forgiving oneself for one's own desperate but shameful need for sexual affirmation and for a vindictive response when one's sexual vanity is wounded is difficult when these have inflicted betrayal trauma on someone who, in retrospect, deserved better. Self-forgiveness requires being able to recognize and own the impact on others of the self-protective things one does to cope with narcissistic vulnerability.

Self-forgiveness is easier if there is some sense that, moving forward, one will live less narcissistically and be less of an emotionally toxic influence in the lives of others. It is difficult to feel like a good person when recognizing the negative impact one's narcissistic (devaluing others), Machiavellian (manipulating others), psychopathic (deceiving others), or borderline (unfairly blaming others) personality tendencies have on other people.

CONCLUSION

Self-forgiveness is challenging when it requires learning to accept disappointment in oneself for failing to live up to a monogamous ideal. Some reject the monogamous ideal as oppressive and unrealistic; in so doing, they may avoid feeling bad about their transgressions. This solution may not be viable for those who still believe in the monogamous ideal despite failing to live up to it. This is particularly a problem for affair partners and the betrayed who remain hopelessly attached to someone who won't recommit to monogamy. It may feel too painful to end the relationship with the unfaithful partner, but it may also be difficult to have to forever share that person with a romantic rival. The next chapter explores how self-acceptance is facilitated when one lacks the emotional independence to end a relationship with an unrepentant philanderer, while also being unable to inspire him or her to recommit to monogamy.

8

THE PROBLEM OF BEGRUDGING PARTNER SHARING: WHEN CHEATERS WON'T LEAVE THEIR SPOUSES

Infidelity cannot happen without a permissive environment that activates adulterous desires and diminishes shame and guilt about acting on those desires. A permissive environment is generated by individuals willing to have sexual relationships with people who are in committed relationships. Evolutionary psychologists call such individuals *mate poachers* (Schmitt & Buss, 2001). The term mate poacher for the affair partner may seem to imply a conscious strategic decision to steal someone's partner. From an evolutionary point of view, having affairs with individuals in sexually exclusive relationships can be adaptive whether it is simply appropriating the unfaithful partner's sperm, eggs, or resources through casual sex or by winning the unfaithful partner's enduring love and commitment for a long-term relationship. Whether the affair partner is the active seducer or the passively seduced, looking for just casual sex or lasting love, he or she is knowingly facilitating another person's infidelity by violating the social taboo against sexual relations with individuals in committed relationships.

http://dx.doi.org/10.1037/0000053-009
The Dynamics of Infidelity: Applying Relationship Science to Psychotherapy Practice, by L. Josephs

The affair partner willingly enters a temporary, if not more enduring, arrangement of sharing the unfaithful partner with the betrayed partner. Humans seem not to mind sharing partners for casual sex as much as they mind sharing long-term romantic partners to whom they are attached. Affair partners become vulnerable to romantic jealousy when they become attached to an unfaithful partner who is unwilling to leave the betrayed partner for them. Affair partners may find themselves in a situation of begrudging partner sharing anytime an affair evolves from something casual to something more serious. An affair may start out as "safe" because it's only about casual sex with an emotionally unavailable person, so it seems as though it can't get too complicated. Such affairs become "dangerous" if they somehow turn into something deeper from which it becomes difficult to extricate oneself.

What infidelity beliefs allow affair partners to embroil themselves in complicated love triangles? Affair partners may believe that unfaithful partners are unhappily married people who would be much happier in a second marriage with someone like themselves or that casual sexual variety and experimentation outside of marriage could make the marriage more viable or even better. Those may seem like "good" reasons for mate poaching that mitigate the sense of wrongdoing, of being a partner in crime who facilitates the unfaithful partner's deceit and betrayal. Empathy need not be extended to the potential hurt and humiliation that the betrayed partner might suffer if construed as a "bad" partner (e.g., cold, critical) who is incapable of making the unfaithful partner happy, sexually or otherwise.

Affair partners who fail to win their unfaithful partners for long-term committed relationships may seem as though they have only have themselves to blame if they can't hold on to the loyalty and devotion of a desirable romantic partner who has been successfully seduced into an affair. It may reflect poorly on the mate poacher if the affair partner recommits to the betrayed partner to recover from infidelity. The mate poacher's self-perceived mate value may plummet if it seems as though the failed love relationship with the unfaithful partner was no more than the symptom of a "marital illness" from which the unfaithful partner needed to "recover" with the betrayed partner's help in couples therapy.

What does it say about oneself that one knowingly initiated a relationship with the kind of person who would break promises of sexual exclusivity and lie about it? What if the unfaithful partner is willing to allow the affair to go on indefinitely without ever leaving the betrayed partner? Does a female affair partner allow herself to become the unfaithful partner's permanent hidden mistress although she would prefer that her lover leave his wife and marry her? This clinical situation even has a name, the *single woman–married man syndrome* (Tuch, 2000), although the *single man–married woman syndrome* has become more frequent with the rising prevalence rate of female infidelity (Drigotas, Safstrom, & Gentilia, 1999; Glass & Wright, 1985; Wiederman, 1997).

A reason that many individuals take a pass on opportunities for affairs with individuals in sexually exclusive relationships is not because it is morally wrong but because they don't want to risk embroiling themselves in a love triangle in which they risk becoming "the odd man (or woman) out." Mate poaching appears to be a conditional mating strategy that individuals deploy when they can't seem to win an unattached partner of sufficient attractiveness (mate value) and resort to trying to win an attached partner of acceptable attractiveness despite the potential costs (Davies, Shackelford, & Hass, 2010).

Would-be mate poachers looking for a life partner as opposed to casual sex assume, naively or perhaps grandiosely, that they will prevail in the rivalry for the unfaithful partner's ultimate commitment. Partner sharing as a temporary state on the road to eventually winning a sexually exclusive long-term relationship with a desirable partner is tolerated, whereas partner sharing as a seemingly permanent arrangement can start feeling like always being what Freud (1910/1957b) called "the injured third party" in a love triangle. Partner sharing in a context in which it seems like one is only an unfaithful lover's second favorite sexual partner can feel like a humiliating downgrade to second-class citizenship that is only begrudgingly tolerated. An affair partner begins to feel like the betrayed partner when their lovers are spending weekends, holidays, and vacations with their partners and their children while "the other woman" (or man) is left all by her lonesome and childless, anxiously waiting for their next secret rendezvous. Does one forgo having a family of one's own to be someone's lifelong mistress?

Such individuals may seek psychotherapy when they are too ashamed to share their predicament with friends and family. Friendly confidants may give affair partners advice that they don't want to hear, saying, for example, that the affair is hopeless and should be ended immediately. Friendly confidantes may also acquire empathy fatigue from listening to endless repetition of the same sad story. Affair partners, just like their unfaithful partners, may engage in anguished ruminative thought on whether to end the affair and seek psychotherapy when there is no one else they can turn to for help without feeling judged.

It is not only affair partners who may find themselves begrudgingly tolerating sexual partner sharing while waiting for the unfaithful partner to commit to a monogamous relationship. Betrayed partners often find themselves in the same boat as the affair partner subsequent to exposed infidelity. Couples therapy for recovery from infidelity is based on the premise that the unfaithful partner is ready to recommit to monogamy and has definitively ended the relationship with the affair partner (Baucom, Snyder, & Gordon, 2009). These are the minimum conditions for the restoration of trust. Yet, subsequent to exposure of infidelity, many unfaithful partners remain ambivalent about ending their extramarital affairs or simply refuse to end them.

Tolerating the unfaithful partner's extramarital sex life might be made a condition of the unfaithful partner's remaining committed to the marriage, if not to sexual exclusivity. Betrayed partners must then make a difficult decision when their unfaithful partners are unwilling to recommit to sexual exclusivity. Should they terminate the relationship, patiently wait for their unfaithful partners to eventually come around and recommit to monogamy, or perhaps begrudgingly resign themselves to accommodating the unfaithful partner's extramarital sex life when they have no interest in being in an open marriage?

Tanya was an African woman married to an African businessman who left his second wife in an African country where polygamy was legal when he was in the United States for work. Tanya periodically sought psychotherapy for depression while she was in the United States with her husband. She didn't know why she was depressed because she realized that she lived a fairly privileged, upper-class lifestyle so shouldn't have any reason to complain. Tanya's psychiatrist referred her for psychotherapy when antidepressants proved ineffective, but Tanya had no idea how talking to someone could be helpful. A year after her initial consultation, Tanya came in to happily report that her husband was divorcing his second wife and that her depression had finally lifted.

Begrudging nonconsensual sexual partner sharing can lead to depression. For such depressed individuals, sexual partner sharing is humiliating and feels like an indignity that diminishes their self-respect for tolerating it. To feel so dependent on an unfaithful partner, emotionally or financially, that one must suffer a chronic humiliation gives rise to bitterness and self-hatred. Affair partners and betrayed partners may harshly blame themselves for their poor judgment in having fallen in love with someone who has proven incapable of committing to sexual exclusivity and then hate themselves for being unable to terminate a relationship with such a "selfish" person. It seems more self-respecting to prefer to be alone while holding out for a partner who is capable of the sexual exclusivity one deserves.

Depressed betrayed partners may also be receiving conflicting cultural messages that are confusing. One message is that mature, sophisticated, and sexually progressive individuals should be more accepting of infidelity because it is such a common and relatively minor moral transgression. Such cultural messages are shaming because they make betrayed individuals feel that they might be shamefully immature, insecure, and unsophisticated for wanting to punish an unfaithful and uncommitted partner by terminating the relationship to regain their own self-respect. Sometimes the unsympathetic advice is that betrayed partners should just enjoy multiple partners, as does the partner unwilling to commit to sexual exclusivity. Such advice is unhelpful when such depressed individuals desire a sexually exclusive relationship with their unfaithful life partners. The desire for lifelong sexual exclusivity can be made to seem like a shamefully naive romantic fantasy that should be outgrown on the road to sexual freedom, liberation, and sophistication.

Unfortunately, betrayed partners and frustrated affairs partners can be "damned if they do and damned if they don't." The opposing cultural message is that one should be ashamed of tolerating a relationship with an unfaithful partner who won't commit to monogamy ("break up with the bum"). Women from cultures in which there is a double standard may get a message, sometimes explicitly stated by their mothers, that all men cheat, so one should remain devoted to an unfaithful husband who is a good provider and father. Yet a more individualistic message is that a strong, independent, and self-respecting woman should terminate a relationship with a man who is incapable of sexual exclusivity and hold out for better, even if it means being alone. The therapist must free patients from the grip of these conflicting "shoulds" so they can make up their own minds and reconcile themselves to their ultimate decisions without excessive self-blame because there is no ideal solution to their troubled love lives.

THE SPECIAL ALLURE OF UNFAITHFUL WIVES AND HUSBANDS

Do unfaithful individuals possess some special magnetic attraction that makes would-be mate poachers irresistibly attracted to them and betrayed partners unable to end relationships with them? How is it that they remain "lovable" despite their capacity for deceit and betrayal and apparent incapacity for sexually exclusive loyalty and devotion? As the song goes, "If loving you is wrong, I don't want to be right." What accounts for the tenacity of strong attachments to disloyal partners who are frustrating an equally deep need for a sexually exclusive partner?

One of the benefits of mate poaching for both sexes is the ego boost that comes from the challenge of winning a desirable person who is already in a committed relationship despite the risks (Davies et al., 2010). Poaching a committed individual for casual sex is not as big a challenge or ego boost as winning that person for a long-term sexually exclusive commitment. There may be reticence to give up relationships with "commitment-phobic" individuals to whom one has become attached, be they married or single, and suffer the ego deflation of being unable to win and maintain that person's exclusive commitment.

In economic decisions, humans appear to be more motivated by "loss aversion" than "risk aversion" (Tversky & Kahneman, 1981). It may be the same when it comes to mate poaching. Individuals may be willing to engage in mate poaching despite the risks because there are feelings of elation and triumph in being able to succeed in doing something risky without paying the cost. That is similar to how people become addicted to gambling. A mate poacher's willingness to assume risk may be associated with an aversion to cutting their losses as it becomes apparent that the gamble is not going to pay off. Unfortunately, the greater the emotional attachment to a risky bet, the greater the loss aversion (Ariely, Huber, & Wertenbroch, 2005). Unavailability appears to be an incentive to keeping one's options open because there is loss aversion to missing out on what may be a golden opportunity (Shin & Ariely, 2004). The emotionally unavailable romantic partner may be perceived as a once-in-a-lifetime opportunity that one doesn't want to miss, despite the accumulating costs. Such individuals may then seek psychotherapy, hoping to find some way to snatch victory from the jaws of defeat and solicit the therapist's assistance in winning what looks like a losing battle. The therapist might privately think "good riddance" because the affair partner doesn't seem like such a desirable catch. Yet the patient finds the thought of losing such a desirable but uncommitted partner intolerable. Why would somebody become so invested in winning an untrustworthy long-term partner when dishonesty and untrustworthiness are generally considered undesirable traits in a long-term partner (Fletcher, Simpson, Thomas, & Giles, 1999)?

THE PORNOGRAPHIC IMAGINATION AND INFIDELITY

There is a genre of male pornography called *MILF* (i.e., mothers I'd like to f–k) that is frequently sought in online searches (Ogas & Gaddam, 2011). "Mom" is the single most popular search term users enter into the PornHub search engine. Clearly, men have a thing for married women, even mothers and middle-aged women. Ogas and Gaddam (2011) found that in sexual searches on dogpile, "teen" and "young" were first and second but "mom" and "MILF" came in third and fourth. Is this simply a reflection of men's Freudian Oedipus complex—the unconscious desire to have sex with their mothers? Regardless of the answer to that question, it would appear that although men generally prefer to fantasize about sexual partners who are young and unattached, they also appear to be more than happy to fantasize about sexual partners who are middle-aged and attached.

Men may view married women as desirable partners for casual sex because there may be an assumption that the sex will come without any expectations of further emotional commitment because that person is already in a committed relationship with someone else. Avoidantly attached men may be especially attracted to such "no strings attached" relationships that provide an opportunity to split lust from love and have a purely sexual relationship without any deeper emotional involvement. Similarly, women, especially those who are avoidantly attached, may also see affairs with married people as sexual opportunities without the complications of sex with someone looking for an emotional commitment. In that sense, married individuals seem like "safe" sexual partners—partners with whom one can have a casual sexual relationship uncomplicated by emotional entanglements.

The underlying evolutionary logic of such preferences is that men can inseminate maternal types who could be good mothers even without paternal support, and women can obtain the "good" genes of mature men who possess a proven track record of accomplishment. Marriage is an advertisement of mate value. Single women expressed more romantic interest in a picture of the same man when told that he was attached rather than unattached (Parker & Burkley, 2009). Winning the commitment of a desirable partner tells the entire world that one is worthy of that partner. Marriage is like a character reference. Family is also an advertisement of mate value that one is fertile and possesses the resources to raise a family. The number and quality of one's children also becomes a character reference that advertises the quality of one's parenting abilities. In contrast, younger and single individuals are unknown qualities whose mate value is yet to be proven. For these underlying reasons, forbidden fruit may taste sweeter because affairs with married people reflect reproductive opportunities with individuals of demonstrated mate value. Why not have an affair with a married person if unattached individuals of equivalent mate value are not obtainable (Davies et al., 2010)?

Mate poaching can also constitute a conditional mating strategy for acquiring a long-term partner as well as recruiting partners for casual sexual relationships. Desirable individuals in committed relationships can always be implicitly looking to "trade up" and might be willing to defect from a committed relationship if the "upgrade" appears to be worth the potential risks and costs. Individuals in "bad" relationships that are not "good enough" (e.g., abusive relationships, empty and superficial relationships lacking intimacy, relationships with irresponsible individuals that are not reciprocal) may use infidelity as a means of getting out of a "bad" relationship and into a genuinely "good-enough" relationship.

Married people may use affairs as a means of replacing their current partner with a better one. Women may do this more so than men because the anxiously attached are more likely unfaithful in an attempt to find the intimacy that is lacking in their current relationship (Allen & Baucom, 2004) and because women tend to be more anxiously attached than men (Del Giudice, 2011). Mate poachers may not want to pass up the opportunity to win a desirable long-term partner despite the costs of mate poaching if the available single alternatives are not as desirable as the married individuals.

The question that arises in psychotherapy is whether, in a particular relationship, mate poaching for the purpose of winning a desirable long-term partner is a long shot or a sure thing. The mate poacher is unsure of the reliability of his own judgment and intuition. Has he correctly perceived that the unfaithful partner is genuinely motivated to leave her marriage, is committed to him, is a compatible long-term partner, and will not be a source of "buyer's remorse?" Or is his judgment clouded by wishful thinking? Will he eventually discover that the unfaithful partner will recommit to her betrayed partner, will eventually leave the marriage but want to date other people, or will prove to be an incompatible life partner in a second marriage that might even go on to be unfaithful to him? Helping patients distinguish fantasy based on wishful thinking from realistic assessment of painful realities has always been a difficult task of psychotherapy. How does one assist a patient with their reality testing in such a situation when patients are intensely curious about what the therapist "really" thinks?

The traditional Freudian psychoanalyst has a standard approach to analyzing such doubts about the wisdom of one's own judgment and the desire for a therapist who will share her superior judgment and reality testing: Remain neutral and poker-faced to avoid imposing one's own biases on the patient to show respect for the patient's autonomous decision-making. The problem with this approach is that the therapist's unconscious biases are likely to slip out nonetheless. Research in the psychology of emotions has suggested that when an emotion is activated, it is likely to be automatically expressed in a person's facial expressions and tone of voice before he or she becomes consciously aware of the emotion and then tries to inhibit its open expression (Oatley, Keltner, & Jenkins, 2006).

More contemporary psychodynamic approaches such as mentalization-based therapy (Bateman & Fonagy, 2004) and brief relational therapy (Safran & Muran, 2003) allow therapist self-disclosure. Therapists may as well acknowledge their biases and try to clarify why they think the way they do if their biases will be unconsciously communicated despite their best efforts to contain the open expression of countertransferential reactions. Therapist self-disclosure (therapists' underlying thoughts, feelings, and attitudes rather than biographical information about the therapist's private life) may facilitate patients in becoming more reflective about the therapist's mind rather than just viewing his or her mental state in ways that are egocentric and are projections of patients' own repudiated self-doubts (e.g., the therapist is a moralistic authority figure that disapproves of mate poaching, the therapist assumes the patient is only imagining that the unfaithful partner genuinely intends to leave the betrayed partner for the affair partner, the therapist assumes that the unfaithful partner is not a good candidate for a long-term relationship become the unfaithful partner would most likely be unfaithful to the patient down the road).

Patients who ruminate about such issues may assume that therapists think in dichotomous either–or ways and so might be able to come up with one correct answer that will enable a patient to decide which side of her inner conflict is correct. Therapist self-disclosure can be helpful when it role models a way of transcending dichotomous thinking by seeing the merits as well as the limitations of opposing points of view. It is the adoption of such a metaperspective that facilitates reflective thought, better affect regulation, and ultimately more adaptive decision making (Fonagy, Gergely, Jurist, & Target, 2002).

In the case of mate poaching: Yes, the therapist thinks stealing someone else's romantic partner and facilitating that person's deceitfulness is wrong, and it is better to go out and find a desirable single partner. That doesn't mean that the therapist is unappreciative of the fact that mate poaching can result in ego-affirming casual sexual experiences and sometimes lead to a successful long-term relationship that in retrospect will seem worth the costs. Sometimes poaching another's mate while being trapped in an abusive relationship becomes a means of extricating oneself. An affair with a married individual while in an abusive relationship might affirm one's self-worth and right to better treatment with someone who seems safe by virtue of not expecting too much. Just because the therapist thinks something is morally wrong doesn't mean his morality is universally valid or that he is a moralistic person who will respond with anger, contempt, and disgust (i.e., moralistically) to violations of his moral values. Or just because a therapist thinks mate poaching is wrong doesn't mean that he thinks mate poaching is a major moral transgression on the same level as murder or child abuse.

Ruminative thought tends to set up false dichotomies. The patient implicitly tries to get the therapist to accept the terms of a false dichotomy. The therapist's job is to recognize the false dichotomy and extricate herself from thinking in those terms by disclosing the metaperspective through which she attempts to transcend dichotomous thinking. The therapist can acknowledge lapsing into dichotomous thinking under stress just as the patient does but then use the search for a synthetic metaperspective as a tool for putting things in broader perspective when things seem confusing and overwhelming. Therapists who self-disclose their thought processes have to clarify that they are sharing a subjective point of view that could be wrong, rather than an objective and omniscient point of view. Therapists can acknowledge that sometimes they possess great conviction in their own points of view, but that doesn't necessarily mean they are right every time they possess a sense of certitude or wrong every time they express a tentative opinion. It can be difficult for ruminative patients to accept a therapist's realistic limitation because they may seek an omniscient authority figure to tell them what to do that uncomfortably coexists with a dread of being misled by bad advice.

Morgan sought psychotherapy subsequent to falling in love with her married professor, Zach, with whom she was having a passionate affair. Zach remained ambivalent about leaving an unhappy marriage to marry to start a family with Morgan. Morgan felt tortured. On the one hand, she deeply felt that there was a special romantic chemistry with Zach that he didn't have with his wife. She felt she could make Zach much happier than his wife could. Morgan reported feeling puzzled and frustrated by what she was doing wrong to successfully free Zach from his unhappy marriage. She thought I might have some sound advice about what she should do. Perhaps she should have Zach see me for either individual or couples therapy with her to help him work through his ambivalence about leaving his wife.

On the other hand, Morgan worried that she might be living in a "fool's paradise," as many of her friends thought. Maybe married men who have affairs string their partners along for years with false promises when they have no real intention of leaving their betrayed wives. Morgan said it was humiliating to always be the "other woman" in Zach's life when the self-respecting thing would be to end the affair and look for a single man capable of commitment. The issue became especially pressurized for Morgan as a woman in her mid-30s who didn't want to run out her biological clock waiting for Zach to leave his wife. Morgan didn't want to forgo having a family of her own to be Zach's long-term mistress. Zach pleaded with Morgan to give him a little bit more time to make up his mind every time she threatened to break up with him if he didn't leave his wife for her.

Morgan wanted to know what I thought, so I decided to share my honest assessment of her situation. I said that I really didn't know whether Zach would ultimately leave his wife for her. I questioned, though, whether, because he already had two children with his wife, Zach would really be that motivated to start a new family with her given that he was already in his 40s and struggling to support the family he already had on a professor's salary. I also said that as a life partner, he seemed to lack empathy for the fact that he was running out Morgan's biological clock in asking her to always give him more time to figure out his own mind. I said he might in fact love her but that it seemed to me a selfish kind of love in asking her to wait for him when he might not ever leave his wife for her, or if he did, he might not want to have any more children.

As I shared my assessment, Morgan looked shocked and crestfallen. She also had a look of consternation, which implicitly said, "I know what you're saying is true, but it makes me angry because I really don't want to hear it." I didn't interpret the "negative transference" because I thought it best to just let her sit with the "bad news" and see how she assimilated it once it had some time to sink in. Eventually, Morgan broke up with Zach, believing that he was only leading her on. Ironically, a year after Morgan broke up with him, he left his wife with the intention of resuming his relationship with Morgan. At that point, she had no interest in resuming the relationship because she had come to understand that he only thought of himself and what he felt he needed; her needs would always be a secondary priority. She didn't want to spend the rest of her life catering to his narcissistic sense of entitlement.

When patients press therapists to give them advice about what to do, all therapists can give is their estimate of how they think things will "probably" play out. That means that some percentage of the time, therapists will be wrong in their speculation. Morgan did not blame me for being wrong in my estimation of the likelihood that Zach would leave his wife for her because in the end, she agreed with my character assessment and didn't want him back. Other patients, however, may have difficulty assuming responsibility for their own life decisions. They press their therapists to offer advice but then blame them for giving bad advice if they accept it and things don't work out as anticipated. For this reason, many therapists are reluctant to give advice at all. Or the patient doesn't take the therapist's advice, things go poorly as the therapist correctly anticipated, and the patient blames the therapist for not having been more successful in persuading the patient to see the error of his or her ways. Unfortunately, the more narcissistic the patient, the more likely the therapist will be scapegoated for what goes wrong in the patient's love life despite the therapist's best efforts to offer well-informed and thoughtful, although not infallible, guidance when it is solicited.

MACHIAVELLI ON THE MAKE

The personality characteristics of many mate poachers are often not that different from the personality characteristics of many unfaithful individuals. They may be high on Dark Triad traits of narcissism, Machiavellian intelligence, and psychopathy. They have difficulty with mate retention and are more likely to allow themselves to be poached as well (Jonason, Li, & Buss, 2010). Assortative mating has been found for the psychopathic dimension of the Dark Triad (C. V. Smith et al., 2014) so that high Dark Triad individuals may have difficulty holding on to the partners who are most likely to allow themselves to be poached.

Mate poachers appear to be better looking than those who don't poach (Sunderani, Arnocky, & Vaillancourt, 2013) because, after all, they need to be especially desirable to lure a potentially unfaithful partner to engage in infidelity. Research has delineated the tactics and techniques that successful mate poachers use to steal other people's romantic partners (Schmitt & Buss, 2001). Some mate poachers are just shameless flirts who have no inhibitions about flirting with individuals in committed relationships. Other strategies are more devious, such as using platonic friendship as a technique of relationship infiltration (Mogilski & Wade, 2013). Sometimes people become more than just friends over time.

The infidelity researcher Shirley Glass (2002) wrote a classic text in the infidelity field called *Not "Just Friends."* Glass noted that as women started entering the workforce in large numbers with changes in the economy, more people began working in coed work settings. The coed workplace offers ample opportunities for friendships to form with colleagues that may evolve into romantic relationships. Desirable individuals who work in the same profession may seem like ideal romantic partners because they share so much in common. Going to lunch, drinks after work, or out-of-town conferences with attractive colleagues provide a conducive environment not only for team building and collegial relationships to develop but also for emotional intimacy and sexual attraction. Mate poachers can use the professional opportunity to develop collegial friendships with attractive individuals in committed relationships as an opportunity to have an affair with a seducible individual in a committed romantic relationship.

Glass (2002) has an insightful theory about what makes for a healthy relationship and why affairs are ultimately bad for a marriage. In a healthy marriage, according to Glass, the couple has an open, honest, and transparent relationship with each other. They know each other's deepest and darkest secrets and can be trusted with them. Couples can be vulnerable with each other and sensitive to each other's vulnerabilities. The couple leaves a "window" open into each other's souls while keeping a "wall" up with everyone else. The couple protects their privacy and is not an open book to their friends and family. They don't air their dirty laundry in public. They don't necessarily divulge their marital problems or marital sex lives to their friends but instead try to work it out among themselves or with the help of a therapist. What the couple has with each other is special and unique and must be protected from family and friends who might be tempted to become overinvolved in ways that could be destructive to the couple (e.g., encouraging their married friend to have an affair as a solution to a marital problem).

Infidelity reverses where the walls and windows are in a relationship. There is now a wall up between the betrayed partner and the unfaithful partner. The betrayed partner is kept in the dark about the unfaithful partner's secret double life, whereas there is an open window with the affair partner, who may know all about the unfaithful partner's marital problems. The affair may have started when the soon-to-be unfaithful partner began confiding his or her marital problems to the soon-to-be affair partner as though he or she were just a good friend—a sympathetic sounding board or surrogate therapist.

Recovery from an affair requires that windows and walls be reestablished in their proper place. The unfaithful partner must break it off and put up a wall that makes the affair partner the "odd man out." A window of brutal honesty and total transparency must be opened up between the betrayed partner and the unfaithful partner to restore trust. From Glass's (2002) perspective, infidelity can never be part of a healthy relationship because of the walls of emotional distance it creates. A healthy relationship is one in which the couple maintains an open window into each other's private thoughts and feelings. Mate poachers may be shut out and rejected precipitously if the unfaithful partner puts up a wall to begin recovering from infidelity. The mate poacher as a symptom of a marital illness may have to be removed like a cancerous tumor from the unfaithful partner's emotional life.

Psychotherapy with affair partners can be challenging because it can be difficult for them to acknowledge that the implicit game-playing strategy through which they hope to steal the unfaithful partner may backfire in ways that can be quite traumatic. Mate poachers may not only suffer sudden abandonment by the unfaithful partner but sometimes suffer angry and shaming confrontations with the betrayed partner after the affair is exposed and his or her vindictive fury is aimed as much at the mate poacher as the unfaithful partner. Love triangles can sometimes degenerate into three game-playing individuals trying to game the others. Mate poachers might not be open to the possibility that their game-playing strategy may be backfiring, and they may respond defensively and angrily if the therapist raises the disturbing possibility that they may have been played for a fool by the unfaithful partner and sometimes even by the betrayed partner, the archrival, as well.

Marianne came to see me because she had been in an affair with a married man for the past 7 years. She was in her early 30s and had begun to worry that her married lover, Martin, might never leave his wife for her and that time was running out if she hoped to have a family. Martin was a work colleague, and the affair had begun with after-work drinks, during which he would confide to her about his marital unhappiness. After he had vented to a sympathetic ear, they would get drunk and then go to Marianne's apartment to have sex. Martin complained that since having children, his wife was no longer any fun, no longer interested in sex, and had become a fussy person in a way that drove him crazy. To win him away from his wife, Marianne hoped to prove that she could be sympathetic, indulgent, and fun in a way his wife couldn't. Martin was successful, good-looking, charming, and seemed like a good father. It didn't occur to Marianne that he might just be looking for a temporary vacation from the stresses of family life without really intending to leave his wife for her.

Listening to Marianne, it dawned on me that both she and Martin seemed to have serious alcohol problems. Both of them were getting drunk almost daily after work, and they never had sex without being thoroughly intoxicated. The honeymoon phase of an extramarital affair can last quite a long time as they are insulated from the stresses and responsibilities of family life. Such affairs can exist in a little bubble of escapist illusion if such affairs never evolve beyond fun and games and are lubricated with alcohol or drugs. In this case, it did not occur to Marianne that perhaps Martin saw his wife as a sober-minded and responsible person who would conscientiously maintain his home life while he went out to party. His wife was what they call an *enabler* in Alcoholics Anonymous—someone who enables a partner's alcoholism by providing the social support that spares the alcoholic from suffering the negative consequences of his alcohol abuse. Quite possibly, Martin's wife was aware of his drunken affairs but looked the other way on the assumption that they didn't mean anything and wouldn't threaten the marriage if she didn't make a big deal about them.

It did not occur to Marianne that Martin wouldn't leave his wife for a "party girl" with a drinking problem who might be fun in bed but perhaps not as suitable a partner as the mother of his children. Of course, a therapist can't easily share such an assessment without risking insulting the patient and risking premature termination of treatment. Yet without such a painful confrontation, the patient might not appreciate that the game-playing strategy might make her less rather than more desirable as a long-term partner and so is ultimately self-defeating. It might work in attracting a married romantic partner looking for an extramarital sexual outlet but not in winning his long-term commitment.

I did confront Marianne with the possibility that both she and Martin had serious drinking problems. I inquired whether she really wanted to bring such drinking problems into her marriage and future family life. Marianne was open to this confrontation because her father had serious drinking problems while she was growing up that were a source of constant marital conflict. She didn't want her children to suffer what she had. As a consequence, Marianne decided she would abstain from drinking but not end the affair. But Martin didn't enjoy drinking alone, and the sexual aspect of the affair began to decline as Marianne found it less appealing when sober, even feeling it was a bit disgusting to have sex with Martin while he was drunk. As the sexual aspect of the relationship declined, Martin began to lose interest in the affair, and they eventually drifted apart. Marianne realized she wanted to live a sober lifestyle that no longer included drunken affairs with married men.

SEDUCED, BETRAYED, AND BEGRUDGINGLY ACCOMMODATING

Recovery from infidelity can't begin until the unfaithful partner is willing to recommit to monogamy (Baucom et al., 2009); an unwillingness to do so only adds insult to injury. Exposure of the affair constitutes a betrayal trauma (Scuka, 2015). Someone loved and trusted has engaged in deception and violated a promise of sexual exclusivity. The hurt, humiliation, and anger run deep to the point of suffering intrusive flashbacks of the traumatic memory of having learned of the sexual betrayal for the first time and the accompanying disturbing image of one's partner having sex with another person. Those flashbacks reawaken the shock, disbelief, hurt, humiliation, and anger in the full and overwhelming intensity of the initial moment of discovery of the sexual betrayal (Lusterman, 2011). On top of the trauma of sexual betrayal, the unfaithful partner may not be contrite but feels that the extramarital affair was justified by the unhappy marital situation. Although the deceit is regrettable, now that everything is out in the open, the unfaithful partner does not feel that recommitment to monogamy is warranted, although he or she does not necessarily want to break up the marriage. The unfaithful partner may now require a more open marital arrangement as a precondition of remaining in the marriage instead of recommitment to monogamy.

Threats or ultimatums by the betrayed partner to break up the marriage are to no avail. The unfaithful partner is willing to let the betrayed partner walk away from the marriage and won't recommit to monogamy just to hold on to the betrayed partner. Some betrayed partners will begrudgingly accommodate their unfaithful partners' extramarital sex lives if that is the only way of holding on to them. They seek psychotherapy because they don't feel like that is a self-respecting approach to take, they hope they can eventually get the unfaithful partner to recommit to monogamy with the right strategy a therapist might provide, they may hope the therapist will help them find the strength to walk away from a marriage that diminishes their self-respect, or they perhaps find a way to tolerate extramarital partner sharing with some measure of self-acceptance rather than self-hatred even when they have no desire for extramarital lovers for themselves. Such betrayed partners may ruminate about what is the "right" thing to do in this situation as they are trying to recover from their betrayal trauma without any help from their unfaithful spouses, who are adamant in their refusal to recommit to monogamy.

Rebecca was in her early 70s and a grandmother of five when she discovered her husband's extramarital affair with a work colleague. When she confronted him, he acknowledged the affair and said he would immediately end it and recommit to monogamy because he didn't want to lose her. At first Rebecca trusted him, but she continued to have sneaking suspicions that it had all been too easy and perhaps he was lying. Unbeknownst to her husband, she did some snooping by obtaining the password to his e-mail account and started monitoring his e-mails. As it turned out, he hadn't ended the affair, but it appeared to be going poorly. His affair partner had begun to demand that he leave his wife for her and threatened that she might expose the affair to his wife. Her husband was responding evasively in asking for more time to make up his mind. Rebecca was reluctant to confront her husband because she felt that if she didn't make a stink, the affair would eventually end on its own if she played her cards right.

Rebecca came for therapy because after a year of surreptitiously tracking her husband's e-mails, she felt tortured waiting for the affair to end. It seemed like the affair partner was not going to let go without a fight despite her ultimatums and that her husband was not going to end it on his own initiative.

Theirs appeared to be a passionate but tempestuous affair. It seemed her husband did not want to give up his comfortable life with his nondemanding wife or scandalize his children and grandchildren by breaking up the family at this late date. Nor did he want to give up his passionate affair with an emotionally demanding affair partner he apparently had no intention of marrying. Rebecca was hoping her husband would give up the affair as his sex drive waned with age, but his affair partner was doing quite well in keeping her husband sexually interested and enthralled.

In psychotherapy Rebecca said that she could not see herself divorcing her husband at her age and adjusting to being a divorced woman. She assumed she would just live out her life alone if she were to divorce her husband over the affair. She didn't want to burden her two adult daughters, who were overwhelmed working mothers with their own marital difficulties, with worrying about her and providing companionship for a lonely old woman. The sexual aspect of the marriage was no longer that important to her, but her husband's sexual fidelity was. Rebecca's working assumption was that sooner or later the affair would end, and they would live out their lives together in a sexless marriage enjoying their leisure time and grandchildren together. Until that time, she had to find some way of managing her jealousy, humiliation, and obsession with surreptitiously tracking the progression of the affair through her husband's e-mail correspondence with his lover.

Psychotherapy centered on helping Rebecca come to accept her situation, in which there were no good options, and wean herself from her obsession with tracking the affair. She couldn't talk to her friends because they would make her feel like the self-respecting thing would be to divorce her husband because he would just lie once again about recommitting to monogamy and just do a better job of covering his tracks next time. Rebecca wanted to find a way to have self-respect while tolerating sharing him with another woman until the affair ended of its own accord. She had already gone the route of angry confrontation and, feeling it wasn't worth the headache, didn't want to go down that path again. She came to terms with the fact that her husband was going to do what he was going to do and there was nothing she could do to fix him or the situation. Rebecca came to feel that she was making the best of a bad situation and there was no point in blaming herself for not having the kind of married life to which she had always aspired. It was a bitter disappointment but preferable to the alternative of growing old alone and feeling like a burden to her adult daughters.

Knowing that I believed honesty is the best policy, Rebecca needed reassurance that I was not privately judging her decision about how best to manage the situation. I acknowledged that my bias was to opt for honesty but that honesty comes with risks because one never knows for sure if a relationship can survive a moment of truth. I said that I respected her decision to avoid assuming a course of action that felt too risky. I added that I would not want to push her to assume a risky course of action because if it backfired, it would be my fault for having given her bad advice. That response appeared to satisfy Rebecca that I could respect her decision even when we had a significant difference of opinion as to whether honesty was always the best policy.

In giving patients advice about their love lives, therapists need to have some sense of the possible risks involved in implementing the advice and share this with the patient. In an ideal world, one would like to have an open, honest, and authentic relationship with one's life partner. In the real world, some relationships cannot survive the revelation of secret betrayals of trust. Patients may need to mourn the loss of never achieving the kind of open honest, and authentic relationship in which they can expose their vulnerabilities to their life partners and be accepted, warts and all.

Sometimes patients come for psychotherapy because they don't like any of their choices. They postpone making a final decision because each choice comes with a serious downside that they would rather not have to face. They hope the therapist will think of some as-yet-unknown third option that will spare them from having to make a painful choice and learning to live with the consequences. They implicitly make the therapist feel that it is her job to spare them the unhappy consequences of their life choices and that she is incompetent and therapy a waste of time if she can't help them achieve a happy ending in their love lives.

Romantic fantasies tend to be utopian visions of living happily ever after with one's soul mate or of enjoying ecstatic orgasms on a regular basis throughout the lifespan with the most desirable partners, as though casual sex will never begin to feel empty. Sadly, in real life, people often have to make painful compromises or risk ending up with nothing. Perfectionists are vulnerable to ending up with nothing if no one is ever good enough to live up to their high expectations. Those high in narcissism tend to have perfectionistic expectations of self and others (M. M. Smith et al., 2016).

Psychotherapy, then, involves helping patients give up perfectionism in their love lives despite their narcissism. That can be a bitter pill to swallow, as in Rebecca's case, when the final outcome is hardly ideal. Patients must tolerate disillusionment with self and others to mourn the loss of their romantic ideal—be it a monogamous, a polyamorous, or a perennial playboy or playgirl ideal—and learn how to make the best of a bad situation. Envy and feelings of inadequacy can be acute when it seems as though others are succeeding in love where one has failed. Trying to make oneself feel better by becoming cynical about love—thinking that deep down, everyone else is miserable too but hiding it from themselves and others—doesn't help when confronting the painful reality that others do indeed enjoy a more satisfying love life. Self-acceptance is challenging when one's game-playing approach has backfired, difficult personality characteristics make stable romantic relationships near impossible despite good looks and social status, or when a relatively low mate value (e.g., poor looks, social insecurity, and poor financial prospects) severely limits the quality of the partners one can attract and hold on to.

Psychotherapists might be blamed for "making" a patient feel depressed and bad about herself when they confront the denial of these frustrating personal realities. Yet the therapist who avoids such confrontations for fear of bursting the patient's bubble colludes in allowing the patient to live in a "fool's paradise" pursuing a pipe dream while self-defeatingly passing up opportunities for pursuing what is realistically attainable. Of course, what is and isn't realistically attainable is not without ambiguity. A therapist might not want to be accused of "underselling" what the patient might realistically achieve and pressuring them to settle, if the patient perceives that the proper encouragement and guidance from the therapist might be what they need to actualize their potential and realize their dreams.

Therapists might be reticent to confront patients' defensive cynicism as well as their romantic perfectionism. Those two traits often coexist, leading patients to feel that if they can't make their romantic dreams come true, they won't believe in romantic dreams at all (dichotomous thinking). The therapist who confronts patients' cynicism could be shamed for being Pollyannaish and unsophisticated if he still naively believes in "love." Patients don't want to be told that they can't have it all, yet if they end up with nothing, they don't want to be made to feel that they should have "settled," because the stable love lives of the "settlers" are boring and fake.

CONCLUSION

Acceptance of oneself and one's life partner is particularly difficult for betrayed partners to achieve when the unfaithful partner has difficulty recommitting to monogamy, and this is especially the case when an unfaithful partner suffers from a sexual addiction. The next chapter explores the challenges of treating infidelity when it is a symptom of sexual addiction.

9

BOYS GONE WILD: CAN INFIDELITY BE A SYMPTOM OF SEX ADDICTION?

What if one discovers, to her shock and disappointment, that she has fallen in love with a sex addict, and recommitment to monogamy requires overcoming a sexual addiction? A significant percentage of male infidelity is not about work friendships turning romantic but about paying for impersonal sexual gratification. Sometimes the male quest for impersonal sexual gratification becomes compulsive and can qualify as a sexual addiction. To understand men's sexual addictions it is first necessary to understand the role that casual sex plays in men's sexual psychology.

Prostitution may be one of the world's oldest professions (Bullough & Bullough, 1978). Exchanging sex for resources may go deep into our evolutionary history. The primatologist Franz de Waal observed a female chimpanzee presenting herself for sex while taking food from the hand of her male consort (de Waal, 2007). Chimpanzees, unlike humans, generally don't share their food with each other. The male chimpanzee appears to have felt that exchanging food for sex was a reasonable exchange. Males' pressing desire for sexual variety

http://dx.doi.org/10.1037/0000053-010
The Dynamics of Infidelity: Applying Relationship Science to Psychotherapy Practice, by L. Josephs

and novelty appears to drive their willingness to exchange resources for casual sex (Baumeister, Catanese, & Vohs, 2001).

Most men would prefer to obtain free casual sex offered by willing and desirable partners. For many men, this is a scarce resource because women on average prefer to have sex within the context of an ongoing relationship that possesses some level of emotional intimacy and commitment. Most gender differences in sexual attitudes and behaviors are small, but exceptions to this include frequency of masturbation, pornography use, and casual sex and attitudes toward casual sex, for which there are medium effect sizes (Petersen & Hyde, 2010). These findings are consistent with the evolutionary idea that men on average are more oriented toward short-term mating strategies than are women (Schmitt et al., 2012) and that men appear to have the stronger sex drive with greater need for sexual variety as well as willingness to pay for sex (Baumeister et al., 2001).

Successful womanizers may be able to obtain casual sex for free on a regular basis, but many men aren't sufficiently skilled in the arts of seduction, attractive enough, or of high enough status to attract desirable women for casual sex as, for example, some male college athletes can regularly do (E. Anderson, 2012). Men who were successful pickup artists in their youth can start to look like "dirty old men" as they age (Walz, 2002) if they are still trying to pick up much younger women in middle-age or beyond. Men who can't obtain casual sex for free might have to resort to paying for casual sex to gratify their desire for sexual variety and novelty rather than learn to make do without. Individual difference variables that predict greater interest in casual sex, such as insecure attachment and narcissism, may distinguish the men who are more likely to pay for casual sex. For example, there appears to be a *psychopathic sexuality* associated with a propensity to fantasize and act out sexual themes that are more anonymous, uncommitted, and nonromantic (Visser, DeBow, Pozzebon, Bogaert, & Book, 2015).

Since the arrival of the Internet, men have had greater opportunities to gratify their desire for sexual variety and novelty because online pornography provides free or affordable ways to feed sexual fantasies (Paul, 2005). Narcissism is associated with more frequent pornography use (Kasper, Short, & Milam, 2015), and passionate attachment to pornography is associated with sexual compulsivity (Rosenberg & Kraus, 2014). Married men are also using the Internet as a means of recruiting affair partners (Dew, Brubaker, & Hays, 2006). Men with more disposable income can take sex vacations in exotic places where they need not worry about getting arrested for engaging in what would be illegal behavior in their own country (Hesse & Tutenges, 2011). Those with moderate levels of disposable income can obtain lap dances at strip clubs or massages with "happy endings" with little risk of getting themselves into legal trouble. It may be expected that young men who work in finance on Wall Street, for example, go to strip clubs for lap dances or hire strippers for private parties because such practices become part of business networking and brokering deals (Jeffreys, 2010).

Sexual education for boys entering puberty is not necessarily from parents or schools (Hyde et al., 2010) or even from friends and *Playboy* magazine, as it may have been for the baby boom generation. The sexual education of young boys may often be through online pornography that allows pubescent boys to feed their masturbatory fantasies and acquire "sexual scripts" that shape their sexual preferences (Sun, Bridges, Johnson, & Ezzell, 2016). The desire for sexual variety and novelty, as well as the sexual curiosity of the uninitiated, can be gratified through Internet pornography without having to learn how to negotiate such issues with a real person. Male sexuality can be strongly activated by visual cues that induce impatience for immediate gratification (Kim & Zauberman, 2013). Indulging in Internet pornography may therefore serve as an effective simulation of and reliable substitute for sexual relations with a real person. Some men may come to prefer pornography to a real sexual relationship if the partners with whom they can actually have sex are not as attractive as porn actresses or are not interested in engaging in "kinky" sexual practices (Paul, 2005).

Some men in committed relationships may see pornography use as commendable because it's not infidelity with an actual person. Many women assume that most men use pornography, but those women are not without ambivalence about this fact of life. Paul (2005) found that women often do experience male pornography use as a kind of infidelity. They may feel unfavorably compared with the actresses in pornography and feel rejected in a humiliating way if it becomes apparent that their romantic partners prefer watching pornography to having sex with them.

Paying for sex while single might not be a problem for long-term monogamous relationships if young men did this only while they were single and "sowing their wild oats." The hope is that young men who spend their youth playing the field and engaging in sexual experimentation will get the desire for casual sex, sexual variety, and sexual novelty out of their systems by the time they are ready to embark on long-term committed relationships and start a family. Yet it is not entirely clear to what extent indulging those desires fulfills a developmental need that can then be outgrown and to what extent indulging those fantasies creates a dependency in which masculine self-esteem and emotion regulation become dependent on regularly actualizing such fantasies.

Some men assume that they will just surreptitiously continue their casual sex lives on the side without mentioning it to their future girlfriends or wives. They know their girlfriends and wives wouldn't approve. Yet their infidelity beliefs rest on the assumption that their private casual sex life is really none of their partner's business and that because it's only impersonal casual sex for tension relief, it doesn't really mean anything and is not an actual threat to the long-term relationship. In their minds, it doesn't constitute infidelity. Their definition of infidelity is restricted to falling in love with another woman with whom they would also have a sexual relationship.

Such men assume that there's no point debating the issue with their partners and getting into an argument. It's best to let sleeping dogs lie and keep one's casual extramarital sex life to oneself. Many men have maintained an extremely active but secret masturbatory sex life facilitated by pornography since puberty, and many started going to strip clubs and paying for sex once they had a job and disposable income to pay for sexual services. Living a secret double sex life comes almost naturally once one starts to date and engage in what is officially a sexually exclusive long-term relationship. It comes as a shock to most women to discover a treasure trove of pornography on their partners' personal computers or to see the credit card debt incurred by going to massage parlors for sexual relief. Discovering men's hidden pornography use appears to threaten women's attachment security in the relationship (Zitzman & Butler, 2009). Not surprisingly, men who are high on the negative personality traits that characterize the Dark Triad are more likely to engage in deception, dishonesty, and lying about their sexual behavior (Baughman, Jonason, Lyons, & Vernon, 2014). Trust will be an issue when anxiously attached women find themselves in relationships with men high on the Dark Triad who maintain an active but secret casual sex life.

OCCASIONAL SLIP-UP OR COMPULSIVE HABIT?

It is always a shock to the system to discover that one's romantic partner has a secret sex life. Exposure of infidelity may begin with what seems to be a single isolated instance of paying for casual sex. The unfaithful partner may quickly apologize, claim that this one instance was a single, isolated case rather than a habitual pattern, was meaningless and not particularly gratifying, and promise to never do it again. The unfaithful partner's hope and expectation is to be forgiven for one regrettable mistake. The betrayed partner may be treated as though he or she is overreacting and unduly moralistic if expressing hurt and anger about what the unfaithful partner believes is only meaningless casual sex.

The betrayed partner naturally worries about what else the unfaithful partner might be hiding. A betrayed woman then has to make a difficult assessment: Is her romantic partner lying or telling the truth? The unfaithful partner has already been caught in a lie, so why should she assume he is telling the truth now that he has been caught red-handed? Maybe he is just engaging in a cover-up in the hope that the full extent of his indiscretions will not be discovered.

What if the exposed instance is not isolated but part of a habitual pattern that may reflect a sexual compulsion or addiction that has gotten out of control? The unfaithful partner may be lying not only to his betrayed partner but also to himself as to the true nature of his extramarital sex life.

Recovery from infidelity requires restoration of trust. It is much easier to trust an unfaithful partner who engaged in one regrettable indiscretion when drunk than an unfaithful partner who has been covering up for years a secret sex life that has become habitual. Such men may hide their secret sex lives from the therapist as well, seeking treatment for help with the emotional fallout of being caught without ever having to expose their extramarital casual sex lives to the therapist, or at least not to its full extent. They assume the therapist wouldn't approve and would try to get them to stop, so it seems best not to tell the therapist, just as they wouldn't tell their wives or girlfriends.

Stan had been seeing me for psychotherapy every other week because he couldn't afford weekly sessions. He was unhappy in his marriage to Fran. They were in a voluntarily childless marriage in which they never had sex and barely spoke to each other. They were more like roommates than married partners. He didn't know what to do about it because it was a comfortable situation, and he didn't think he could do much better than Fran. In addition, Stan was frustrated in his career as an accountant, which never really took off. He said he couldn't even afford a divorce because he would suffer downward mobility without pooling his income with Fran, who was a somewhat successful real estate agent. Stan sought psychotherapy because he was depressed about his life situation and was hoping I would have some practical advice about how to go about fixing it.

After 6 months of treatment, Stan came in and told me that he had to be completely honest with me. He confided that the reason he couldn't afford weekly sessions is that twice a month, he went for massages with happy endings. It was an expensive habit because he went to a high-end place in which all the women were college graduates who were quite good-looking. Stan dryly noted that as a not particularly attractive, balding, middle-aged overweight man who was not that financially successful, there was no way he could have a sexual encounter with a young, attractive woman without having to pay for it.

Stan noted that the only time he was happy and felt temporary relief from his lifelong chronic depression was when receiving a massage with a happy ending from a beautiful and intelligent young woman. Stan claimed that a massage with a happy ending was money well spent because it was a better antidepressant than weekly psychotherapy and Prozac combined. It was basically the only thing he had to look forward to in his life. Stan said that if Fran ever caught him and demanded that he stop, he would rather end the marriage than give up his extramarital sex life. He didn't think it would come to that because he believed his wife would just continue to look the other way.

Such cases challenge a therapist to think through what is a healthful or an unhealthful expression of human sexuality and try to transcend dichotomous either–or thinking on the topic. In Stan's case, there were certainly financial repercussions of his extramarital sex life, as he was spending a significant amount of money for something he could not easily afford. In an ideal world, Stan could improve his marital intimacy and sex life and make better progress on his lifelong treatment-resistant depression. In the real world, he may have found a kind of maintenance therapy that stabilized both his mood and his marriage. Stan accepted his situation, but he was reluctant to openly share his coping strategy because he assumed I wouldn't approve. Only after building up trust in my nonjudgmental and accepting attitude toward his life situation did he feel comfortable being truthful with me because he knew I would have preferred he attend weekly sessions.

There is always a side of the patient that would like to be honest and have the kind of trustworthy and intimate relationships that only honest self-disclosure of emotional vulnerabilities can create. Being honest and openly vulnerable with the therapist is at least a step in the right direction. That doesn't always translate into being more open, honest, and vulnerable with the betrayed partner, however. Sometimes therapists are the only people with whom such individuals feel sufficiently safe to be emotionally intimate, and hence they may use psychotherapy to get their intimacy needs met in a limited way. The therapist then becomes the one person with whom they can be themselves. Is the therapist then an "enabler" of a self-defeating pattern that makes that habitual pattern more sustainable by mitigating its negative consequences? Or perhaps the therapist is providing the necessary emotional support that will enable the patient to one day find the courage to live a life that is more honest and authentic? Perhaps only time will tell, as psychotherapy outcome research has yet to investigate such issues.

I CAN'T HELP MYSELF: THE PSYCHOLOGY OF SEXUAL ADDICTION

How much sex is too much sex? Many young men masturbate daily or every other day. When does masturbation become compulsive: twice a day, three times a day, or more? Many people would think that a monogamous couple that had sex daily were having a great sex life but that someone who had casual sex daily with a different person each day was pathologically promiscuous. It is difficult to establish clear lines in the sand between healthy sexuality and compulsive sexuality; it's also difficult to know when labeling a sexual behavior as pathological is just a rationalization for an oppressive, moralizing attitude. Such distinctions are important if a couple hopes to recover from infidelity and the unfaithful partner is promising to recommit to sexual exclusivity. The unfaithful partner's ability to honor his commitment to whatever sexual ground rules have been agreed on is dependent on his ability to curb the impulse to break those ground rules and then lie about it.

Individuals with weak self-control may have difficulty sticking with a diet or abstaining from alcohol. Similarly, individuals who are trying to recommit to sexual exclusivity might have difficulty honoring that commitment in the face of temptations to break the sex rules despite their best intentions. Restoring trust after exposed sexual betrayal requires that the betrayed partner trusts that the unfaithful partner possesses self-control to restrain himself or herself from future unfaithful behavior in the face of serious temptation. It's not enough to trust in the unfaithful partner's good intentions; there must be trust in the partner's capacity to execute those good intentions.

Is sex addiction a real condition, or is it only a moralistic judgment made by sexually conservative individuals who disapprove of an extremely active casual sex life? From the point of view of infidelity, the issue is not whether a need to engage in a high frequency of casual sex with multiple partners is morally bad or addictive. The issue is whether a partner is willing and capable of sacrificing the gratification of that desire for the sake of a long-term relationship with a person who desires an honest and genuinely monogamous partner who can abide by the mutually agreed-on sex rules. Unfaithful partners are always free to end a relationship to conduct their sex lives without being under the surveillance of a sexually restrictive and disapproving partner or to find a new long-term partner who shares a less restrictive attitude toward extramarital sexual activities.

As the price of continuing a relationship, betrayed partners may require their unfaithful partners to relinquish a habit they might not possess the self-control to stop. It's one thing to remain loyal to an alcoholic spouse who is trying to recover from alcoholism and sticking with her through multiple relapses until she achieves a stable, longer term abstinence. It's another thing to remain loyal to a sexually addicted spouse through multiple relapses because each relapse into sex addiction also constitutes an act of sexual betrayal.

In recovery from infidelity, many unfaithful partners who struggle with their compulsive sexuality do want to recommit to monogamy. When push comes to shove, for many people, it seems more important to save the marriage than to maintain an extramarital sex life that seems out of control. Such individuals may find that it is easier said than done to recommit to monogamy because having an extramarital sex life has become such an entrenched habit over the years. Behavior begins to seem compulsive or addictive when people try to refrain from excessive eating, drinking, drugs, or sex but then discover that they don't have the willpower to stick to their resolve. They fall back into old habits they can't seem to break and then cover them up out of shame at their lack of self-control.

Sex addiction is not yet an official psychiatric diagnosis, but there is increasing recognition that sexual behavior can become compulsive (Tepper, Owens, Coleman, & Carnes, 2007). Various definitions of sexual addiction, or what has also been called *compulsive* or *hypersexual* behavior, have been offered. In fact, the problem was recognized by the medical community back in the 19th century. In his 1812 book *Medical Inquiries and Observations Upon the Diseases of the Mind*, Benjamin Rush described a case of a man whose "excessive" sexual appetite caused him psychological distress to the point of requesting that he be medically rendered impotent (Rush, 1812). In 1886, the famous sexologist von Krafft-Ebing made a case that pathological sexuality is indeed a real psychiatric illness (von Krafft-Ebing, 1886/1965). Orford (1978) proposed that hypersexuality should be considered an addictive disorder. Clinicians agree that individuals who are distressed by sexuality that seems out of control should get help. Yet those same clinicians disagree as to whether such sexual behavior is better conceptualized as a genuine addiction or a compulsion (Tepper et al., 2007). For some practitioners, whether a problematic behavior is labeled an addiction or a compulsion may seem like a distinction without a difference because it's not clear that the treatment approach would be any different depending on the label.

Many years ago, a patient of mine who went to self-help groups for sex and love addicts told me that P. J. Carnes (1991) had written the bible for sexual addiction, *Don't Call It Love: Recovery From Sexual Addiction*. Carnes was one of the first clinicians to apply the 12-step approach to recovery from sexual addiction. Carnes provided the following definition of sexual addiction:

> 1. a pattern of out-of-control behavior;
> 2. severe consequences due to sexual behavior;
> 3. inability to stop despite adverse consequences;
> 4. persistent pursuit of self-destructive or high-risk behavior;
> 5. ongoing desire or effort to limit sexual behavior;
> 6. sexual obsession and fantasy as a primary coping strategy;
> 7. increasing amounts of sexual experience because the current level of activity is no longer sufficient;
> 8. severe mood changes around sexual activity;
> 9. inordinate amounts of time spent in obtaining sex, being sexual, or recovering from sexual experiences; and
> 10. neglect of important social, occupational, or recreational activities because of sexual behavior. (pp. 11–12)

Addictions as well as other psychopathologies have been conceptualized as expressions of maladaptive emotion-regulation strategies such as rumination, avoidance, and suppression (Aldao, Nolen-Hoeksema, & Schweizer, 2010). Risky sexual behavior has been associated with problems of emotional regulation (Tull, Weiss, Adams, & Gratz, 2012). Sex addiction may be a maladaptive emotion-regulation strategy. Dealing with stress, depression, anxiety, and anger is part of life for everybody. The more chronic stress one experiences or the more trauma one has been subjected to, the more depression, anxiety, and anger one will have to learn how to manage. When the stresses and strains of life seem overwhelming, it is only natural to look for a quick fix. Anything that makes one feel good in the moment (i.e., immediate gratification) provides a temporary fix for one's troubles. Thus, alcohol, drugs, food, and sex possess the potential to become forms of self-medication that produces an immediate result by generating a transient state of euphoria, comfort, or relaxation that provides a temporary escape from overwhelming depression, anxiety, and anger.

Growing dependence on alcohol, drugs, food, or sex for emotion regulation makes it extremely difficult to give up these regulatory behaviors without making oneself vulnerable to reexperiencing overwhelming levels of anxiety, depression, and anger. Dependence on maladaptive emotion-regulation strategies for immediate stress relief prevents the acquisition of more adaptive stress management strategies, such as learning to manage one's feelings by stepping back and putting them in broader perspective (i.e., cognitive reappraisal), reaching out to others for social support, learning different relaxation techniques, sticking to a healthy diet and exercise routine, or finding spiritual values that inspire one to endure in difficult circumstances by learning to mindfully tolerate and accept painful emotions. Unfortunately, the more adaptive strategies are coping skills that one must work at acquiring and take time to develop. In addition, they don't generate intense immediate states of euphoria or contentment. Adaptive coping skills contribute to a more peaceful state of mind by dialing down (i.e., down-regulating) the troubling emotion to a more manageable level. Adaptive coping skills do not entirely turn off anxiety, depression, and anger but simply lower the intensity of the emotion.

In contrast, addictive behaviors actively turn on the pleasure centers in the brain and so for the moment do effectively turn off depression, anxiety, and anger like a light switch and replace it with a temporary state of bliss. It's hard for individuals who are feeling overwhelmed by their emotions and hoping for immediate relief not to take the path of least resistance. Nevertheless, what makes such emotion-regulation strategies maladaptive is that they are associated with negative long-term consequences, such as impairments in occupational and social functioning, as well as physical diseases such as lung cancer, diabetes, and sexually transmitted diseases. Adaptive emotion-regulation strategies contribute to successful occupational and social functioning and lifestyles more conducive to physical and mental health.

The ecstasy generated by sexual gratification or romantic infatuation is difficult to surpass in intensity. The bliss generated by sexual gratification and romantic love provides an extremely effective although transient antidepressant. Men's strong sex drive makes them more vulnerable than women to becoming dependent on sexual gratification as a maladaptive form of emotion regulation. This can begin in adolescence with compulsive masturbation as a kind of self-soothing for a depressed or anxious adolescent boy. I have had patients who dealt with their adolescent loneliness and low self-esteem by masturbating up to five times a day, 7 days a week, while looking at pornography and sometimes high on marijuana. When they grow up and try to enter mature, long-term relationships, it may not be easy for them to adjust to having sex only several times a week with their girlfriends. Sexual addiction also dramatically increases the problem of habituation that is present in all long-term sexual relationships so that sex addicts are more predisposed to lose interest in having sex with their long-term partners.

Women tend to score higher on measures of disgust than do men on average (Skolnick, Bascom, & Wilson, 2013). Certainly, men are also prone to disgust reactions upon discovery of a female partner's infidelity and might think she is a "slut." Discovery of the full extent of a partner's immersion in various forms of impersonal casual sex is not only shocking but often disgusting as well. The betrayed partner's disgust shames the unfaithful partner for their "perverted" sexuality. Shame appears to be related to self-disgust, as self-directed disgust shames the self (Terrizzi, 2014). Disgust aroused as a consequence of violations of sexual morality appears closely associated with judgments of abnormality (Giner-Sorolla, Bosson, Caswell, & Hettinger, 2012). Disclosure of sex addiction is risky because half of partners subsequently threaten to leave a relationship and a quarter actually do leave (Corley, Schneider, & Hook, 2012).

Recovery from sexual addiction becomes more challenging if the unfaithful partner feels shamed for his extramarital sexuality and is therefore more likely to minimize and cover up his impaired self-control. By the same token, women who are disgusted by their partners' extramarital sexuality shouldn't be shamed for their sexual aversions either. They trusted their partners' apparent commitment to sexual exclusivity. They may well have taken a pass if they had known the full extent of their partners' pornography use or casual sex life when they first started to become emotionally involved with their sexually addicted partners. Thus, sex addicts may have obtained their partners on the basis of false pretenses by pretending to be more monogamous than they actually were and currently are.

The question moving forward is if a betrayed partner remains willing to commit to working with an unfaithful partner whose infidelity was an outgrowth of his sex addiction. If so, the betrayed wife or partner has to work on overcoming her moral disgust with her unfaithful partner's sexuality to see the addiction as an illness requiring treatment. The question is then one of how committed the unfaithful partner is to recovering from sex addiction, and, if committed, what is the unfaithful partner's capacity to achieve a stable recovery. Relapse rates of 50% have been reported for sex addicts who disclosed their sex addiction and then had to make decisions about whether to report relapsing (Corley et al., 2012). Is the betrayed partner willing to deal with the possibility of relapse because an expectation of long-term abstinence without relapse is not always realistic? The betrayed partner would have to live with uncertainty about how successful the unfaithful partner's recovery will be and how long it will take to get there.

Male sex addiction is associated with insecure attachment (Zapf, Greiner, & Carroll, 2008). It is understandable that insecurely attached men would like to hold on to their betrayed partners as their secure home base and might be frightened of losing them after the exposure of sexual betrayal. Thus, there is incentive to recover from sex addiction to form a more securely attached relationship with the betrayed partner.

Sex addicts' claims that casual extramarital sex is just sex and doesn't really mean anything may possess a kernel of truth if the sex is an impersonal form of tension release on which the addict has become dependent for stress management. What about "love addiction," the need to always be infatuated with someone, which can lead to romantic obsessions, stalking, and compulsively finding new objects of romantic infatuation once the honeymoon phase subsides with the current partner (Sussman, 2010)? Even love addicts may believe that their extramarital infatuations pose no threat to maintaining a long-term relationship with a stable attachment partner. Love addicts appreciate that their emotional affairs will eventually run their course as the honeymoon phase of the love affair wanes. Marriage provides the love addict with ongoing emotional security and stability, while serial extramarital romances provide them with excitement, validation, and bliss. Such unfaithful partners do not so much split love and lust but rather split romantic love from the need for secure attachment.

Sexual addiction as a disease of denial, rationalization, and minimization may lead the unfaithful partner to try to convince himself that his sexuality is neither abnormal nor out of control but only a man gratifying a healthy sex drive of which a moralistic and sexually repressive society does not approve. Regardless of whether there is any merit to this viewpoint, his betrayed wife most likely does not see it that way, no matter what arguments he makes. A betrayed wife, upon discovery of a husband's sexual addiction, is unlikely to feel compassion for his impaired capacity for adaptive emotion regulation. The therapist's job is to help the sex addict assume responsibility for his impaired emotion regulation but with self-compassion rather than self-disgust. Part of assuming responsibility is acquiring some empathy for the negative impact of his sex addiction on his betrayed partner and then trying to repair the emotional damage done to the degree possible.

Ariana began to suspect that her husband, Craig, might be surreptitiously using porn when one day he wanted to pretend to strangle her while having sex and talking dirty to her. Ariana refused and Craig accused her of only liking boring sex. Ariana snooped around a bit and discovered a treasure trove of pornography on his computer. She confronted Craig by expressing her disgust with the kind of sadomasochistic pornography that degraded women that Craig appeared to enjoy. Craig responded defensively and then withdrew in anger. Their sex life stopped, to Ariana's relief. Nevertheless, Ariana came for therapy because she wanted to start a family and realized they obviously couldn't unless they resumed their marital sex life. Ariana would need to overcome her sexual disgust with the thought of having even regular sex with a husband she no longer respected, and Craig would have to assume responsibility for the emotional impact his secret sex life had on Ariana.

I recommended they go for couples therapy. I coached Ariana about how to express her hurt and anger in ways that didn't shame Craig for his sexual preferences while asserting her right to have her own preferences and aversions treated respectfully. Relieved from being shamed for his sexuality, Craig tearfully said he didn't want to lose Ariana, would stop the pornography use, and try to treat her sexual preferences more respectfully. They resumed a more "vanilla" marital sex life, and Ariana became pregnant.

THE CHALLENGE OF LOVING A SEX ADDICT

Because the sex a sex addict requires is often impersonal, like a massage with a happy ending, the betrayal might not seem as "bad" as an isolated love affair. But on the other hand, because the behavior is compulsive, it might be significantly more difficult to stop. Wives of sex addicts might understand that they are still the love of their husbands' lives, yet have difficulty not being disgusted and repulsed by their husbands' sexuality and trusting that the sex addict can achieve a stable recovery that will insulate them from future betrayal trauma. Every time a recovered sex addict relapses is another betrayal trauma for the wife that pours more salt in a wound that has yet to heal.

Individual treatment for sexual addiction is not unlike individual treatment for any other addiction. Twelve-step approaches involve regular attendance at self-help support groups for sex or love addicts plus checking in with a sponsor on an as-needed basis (Corley et al., 2012). Individual psychotherapy for sex addicts in committed relationships has to help not only with the sexual addiction but also with the emotional fallout of the sex addiction for the relationship. Honesty and transparency were crucial characteristics of those sex addicts who are able to abstain from their compulsive sexual behavior as well as those couples able to recover from the infidelity (Corley et al., 2012). Being honest and transparent with the betrayed partner seems quite risky to the sex addict because it makes him vulnerable to being shamed as an object of disgust and to threats and ultimatums from his betrayed partner about terminating the relationship.

Recovery from sex addiction and from the infidelity caused by the sex addiction is facilitated when betrayed partners receive help dealing with their betrayal trauma. Betrayed partners need help finding constructive ways of expressing their hurt and anger at sexual betrayal. Ultimatums expressed by the betrayed partner do not seem to prevent relapse. They may in fact may make relapse more likely in exacerbating the sex addict's dread of abandonment, an overwhelming dread that may be self-medicated through sexual acting out. Expressing disgust with the sex addict's sexuality by shaming the sex addict may also make relapse more likely as damaged self-worth is restored in a compensatory way by reverting to addictive sexual behavior. Individual and couples therapists must find a way of breaking this vicious interpersonal cycle. Sexual betrayal brings out a shaming and threatening side of the betrayed partner, while ultimatums and shaming trigger relapse.

Sex addicts generally feel shame, self-loathing, and self-disgust for being out of control and engaging in sexual behavior that does not live up to their own moral standards. Anything that exacerbates their self-hatred makes relapse more likely because the addiction is driven by an inability to adaptively tolerate feelings that seem overwhelming and unbearable. Betrayed partners are also understandably overwhelmed by feelings of hurt, humiliation, and anger and feel justified in venting those feelings on the person who caused their suffering. Unfortunately, that just exacerbates the addicts' overwhelming feelings of guilt and shame, making relapse all the more likely.

Ned and Alicia had recently had a beautiful baby girl. They were a dual-career professional couple with high-powered careers, so they were quite busy. They simply stopped having sex without discussing it. Alicia had lost her sex drive and assumed it would come back as they settled into their new routine. She figured that Ned could wait at least a few months until their daughter could sleep through the night before resuming their marital sex life. But a few months had turned into half a year without sex or any discussion about it. Ned understood that Alicia was overwhelmed with responsibilities, so he didn't want to burden her with complaints about their nonexistent sex life. He felt that he was being a sensitive and considerate husband not to pester her for sex when she clearly wasn't in the mood.

One day, Ned stopped for a massage at one of the many massage parlors located not far from where he worked in the financial district. His sexual tension was building, and he figured he would just get some relief. As a single man, he had occasionally gone for massages with happy endings when not much was going on in his sex life. It seemed like a harmless form of tension relief that didn't mean anything. Nevertheless, he found himself going weekly and sometimes twice a week as a routine habit. In fact, he would do it in a kind of trancelike state of mind, like driving a car on automatic pilot. He just didn't think too much about the implications of what he was doing because if he did, he would have recognized that it was wrong, felt guilt-ridden, and made some effort to stop. But he did it in a distracted, mindless way so that he didn't really feel responsible for his behavior. It was like temporarily forgetting that one is on a special diet and can't eat certain restricted food and then after the fact, there might be a naughty feeling of "oops, I did it again, but I'll remember next time."

Ned also routinely charged the massages on his credit card, forgetting that even though he paid the bills, there was certainly some possibility that his wife might take a look at the statements when they came in the mail. And that is exactly what happened. One day Alicia casually opened their credit card bill to see how much debt they were accumulating because she was worried if they were making enough money to afford their expensive lifestyle. To her shock, she discovered they certainly couldn't afford the accumulating expense of weekly or biweekly massages. Alicia felt betrayed, but her self-esteem also took a big hit. She worried that she was no longer attractive to her husband or that she wasn't good in bed. She couldn't understand why he would pay for sex when he could have it for free at home. And she couldn't understand why he wouldn't have asked for sex, as she would have freely given him oral sex even if she wasn't in the mood for vaginal sex. It must be that he had lost sexual interest in her.

Infidelity is often exposed when unfaithful men are not that careful in covering their tracks. Do they unconsciously want to be caught due to a guilt-ridden conscience or perhaps to sadistically inflict a betrayal trauma on their partner for frustrating them? Or are they just "stupid"? Some research has suggested that sexual arousal can impair working memory (Laier, Schulte, & Brand, 2013) and decision-making (Laier, Pawlikowski, & Brand, 2014). So it may be that smart men do stupid things that lead to getting caught because, under the influence of their sexual obsessions, their working memory and decision-making are impaired, although they may rationalize such errors of judgment after the fact.

In therapy, it turned out that Ned had avoidant attachment style. It was easy for him to separate love and sex, and in fact, this was preferable for him. He didn't like the feeling of being a needy and emotionally demanding little boy who had to ask for sex. It was more comfortable to go to a massage parlor where it was all business. He received the tension relief he needed so that he could concentrate and focus at work without being distracted by pressing sexual desires and fantasies. He was stressed worrying about money, and going to massage parlors enabled him to forget his ruminative worries.

It was difficult for Ned to admit that his behavior had gotten out of control and that he had become emotionally dependent on going to massage parlors to avoid and suppress his worries. It was shameful to think of his behavior as addictive and even more shameful to have to admit it to his wife. Initially, when I suggested that he might have a sexual addiction, he was skeptical and offended, but as I clarified the diagnostic criteria for sex addiction he began to admit that his sexual behavior seemed to fit the classic pattern. Ironically, it was easier for Ned to own the infidelity than the sex addiction because owning the addiction meant he would have to work on relapse prevention. Viewing his sexual behavior as only an isolated instance of infidelity that he would never repeat was less of a threat to his self-concept than thinking of himself as someone at risk for becoming a serial philanderer due to his impaired self-control.

Some men who are in recovery from sex addiction try to be open and honest in their dating relationships about the fact that they have struggled with compulsive sexuality in the past. Their dating partners are understandably concerned about their relapsing once a committed sexually exclusive relationship has been initiated. Sometimes recovering sex addicts and their romantic partners seek couples therapy not so much because infidelity has happened, but because their partners live in dread that infidelity might happen when the recovering sex addict relapses. These women want some reassurance from the therapist that their recovering partner won't fall back into his pattern of sex addiction even though they understand that the therapist can't predict the future. Every time there is a decline in their sex lives, these women worry that their partners might be relapsing but covering it up. It also makes them feel insecure about their sexual desirability or how good they are in bed if their partners need an extra-relationship sexual outlet.

Jonathan was a struggling actor who had suffered an addiction to pornography. He also obsessed about becoming a porn actor. He attended Sex and Love Addicts Anonymous regularly and had not looked at pornography in years. Yet he still suffered ruminative worries that he might give in to his temptations to look for acting jobs in the pornography industry. Jonathan's relationships with his girlfriends remained superficial because he felt he could not be honest about who he was without being rejected for being a creepy guy who might engage in unsavory forms of sexuality. Jonathan realized that if he were ever to have a truly intimate relationship with a woman, he would have to be honest about his struggles with sex addiction and see who was willing to stick around. Finally, Jonathan found Dorothy, a rather unconventional woman who didn't seem like she would be judgmental about the "kinky" aspects of his sexuality. After 6 months of dating, Jonathan finally found the courage to be honest with Dorothy after she intuited that he was keeping some sort of secret from her. It was not a deal-breaker for Dorothy, and soon they moved in together.

Over the months, however, Dorothy found herself ruminating about Jonathan's sexuality and feared not simply that he might be unfaithful but that one day she might discover the infidelity by seeing him in a porn video. It emerged that Jonathan had been sexually abused by a female babysitter during childhood, and his obsession with appearing in a porn video appeared to be a symptom of his posttraumatic stress disorder subsequent to having been sexually molested. Jonathan lived in dread that his temptation to exhibit himself in a porn video would get out of control and that he would be publicly humiliated as his perverted sexuality was exposed to the world. As the couple began to appreciate that his obsession did not so much represent his underlying forbidden desire as his worst fear, they were both better able to contain their worry that Jonathan's sexuality could get out of control.

Sex addicts who rated their spouses as supportive were more likely to have positive relationship outcomes (Pollard, Hook, Corley, & Schneider, 2014). Nevertheless, betrayed partners cannot be made to feel by either their spouses or their therapists that it is somehow their responsibility to prevent relapse, and not that of the unfaithful partner, who must assume responsibility for his own recovery without blaming his spouse for slip-ups. Of course, many betrayed spouses will not want to recover from infidelity if recovery requires learning to live with a recovering sex addict who is at a significant risk of relapse.

CONCLUSION

Recovery from infidelity can mean learning how to have constructive discussions of acutely shame-sensitive issues, such as the unfaithful partner's sexual addiction and potential for relapse. How do couples learn to have discussions about such touchy issues without having the conversation escalate into an ugly quarrel? Communication skills—being able to have a constructive discussion about shame-sensitive issues—appear to provide some immunity to the risk of infidelity. Couples that avoid such discussions and sweep shame-sensitive issues under the rug or can't discuss shame-sensitive issues without getting defensive and argumentative are at much greater risk of infidelity. The next chapter addresses the science of marital communication.

10

MARITAL COMMUNICATION STYLES THAT PREDICT BETRAYAL

Infidelity arises in a relational context that is created by two people, with their respective personality styles, in interaction with each other. Those individuals may bring out the best or the worst in each other. One is not responsible for a partner's "bad" behavior, whether it results from a sexual addiction or the need to flirt with others for validation. Yet the way one relates to one's partner may exacerbate or attenuate their worst tendencies.

Marital researchers (Christensen & Heavey, 1993; Christensen & Jacobson, 1998; J. M. Gottman, 1999) have identified the communication patterns that reveal how couples bring out the best or the worst in each other. Infidelity may be motivated by a search for a partner who will bring out one's best self—be it one's sexiest, most virile or feminine self or one's most intimate, open, and self-revealing self. Relationships are like mirrors that reveal who we are. We are motivated to search for a new partner who will reflect a more flattering view of ourselves when we look at our current partners and see a reflection of ourselves that we don't like.

http://dx.doi.org/10.1037/0000053-011
The Dynamics of Infidelity: Applying Relationship Science to Psychotherapy Practice, by L. Josephs

John Gottman (1994) initiated a line of research in his marriage laboratory that began to explain why marriages succeed or fail. He designed his laboratory to look like a living room—not an ordinary living room, but one with cameras and microphones that would record the participant couples' every word, facial expression, and body posture. In addition, each member of a couple was hooked up to various physiological measures to assess his or her level of physiological arousal. The participants were instructed to have a 20-minute discussion about a problem with which they grappled. Gottman wanted to observe how well or how poorly a couple negotiated conflict with each other and how strongly their communications patterns were associated with eventual divorce. What Gottman discovered enabled him to accurately predict which couples were most likely to be divorced from the couple's particular pattern of marital communication.

J. M. Gottman's (1999) research led to an approach to couples therapy based on marital communication skills training. A meta-analysis found that couples therapy that includes communication skills training is effective in increasing relationship quality as well as communication skills (Hawkins, Blanchard, Baldwin, & Fawcett, 2008).

THE SCIENCE OF TRUST

J. M. Gottman (2011) established what he called the *science of trust* from his analysis of patterns of marital communication. Are there ways that couples talk to each other that create romantic intimacy or distance? Gottman discovered patterns of marital communication that generate so much animosity or distance that these increasingly entrenched communication patterns may eventually lead to divorce. He called these destructive patterns of marital communication the "Four Horsemen of the Apocalypse" (J. M. Gottman, 1994, p. 68): criticism, defensiveness, stonewalling, and contempt. *Criticism* more precisely refers to destructive criticism that attacks a partner's basic personality and sense of self, in contrast to constructive criticism. Rather than complain about a specific behavior that could be changed, this kind of criticism involves complaining about a partner's core personality characteristics (i.e., character assassination).

Christensen and Jacobson (1998) noted that individuals can't quickly or easily change their basic personalities no matter how frequently their partners complain about them. Personality is who we are in some core way. It is built on the substrate of a genetically heritable temperament interacting with early childhood experiences (Thomas, Chess, & Birch, 1970). As a consequence, complaining about someone's personality and expecting him to quickly change it will only succeed in making that person feel bad about himself—that he isn't accepted for who he is despite his imperfections.

Such destructive critical thinking may be a symptom of low mentalization. This particular kind of teleological communication is characterized by the effort to change someone's behavior without accurately understanding the mental states that motivate it (Bateman & Fonagy, 2004). Frustrated partners mistakenly think, "If you really loved me, you would change" once they have pointed out problematic behaviors. "You either don't love me or are stubbornly obtuse if you don't make the behavior changes I need to feel happy in the relationship." This lack of reflection fails to recognize that one's basic personality is not a matter of volitional choice but an automatic and unreflective way of being that people can't turn on and off like a light switch. One can't stop being an angry person, a depressed person, an anxious person, a sexually driven person, or an asexual person just because a partner complains about it even if one would genuinely wish to be another type of person. Cognitive reframing is required to overcome the kind of teleological thinking that mistakenly assumes a valid measure of love is a partner's willingness and ability to change his or her basic personality.

It's easy to wonder why one's partner got married in the first place or whether one's partner regrets his or her decision to marry if all one ever hears, day in and day out, are complaints about his or her personality (e.g., you're a slob, you're a bitch, you're stupid, you're insensitive, you're a control freak, you're rude, you're disgusting, you're inconsiderate, you don't love me because you don't change your behavior despite seeing how much I suffer from it). Character assassination may derive from a tendency to engage in dichotomous thinking when frustrated. The partner is critiqued as "all bad" (e.g., an asshole, a bitch, stupid, a slob, a loser) in an insulting way and is contrasted with an ideal partner who is "all good" (e.g., a winner, the love of my life, a sweetie pie) who is looked at adoringly. Such dichotomous thinking is another indication of low reflective functioning to be remediated by learning to look at one's romantic partner as a whole individual with both good and bad aspects (Kernberg, 1996).

Most of us respond defensively when people complain about our personalities, and we try to justify ourselves to prove we are not really as bad as our partners are trying to make us out to be. That generates an argument that may potentially escalate out of control. The person making the complaint feels it's a legitimate one that is based on months, years, or decades of objective and intimate observations living with a person day in and day out. The complainant isn't aware that the critique is an unflattering overgeneralization that is punitively shaming. Instead, he or she feels that the critique contains more than a kernel of truth, and it is understandable if, when frustrated, one expresses oneself with a bit of hyperbolic overstatement for dramatic effect to get a point across to a defensively obtuse person.

Responding defensively to unfair criticism when attacked reflects a defense mechanism referred to as *externalization of blame*, a way to deflect self-criticism and a sense of responsibility by turning the tables on the critic to shame and silence her or him through countercomplaint (J. M. Gottman, 1994; Stuewig, Tangney, Heigel, Harty, & McCloskey, 2010). This defense mechanism is commonly found among those with borderline, narcissistic, and paranoid tendencies, who may often construe themselves as innocent victims of unfair criticism to diminish their own sense of guilt (Peters & Geiger, 2016).

Externalizing blame allows people to avoid responsibility for their role in a conflict by shifting all blame to the other party. The bearer of bad news, be it a partner or a therapist, is attacked if he or she notes the angry overgeneralization, the contemptuous and mocking manner in which the criticism was made, and the hypocrisy of pointing out flaws in someone else that the critic actually possesses. Externalization of blame precludes acknowledging the kernel of truth in the complaint and any empathy for the hurt feelings behind the angry criticism. It is overlooked that individuals often use overgeneralization and hyperbole to make a point in bold primary colors when it seems that a more measured or nuanced way of expressing oneself isn't getting through. It is overlooked that one's own obtuseness may provoke others to make points more forcefully, bluntly, and authoritatively than they otherwise would if one were more receptive and understanding.

The person who responds defensively to criticism, be it fair or unfair, by externalizing blame feels deeply misunderstood and mischaracterized. The externalizer perceives criticism as no more than a power play by the critic to put him in the one-down position by trying to assume the moral high ground as the arbiter of objective reality and of moral rectitude. The externalizer rationalizes that any self-respecting person would defend himself or herself in the face of patently unfair criticism and engage in what J. M. Gottman (1999) called *countercomplaint* to expose the critic's hypocrisy. After all, as they say, people who live in glass houses shouldn't throw stones. Character assassination is met with counter–character assassination in a game of tit for tat, giving rise to a potentially escalating power struggle until someone gives in.

Fighting with one's partner is unpleasant, so some people just try to avoid conflict by *stonewalling*. Rather than argue, hostility is expressed indirectly by giving the critical partner the cold shoulder, often denying the implicit hostility expressed through withdrawal. The punishment for complaining about a partner's personality may be the silent treatment until the criticism ceases. Stonewalling would be the preferred strategy for more avoidantly attached individuals who would rather avoid conflict and the emotional intimacy of having a deep discussion about touchy issues that make them feel uncomfortably exposed and vulnerable (Overall, Simpson, & Struthers, 2013). Unfortunately, stonewalling activates fears of abandonment in more anxiously attached individuals, only increasing their separation protest and angry demands to continue a conflict discussion until some resolution is achieved that quells their fear of abandonment (Rodriguez, 2000).

The final and apparently most deadly horseman of the apocalypse is a look or tone of *contempt* (J. M. Gottman, Levenson, & Woodin, 2001). Contempt expresses a feeling that one is superior to and looks down on the partner. The implication is that one is better than one's partner and deserves someone better, someone more one's equal. Contempt may imply that the partner is perceived as stupid, disgusting, unattractive, clueless, or a hopeless case. Contempt has been associated with dominance and superiority (Matsumoto & Ekman, 2004), avoidant attachment style (Magai, Distel, & Liker, 1995), and narcissism (Morrison, 2011).

Gottman's Four Horsemen of the Apocalypse should be familiar to all readers who have been in long-term relationships. All couples argue this way to some degree when frustrated with each other and feeling unfairly attached. That doesn't necessarily mean the marriage is headed toward divorce; J. M. Gottman (1994) discovered that couples are only in real danger when the percentage of these negative interactions significantly exceeds the percentage of positive interactions.

J. M. Gottman (2011) discovered that many couples that fight in this manner have ways of reconciling after an argument that bring them closer together. A bid for reconnection is made that, if accepted, leads to reconciliation. Rejection of a bid for connection leads to that bid being withdrawn, and the couple remains alienated and detached from each another. Trust is diminished when bids for connection are rejected and restored when they are accepted. Couples that don't know how to reconcile after a difficult argument may just sweep problems under the rug and pretend everything is fine after an argument that ends in stalemate. They become what J. M. Gottman (1994) called *conflict-avoiding couples*. Couples that never reconcile after an argument tend to grow apart in ways that can become a risk factor for infidelity.

Stewart came for psychotherapy because he had been having an affair for the past 2 years with a woman he had met at his country club, where he played golf on weekends. He felt a real connection with his affair partner that he had never had with his wife. Stewart felt frustrated that no matter how he tried to get through to his wife, Julie, she just didn't get it. Initially, Julie would respond defensively to Stewart's complaints about what he felt were her irresponsible ways of managing the household and raising their two teenage girls. When Stewart began to lose his temper, Julie would back down and say she would try to change. Yet from Stewart's perspective, she never did. In retrospect, it seemed that Julie was just humoring him, telling him what he wanted to hear so he would get off her case, a subtle form of stonewalling. Julie defended herself by saying she was doing her best and would just try harder. She never empathized with Stewart's frustration, his feeling that he was hitting his head against a brick wall every time he tried to get through to her. Eventually, he just gave up trying, but he felt a deep need for a woman who would listen patiently and sympathetically.

Stewart met Caroline while playing golf. Caroline was married to a successful but aloof man with whom she did not seem to have much of an emotional connection. Stewart and Caroline began confiding in each other about their marital frustrations on the golf course as "just friends," but eventually the relationship became romantic when they both had had a little too much to drink after they finished their golf game and their self-control was impaired. Because talking with each other was so much easier than talking with their respective spouses, they continued with the affair, although both were guilt-ridden about it. They spoke to each other daily on the phone but would only have sex together every few months. Nevertheless, Stewart and Caroline began bickering as they started trying to figure out where the affair was going. Neither could see having a long-term affair because neither relished living a lie indefinitely; yet for both financial and emotional reasons, neither could see breaking up their families, nor could they see ending the affair and being left to live lives of silent despair, married to their uncommunicative, conflict-avoiding spouses from whom they had become alienated.

The fights that Stewart and Caroline had about the future of the affair didn't go anywhere, and they started avoiding such discussions even though the future of the affair became their unspoken and unresolved dilemma as they lived in constant fear of exposure. It was not lost on Stewart that his relationship with his affair partner was beginning to show some striking similarities to his relationship with his wife. It began to dawn on him that maybe some of the ways he tried to fix his wife, and now his affair partner, had backfired, in his attempt to force changes he believed were for the best. Stewart began to appreciate that he had a tendency to try to fix his romantic partners, forcing them to be who he thought they "should" be, rather than accepting them for who they were. Due to his narcissism, he assumed that he was always right and his partners were always wrong, and due to his teleological thinking, he assumed his partners were just stubborn, proud, and unreasonably entitled individuals (i.e., seeing the repudiated narcissism in others that he didn't see in himself) who didn't care enough about his feelings to make the behavior changes that would make him happy.

Stewart was a controlling person who became belligerent when he didn't get his way. Trying to pressure his romantic partners to make changes that they weren't emotionally prepared to make usually evoked passive–aggressive resistance. His romantic partners didn't want to disappoint him, so they couldn't just tell him to back off and be patient while they figured things out for themselves. Instead, they just went on a sit-down strike because they weren't going to be coerced into making changes they weren't sure were really for the best. Yet because his partners were conflict-avoiding people, they couldn't stand up to Stewart's implicit bullying in a more assertive way. Stewart didn't see the impact of his own narcissism on either of his partners' mental states. As a consequence, he developed the same relational problems with his affair partner as he had with his wife.

In individual psychotherapy, I started teaching Stewart about Gottman's Four Horses of the Apocalypse and suggested constructive alternatives like listening sympathetically and nondefensively while his partners vented their feelings of frustration with him and their situation rather than needing to angrily rebut every point they made that differed from his own opinion. Not surprisingly, Stewart responded argumentatively to my attempt to do communication skills training. He protested that even if the training might work with "normal" people, it wouldn't work with the impossibly difficult women in his life. He exhibited with me the same maladaptive communication pattern that he had with his partners by debating me on every point to justify his unwillingness to try my suggestions. I pointed out that the pattern was now playing out with me, but he remained skeptical.

One day Stewart started complaining that his two teenage girls seemed to avoid talking to him. I suggested that maybe they walked on eggshells with him because they were frightened that if they expressed their opinions, he would start angrily debating them until he won the argument. Stewart looked both stunned and sheepish, as it finally got through to him how his domineering and overbearing way of expressing himself might affect other people, including his own children.

Stewart finally said he would give Gottman's approach a try. He reported that it did reduce arguments with his wife, but then they fell back into going through the motions and their uncommunicative way of relating, with which he was dissatisfied. Stewart said that he was tired of trying and failing to connect to her. In contrast, Stewart reported that Gottman's approach also reduced arguments with his affair partner, but in contrast to communications with his wife, they were now able to have deep and meaningful discussions. Ironically, marital communication skills training worked better with his affair partner than with his wife. Second marriages to affair partners can potentially be more successful than first marriages if a more constructive communication pattern is achieved.

COMMUNICATION STYLE AS A RISK FACTOR FOR INFIDELITY

J. M. Gottman (1994, 1999) discovered that there are three basic styles of marital communication: volatile, validating, and conflict-avoiding. *Volatile* couples fight all the time and don't make any effort to hide their marital spats from others. It seems on the surface that volatile couples should be the ones headed toward divorce and among whom infidelity would be most likely, but this is not necessarily the case. Many volatile couples are good at reconciling with each other after an angry spat and might even have good makeup sex. Gottman found that many volatile couples had a passionate sex life after decades. It seems that some volatile couples are engaging each other at a deep emotional level and working things out successfully. Other volatile couples degenerate into verbally abusive interchanges that might turn physical and suffer a deteriorating marital situation in which nothing is being worked through.

Validating couples do what healthy couples are supposed to do. They listen patiently and sympathetically. They demonstrate respect and show empathy for each other's viewpoints even if they don't agree with their partner. Even if they think that their partners' viewpoints are stupid, uninformed, or dead wrong, they appreciate that it's a free country and everyone is entitled to express their opinion no matter how offensive it may seem. They use humor to diffuse tension and try not to take things too personally. They try not to say mean things they might later regret. They are generally supportive of each other's aspirations and sympathetic to each other's stresses.

Even validating couples can have problems if they are always being "nice" to each other because they don't trust that they can openly express how hurt and angry they really are. They don't avoid conflict discussions, but they might have some that are "too nice." They are frightened of having a heated exchange in which feelings might get bruised, so they avoid the kind of passionate give-and-take in which volatile couples engage. With validating couples, there can sometimes be too much of a good thing.

Conflict-avoiding couples can often pass as "normal" to others and to themselves. They generally avoid open marital conflict, so that they can pride themselves on being a couple that rarely fights. Yet the reason they don't fight is because the few times they have had spats, it's been a frustrating and upsetting experience that doesn't go anywhere. It never leads to any kind of meaningful resolution or reconciliation, so they studiously avoid all upsetting discussions and assume such avoidance is a good thing for keeping the peace. As a consequence, conflict-avoiding couples tend to have a superficial relationship with each other in which the underlying issues never get aired or worked through. Instead, the underlying issues fester, leading to increasing alienation in the marriage despite the pretense of normality. Occasionally, the underlying conflicts erupt, for example, when they have had a bit too much to drink. But the morning after, they pretend the drunken argument the night before never even happened and the upsetting issues that erupted aren't really of any major import.

A risk factor for infidelity arises when one or both members of a conflict-avoiding couple feels sexually rejected and frustrated in the marriage. Such individuals may seek sexual satisfaction outside the marriage and not see anything wrong with it given that their avoidant partners seem indifferent to their sexual needs and frustrations. Avoidant couples may drift into having an infrequent and passionless sex life and avoid having any meaningful discussion about the incremental deterioration in their sexual relationship. The emotional distance, the lack of communication, and the impersonal, infrequent marital sex life creates an emotional distance in which the unfaithful partner can have an active extramarital sex life without being detected. Conflict-avoiding couples normalize a superficial, emotionally distant, and going-through-the-motions relationship that they convince themselves is a good marriage because they rarely fight. They overlook the fact that when they do fight, it emerges how alienated they have become from each other. They rationalize that the lack of passion, humor, and affection is just what happens to all couples once the honeymoon phase wanes. They overlook the fact that successful couples do retain delight in each other's company and sexual chemistry in a long-term relationship (Lodge, 2015).

The reason betrayed partners are often shocked by exposure of the infidelity is not simply because unfaithful partners are so good at the cover-up. It's because the relationship is already so emotionally distant by the time the affair happens, there isn't much to detect that is dramatically different from the way things usually are. By the time an affair happens, conflict-avoiding couples may not be having that much sex, may not be that affectionate with one another, may no longer be amusing each other, and may not even be spending all that much time with each other. Preoccupation with work, children, or hobbies can lead the couple to live separate and parallel lives. Betrayed partners assume that their partners are just too busy with child care, work, or recreational activities to have any time for an extramarital sex life. Conflict-avoiding couples may be proud of the fact that they are two independent people who give each other considerable space to live their independent lives, mistakenly trusting that their partners wouldn't abuse that zone of privacy to cultivate a secret extramarital sex life.

ACCEPTANCE, MINDFULNESS, AND MARITAL FRUSTRATION

Marital communications skills training is a powerful intervention because couples with good communication skills are able to manage their perpetual conflicts without letting conflicts escalate out of control or being so conflict avoidant to the point that an unbridgeable emotional distance arises. Some couples have difficulty learning such skills, while others that have improved their communication skills still relapse and fall back into old patterns of communicating when feeling emotionally flooded by their conflicts. Constructive marital communication doesn't seem to come naturally to anybody when they are feeling hurt, frustrated, and insecure. In those vulnerable moments, it seems almost instinctive to relate in defensive ways such as dumping one's feelings of frustration on one's romantic partner, blaming romantic partners for marital problems as though one is an innocent victim, withholding affection as punishment, and treating one's partner as an object of contempt and disgust who isn't good enough.

Communicating in defensive ways when feeling threatened, vulnerable, and self-protective may just be a part of human nature that has to be accepted and managed. Maybe it isn't something that can be entirely unlearned and eliminated through communication skills training. As a consequence, maladaptive patterns of marital communication can be treatment resistant. That treatment resistance will be all the more severe for individuals who possess low frustration tolerance, limited self-awareness, and difficulty recognizing and empathizing with the impact of their destructive communication style on a partner's mental states. Building up one or both partners' frustration tolerance, self-awareness, and empathy means changing basic personality traits for which there is no short-term treatment. Patients with such deficits often need a longer term ego-building treatment to acquire such ego strengths. The more severe the ego deficits as in narcissistic, borderline, or paranoid personality disorders, the longer it will take to build such ego strengths. For these reasons, couples aren't always ready to change their ways of relating because it requires altering basic aspects of their personalities that can only be transformed in slow, incremental ways with hard work. How do therapists help patients learn to tolerate the frustrating reality that sometimes there are no quick fixes for entrenched personality issues?

Christensen and Jacobson (1998) developed an approach they called *integrative couples therapy*. They are behavioral marital therapists, but they discovered that marital communications skills training is not always effective because couples are not always ready to change their behavior, despite the best instruction as to how to accomplish that goal. They advised that when couples aren't ready to change, it's best for therapists to accept that fact and avoid getting embroiled in power struggles with patients. The therapeutic task is then to facilitate couples in learning how to accept that change, or at least rapid change, is not always possible.

Acceptance can derive from the Buddhist practice of *mindfulness* (Gambrel & Keeling, 2010; Keng, Smoski, & Robins, 2016). In mindfulness meditation, one learns simply to observe what's on one's mind without trying to judge or control it. One can then discover that aversive thoughts and feelings are transitory phenomena that eventually pass. Learning to wait for aversive states of mind to pass can lead to feelings of acceptance and the peace of mind that comes with learning to accept things as they are rather than as one wishes they were. In addition, one can cultivate the capacity to observe thoughts and feelings not only objectively from a place of emotional distance or detachment but also with compassion. According to Buddhism, life is suffering. The challenge of being alive is not simply to find ways of patiently enduring the suffering that being a conscious sentient being entails but to also develop compassion for others, as well as for oneself, for the suffering to which we are made vulnerable by our attachment to our needs and desires. Psychotherapists can facilitate patients to become more mindful toward the psychological suffering that they and their romantic partners experience. Couples can learn to live more mindfully with each other's annoying personality characteristics and conflicting viewpoints so that they can be on the same page about how to live their life together.

Couples tend to continue to mistakenly believe that their partner's frustrating traits should be amenable to swift change, despite daily experience to the contrary. Daily life demonstrates time and time again that partners' minds and personalities do not change easily despite repeated and frustrating attempts to make this happen. Couples therapy is often sought because romantic partners believe a marital therapist has some magical formula for quickly changing their partner and fixing his or her character flaws. They have given it their best shot, and it wasn't good enough, but perhaps a couples therapist is more skilled at this. Such expectations put considerable pressure on the therapist to be a miracle worker.

Psychotherapists, whether in couples or individual psychotherapy, can facilitate patients' acceptance that they cannot change their partner's personality or mind. Psychodynamic psychotherapists in particular believe that personality only changes in slow and incremental ways, if at all. Psychodynamic psychotherapists have always been skeptical of quick fixes that treat symptoms that are prone to relapse without treating the cause (Josephs & Weinberger, 2013). Patients can be helped to see and accept that their marital suffering derives from having to learn to live with certain frustrating features of their partner's personality and that it is unrealistic to expect quick change in those personality characteristics. Christensen and Jacobson (1998) noted that personality is much more likely to change in a relationship in which one feels accepted despite one's character flaws than in a relationship in which one feels rejected for those character flaws. Secure attachment facilitated by acceptance enables one to find the courage to engage in intimate risk taking that exposes emotional vulnerabilities, a key therapeutic process in emotion-focused couples therapy (Johnson, 2004).

Patients with low reflective functioning and teleological thinking (Bateman & Fonagy, 2004) may possess the naive expectation that if they simply point out their partner's character flaws, attribute those flaws to childhood experiences or misguided gender role conditioning, and suggest constructive alternatives that they are giving constructive criticism for their partner's self-improvement, just like a therapist would, and that their partner should be appreciative. It is not recognized that when therapists provide identical feedback to patients, it is solicited from someone whom they assume has their best interest at heart. When patients provide their partner with seemingly therapeutic feedback, it is seen as unsolicited feedback from an angry, presumably biased person with a hidden agenda. Patients don't appreciate the radically different impact of feedback that is solicited versus unsolicited and whether the "bearer of bad news" is assumed to be a biased or unbiased observer.

Disgruntled partners may complain in couples therapy that it bothers them when their partner gratefully accepts feedback from a therapist that was angrily rejected when they made exactly the same observation. Romantic partners feel hurt and wounded when their insightful observations are met with defensiveness, thereby invalidating their hard-won insights into their partner's personality. An argument ensues as patients try to prove to their partner that their insights are indeed correct and useful. Thus, the very thing patients do to fix their romantic partner comes across as antagonistic and makes a bad situation worse by implicitly shaming the partner for his or her character flaws.

Individuals who are egocentric and possess low reflective functioning have difficulty accepting that partners in a relationship are entitled to have a mind of their own no matter how wrong-headed and misguided their view of reality appears to be (Bateman & Fonagy, 2004). From patients' perspectives, their partners possess a distorted view of reality that is simply rationalizing character flaws. In sharp contrast, their partners believe that they don't possess the character flaws being attributed to them (e.g., their partners are imagining things, are projecting their own repudiated issues, or are hypersensitive) or they do indeed possess those character traits but those traits are assets rather than flaws (e.g., their presumed arrogance is actually healthful self-confidence, their presumed abusiveness is healthful self-assertiveness, their presumed hostile withdrawal is healthfully deescalating a conflict, their presumed faultfinding is just constructive criticism). It doesn't matter if nobody, including the therapist, shares the person's own high opinion of himself or herself because sometimes the popular majority unfairly judges minorities of one. The popular majority isn't always right but can be blinded by conventional biases or a herd mentality.

Therapists can help patients accept that constructive dialogue is not about winning a debate that will change a partner's mind. It requires respectfully expressing different viewpoints, looking for areas of consensus, and finally agreeing to disagree so an irreconcilable difference of opinion doesn't escalate into an angry argument. The therapeutic task is to learn how to disagree without becoming disagreeable. Accepting a partner's point of view doesn't mean agreeing with it or even empathizing with it but accepting that a partner's mind won't be changed through angry debate. For example, a wife must learn how to live with a viewpoint that she may strongly believe is wrong-headed or offensive. A husband isn't going to talk his wife out of the unflattering opinion she has formed about his character flaws no matter how insulted he is by what feels like an unfair character assassination.

Communication skills training can stop the partner from angrily voicing an unflattering character analysis that might be an overgeneralization despite possessing some truth. Yet communication skills training can't stop someone who is hurt and angry from privately thinking about their partner in an unflattering light. Partners usually know each other well enough to recognize and feel insulted by what they privately think but don't necessarily say out loud. That's why it seems so important to change their partners' mind and behavior: They are just as troubled by the secret criticism their partners may harbor as by the offensive thoughts they openly verbalize.

Infidelity is perhaps the ultimate expression of privately critical thoughts that have gone unsaid: that the partner isn't good in bed, the partner's personality is insufferable, or the partner doesn't have a clue as to one's true self. Finding an affair partner who is good in bed, has a wonderful personality, and appreciates and understands one at a deep level is confirmation that the critical thoughts harbored toward the betrayed partner are indeed astute and valid. Infidelity validates the unfaithful partner's view of the marital situation that the problem is with the betrayed partner rather than with oneself because he or she can achieve sexual satisfaction and romantic intimacy with another person who doesn't possess the same personal deficiencies that the betrayed partner possesses.

Mindfulness in a marital context requires learning to look at a partner's unflattering view of oneself from an emotional distance and not take it personally:

> My partner is entitled to his or her view of me, and I'm entitled to my own view of myself. Maybe we just have to agree to disagree about which is the "real" me. I'd like validation of my view of myself but I'll just have to learn to live without it.

In addition, mindfulness also requires developing compassion for the fact that people suffer what they believe are their partners' character flaws, whether those character flaws are objectively perceived or imagined. The flaw of denying or rationalizing one's character flaws to maintain a grandiose delusion of one's flawlessness may be especially troubling.

Marriage means suffering a partner's character flaws. It becomes apparent that character flaws do not easily change even when partners acknowledge their flaws and go into psychotherapy to try to fix them. Personality reflects automatic dispositions that are based in temperament as well as in childhood experience, sometimes highly traumatic experience, and cultural conditioning. Self-awareness creates the possibility of altering automatic patterns of thought, feeling, and behavior but doesn't guarantee it; people tend to fall back into old behavior patterns in stressful situations. To remain self-aware and thoughtful (i.e., mindful) in stressful situations is an ego strength that can only be slowly cultivated over time. Acceptance may require learning to accept the limitations on how much personality and minds can change despite one's best efforts. There will always be residue of the original character flaws, even among individuals who have grown as individuals through a lot of hard work. Such individuals won't appreciate it if their partners continue to fault them for the frustrating residue of their character flaws rather than credit them for the improvements they have made with great difficulty to make their partners—and themselves—happier.

Appreciating that a partner won't "get fixed" requires a difficult personal choice. Can I learn to live with a partner's character flaws, sexual preferences, and sexual aversions if they can't be changed? The relationship may be over if the answer is no. When the answer is yes, it requires cultivating mindfulness and compassion to better cope with a disappointing and frustrating circumstance that cannot be changed. The benefit of acceptance is that it diffuses power struggles within a relationship. Sometimes the diffusion of the power struggle about trying to fix each other's character flaws is the difference between a relationship that works and is gratifying and one that isn't. Maybe it's not so bad to live with a partner's character flaws once one has given up the exercise in futility of trying to fix them.

Acceptance creates a moment of truth: Is the relationship minus the never-ending power struggles good enough to remain committed? Patients may resist acceptance because they are frightened of confronting that moment of truth—their fear that the relationship minus the power struggles won't be good enough to remain committed. The fantasy of someday winning the power struggle keeps hope alive that someday one's partner will be fixed to one's liking. Ending the power struggle means accepting one's partner won't get fixed someday and one will have to decide if one's partner, "warts and all," is good enough to warrant continuing lifelong commitment. The painful loss of ending the relationship will have to be confronted if their worst fears are proved true (e.g., the partner is just too untrustworthy to ever feel securely attached, their sexual dispositions are too incompatible, their frustrating traits are too insufferable to endure any longer, the loss of self-respect in tolerating demeaning treatment is not worth whatever dependency needs that are gratified).

Recovery from infidelity—personally healing oneself, if not the relationship—sometimes means accepting the end of the relationship. The unfaithful partner may realize that the affair was a way of getting out of an unhappy marriage that she is no longer committed to working on. The betrayed partner may realize his partner is just not the person she seemed to be and he is no longer interested in fixing or living with her. One or both partners may eventually call it quits when the work of fixing a marriage marred by infidelity is just too much work for too little payoff.

Donald and Maxine came for couples therapy to recover from infidelity. Donald had confessed to having had a drunken fling with a work colleague after having drinks with a group of professionals who mixed work with socializing. Maxine felt she could no longer trust Donald, who still came home drunk late at night. Donald insisted that the affair was over and he wouldn't be unfaithful again. Yet Donald insisted that in his profession, deals were made after work over drinks with colleagues. He didn't think he had a drinking problem, and he wasn't going to stop an activity that he felt was crucial to his business success. After a year of trying to negotiate this issue in couples therapy to no avail, they decided to separate. Maxine felt she would never be able to trust that Donald wouldn't slip up again, and Donald no longer wanted to live under the constant surveillance of a mistrustful and watchful eye. By the end of couples therapy, they no longer had screaming matches about this touchy issue, so their communication skills were much improved. Nevertheless, they regrettably came to feel that their differences were not reconcilable, and neither wanted to go on living with the status quo.

YOU CAN'T GO HOME AGAIN

From a Freudian perspective, there is a reason that all individuals go into marriage with unrealistic expectations. Freud (1910/1957b, 1912/1958, 1924/1961) was the first to note that what motivates adult romantic relationships is the unconscious search for a good mother or father to substitute for the loss of the relationships with parents as we grow up and eventually leave the nest. We can't grow up to marry our parents, although young children may openly express that sentiment during the oedipal phase between 3 and 6 years of age (Watson & Getz, 1990a, 1990b). Romantic love is therefore based on a fantasy that we have found the perfect substitute parent, a parent who will make our lives blissfully happy and compensate us for all our childhood disappointments, frustrations, and traumas. We hope to be healed in a deep and enduring way by the best sex of one's life and romantic love that will magically banish all issues with self-esteem and fear of rejection.

Culture may reinforce unrealistic romantic fantasies about marriage, but, according to Freud, it doesn't create such fantasies because such unrealistic fantasies are just part of the human condition. Long-term relationships are inherently frustrating and disappointing because we go into them with unrealistic expectations. Part of the work of marriage is coming to terms with one's unrealistic expectations. Acceptance, mindfulness, and compassion are tools for coming to terms with such unrealistic expectations. From a Freudian perspective, power struggles are futile attempts to actualize sexual and romantic fantasies of an unrealistic nature rather than learn to accept the painful realities of long-term romantic relationships.

Freud (1910/1957b, 1924/1961) links the psychological dynamics of adult romantic relationships to the oedipal conflict—the primal love triangle. Freud hypothesized that a child fantasizes marrying the opposite-sex parent if heterosexual or the same-sex parent if homosexual. As a result, the other parent is perceived as a rival for the desired parent's love and affection. The desired parent is experienced as unfaithful because in the end, the desired parent favors the other parent over the child as his or her life partner. The child is reduced to an injured third party in a love triangle, experiencing the hurt, humiliation, jealousy, insecurity, anger, and vindictiveness that an adult would experience in a love triangle (Josephs, 2006). According to Freud, the oedipal complex is unconsciously worked through in adult romantic relationships (for experimental validation of this Freudian hypothesis, see Hunyady, Josephs, & Jost, 2008).

From an evolutionary perspective, it might be adaptive to develop a working model of adult love triangles in childhood and thus be better prepared to adapt to the sexual rivalries of adulthood (Josephs, 2010). The parents are role models of how to negotiate love triangles. They may role model successful monogamy by showing how a couple can remain faithful and reasonably happy in a monogamous arrangement by dealing with perpetual conflict through constructive forms of marital communication. As implicit mate poachers, children intrude on the parents' romantic happiness by making all kinds of pressing emotional demands for attention, resources, and affection—even sleeping in the parents' bed, further complicating the parents' postpartum sexual relationship. Raising a family together is usually the fulfillment of a couple's romantic fantasies, but—and perhaps it goes without saying—the arrival of children ends the honeymoon phase of any romantic relationship. Two is company, and three is a crowd. The child is an interloper who spoils a couple's romantic bliss, and this may be why marital satisfaction may increase once couples are left with an empty nest (Gorchoff, John, & Helson, 2008).

According to Freud, the lasting legacy of the oedipal conflict is this: Ultimately, we are all oedipal losers because none of us grow up to live happily ever after with the desired parent. Adult romantic relationships provide an imagined opportunity to be an oedipal winner in at least a symbolic way with a romantic partner as a parental substitute. Acceptance means realizing that, in the end, adult romantic relationships can't entirely compensate for the disappointments of one's childhood relationship with one's parents. The child's unrealistic fantasy is of being loved and protected forever and without ever having to grow up, like Peter Pan, who can spend life engaged in imaginative play without ever having to accept the depressing realities, privations, and responsibilities of adulthood. There can be a brief honeymoon phase in which it seems as though all of one's romantic fantasies will come true. Yet, ultimately, adult romantic relationships become an emotionally trying exercise in learning to constructively accept a set of frustrating realities and onerous responsibilities. From this perspective, infidelity is a symptom of a couple's inability to do just that.

ACHIEVING MARITAL SERENITY

The serenity prayer of Alcoholics Anonymous is relevant to the psychology of long-term romantic relationships:

> God, grant me the serenity to accept the things I cannot change,
> The courage to change the things I can,
> And the wisdom to know the difference.

Communication patterns are amenable to change, at least when one is not feeling emotionally overwhelmed, because such patterns can be subject to volitional control once they are pointed out in a constructive way. One can make a choice to refrain from engaging in Gottman's Four Horses of the Apocalypse and try to engage in more constructive ways, at least when in a relatively calm frame of mind. What must be accepted is that character flaws and relapsing into defensive communication patterns under stress might change only gradually, if at all. The wisdom to know the difference between what can be changed and what cannot doesn't come from the therapist; couples must develop that wisdom for themselves in learning through trial and error what works and what doesn't to diffuse their destructive power struggles (i.e., the relative balance of change and acceptance). The therapist's job is to facilitate such trial-and-error learning so that couples can learn from their mistakes as best they can and then see how they feel about each other once their power struggles have been successfully diffused.

CONCLUSION

As we near the end of this book, the reader could feel both overwhelmed and depressed by all the things that can go wrong in a sexually exclusive long-term relationship that increase the risk of infidelity. Readers prone to catastrophizing could even become a little paranoid because these risk factors exist to some degree in all long-term relationships. Increased awareness of these risk factors could activate ruminative worry about the potential for infidelity in one's own long-term relationships. There is no reason to think that the prevalence rates of infidelity among therapists who treat infidelity is any different from those rates among their patients. Therapists are often what Carl Jung called *wounded healers* (Sedgwick, 1994). With this in mind, the Conclusion ends on a more positive note, with a focus on the personality variables that decrease the risk of infidelity and increase the probability of enjoying a long-term relationship characterized by trust, authenticity, and emotional intimacy.

CONCLUSION: WHY PEOPLE REMAIN FAITHFUL

What enables people to remain faithful in long-term relationships despite the deep human ambivalence about long-term monogamous commitments and the universal difficulty humans have accepting, with compassion and without moralistic judgment, the frustrating realities of long-term sexually exclusive adult romantic relationships? What personality variables might enable individuals to best tolerate the conflicts, frustrations, and disappointments of such relationships if insecure attachment and high narcissism contribute to intolerance?

MENTALIZATION AND SECURE ATTACHMENT

Being a reflective person with a sophisticated theory of mind may inhibit infidelity because of the deeper appreciation of the negative impact that sexual betrayal has on a partner's mental states (Josephs, 2015a). Secure

http://dx.doi.org/10.1037/0000053-012
The Dynamics of Infidelity: Applying Relationship Science to Psychotherapy Practice, by L. Josephs

attachment is facilitated when couples possess the metacognition to appreciate how their defenses against attachment injury negatively affect each other (Johnson, 2004). Unfortunately, stressed couples tend to scapegoat each other for their unhappiness in life, as though all their misery is the other partner's fault. Couples may use each other as an emotional dumping ground for their frustrations and worries, as though a partner's job is to somehow absorb and manage all the frustrations and worries that someone seems unable to manage. Many people don't appreciate that using their partner as a vehicle for emotional catharsis only increases their own emotional dysregulation (Bushman, 2002) and floods their partner with overwhelming feelings that he or she may be unable to sympathetically contain.

Couples may focus on each other's deficits rather than their assets, with both people thinking that they are only engaging in constructive criticism that is for their partner's own good. Being unreflective means never considering how treating someone as a "fixer-upper" adversely affects a partner's mental state and brings out the worst rather than the best in a partner who may resent more than welcome being fixed "for their own good." Such criticism brings out a defensively self-justifying side rather than an empathetic side, thereby exacerbating the very problems about which frustrated partners complain.

Infidelity becomes an escape from an unhappy relationship in which one may feel scapegoated, emotionally dumped on, and treated like an unfinished project. It may be an extreme instance of the demand–withdraw pattern of marital communication (Christensen & Heavey, 1993) in which withdrawal is taken to the extreme of seeking a replacement for the overly demanding partner or the emotionally unavailable partner. Unfortunately, infidelity only exacerbates the problem by creating emotional distance when undetected and profound hurt, anger, and distrust if exposed. Being reflective means being able to appreciate that what seems like a solution in the moment may only create further headaches down the road because of the lasting emotional damage it inflicts on the betrayed partner. Being reflective means appreciating that exposed infidelity will exacerbate insecure attachment by making the partner jealous and mistrustful. Being reflective about long-term consequences means appreciating that infidelity inflicts psychological damage that may be difficult to heal because it damages the betrayed partner's sense of self-worth and ability to be trusting. Being reflective means possessing the foresight to appreciate that the short-term rewards of infidelity may not be worth the long-term negative consequences for oneself, one's partner, or one's children. Unreflective individuals are not as burdened with such worries about the future, so they are better able to live in and enjoy the adulterous moment.

Reflective individuals appreciate that infidelity might not be the most constructive or honorable way to extricate oneself from an unhappy marriage.

It can be anticipated that casual sex outside of a marriage one doesn't plan on ending could be seen by one's partner as a selfish self-indulgence, reflecting an unwillingness to make the personal sacrifices one's partner needs to feel securely attached. Being deceitful to protect a partner's feelings creates the potential for an even bigger hurt once a lie is exposed and the partner comes to believe—justifiably—that one is not an honest or trustworthy individual. Keeping a long-term affair partner around without ever leaving the betrayed partner hurts both the affair partner and the betrayed partner, because the affair partner is fated to always be the "other woman" or "other man" who lives in the shadows. And of course, exposed infidelity is not good role modeling of how to have a stable and successful long-term relationship for one's children.

People with high reflective functioning are likely to know all these things intuitively even if they can't articulate them quite so clearly. Owen, Rhoades, and Stanley (2013) found that more thoughtful decision-makers were not only more dedicated to their partners and less likely to be unfaithful but also reported higher relationship satisfaction. A special type of thoughtfulness is required to be successful in long-term relationships. It is the ability to be reflective about one's own impact on the mental state of a partner. It is appreciating that one's character flaws negatively affect a partner's mental states: One's character flaws may bring out the worst rather than the best in one's partner. It is rarely appreciated that when complaining about a romantic partner's insufferable character flaws one is implicitly complaining about a Frankenstein monster that is at least partially of one's own creation. Individuals rarely see how they bring out the worst in their partners though they may incessantly complain about the worst in their partners looking for sympathy. They don't see how their own character flaws exacerbate the problems of which they complain.

Therapists can help patients be reflective not just about their own mental states but about their partner's as well; they can also help their patients understand how their character traits affect a partner's mental states for better or for worse. It is human nature to wish to be accepted and appreciated for being one's uncensored and authentic self, but the reality is often the exact opposite of that. That wish is frustrated in long-term relationships because nobody enters one possessing Buddha-like compassion for their partner's character flaws that seem to cause them so much suffering. Buddhists say that your enemy is your teacher (Wallace, 2001). It's easy to have compassion for the suffering of someone who treats us well, but it's quite difficult to have compassion for someone who appears to be the cause of our suffering but angrily denies any role in it.

Guilt-ridden unfaithful partners do not find it easy to assume responsibility for the fact that sexual betrayal inflicts a type of posttraumatic stress disorder on the betrayed that takes time to heal, if it does at all. Betrayed partners who feel shamed by the betrayal do not find it easy to assume responsibility for their role in the problems that might have led the unfaithful partner to have an affair as a potential solution to marital unhappiness. They may feel like "you broke me, so you're responsible for fixing me and making me whole again." Unfaithful partners may be flooded and overwhelmed by having to sympathetically manage the emotional dysregulation precipitated by a betrayal trauma that they inflicted. But to betrayed partners, it simply doesn't seem fair that they now have to assume responsibility for limiting the negative emotional impact of their PTSD on the person who caused it.

Humiliated affair partners ("mate poachers") do not find it easy to assume responsibility for the emotional pain that infidelity may cause the betrayed partner and the unfaithful partner's children or that the unfaithful partner may not have been unfaithful were it not for the permissive environment that a seductive affair partner intentionally provided. Unfaithful partners have difficulty assuming responsibility for the pain they cause their affair partners, who may have been seduced into being a partner in crime, which in retrospect they may come to regret. Human nature finds it difficult to bear the guilt that awareness of one's destructive impact on a partner's mental state entails, then to assume responsibility for finding some constructive way to repair the damage done (Klein, 1937/1998). Assuming responsibility requires the self-awareness necessary to insulate a partner as best one can from the negative impact of one's character flaws moving forward into the future.

AUTHENTICITY AND SECURE ATTACHMENT

Another variable that may be essential to successful long-term relationships is a trait that humanistic psychologists like Carl Rogers (1961) and Abraham Maslow (1968) called *authenticity*. Being authentic involves striving for openness and honesty in one's close relationships (Kernis & Goldman, 2006). Authenticity is associated with secure attachment in long-term relationships (Leak & Cooney, 2001) and with partaking in healthy relationship behaviors that predict positive relationship outcomes (Brunell et al., 2010). It has also been related to higher mindfulness and lesser verbal defensiveness (Lakey, Kernis, Heppner, & Lance, 2008). Authenticity within an intimate relationship has been related to two subcomponents: a willingness to risk being vulnerable and the unacceptability of deception (Lopez & Rice, 2006).

Being authentic is being yourself, being someone whose thoughts and feelings are relatively transparent and someone who doesn't play games with people. Authenticity is the opposite of narcissistic game-playing. An authentic person is a straightforward and down-to-earth person who is trustworthy (Wickham, Reed, & Williamson, 2015). An authentic person is what's called in Yiddish a *mensch*—a decent human being. Authentic individuals are trustworthy because we know where we stand with them. They aren't trying to con or manipulate their romantic partners, unlike those with the personality characteristics that make up the Dark Triad. Authenticity appears to be the antithesis of the Dark Triad.

Authentic individuals for whom deception within an intimate relationship is unacceptable would be less inclined to be unfaithful, because they would then have to live a lie. Authenticity is a state of mind as well as a character trait (Lenton, Bruder, Slabu, & Sedikides, 2013). Infidelity can generate a disturbing sense of deceptiveness and inauthenticity that is painful to endure. Individuals high in trait authenticity are intolerant of the unpleasant feeling of not being true to themselves and of having to live a lie. Being authentic reflects a kind of moral integrity (Schlenker, 2008). It reflects the courage to live one's life without hypocrisy and acceptance of the potential for social disapproval for being true to oneself.

Others may not like it if being true to oneself requires being politically incorrect in standing up for unpopular opinions or exposing the emperor's new clothes. Authentic people make themselves vulnerable to criticism and rejection because they are not necessarily conforming to what others expect of them if those expectations require them to violate their core values and heartfelt beliefs. Individuals who are frightened of rejection for being authentic become conformist. They accommodate to the expectations of others to fit in even if it means that they are living falsely. For example, playing hard to get, a game-playing approach to dating, is fostered when rejection-sensitive individuals are made to feel that they will be rejected for being themselves (Weinberg & Josephs, 2014).

State authenticity may be pleasurable in part because it appears to be associated with using cognitive reappraisal (i.e., mentalization) to regulate emotions (English & John, 2013). Inauthenticity requires hiding one's true feelings from others so that there is a certain kind of chronic stress in having to ensure that one's true feelings don't accidentally come out. In contrast, authentic people feel free to show their true feelings so they don't have to worry about being caught in a lie. They use cognitive reappraisal rather than emotion suppression as their predominant emotion regulation strategy. Unfaithful partners must often resort to emotion suppression so the truth doesn't unwittingly leak out. Many affairs have been exposed to betrayed spouses because of subtle forms of "leakage" that revealed the truth, like a Freudian slip in which one calls the betrayed partner by the affair partner's name in the heat of an argument when one's self-control and self-monitoring are diminished. Hiding an affair creates what experimental psychologists call a *cognitive load*, a burden of information processing in having to keep track of all of one's lies that may impair one's ability to regulate underlying emotional processes.

Authentic people are therefore trustworthy romantic partners with whom one can feel securely attached. They might not always be pleasant to be around if they have a penchant for being brutally honest to the point of emotional insensitivity, but at least one always knows where one stands with such a person. They can't tell a lie because they are intolerant of suppressing their true selves. Of course, a person such as this might sound a bit insufferable, but being authentic doesn't require being tactless. It doesn't require being blunt in a way that is insensitive to the feelings of others. It means being truthful, as least as one sees it, with respect for those who see things differently. People who are both authentic and reflective can be themselves in a way that is sensitive to the feelings of others. People who are authentic without being reflective or thoughtful can be indifferent to the feelings of others, priding themselves on their brutal honesty while oblivious to their lack of empathy or tact. Thus, the people least likely to be unfaithful may be high in reflective functioning and authenticity because they are the people most likely to address conflictual issues forthrightly rather than avoidantly and empathetically rather than insensitively.

Carl Rogers (1961) was the first to point out the importance of authenticity in psychotherapy. He discovered that therapists who are congruent (i.e., are authentic because their words match their deeds), provide unconditional positive regard (i.e., are essentially affirmative of the patient's intrinsic worth and dignity as a human being), and empathetic achieve better results than therapists who don't possess those qualities. Recent research (Wampold & Imel, 2015) suggests that Rogers was right about the relational factors that lead to successful psychotherapy outcome. Psychotherapy facilitates patients' authenticity in a variety of ways. For example, therapists are role models of authenticity, especially to the degree that they strive to be transparent and honest in openly sharing their clinical thinking, opinions, and perspectives as pertains to the patient. Further, therapists strive to provide a therapeutic atmosphere in which authenticity is rewarded rather than punished. Therapists hope to provide a therapeutic relationship in which patients feel free to express their socially unacceptable thoughts and feelings without fear of being judged. That includes openly expressing what psychodynamic psychotherapists call *negative transference* (Freud, 1912/1958), the patient's unflattering and potentially offensive characterization of the therapist's clinical approach and personality.

Can the therapist nondefensively tolerate being characterized or perhaps mischaracterized as incompetent and ineffective; as a cold, uncaring sadist; or perhaps even as a secret philanderer? For example, I practice in the same suite of offices as my wife, who is also a clinical psychologist. It is not uncommon that patients dealing with conflicts around infidelity notice that I don't wear a wedding ring and speculate that perhaps I pretend to be an unmarried man so that I can have affairs with unsuspecting women. Patients may hope that the therapist is an authentic person yet dread that perhaps he or she is not and that the therapist's therapeutic persona is only a false pretense.

The therapist must practice what he or she preaches when it comes to communication skills. How does the therapist respond when the patient engages in therapist character assassination, treats the therapist with contempt, responds with defensive self-justification as if all therapist observations of self-defeating patterns constituted unfair criticism, and finally withdraws in anger by giving the therapist the silent treatment, missing sessions, or arriving late? Does the therapist retaliate in kind or respond in a more constructive fashion? Does the therapist "own" lapses into defensive responding when the patient succeeds in pressing the therapist's hot-button issues? Can the therapist tolerate perpetual conflict in the therapeutic relationship when the patient resists more cooperative engagement? In couples therapy, does the therapist become as flooded and overwhelmed as the couple is when an ugly spat erupts in the consulting room or implicitly side with one partner against the other?

The therapist is being implicitly tested by these emotional challenges. Just how authentic is the therapist when put to the test—when the patient unconsciously treats or mistreats the therapist as the patient has felt mistreated by others? Do therapists protect their vulnerable selves in the same self-protective ways as everybody else, or do they role model somehow being able to transcend their own defensive reactions to insensitive, if not emotionally abusive, treatment by patients? The most useful and inspirational role modeling is seeing how someone copes when seriously challenged by trying circumstances. Perhaps this is why there are no "easy" patients—because patients learn by being difficult patients and then observing how their therapist copes with a difficult person. Weiss (1995) discovered that psychotherapy outcome is better when therapists pass these unconscious tests.

COOPERATIVE CHILDCARE, SEXUAL FIDELITY, AND GENERATIVITY

From an evolutionary perspective, romantic pair bonding for biparental care may be the most cooperative and altruistic long-term relationship in which humans engage. Being reflective and authentic may be adaptations for having successful long-term cooperative relationships with others. If there is assortative mating for such personality traits, it would mean that the most reflective and authentic people tend to pair off and reproduce with each other, while the least authentic, least reflective people tend to pair off and reproduce with one another. Children of reflective, authentic, and securely attached parents may be inheriting those personality traits to the degree that those traits possess some hereditability and are role modeled by their parents throughout their childhoods. The children of unreflective, inauthentic, and insecurely attached parents are getting the opposite—a childhood more likely to be characterized by parental infidelity, divorce, high parental conflict, and the emotional distance of conflict-avoiding couples. As a consequence, evolutionary conflict may be playing out before our very eyes as two alternative reproductive strategies compete for dominance among the human population as well as within the hearts of each of us. It is not apparent whether the most or the least cooperative reproductive strategy will eventually emerge a clear winner in the future course of human evolution.

Psychotherapy for infidelity might ultimately facilitate what Erik Erikson (1963) called *generativity*: Generativity versus stagnation is Erikson's seventh stage of psychosocial development, which occurs during middle age. It is a time that adults strive to create or nurture things that will outlast them by having children and contributing to positive changes that benefit other people. Generativity epitomizes human cooperation because it means doing something for the good of others that might have its beneficial long-term impact after one has been long dead and gone.

Generativity is the developmental challenge that comes after the sixth stage of psychosocial development, intimacy versus isolation, which occurs during young adulthood in the quest for a long-term adult romantic relationship. Infidelity appears to be a symptom of the inability to form the kind of stable long-term intimate relationship that facilitates successful generativity rather than stagnation. Infidelity suggests that one is still stuck working through issues around romantic intimacy and is not fully engaged in the challenges of generativity, of fully investing in the survival of something that will outlast oneself. The more one is bogged down in negotiating issues around intimacy, the less time and energy are left to confront the challenges of generativity.

Individuals may retreat from the challenges of generativity when they become too daunting. It can seem overwhelming to learn how to have a successful long-term relationship, raise emotionally stable and responsible children, and make enough money to support a family in a difficult economy. Infidelity can be an escape from responsibilities that seem too much to bear. Intimacy without generativity may ultimately feel meaningless, which may be why affairs that don't lead to successful second marriages are often regretted in retrospect. Affairs that are not generative seem in retrospect to be part of the problem rather than part of the solution.

Psychotherapy has always been seen as a practice that can help patients overcome fears of intimacy. Psychotherapy may also need to facilitate intimacy that results in generativity because romantic intimacy that doesn't lead to generativity may ultimately lead to feelings of meaningless and purposelessness.

Not everyone has to be a "breeder" to live a meaningful life, but those who do reproduce often feel that raising a family together gives a romantic relationship a deeper meaning and purpose compared with the satisfaction of one's personal needs for sex and emotional intimacy. As cooperative breeders, humans can live generative lives by being of help to their communities or to humanity in general without having to sire children themselves. In addition, generative families could potentially be based on both consensual nonmonogamy and consensual monogamy, although this issue has yet to be adequately researched because polyamorous parents tend to be marginalized (Pallotta-Chiarolli, Haydon, & Hunter, 2013).

A couple or family that functions as a cooperative team based on mutual trust, respect, and understanding is more likely to facilitate generativity than couples or families that lack those qualities. Psychotherapists who facilitate acceptance, mentalization, secure attachment, constructive communication, and authenticity are facilitating the cultivation of the personality traits most likely to contribute to having the kind of cooperative long-term romantic relationship based on trust and secure attachment that enables meaningful generativity.

REFERENCES

Acevedo, B. P., & Aron, A. (2009). Does a long-term relationship kill romantic love? *Review of General Psychology, 13*, 59–65. http://dx.doi.org/10.1037/a0014226

Acevedo, B. P., Aron, A., Fisher, H. E., & Brown, L. L. (2012). Neural correlates of long-term intense romantic love. *Social Cognitive and Affective Neuroscience, 7*, 145–159. http://dx.doi.org/10.1093/scan/nsq092

Achim, A. M., Guitton, M., Jackson, P. L., Boutin, A., & Monetta, L. (2013). On what ground do we mentalize? Characteristics of current tasks and sources of information that contribute to mentalizing judgments. *Psychological Assessment, 25*, 117–126. http://dx.doi.org/10.1037/a0029137

Adams, H. E., Wright, L. W., Jr., & Lohr, B. A. (1996). Is homophobia associated with homosexual arousal? *Journal of Abnormal Psychology, 105*, 440–445. http://dx.doi.org/10.1037/0021-843X.105.3.440

Ainsworth, M. D. S. (1967). *Infancy in Uganda: Infant care and the growth of love*. Oxford, England: Johns Hopkins Press.

Ainsworth, M. D. S., Blehar, M. C., Waters E., & Wall, S. (1978). *Patterns of attachment: A psychological study of the strange situation*. Oxford, England: Erlbaum.

Alberts, H. J. E. M., Thewissen, R., & Raes, L. (2012). Dealing with problematic eating behaviour. The effects of a mindfulness-based intervention on eating behaviour, food cravings, dichotomous thinking and body image concern. *Appetite, 58*, 847–851. http://dx.doi.org/10.1016/j.appet.2012.01.009

Aldao, A., Nolen-Hoeksema, S., & Schweizer, S. (2010). Emotion-regulation strategies across psychopathology: A meta-analytic review. *Clinical Psychology Review, 30*, 217–237. http://dx.doi.org/10.1016/j.cpr.2009.11.004

Al-Krenawi, A. (2001). Women from polygamous and monogamous marriages in an out-patient psychiatric clinic. *Transcultural Psychiatry, 38*, 187–199. http://dx.doi.org/10.1177/136346150103800203

Al-Krenawi, A., Graham, J. R., & Al-Krenawi, S. (1997). Social work practice with polygamous families. *Child & Adolescent Social Work Journal, 14*, 445–458. http://dx.doi.org/10.1023/A:1024571031073

Allen, E. S., & Atkins, D. C. (2012). The association of divorce and extramarital sex in a representative U.S. Sample. *Journal of Family Issues, 33*, 1477–1493. http://dx.doi.org/10.1177/0192513X12439692

Allen, E. S., & Baucom, D. H. (2004). Adult attachment and patterns of extradyadic involvement. *Family Process, 43*, 467–488. http://dx.doi.org/10.1111/j.1545-5300.2004.00035.x

Allen, J. G. (2013). *Restoring mentalizing in attachment relationships: Treating trauma with plain old therapy*. Arlington, VA: American Psychiatric Publishing.

Amato, P. R. (2001). Children of divorce in the 1990s: An update of the Amato and Keith (1991) meta-analysis. *Journal of Family Psychology, 15*, 355–370. http://dx.doi.org/10.1037/0893-3200.15.3.355

American Psychiatric Association. (2013). *Diagnostic and statistical manual of mental disorders* (5th ed.). Washington, DC: American Psychiatric Association Press.

Anders, S. L., & Tucker, J. S. (2000). Adult attachment style, interpersonal communication competence, and social support. *Personal Relationships, 7*, 379–389. http://dx.doi.org/10.1111/j.1475-6811.2000.tb00023.x

Andersen, S. M., & Przybylinski, E. (2012). Experiments on transference in interpersonal relations: Implications for treatment. *Psychotherapy, 49*, 370–383. http://dx.doi.org/10.1037/a0029116

Anderson, E. (2012). *The monogamy gap: Men, love, and the reality of cheating*. New York, NY: Oxford University Press. http://dx.doi.org/10.1093/acprof:oso/9780199777921.001.0001

Anderson, K. G. (2006). How well does paternity confidence match actual paternity? Evidence from worldwide nonpaternity rates. *Current Anthropology, 47*, 513–520. http://dx.doi.org/10.1086/504167

Andersson, M. (1994). *Monographs in behavior and ecology: Sexual selection*. Princeton, NJ: Princeton University Press.

Ard, B. N. (1977). Sex in lasting marriages: A longitudinal study. *Journal of Sex Research, 13*, 274–285. http://dx.doi.org/10.1080/00224497709550985

Ariely, D., Huber, J., & Wertenbroch, K. (2005). When do losses loom larger than gains? *Journal of Marketing Research, 42*, 134–138. http://dx.doi.org/10.1509/jmkr.42.2.134.62283

Ariely, D., & Loewenstein, G. (2006). The heat of the moment: The effect of sexual arousal on sexual decision making. *Journal of Behavioral Decision Making, 19*, 87–98. http://dx.doi.org/10.1002/bdm.501

Aron, A., Fisher, H., Mashek, D. J., Strong, G., Li, H., & Brown, L. L. (2005). Reward, motivation, and emotion systems associated with early-stage intense romantic love. *Journal of Neurophysiology, 94*, 327–337. http://dx.doi.org/10.1152/jn.00838.2004

Asayama, S. (1975). Adolescent sex development and adult sex behavior in Japan. *Journal of Sex Research, 11*, 91–112. http://dx.doi.org/10.1080/00224497509550883

Asendorpf, J. B., Penke, L., & Back, M. D. (2011). From dating to mating and relating: Predictors of initial and long-term outcomes of speed-dating in a community sample. *European Journal of Personality, 25*, 16–30. http://dx.doi.org/10.1002/per.768

Ash, J., & Gallup, G. (2008). Brain size, intelligence, and Paleolithic variation. In G. Geher & G. Miller (Eds.), *Mating intelligence: Sex, relationships, and the mind's reproductive system* (pp. 313–336). New York, NY: Erlbaum.

Atkins, D. C., Baucom, D. H., & Jacobson, N. S. (2001). Understanding infidelity: Correlates in a national random sample. *Journal of Family Psychology, 15*, 735–749. http://dx.doi.org/10.1037/0893-3200.15.4.735

Atkins, D. C., Marín, R. A., Lo, T. T., Klann, N., & Hahlweg, K. (2010). Outcomes of couples with infidelity in a community-based sample of couple therapy. *Journal of Family Psychology, 24*, 212–216.

Atkins, D. C., Yi, J., Baucom, D. H., & Christensen, A. (2005). Infidelity in couples seeking marital therapy. *Journal of Family Psychology, 19*, 470–473. http://dx.doi.org/10.1037/0893-3200.19.3.470

Back, M. D., Schmukle, S. C., & Egloff, B. (2010). Why are narcissists so charming at first sight? Decoding the narcissism-popularity link at zero acquaintance. *Journal of Personality and Social Psychology, 98*, 132–145. http://dx.doi.org/10.1037/a0016338

Bagemihl, B. (1999). *Biological exuberance: Animal homosexuality and natural diversity*. New York, NY: St. Martins Press.

Balicki, A. (1970). *The Netsilik Eskimo*. Garden City, NY: Natural History Press.

Barash, D. P., & Lipton, J. E. (2001). *The myth of monogamy: Fidelity and infidelity in animals and people*. New York, NY: Freeman.

Barber, N. (1999). Women's dress fashions as a function of reproductive strategy. *Sex Roles, 40*, 459–471. http://dx.doi.org/10.1023/A:1018823727012

Barkow, J. H., Cosmides, L., & Tooby, J. (Eds.). (1992). *The adapted mind: Evolutionary psychology and the generation of culture*. New York, NY: Oxford University Press.

Baron-Cohen, S. (2003). *The essential difference: Male and female brains and the truth about autism*. New York, NY: Basic Books.

Bartz, J. A., Lydon, J. E., Kolevzon, A., Zaki, J., Hollander, E., Ludwig, N., & Bolger, N. (2015). Differential effects of oxytocin on agency and communion for anxiously and avoidantly attached individuals. *Psychological Science, 26*, 1177–1186. http://dx.doi.org/10.1177/0956797615580279

Bateman, A., & Fonagy, P. (2004). *Psychotherapy for borderline personality disorder: Mentalization-based treatment*. Oxford, England: Oxford University Press. http://dx.doi.org/10.1093/med:psych/9780198527664.001.0001

Baucom, D. H., Snyder, D. K., & Gordon, K. C. (2009). *Helping couples get past the affair*. New York, NY: Guilford Press.

Baughman, H. M., Jonason, P. K., Lyons, M., & Vernon, P. A. (2014). Liar liar pants on fire: Cheater strategies linked to the Dark Triad. *Personality and Individual Differences, 71*, 35–38. http://dx.doi.org/10.1016/j.paid.2014.07.019

Baumeister, R. F., & Bratslavsky, E. (1999). Passion, intimacy, and time: Passionate love as a function of change in intimacy. *Personality and Social Psychology Review, 3*, 49–67. http://dx.doi.org/10.1207/s15327957pspr0301_3

Baumeister, R. F., Catanese, K. R., & Vohs, K. D. (2001). Is there a gender difference in strength of sex drive? Theoretical views, conceptual distinctions, and a review of relevant evidence. *Personality and Social Psychology Review, 5*, 242–273. http://dx.doi.org/10.1207/S15327957PSPR0503_5

Baumeister, R. F., Smart, L., & Boden, J. M. (1996). Relation of threatened egotism to violence and aggression: The dark side of high self-esteem. *Psychological Review, 103*, 5–33. http://dx.doi.org/10.1037/0033-295X.103.1.5

Beckerman, S., Lizarraide, R., & Lizarraide, M. (2002). The Bari partible paternity project, Phase One. In S. Beckerman & P. Valentine (Eds.), *Cultures of multiple fathers: The theory and practice of partible paternity in lowland South America* (pp. 27–41). Gainesville: University of Florida Press.

Beckerman, S., & Valentine, P. (2002). *Cultures of multiple fathers: The theory and practice of partible paternity in lowland South America.* Gainesville: University of Florida Press.

Behne, T., Liszkowski, U., Carpenter, M., & Tomasello, M. (2012). Twelve-month-olds' comprehension and production of pointing. *British Journal of Developmental Psychology, 30*, 359–375. http://dx.doi.org/10.1111/j.2044-835X.2011.02043.x

Belsky, J. (2000). Conditional and alternative reproductive strategies: Individual differences in susceptibility to rearing experience. In J. Rodgers, D. Rowe, & W. Miller (Eds.), *Genetic influences on human fertility and sexuality: Theoretical and empirical contributions from the biological and behavioral sciences* (pp. 127–146). Boston, MA: Kluwer.

Belsky, J., Steinberg, L., & Draper, P. (1991). Childhood experience, interpersonal development, and reproductive strategy: And evolutionary theory of socialization. *Child Development, 62*, 647–670. http://dx.doi.org/10.2307/1131166

Bergling, T. (2007). *Chasing Adonis: Gay men and the pursuit of perfection*. Binghamton, NY: Harrington Park Press/The Haworth Press.

Bergström-Walan, M.-B., & Nielsen, H. H. (1990). Sexual expression among 60–80-year-old men and women: A sample from Stockholm, Sweden. *Journal of Sex Research, 27*, 289–295. http://dx.doi.org/10.1080/00224499009551558

Besser, A., & Priel, B. (2008). Attachment, depression, and fear of death in older adults: The roles of neediness and perceived availability of social support. *Personality and Individual Differences, 44*, 1711–1725. http://dx.doi.org/10.1016/j.paid.2008.01.016

Betzig, L. L. (1986). *Despotism and differential reproduction: A Darwinian view of history*. New Brunswick, NJ: Aldine Transaction.

Birnbaum, G. E., Reis, H. T., Mikulincer, M., Gillath, O., & Orpaz, A. (2006). When sex is more than just sex: Attachment orientations, sexual experience, and relationship quality. *Journal of Personality and Social Psychology, 91*, 929–943. http://dx.doi.org/10.1037/0022-3514.91.5.929

Blurton Jones, N. G., Marlowe, F., Hawkes, K., & O'Connell, J. F. (2000). Paternal investment and hunter-gatherer divorce rates. In L. Cronk, W. Irons, & N. Chagnon (Eds.), *Adaptation and human behavior: An anthropological perspective* (pp. 69–90). New York, NY: Aldine de Gruyter.

Boehm, C. (2012). *Moral origins: The evolution of virtue, altruism, and shame*. New York, NY: Basic Books.

Bowins, B. (2013). Cognitive regulatory control therapies. *American Journal of Psychotherapy, 67*, 215–236.

Bowlby, J. (1944). Forty-four juvenile thieves: Their characters and home-life (II). *The International Journal of Psychoanalysis, 25*, 107–128.

Bowlby, J. (1951). *Maternal care and mental health.* World Health Organization Monograph Series No. 2. Geneva, Switzerland: World Health Organization.

Bowlby, J. (1969). *Attachment and loss: Vol. 1. Attachment.* New York, NY: Basic Books.

Bowlby, J. (1973). *Attachment and loss: Vol. 2. Separation: Anxiety and anger.* New York, NY: Basic Books.

Bowlby, J. (1980). *Attachment and loss: Vol. 3. Loss: Sadness and depression.* New York, NY: Basic Books.

Bowlby, J. (1988). *A secure base: Clinical applications of attachment theory.* London, England: Routledge.

Brand, R. J., Markey, C. M., Mills, A., & Hodges, S. D. (2007). Sex differences in self-reported infidelity and its correlates. *Sex Roles, 57,* 101–109. http://dx.doi.org/10.1007/s11199-007-9221-5

Brase, G. L., & Guy, E. C. (2004). The demographics of mate value and self-esteem. *Personality and Individual Differences, 36,* 471–484. http://dx.doi.org/10.1016/S0191-8869(03)00117-X

Brassard, A., Shaver, P. R., & Lussier, Y. (2007). Attachment, sexual experience, and sexual pressure in romantic relationships: A dyadic approach. *Personal Relationships, 14,* 475–493. http://dx.doi.org/10.1111/j.1475-6811.2007.00166.x

Bredow, C. A. (2015). Chasing Prince Charming: Partnering consequences of holding unrealistic standards for a spouse. *Personal Relationships, 22,* 476–501. http://dx.doi.org/10.1111/pere.12091

Brennan, K. A., Clark, C. L., & Shaver P. R. (1998). Self-report measurement of adult attachment: An integrative overview. In J. A. Simpson & W. S. Rholes (Eds.), *Attachment theory and close relationships* (pp. 46–76). New York, NY: Guilford Press.

Brennan, K. A., & Shaver, P. R. (1995). Dimensions of adult attachment, affect regulation, and romantic relationship functioning. *Personality and Social Psychology Bulletin, 21,* 267–283. http://dx.doi.org/10.1177/0146167295213008

Brenner, C. (2002). Conflict, compromise formation, and structural theory. *The Psychoanalytic Quarterly, LXXI,* 397–417. http://dx.doi.org/10.1002/j.2167-4086.2002.tb00519.x

Brewer, G., & Abell, L. (2015). Machiavellianism and sexual behaviour: Motivations, deception and infidelity. *Personality and Individual Differences, 74,* 186–191. http://dx.doi.org/10.1016/j.paid.2014.10.028

Brodsky, B. S., & Stanley, B. (2013). *The dialectical behavior therapy primer: How DBT can inform clinical practice.* New York, NY: Wiley. http://dx.doi.org/10.1002/9781118556603

Brown, D. (1991). *Human universals.* New York, NY: McGraw-Hill.

Brown, M., & Auerback, A. (1981). Communication patterns in initiation of marital sex. *Medical Aspects of Human Sexuality, 15,* 105–117.

Brunell, A., Kernis, M., Goldman, B., Heppner, W., Davis, P., Cascio, E., & Webster, G. (2010). Dispositional authenticity and romantic relationship functioning.

Personality and Individual Differences, *48*, 900–905. http://dx.doi.org/10.1016/j.paid.2010.02.018

Bullough, V. L. (1976). *Sexual variance in society and history*. Chicago, IL: University of Chicago Press.

Bullough, V. L., & Bullough, B. (1978). *Prostitution: An illustrated social history*. New York, NY: Crown.

Burlingham, D., & Freud, A. (1949). *Kriegskinder* [War children]. Oxford, England: Imago.

Burt, S. A., & Donnellan, M. B. (2015). Toward a developmentally sensitive and genetically informed perspective on popularity. In B. N. Horwitz & J. M. Neiderhiser (Eds.), *Gene–environment interplay in interpersonal relationships across the lifespan. Advances in behavior genetics* (pp. 151–169). New York, NY: Springer Science + Business Media. http://dx.doi.org/10.1007/978-1-4939-2923-8_7

Bushman, B. J. (2002). Does venting anger feed or extinguish the flame? Catharsis, rumination, distraction, anger and aggressive responding. *Personality and Social Psychology Bulletin*, *28*, 724–731. http://dx.doi.org/10.1177/0146167202289002

Bushman, B. J., & Baumeister, R. F. (1998). Threatened egotism, narcissism, self-esteem, and direct and displaced aggression: Does self-love or self-hate lead to violence? *Journal of Personality and Social Psychology*, *75*, 219–229. http://dx.doi.org/10.1037/0022-3514.75.1.219

Bushman, B. J., Baumeister, R. F., & Stack, A. D. (1999). Catharsis, aggression, and persuasive influence: Self-fulfilling or self-defeating prophecies? *Journal of Personality and Social Psychology*, *76*, 367–376. http://dx.doi.org/10.1037/0022-3514.76.3.367

Buss, D. M. (1989). Sex differences in human mate preferences: Evolutionary hypotheses tested in 37 cultures. *Behavioral and Brain Sciences*, *12*, 1–49. http://dx.doi.org/10.1017/S0140525X00023992

Buss, D. M. (2000). *The dangerous passion: Why jealousy is as necessary as love and sex*. London, England: Bloomsbury.

Buss, D. M. (2003). *The evolution of desire: Strategies of human mating* (revised ed.). New York, NY: Basic Books.

Buss, D. M., & Hawley, P. H. (Eds.). (2011). *The evolution of personality and individual differences*. New York, NY: Oxford University Press.

Buss, D. M., & Schmitt, D. P. (1993). Sexual strategies theory: An evolutionary perspective on human mating. *Psychological Review*, *100*, 204–232. http://dx.doi.org/10.1037/0033-295X.100.2.204

Buss, D. M., & Shackelford, T. K. (1997). From vigilance to violence: Mate retention tactics in married couples. *Journal of Personality and Social Psychology*, *72*, 346–361. http://dx.doi.org/10.1037/0022-3514.72.2.346

Buss, D. M., & Shackelford, T. K. (2008). Attractive women want it all: Good genes, economic investment, parenting proclivities, and emotional commitment. *Evolutionary Psychology*, 6, 134–146. http://dx.doi.org/10.1177/147470490800600116

Call, V., Sprecher, S., & Schwartz, P. (1995). The incidence and frequency of marital sex in a national sample. *Journal of Marriage and the Family*, *57*, 639–652. http://dx.doi.org/10.2307/353919

Cameron, C., Oskamp, S., & Sparks, W. (1977). Courtship American style: Newspaper ads. *The Family Coordinator*, *26*, 27–30. http://dx.doi.org/10.2307/581857

Campbell, W. K. (1999). Narcissism and romantic attraction. *Journal of Personality and Social Psychology*, *77*, 1254–1270. http://dx.doi.org/10.1037/0022-3514.77.6.1254

Campbell, W. K., Foster, C. A., & Finkel, E. J. (2002). Does self-love lead to love for others? A story of narcissistic game playing. *Journal of Personality and Social Psychology*, *83*, 340–354. http://dx.doi.org/10.1037/0022-3514.83.2.340

Carlsmith, K. M., Wilson, T. D., & Gilbert, D. T. (2008). The paradoxical consequences of revenge. *Journal of Personality and Social Psychology*, *95*, 1316–1324. http://dx.doi.org/10.1037/a0012165

Carnes, P. (1991). *Don't call it love*. New York, NY: Bantam.

Carter, C. S., DeVries, A. C., & Getz, L. L. (1995). Physiological substrates of mammalian monogamy: The prairie vole model. *Neuroscience and Biobehavioral Reviews*, *19*, 303–314. http://dx.doi.org/10.1016/0149-7634(94)00070-H

Castonguay, L. G., & Hill, C. E. (Eds.). (2012). *Transformation in psychotherapy: Corrective experiences across cognitive behavioral, humanistic, and psychodynamic approaches*. Washington, DC: American Psychological Association. http://dx.doi.org/10.1037/13747-000

Cerda-Flores, R. M., Barton, S. A., Marty-Gonzalez, L. F., Rivas, F., & Chakraborty, R. (1999). Estimation of nonpaternity in the Mexican population of Nuevo Leon: A validation study with blood group markers. *American Journal of Physical Anthropology*, *109*, 281–293. http://dx.doi.org/10.1002/(SICI)1096-8644(199907)109:3<281::AID-AJPA1>3.0.CO;2-3

Chapais, B. (2008). *Primeval kinship: How pair-bonding gave birth to human society*. Cambridge, MA: Harvard University Press.

Chapman, A. L., & Compton, J. S. (2003). From traditional behavioral couple therapy to integrative behavioral couple therapy: New research directions. *The Behavior Analyst Today*, *4*, 17–25. http://dx.doi.org/10.1037/h0100007

Charnov, E. (1993). *Life history invariants*. Oxford, England: Oxford University Press.

Charny, I. W., & Asineli-Tal, S. (2004). Study of "sex-less" (sex-avoidant) young couples. *Journal of Family Psychotherapy*, *15*, 197–217. http://dx.doi.org/10.1300/J085v15n01_15

Chesney, A. P., Blakeney, P. E., Chan, F. A., & Cole, C. M. (1981). The impact of sex therapy on sexual behaviors and marital communication. *Journal of Sex & Marital Therapy*, *7*, 70–79. http://dx.doi.org/10.1080/00926238108403442

Chesney, A. P., Blakeney, P. E., Cole, C. M., & Chan, F. A. (1981). A comparison of couples who have sought sex therapy with couples who have not. *Journal of Sex & Marital Therapy*, *7*, 131–140. http://dx.doi.org/10.1080/00926238108406099

Christensen, A., & Heavey, C. L. (1993). Gender differences in marital conflict: The demand/withdraw interaction pattern. In S. Oskamp & M. Costanzo (Eds.), *Claremont Symposium on Applied Social Psychology: Vol. 6. Gender issues in contemporary society* (pp. 113–141). Thousand Oaks, CA: Sage.

Christensen, A., & Jacobson, N. (1998). *Acceptance and change in couple therapy: A therapist's guide to transforming relationships*. New York, NY: Norton.

Christie, R., & Geis, F. L. (1970). *Studies in Machiavellianism*. London, England: Academic Press.

Clark, L. A. (2005). Temperament as a unifying basis for personality and psychopathology. *Journal of Abnormal Psychology, 114*, 505–521. http://dx.doi.org/10.1037/0021-843X.114.4.505

Cleckley, H. (2015). *The mask of sanity: An attempt to clarify some issues about the so-called psychopathic personality*. New York, NY: Martino Fine Books. (Original work published 1941)

Conroy-Beam, D., & Buss, D. M. (2016). Do mate preferences influence actual mating decisions? Evidence from computer simulations and three studies of mate couples. *Journal of Personality and Social Psychology, 111*, 53–66. http://dx.doi.org/10.1037/pspi0000054

Cooper, M. L., Pioli, M., Levitt, A., Telley, A. E., Micheas, L., & Collins, N. L. (2006). Attachment styles, sex motives, and sexual behavior. In M. Mikulincer & G. S. Goodman (Eds.), *Dynamics of romantic love: Attachment, caregiving, and sex* (pp. 243–274). New York, NY: Guilford Press.

Corley, M. D., Schneider, J. P., & Hook, J. N. (2012). Partner reactions to disclosure of relapse by self-identified sexual addicts. *Sexual Addiction & Compulsivity, 19*, 265–283.

Cortes, B. P., Demoulin, S., Rodriguez, R. T., Rodriguez, A. P., & Leyens, J. P. (2005). Infrahumanization or familiarity? Attribution of uniquely human emotions to the self, the ingroup, and the outgroup. *Personality and Social Psychology Bulletin, 31*, 243–253. http://dx.doi.org/10.1177/0146167204271421

Cosmides, L., & Tooby, J. (1992). Cognitive adaptations for social exchange. In J. Barkow, L. Cosmides, & J. Tooby (Eds.), *The adapted mind: Evolutionary psychology and the generation of culture* (pp. 163–228). New York, NY: Oxford University Press.

Costa, P. T., Jr., Terracciano, A., & McCrae, R. R. (2001). Gender differences in personality traits across cultures: Robust and surprising findings. *Journal of Personality and Social Psychology, 81*, 322–331. http://dx.doi.org/10.1037/0022-3514.81.2.322

Crocker, W. H. (2002). Canela "Other fathers": Partible paternity and its changing practices. In S. Beckerman & P. Valentine (Eds.), *Cultures of multiple fathers: The theory and practice of partible paternity in lowland South America* (pp. 86–104). Gainesville: University of Florida Press.

Cronk, L., Chagnon, N., & Irons, W. (Eds.). *Behavior: An anthropological perspective* (pp. 69–90). New York, NY: Aldine.

Crowell, J. A., Fraley, R. C., & Shaver, P. R. (1999). Measurement of individual differences in adolescent and adult attachment. In J. Cassidy & P. R. Shaver (Eds.), *Handbook of attachment: Theory, research, and clinical applications* (pp. 434–465). New York, NY: Guilford Press.

Cruces, J. M. S., Hawrylak, M. F., & Delegido, A. (2015). Interpersonal variability of the experience of falling in love. *International Journal of Psychology & Psychological Therapy, 15*, 87–100.

Cummings, E. M., & Davies, P. T. (2011). *Marital conflict and children: An emotional security perspective*. New York, NY: Guilford Press.

Cummings, E. M., Zahn-Waxler, C., & Radke-Yarrow, M. (1981). Young children's responses to expressions of anger and affection by others in the family. *Child Development, 52*, 1274–1282. http://dx.doi.org/10.2307/1129516

Cummins, D. (2005). Dominance, status, and social hierarchies. In D. M. Buss (Ed.), *The handbook of evolutionary psychology* (pp. 676–697). Hoboken, NJ: Wiley.

Dabbs, J. M. (2000). *Heroes, rogues, and lovers: Testosterone and behavior*. New York, NY: McGraw-Hill.

Dakanalis, A., Clerici, M., & Carrà, G. (2016). Narcissistic vulnerability and grandiosity as mediators between insecure attachment and future eating disordered behaviors: A prospective analysis of over 2,000 freshmen. *Journal of Clinical Psychology, 72*, 279–292. http://dx.doi.org/10.1002/jclp.22237

Daly, M., & Wilson, M. (1999). An evolutionary psychological perspective on homicide. In M. D. Smith & M. A. Zahn (Eds.), *Homicide: A sourcebook of social research* (pp. 58–71). Thousand Oaks, CA: Sage.

Daly, M., Wilson, M., & Weghorst, S. J. (1982). Male sexual jealousy. *Ethology & Sociobiology, 3*, 11–27. http://dx.doi.org/10.1016/0162-3095(82)90027-9

Darwin, C. (1871). *The descent of man and selection in relation to sex*. London, England: Murray.

Davidov, M., Zahn-Waxler, C., Roth-Hanania, R., & Knafo, A. (2013). Concern for others in the first year of life: Theory, evidence, and avenues for research. *Child Development Perspectives, 7*, 126–131. http://dx.doi.org/10.1111/cdep.12028

Davies, A. P. C., Shackelford, T. K., & Hass, R. G. (2010). Sex differences in perceptions of benefits and costs of mate poaching. *Personality and Individual Differences, 49*, 441–445. http://dx.doi.org/10.1016/j.paid.2010.04.014

Davis, D., Shaver, P. R., Widaman, K. F., Vernon, M. L., Follette, W. C., & Beitz, K. (2006). "I can't get no satisfaction": Insecure attachment, inhibited sexual communication, and sexual dissatisfaction. *Personal Relationships, 13*, 465–483. http://dx.doi.org/10.1111/j.1475-6811.2006.00130.x

Dawkins, R. (1976). *The selfish gene*. New York, NY: Oxford University Press.

DeLamater, J. D., & Sill, M. (2005). Sexual desire in later life. *Journal of Sex Research, 42*, 138–149. http://dx.doi.org/10.1080/00224490509552267

Del Giudice, M. (2009). Sex, attachment, and the development of reproductive strategies. *Behavioral and Brain Sciences*, *32*, 1–21. http://dx.doi.org/10.1017/S0140525X09000016

Del Giudice, M. (2011). Sex differences in romantic attachment: A meta-analysis. *Personality and Social Psychology Bulletin*, *37*, 193–214. http://dx.doi.org/10.1177/0146167210392789

Del Giudice, M. (2014). An evolutionary life history framework for psychopathology. *Psychological Inquiry*, *25*, 261–300. http://dx.doi.org/10.1080/1047840X.2014.884918

Deri, J. (2015). *Love's refraction: Jealousy and compersion in queer women's polyamorous relationships*. Toronto, Ontario, Canada: University of Toronto Press.

Devine, M. (1991). *Baby talk: The art of communicating with infants and toddlers*. New York, NY: Insight Books/Plenum Press.

Dew, B., Brubaker, M., & Hays, D. (2006). From the altar to the Internet: Married men and their online sexual behavior. *Sexual Addiction & Compulsivity*, *13*, 195–207. http://dx.doi.org/10.1080/10720160600870752

de Waal, F. (1990). Sociosexual behavior used for tension regulation in all age and sex combinations among bonobos. In J. R. Feierman (Ed.), *Pedophilia: Biosocial dimensions* (pp. 378–393). New York, NY: Springer-Verlag. http://dx.doi.org/10.1007/978-1-4613-9682-6_15

de Waal, F. (2007). *Chimpanzee politics: Power and sex among the apes*. Baltimore, MD: Johns Hopkins.

de Waal, F., & Lanting, F. (1997). *Bonobo: The forgotten ape*. Berkley: University of California Press.

Dhawan, N., Kunik, M. E., Oldham, J., & Coverdale, J. (2010). Prevalence and treatment of narcissistic personality disorder in the community: A systematic review. *Comprehensive Psychiatry*, *51*, 333–339. http://dx.doi.org/10.1016/j.comppsych.2009.09.003

Diamond, D., & Meehan, K. B. (2013). Attachment and object relations in patients with narcissistic personality disorder: Implications for therapeutic process and outcome. *Journal of Clinical Psychology*, 69, 1148–1159. http://dx.doi.org/10.1002/jclp.22042

Diamond, L. M. (2004). Emerging perspectives on distinctions between romantic love and sexual desire. *Current Directions in Psychological Science*, *13*, 116–119. http://dx.doi.org/10.1111/j.0963-7214.2004.00287.x

Dixson, A. F. (1998). *Primate sexuality: Comparative studies of the prosimians, monkeys, apes and human beings*. New York, NY: Oxford University Press.

Dixson, A. F. (2009). *Sexual selection and the origins of human mating systems*. New York, NY: Oxford University Press.

Domingue, R., & Mollen, D. (2009). Attachment and conflict communication in adult romantic relationships. *Journal of Social and Personal Relationships*, *26*, 678–696. http://dx.doi.org/10.1177/0265407509347932

Doumas, D. M., Pearson, C. L., Elgin, J. E., & McKinley, L. L. (2008). Adult attachment as a risk factor for intimate partner violence: The "mispairing" of partners' attachment styles. *Journal of Interpersonal Violence, 23*, 616–634. http://dx.doi.org/10.1177/0886260507313526

Dozier, M., & Roben, C. K. P. (2015). Attachment-related preventive interventions. In J. Simpson & W. S. Rholes (Eds.), *Attachment theory and research: New directions and emerging themes* (pp. 374–392). New York, NY: Guilford Press.

Drigotas, S., Safstrom, A., & Gentilia, T. (1999). An investment model prediction of dating infidelity. *Journal of Personality and Social Psychology, 77*, 509–524. http://dx.doi.org/10.1037/0022-3514.77.3.509

Druckerman, P. (2007). *Lust in translation: Infidelity from Tokyo to Tennessee*. New York, NY: Penguin.

Dubrow-Eichel, S. K. (1993). The cultural context of sex and love addiction recovery. In E. Griffin-Shelley (Ed.), *Outpatient treatment of sex and love addicts* (pp. 113–135). Westport, CT: Praeger/Greenwood.

Duncombe, J., & Marsden, D. (2004). Affairs and children. In J. Duncombe, K. Harrison, G. Allan, & D. Marsden (Eds.), *The state of affairs: Explorations in infidelity and commitment* (pp. 103–120). Mahwah, NJ: Erlbaum.

Durante, K. M., Griskevicius, V., Simpson, J. A., Cantú, S. M., & Tybur, J. M. (2012). Sex ratio and women's career choice: Does a scarcity of men lead women to choose briefcase over baby? *Journal of Personality and Social Psychology, 103*, 121–134. http://dx.doi.org/10.1037/a0027949

D'Zurilla, T. J., & Nezu, A. M. (2007). *Problem-solving therapy: A positive approach to clinical intervention* (3rd ed.). New York, NY: Springer.

Eagle, M. (2007). Attachment and sexuality. In D. Diamond, S. J. Blatt, & J. D. Lichtenberg (Eds.), *Attachment and sexuality* (pp. 27–50). Hillsdale, NJ: Analytic Press.

Easton, D., & Hardy, J. W. (2009). *The ethical slut: A practical guide to polyamory, open relationships & other adventures* (2nd ed.). New York, NY: Greenery Press.

Eastwick, P. W., & Hunt, L. L. (2014). Relational mate value: Consensus and uniqueness in romantic evaluations. *Journal of Personality and Social Psychology, 106*, 728–751. http://dx.doi.org/10.1037/a0035884

Ein-Dor, T., Perry-Paldi, A., Hirschberger, G., Birnbaum, G. E., & Deutsch, D. (2015). Coping with mate poaching: Gender differences in detection of infidelity-related threats. *Evolution and Human Behavior, 36*, 17–24. http://dx.doi.org/10.1016/j.evolhumbehav.2014.08.002

Ekman, P. (1992). Are there basic emotions? *Psychological Review, 99*, 550–553. http://dx.doi.org/10.1037/0033-295X.99.3.550

Elise, D. (2012). The danger in deception: Oedipal betrayal and the assault on truth. *Journal of the American Psychoanalytic Association, 60*, 679–705. http://dx.doi.org/10.1177/0003065112449187

English, T., & John, O. P. (2013). Understanding the social effects of emotion regulation: The mediating role of authenticity for individual differences in suppression. *Emotion, 13*, 314–329. http://dx.doi.org/10.1037/a0029847

Erikson, E. H. (1963). *Childhood and society* (2nd ed.). New York, NY: Norton.

Erikson, P. (2002). Several fathers in one's cap: Polyandrous conception among the Panoan Matis (Amazonas, Brazil). In S. Beckerman & P. Valentine (Eds.), *Cultures of multiple fathers: The theory and practice of partible paternity in lowland South America* (pp. 123–136). Gainesville: University of Florida Press.

Evraire, L. E., Ludmer, J. A., & Dozois, D. J. A. (2014). The influence of priming attachment styles on excessive and negative reassurance seeking and negative feedback seeking in depression. *Journal of Social and Clinical Psychology, 33*, 295–318. http://dx.doi.org/10.1521/jscp.2014.33.4.295

Exline, J. J., Baumeister, R. F., Bushman, B. J., Campbell, W. K., & Finkel, E. J. (2004). Too proud to let go: Narcissistic entitlement as a barrier to forgiveness. *Journal of Personality and Social Psychology, 87*, 894–912. http://dx.doi.org/10.1037/0022-3514.87.6.894

Feeney, J. A. (1994). Attachment style, communication patterns, and satisfaction across the life cycle of marriage. *Personal Relationships, 1*, 333–348. http://dx.doi.org/10.1111/j.1475-6811.1994.tb00069.x

Feeney, J. A. (1999). Issues of closeness and distance in dating relationships: Effects of sex and attachment style. *Journal of Social and Personal Relationships, 16*, 571–590. http://dx.doi.org/10.1177/0265407599165002

Feeney, J. A., Kelly, L., Gallois, C., Peterson, C., & Terry, D. J. (1999). Attachment style, assertive communication, and safer-sex behavior. *Journal of Applied Social Psychology, 29*, 1964–1983. http://dx.doi.org/10.1111/j.1559-1816.1999.tb00159.x

Feldman, S. S., & Cauffman, E. (1999). Your cheatin' heart: Attitudes, behaviors, and correlates of sexual betrayal in late adolescence. *Journal of Research on Adolescence, 9*, 227–252. http://dx.doi.org/10.1207/s15327795jra0903_1

Fife, S. T., Weeks, G. R., & Stellberg-Filbert, J. (2013). Facilitating forgiveness in the treatment of infidelity: An interpersonal model. *Journal of Family Therapy, 35*, 343–367.

Figueredo, A. J., Vásquez, G., Brumbach, B. H., & Schneider, S. M. R. (2004). The heritability of life history strategy: The K-factor, covitality, and personality. *Social Biology, 51*, 121–143. http://dx.doi.org/10.1080/19485565.2004.9989090

Figueredo, A. J., Wolf, P. S. A., Olderbak, S. G., Sefcek, J. A., Frías-Armenta, M., Vargas-Porras, C., & Egan, V. (2015). Positive assortative pairing in social and romantic partners: A cross-cultural observational field study of naturally occurring pairs. *Personality and Individual Differences, 84*, 30–35. http://dx.doi.org/10.1016/j.paid.2014.12.060

Fischer, A. H., & Roseman, I. J. (2007). Beat them or ban them: The characteristics and social functions of anger and contempt. *Journal of Personality and Social Psychology, 93*, 103–115. http://dx.doi.org/10.1037/0022-3514.93.1.103

Fisher, H. E. (2004). *Why we love: The nature and chemistry of romantic love*. New York, NY: Owl Books.

Fisher, H. E. (2014). The tyranny of love: Love addiction—An anthropologist's view. In K. P. Rosenberg & L. Curtiss Feder (Eds.), *Behavioral addictions: Criteria, evidence, and treatment* (pp. 237–265). San Diego, CA: Elsevier Academic Press. http://dx.doi.org/10.1016/B978-0-12-407724-9.00010-0

Fisher, M., Cox, A., Bennett, S., & Gavric, D. (2008). Components of self-perceived mate value. *Journal of Social, Evolutionary, and Cultural Psychology*, *2*, 156–168. http://dx.doi.org/10.1037/h0099347

Fletcher, G. J., Simpson, J. A., Thomas, G., & Giles, L. (1999). Ideals in intimate relationships. *Journal of Personality and Social Psychology*, *76*, 72–89. http://dx.doi.org/10.1037/0022-3514.76.1.72

Fletcher, G. J., Tither, J. M., O'Loughlin, C., Friesen, M., & Overall, N. (2004). Warm and homely or cold and beautiful? Sex differences in trading off traits in mate selection. *Personality and Social Psychology Bulletin*, *30*, 659–672. http://dx.doi.org/10.1177/0146167203262847

Florsheim, P., & McArthur, L. (2009). An interpersonal approach to attachment and change. In J. H. Obegi & E. Berant (Eds.), *Attachment theory and research in clinical work with adults* (pp. 379–409). New York, NY: Guilford Press.

Fonagy, P., Gergely, G., Jurist, E. L., & Target, M. (2002). *Affect regulation, mentalization, and the development of the self*. New York, NY: Other Press.

Fonagy, P., Luyten, P., & Bateman, A. (2015). Translation: Mentalizing as treatment target in borderline personality disorder. *Personality Disorders*, *6*, 380–392. http://dx.doi.org/10.1037/per0000113

Fonagy, P., Steele, H., & Steele, M. (1991). Maternal representations of attachment during pregnancy predict the organization of infant–mother attachment at one year of age. *Child Development*, *62*, 891–905. http://dx.doi.org/10.2307/1131141

Fonagy, P., Target, M., Gergely, G., Allen, J. G., & Bateman, A. W. (2003). The developmental roots of borderline personality disorder in early attachment relationships: A theory and some evidence. *Psychoanalytic Inquiry*, *23*, 412–459. http://dx.doi.org/10.1080/07351692309349042

Fonagy, P., Target, M., Steele, H., & Steele, M. (1998). *Reflective functioning manual: Version 5 for application to Adult Attachment Interview*. London, England: University College.

Fossati, A., Feeney, J., Pincus, A., Borroni, S., & Maffei, C. (2015). The structure of pathological narcissism and its relationships with adult attachment styles: A study of Italian nonclinical and clinical adult participants. *Psychoanalytic Psychology*, *32*, 403–431. http://dx.doi.org/10.1037/a0037175

Fraley, R. C. (2002). Attachment stability from infancy to adulthood: Meta-analysis and dynamic modeling of developmental mechanisms. *Personality and Social Psychology Review*, *6*, 123–151. http://dx.doi.org/10.1207/S15327957PSPR0602_03

Fraley, R. C., & Marks, M. J. (2010). Westermarck, Freud, and the incest taboo: Does familial resemblance activate sexual attraction? *Personality and Social Psychology Bulletin, 36,* 1202–1212. http://dx.doi.org/10.1177/0146167210377180

Frayser, S. G. (1985). *Varieties of sexual experience: An anthropological perspective on human sexuality*. New Haven, CT: Human Relations Area Files.

Frayser, S. G. (1989). Sexual and reproductive relationships: Cross-cultural evidence and biosocial implications. *Medical Anthropology, 11,* 385–407. http://dx.doi.org/10.1080/01459740.1989.9966005

Freud, S. (1953). Three essays on the theory of sexuality. In J. Strachey (Ed. & Trans.), *The standard edition of the complete psychological works of Sigmund Freud* (Vol. 7, pp. 125–245). London, England: Hogarth Press. (Original work published 1905)

Freud, S. (1955a). Beyond the pleasure principle. In J. Strachey (Ed. & Trans.), *The standard edition of the complete psychological works of Sigmund Freud* (Vol. 18, pp. 1–64). London, England: Hogarth Press. (Original work published 1920)

Freud, S. (1955b). Some neurotic mechanisms in jealousy, paranoia and homosexuality. In J. Strachey (Ed. & Trans.), *The standard edition of the complete psychological works of Sigmund Freud* (Vol. 18, pp. 221–234). London, England: Hogarth Press. (Original work published 1922)

Freud, S. (1957a). On narcissism: An introduction. In J. Strachey (Ed. & Trans.), *The standard edition of the complete psychological works of Sigmund Freud* (Vol. 14, pp. 73–102). London, England: Hogarth Press. (Original work published 1914)

Freud, S. (1957b). A special type of choice of object made by men. In J. Strachey (Ed. & Trans.), *The standard edition of the complete psychological works of Sigmund Freud* (Vol. 11, pp. 163–175). London, England: Hogarth Press. (Original work published 1910)

Freud, S. (1958). The dynamics of transference. In J. Strachey (Ed. & Trans.), *The standard edition of the complete psychological works of Sigmund Freud* (Vol. 12, pp. 97–108). London, England: Hogarth Press. (Original work published 1912)

Freud, S. (1961). The dissolution of the Oedipus complex. In J. Strachey (Ed. & Trans.), *The standard edition of the complete psychological works of Sigmund Freud* (Vol. 19, pp. 173–182). London, England: Hogarth Press. (Original work published 1924)

Frith, C. D., & Frith, U. (2006). The neural basis of mentalizing. *Neuron, 50,* 531–534. http://dx.doi.org/10.1016/j.neuron.2006.05.001

Frith, U., & Frith, C. D. (2003). Development and neurophysiology of mentalizing. *Philosophical Transactions of the Royal Society of London. Series B, Biological Sciences, 358,* 459–473. http://dx.doi.org/10.1098/rstb.2002.1218

Funder, D. C. (1995). On the accuracy of personality judgment: A realistic approach. *Psychological Review, 102,* 652–670. http://dx.doi.org/10.1037/0033-295X.102.4.652

Gambrel, L. E., & Keeling, M. L. (2010). Relational aspects of mindfulness: Implications for the practice of marriage and family therapy. *Contemporary Family Therapy, 32,* 412–426. http://dx.doi.org/10.1007/s10591-010-9129-z

Gangestad, S. W., Garver-Apgar, C. E., Cousins, A. J., & Thornhill, R. (2014). Intersexual conflict across women's ovulatory cycle. *Evolution and Human Behavior*, *35*, 302–308. http://dx.doi.org/10.1016/j.evolhumbehav.2014.02.012

Gangestad, S. W., Haselton, M. G., & Buss, D. M. (2006). Evolutionary foundations of cultural variation: Evoked culture and mate preferences. *Psychological Inquiry*, *17*, 75–95. http://dx.doi.org/10.1207/s15327965pli1702_1

Gangestad, S. W., Thornhill, R., & Garver-Apgar, C. E. (2010). Men's facial masculinity predicts changes in their female partners' sexual interests across the ovulatory cycle, whereas men's intelligence does not. *Evolution and Human Behavior*, *31*, 412–424. http://dx.doi.org/10.1016/j.evolhumbehav.2010.06.001

Geher, G. (2009). Accuracy and oversexualization in cross-sex mind-reading: An adaptionist approach. *Evolutionary Psychology*, *7*, 331–347. http://dx.doi.org/10.1177/147470490900700214

Genest, A. A., & Mathieu, C. (2014). Intimate partner violence: The role of attachment on men's anger. *Partner Abuse*, *5*, 375–387. http://dx.doi.org/10.1891/1946-6560.5.4.375

George, C., Kaplan, N., & Main, M. (1984). *Adult Attachment Interview*. Unpublished protocol, University of California, Berkeley.

George, C., Kaplan, N., & Main, M. (1985). *Adult Attachment Interview*. Unpublished protocol, University of California, Berkeley.

George, C., Kaplan, N., & Main, M. (1996). *Adult Attachment Interview*. Unpublished protocol, University of California, Berkeley.

Gerber, M. M., & Jackson, J. (2013). Retribution as revenge and retribution as just deserts. *Social Justice Research*, *26*, 61–80. http://dx.doi.org/10.1007/s11211-012-0174-7

Giammarco, E. A., & Vernon, P. A. (2014). Vengeance and the Dark Triad: The role of empathy and perspective taking in trait forgiveness. *Personality and Individual Differences*, *67*, 23–29. http://dx.doi.org/10.1016/j.paid.2014.02.010

Gillath, O., Adams, G., & Kunkel, A. (2012). *Relationship science: Integrating evolutionary, neuroscience, and sociocultural approaches*. Washington, DC: American Psychological Association.

Gillath, O., Sesko, A. K., Shaver, P. R., & Chun, D. S. (2010). Attachment, authenticity, and honesty: Dispositional and experimentally induced security can reduce self- and other-deception. *Journal of Personality and Social Psychology*, *98*, 841–855. http://dx.doi.org/10.1037/a0019206

Gilmer, W. S., & McKinney, W. T. (2003). Early experience and depressive disorders: Human and non-human primate studies. *Journal of Affective Disorders*, *75*, 97–113. http://dx.doi.org/10.1016/S0165-0327(03)00046-6

Giner-Sorolla, R., Bosson, J. K., Caswell, T. A., & Hettinger, V. E. (2012). Emotions in sexual morality: Testing the separate elicitors of anger and disgust. *Cognition and Emotion*, *26*, 1208–1222. http://dx.doi.org/10.1080/02699931.2011.645278

Glass, S. P. (2002). *Not "just friends": Rebuilding trust and recovering your sanity after infidelity*. New York, NY: Free Press.

Glass, S. P., & Wright, T. (1985). Sex differences in type of extramarital involvement and marital dissatisfaction. *Sex Roles, 12*, 1101–1120. http://dx.doi.org/10.1007/BF00288108

Glenn, N., & Kramer, K. (1987). The marriages and divorces of the children of divorce. *Journal of Marriage and the Family, 49*, 811–825. http://dx.doi.org/10.2307/351974

Good, K. (1997). *Into the heart: One man's pursuit of love and knowledge among the Yanomami*. New York, NY: Addison-Wesley.

Gorchoff, S. M., John, O. P., & Helson, R. (2008). Contextualizing change in marital satisfaction during middle age: An 18-year longitudinal study. *Psychological Science, 19*, 1194–1200. http://dx.doi.org/10.1111/j.1467-9280.2008.02222.x

Gordon, D. S., & Platek, S. M. (2009). Trustworthy? The brain knows: Implicit neural responses to faces that vary on in the Dark Triad personality characteristics and trustworthiness. *Journal of Social, Evolutionary, and Cultural Psychology, 3*, 182–200. http://dx.doi.org/10.1037/h0099323

Gottman, J. M. (1994). *Why marriages succeed or fail*. New York, NY: Simon & Schuster.

Gottman, J. M. (1999). *The marriage clinic: A scientifically based marital therapy*. New York, NY: Norton.

Gottman, J. M. (2011). *The science of trust: Emotional attunement for couples*. New York, NY: Norton.

Gottman, J. M., Levenson, R., & Woodin, E. (2001). Facial expressions during marital conflict. *Journal of Family Communication, 1*, 37–57. http://dx.doi.org/10.1207/S15327698JFC0101_06

Gottman, J. S. (2004). Extramarital affairs: The pearl in the oyster. In J. S. Gottman (Ed.), *The marriage clinic casebook* (pp. 47–68). New York, NY: Norton.

Gray, P. B., & Anderson, K. G. (2010). *Fatherhood: Evolution and human paternal behavior*. Cambridge, MA: Harvard University Press.

Green, M. F., Penn, D. L., Bentall, R., Carpenter, W. T., Gaebel, W., Gur, R. C., . . . Heinssen, R. (2008). Social cognition in schizophrenia: An NIMH workshop on definitions, assessment, and research opportunities. *Schizophrenia Bulletin, 34*, 1211–1220. http://dx.doi.org/10.1093/schbul/sbm145

Grijalva, E., Newman, D. A., Tay, L., Donnellan, M. B., Harms, P. D., Robins, R. W., & Yan, T. (2015). Gender differences in narcissism: A meta-analytic review. *Psychological Bulletin, 141*, 261–310. http://dx.doi.org/10.1037/a0038231

Haidt, J. (2012). *The righteous mind: Why good people are divided by politics and religion*. New York, NY: Pantheon Books.

Hall, J. H., & Fincham, F. D. (2006). Relationship dissolution following infidelity: The roles of attributions and forgiveness. *Journal of Social and Clinical Psychology, 25*, 508–522. http://dx.doi.org/10.1521/jscp.2006.25.5.508

Hamilton, W. D. (1964). The genetical evolution of social behaviour. I. *Journal of Theoretical Biology, 7*, 1–16. http://dx.doi.org/10.1016/0022-5193(64)90038-4

Haney, C., & Zimbardo, P. G. (2009). Persistent dispositionalism in interactionist clothing: Fundamental attribution error in explaining prison abuse. *Personality and Social Psychology Bulletin*, *35*, 807–814. http://dx.doi.org/10.1177/0146167208322864

Harrington, L., Siegert, R. J., & McClure, J. (2005). Theory of mind in schizophrenia: A critical review. *Cognitive Neuropsychiatry*, *10*, 249–286. http://dx.doi.org/10.1080/13546800444000056

Harris, C. R., & Prouvost, C. (2014). Jealousy in dogs. *PLoS One*, 9, e94597. http://dx.doi.org/10.1371/journal.pone.0094597

Hart, S., & Carrington, H. (2002). Jealousy in 6-month-old infants. *Infancy*, *3*, 395–402. http://dx.doi.org/10.1207/S15327078IN0303_6

Hart, S. L., & Behrens, K. Y. (2013). Affective and behavioral features of jealousy protest: Associations with child temperament, maternal interaction style, and attachment. *Infancy*, *18*, 369–399. http://dx.doi.org/10.1111/j.1532-7078.2012.00123.x

Hart, S. L., Carrington, H. A., Tronick, E. Z., & Carroll, S. R. (2004). When infants lose exclusive maternal attention: Is it jealousy? *Infancy*, 6, 57–78. http://dx.doi.org/10.1207/s15327078in0601_3

Haselton, M. G., & Buss, D. M. (2000). Error management theory: A new perspective on biases in cross-sex mind reading. *Journal of Personality and Social Psychology*, *78*, 81–91. http://dx.doi.org/10.1037/0022-3514.78.1.81

Haselton, M. G., Buss, D. M., Oubaid, V., & Angleitner, A. (2005). Sex, lies, and strategic interference: The psychology of deception between the sexes. *Personality and Social Psychology Bulletin*, *31*, 3–23. http://dx.doi.org/10.1177/0146167204271303

Haslam, C., & Montrose, V. (2015). Should have known better: The impact of mating experience and the desire for marriage upon attraction to the narcissistic personality. *Personality and Individual Differences*, *82*, 188–192. http://dx.doi.org/10.1016/j.paid.2015.03.032

Haslam, N. (2011). The return of the anal character. *Review of General Psychology*, *15*, 351–360. http://dx.doi.org/10.1037/a0025251

Hawkes, K., O'Connell, J. F., & Jones, N. G. B. (2003). Human life histories: Primate trade-offs, grandmothering socioecology, and the fossil record. In P. M. Kappeler & M. E. Pereira (Eds.), *Primate life histories and socioecology* (pp. 204–227). Chicago, IL: University of Chicago Press.

Hawkins, A. J., Blanchard, V. L., Baldwin, S. A., & Fawcett, E. B. (2008). Does marriage and relationship education work? A meta-analytic study. *Journal of Consulting and Clinical Psychology*, *76*, 723–734. http://dx.doi.org/10.1037/a0012584

Hazan, C., Campa, M., & Gur-Yaish, N. (2006). What is adult attachment? In M. Mikulincer & G. S. Goodman (Eds.), *Dynamics of romantic love: Attachment, caregiving, and sex* (pp. 47–70). New York, NY: Guilford Press.

Hazan, C., & Shaver, P. (1987). Romantic love conceptualized as an attachment process. *Journal of Personality and Social Psychology*, *52*, 511–524. http://dx.doi.org/10.1037/0022-3514.52.3.511

Hazan, C., & Zeifman, D. (1994). Sex and the psychological tether. In K. Bartholomew & D. Perlman (Eds.), *Advances in personal relationships: Vol. 5. Attachment processes in adulthood* (pp. 151–178). London, England: Jessica Kingsley.

Heintzelman, A., Murdock, N. L., Krycak, R. C., & Seay, L. (2014). Recovery from infidelity: Differentiation of self, trauma, forgiveness, and posttraumatic growth among couples in continuing relationships. *Couple and Family Psychology: Research and Practice, 3*, 13–29. http://dx.doi.org/10.1037/cfp0000016

Hesse, M., & Tutenges, S. (2011). Young tourists visiting strip clubs and paying for sex. *Tourism Management, 32*, 869–874. http://dx.doi.org/10.1016/j.tourman.2010.08.002

Hill, S., & Reeve, H. (2004). Mating games: The evolution of human mating transactions. *Behavioral Ecology, 15*, 748–756. http://dx.doi.org/10.1093/beheco/arh073

Hook, J. N., Davis, D. E., Owen, J., Worthington, E. L., Jr., & Utsey, S. O. (2013). Cultural humility: Measuring openness to culturally diverse clients. *Journal of Counseling Psychology, 60*(3), 353–366. http://dx.doi.org/10.1037/a0032595

Horney, K. (1928). The problem of the monogamous ideal. *The International Journal of Psycho-Analysis, 9*, 316–331.

Howell, N. (1979). *Demography of Dobe !Kung*. New York, NY: Academic Press.

Hrdy, S. B. (1999). *Mother nature: Maternal instincts and how they shape the human species*. New York, NY: Ballantine Books.

Hrdy, S. B. (2009). *Mother and others: The evolutionary origins of mutual understanding*. Cambridge, MA: Harvard University Press.

Hromatko, I., Bajoghli, H., Rebernjak, B., Joshaghani, N., & Tadinac, M. (2015). Relationship satisfaction as a function of mate value. *Evolutionary Behavioral Sciences, 9*, 242–256. http://dx.doi.org/10.1037/ebs0000055

Hunyady, O., Josephs, L., & Jost, J. (2008). Priming the primal scene: Betrayal trauma, narcissism, and attitudes toward infidelity. *Self and Identity: The International Journal of Self and Identity, 7*, 278–294. http://dx.doi.org/10.1080/15298860701620227

Huston, T. L., & Burgess, R. L. (1979). Social exchange in developing relationships: An overview. In R. L. Burgess & T. L. Huston (Eds.), *Social exchange in developing relationships* (pp. 3–28). New York, NY: Academic Press. http://dx.doi.org/10.1016/B978-0-12-143550-9.50007-0

Hutcherson, C. A., & Gross, J. J. (2011). The moral emotions: A social-functionalist account of anger, disgust, and contempt. *Journal of Personality and Social Psychology, 100*, 719–737. http://dx.doi.org/10.1037/a0022408

Hyde, A., Carney, M., Drennan, J., Butler, M., Lohan, M., & Howlett, E. (2010). The silent treatment: Parents' narratives of sexuality education with young people. *Culture, Health & Sexuality, 12*, 359–371. http://dx.doi.org/10.1080/13691050903514455

Illouz, E. (2012). *Why love hurts: A sociological explanation*. Cambridge, England: Polity Press.

Jankowiak, W. H. (1995). *Romantic passion*. New York, NY: Columbia University Press.

Jeffreys, S. (2010). The sex industry and business practice: An obstacle to women's equality. *Women's Studies International Forum, 33*, 274–282. http://dx.doi.org/10.1016/j.wsif.2010.03.001

Johannes, C. B., & Avis, N. E. (1997). Gender differences in sexual activity among mid-aged adults in Massachusetts. *Maturitas, 26*, 175–184. http://dx.doi.org/10.1016/S0378-5122(97)01102-X

Johns, K. N., Allen, E. S., & Gordon, K. C. (2015). The relationship between mindfulness and forgiveness of infidelity. *Mindfulness, 6*, 1462–1471. http://dx.doi.org/10.1007/s12671-015-0427-2

Johnson, S. M. (2004). *The practice of emotionally focused couple therapy: Creating connection* (2nd ed.). New York, NY: Brunner-Routledge.

Johnson, S. M., & Makinen, J. A. (2003). Posttraumatic stress. In D. K. Snyder & M. A. Whisman (Eds.), *Treating difficult couples* (pp. 208–329). New York, NY: Guilford Press.

Jokela, M., Rotkirch, A., Rickard, I. J., Pettay, J., & Lummaa, V. (2010). Serial monogamy increases reproductive success in men but not in women. *Behavioral Ecology, 21*, 906–912. http://dx.doi.org/10.1093/beheco/arq078

Jolly, A. (1999). *Lucy's legacy: Sex and intelligence in human evolution*. Cambridge, MA: Harvard University Press.

Jonason, P. K., Garcia, J. R., Webster, G. D., Li, N. P., & Fisher, H. E. (2015). Relationship dealbreakers: Traits people avoid in potential mates. *Personality and Social Psychology Bulletin, 41*, 1697–1711.

Jonason, P. K., & Kavanagh, P. (2010). The dark side of love: Love styles and the Dark Triad. *Personality and Individual Differences, 49*, 606–610. http://dx.doi.org/10.1016/j.paid.2010.05.030

Jonason, P. K., & Krause, L. (2013). The emotional deficits associated with the Dark Triad traits: Cognitive empathy, affective empathy, and alexithymia. *Personality and Individual Differences, 55*, 532–537. http://dx.doi.org/10.1016/j.paid.2013.04.027

Jonason, P. K., Li, N. P., & Buss, D. M. (2010). The costs and benefits of the Dark Triad: Implications for mate poaching and mate retention tactics. *Personality and Individual Differences, 48*, 373–378. http://dx.doi.org/10.1016/j.paid.2009.11.003

Jonason, P. K., Li, N., Webster, G., & Schmitt, D. (2009). The dark triad: Facilitating a short-term mating strategy in men. *European Journal of Personality, 23*, 5–18. http://dx.doi.org/10.1002/per.698

Jonason, P. K., Lyons, M., Bethell, E. J., & Ross, R. (2013). Different routes to limited empathy in the sexes: Examining the links between the Dark Triad and empathy. *Personality and Individual Differences, 54*, 572–576. http://dx.doi.org/10.1016/j.paid.2012.11.009

Jonason, P. K., Lyons, M., & Blanchard, A. (2015). Birds of a "bad" feather flock together: The Dark Triad and mate choice. *Personality and Individual Differences*, *78*, 34–38. http://dx.doi.org/10.1016/j.paid.2015.01.018

Jones, D. N., & Weiser, D. A. (2014). Differential infidelity patterns among the Dark Triad. *Personality and Individual Differences*, *57*, 20–24. http://dx.doi.org/10.1016/j.paid.2013.09.007

Josephs, L. (1994). Empathic character analysis. *The American Journal of Psychoanalysis*, *54*, 41–54. http://dx.doi.org/10.1007/BF02741907

Josephs, L. (2006). The impulse to infidelity and oedipal splitting. *The International Journal of Psychoanalysis*, *87*, 423–437. http://dx.doi.org/10.1516/5A5V-WLPB-4HJ3-329J

Josephs, L. (2010). The evolved function of the oedipal conflict. *The International Journal of Psychoanalysis*, *91*, 937–958. http://dx.doi.org/10.1111/j.1745-8315.2010.00280.x

Josephs, L. (2012). The adaptive functions of sexual plasticity: The suppression and surreptitious expression of human sociosexuality. *Psychodynamic Psychiatry*, *40*, 243–274. http://dx.doi.org/10.1521/pdps.2012.40.2.243

Josephs, L. (2015a). The challenge of mentalizing sexual betrayal. In J. M. Thompson & R. Tuch (Eds.), *Stories we tell ourselves: Mentalizing tales of dating and marriage* (pp. 234–255). London, England: Routledge.

Josephs, L. (2015b). How children learn about sex: A cross-cultural and cross-species perspective. *Archives of Sexual Behavior*, *44*, 1059–1069. http://dx.doi.org/10.1007/s10508-015-0498-0

Josephs, L., & McLeod, B. (2014). A theory of mind–focused approach to anger management. *Psychoanalytic Psychology*, *31*, 68–83. http://dx.doi.org/10.1037/a0034175

Josephs, L., Sanders, A., & Gorman, B. S. (2014). Therapeutic interaction with an older personality disordered patient. *Psychodynamic Psychiatry*, *42*, 151–172. http://dx.doi.org/10.1521/pdps.2014.42.2.151

Josephs, L., & Weinberger, J. (2013). Psychodynamic psychotherapy. In I. Weiner & G. Stricker (Eds.), *Handbook of psychology* (Vol. 8, pp. 265–290). Hoboken, NJ: Wiley.

Jurkovic, G. J. (1997). *Lost childhoods: The plight of the parentified child.* New York, NY: Brunner/Mazel.

Kammrath, L. K., & Peetz, J. (2012). You promised you'd change: How incremental and entity theorists react to a romantic partner's promised change attempts. *Journal of Experimental Social Psychology*, *48*, 570–574. http://dx.doi.org/10.1016/j.jesp.2011.10.015

Kaplan, H. S., & Gangestad, S. W. (2005). Life history theory and evolutionary psychology. In D. M. Buss (Ed.), *The handbook of evolutionary psychology* (pp. 68–95). Hoboken, NJ: Wiley.

Kasper, T. E., Short, M. B., & Milam, A. C. (2015). Narcissism and Internet pornography use. *Journal of Sex & Marital Therapy, 41*, 481–486. http://dx.doi.org/10.1080/0092623X.2014.931313

Keng, S., Smoski, M. J., & Robins, C. J. (2016). Effects of mindful acceptance and reappraisal training on maladaptive beliefs about rumination. *Mindfulness, 7*, 493–503.

Kernberg, O. F. (1984). *Severe personality disorders: Psychotherapeutic strategies*. New Haven, CT: Yale University Press.

Kernberg, O. F. (1996). A psychoanalytic theory of personality disorders. In J. F. Clarkin & M. F. Lenzenweger (Eds.), *Major theories of personality disorder* (pp. 106–140). New York, NY: Guilford Press.

Kernberg, O. F. (2009). Narcissistic personality disorders: Part 1. *Psychiatric Annals, 39*, 105–167. http://dx.doi.org/10.3928/00485713-20090301-04

Kernis, M. H., & Goldman, B. M. (2006). A multicomponent conceptualization of authenticity: Theory and research. In M. P. Zanna (Ed.), *Advances in experimental social psychology* (Vol. 38, pp. 284–357). San Diego, CA: Academic Press. http://dx.doi.org/10.1016/S0065-2601(06)38006-9

Kim, B. K., & Zauberman, G. (2013). Can Victoria's Secret change the future? A subjective time perception account of sexual-cue effects on impatience. *Journal of Experimental Psychology: General, 142*, 328–335. http://dx.doi.org/10.1037/a0028954

King, S. (2015). Attachment security: Polyamory and monogamy a comparison analysis. *Dissertation Abstracts International: Section B. The Sciences and Engineering, 75*(10), n.p.

Kinnunen, U., & Pulkkinen, L. (2003). Childhood socio-emotional characteristics as antecedents of marital stability and quality. *European Psychologist, 8*, 223–237. http://dx.doi.org/10.1027//1016-9040.8.4.223

Kinsey, A. C., Pomeroy, W. B., & Martin, C. E. (1948). *Sexual behavior in the human male*. Philadelphia, PA: Saunders.

Kinsey, A. C., Pomeroy, W. B., Martin, C. E., & Gebhard, P. H. (1953). *Sexual behavior in the human female*. Philadelphia, PA: Saunders.

Kirkpatrick, L. A., & Ellis, B. J. (2001). An evolutionary-psychological approach to self-esteem: Multiple domains and multiple functions. In G. J. O. Fletcher & M. S. Clark (Eds.), *Blackwell handbook of social psychology: Interpersonal processes* (pp. 411–436). Malden, MA: Blackwell.

Kirsner, B. R., Figueredo, A. J., & Jacobs, W. J. (2003). Self, friends, and lovers: Structural relations among Beck Depression Inventory scores and perceived mate values. *Journal of Affective Disorders, 75*, 131–148. http://dx.doi.org/10.1016/S0165-0327(02)00048-4

Klein, M. (1998). Love, guilt and reparation. In R. Money-Kyrle (Ed.), *Love, guilt and reparation: And other works 1921–1945* (The Writings of Melanie Klein) (pp. 1–468). London, England: The Hogarth Press. (Original work published 1937)

Knauft, B. M. (1991). Violence and sociality in human evolution. *Current Anthropology, 32*, 391–428.

Knee, C. R., Patrick, H., & Lonsbary, C. (2003). Implicit theories of relationships: Orientations toward evaluation and cultivation. *Personality and Social Psychology Review, 7*, 41–55. http://dx.doi.org/10.1207/S15327957PSPR0701_3

Knoke, J., Burau, J., & Roehrle, B. (2010). Attachment styles, loneliness, quality, and stability of marital relationships. *Journal of Divorce & Remarriage, 51*, 310–325. http://dx.doi.org/10.1080/10502551003652017

Kohut, H. (1971). *The analysis of the self. A systematic approach to the treatment of narcissistic personality disorders*. New York, NY: International Universities Press.

Koleva, S., Selterman, D., Iyer, R., Ditto, P., & Graham, J. (2014). The moral compass of insecurity: Anxious and avoidant attachment predict moral judgment. *Social Psychological and Personality Science, 5*, 185–194. http://dx.doi.org/10.1177/1948550613490965

Konner, M. (2005). Hunter-gatherer infancy and childhood: The !Kung and others. In B. S. Hewlett & M. E. Lamb (Eds.), *Hunter-gatherer childhoods: Evolutionary, developmental, and cultural perspectives* (pp. 19–64). New Brunswick, NJ: Aldine Transaction.

Konner, M. (2010). *The evolution of childhood: Relationships, emotion, mind*. Cambridge, MA: Harvard University Press.

Kris, A. O. (1990). Helping patients by analyzing self-criticism. *Journal of the American Psychoanalytic Association, 38*, 605–636. http://dx.doi.org/10.1177/000306519003800304

Kruger, D. J., & Fisher, M. L. (2005). Alternative male mating strategies are intuitive to women. *Current Research in Social Psychology, 11*, 39–50.

Labriola, K. (2013). *The jealousy workbook: Exercises and insights for managing open relationships*. Emeryville, CA: Greenery Press.

Laier, C., Pawlikowski, M., & Brand, M. (2014). Sexual picture processing interferes with decision-making under ambiguity. *Archives of Sexual Behavior, 43*, 473–482. http://dx.doi.org/10.1007/s10508-013-0119-8

Laier, C., Schulte, F. P., & Brand, M. (2013). Pornographic picture processing interferes with working memory performance. *Journal of Sex Research, 50*, 642–652. http://dx.doi.org/10.1080/00224499.2012.716873

Lakey, C. E., Kernis, M. H., Heppner, W. L., & Lance, C. E. (2008). Individual differences in authenticity and mindfulness as predictors of verbal defensiveness. *Journal of Research in Personality, 42*, 230–238. http://dx.doi.org/10.1016/j.jrp.2007.05.002

Lamkin, J., Campbell, K., vanDellen, M., & Miller, J. (2015). An exploration of the correlates of grandiose and vulnerable narcissism in romantic relationships: Homophily, partner characteristics, and dyadic adjustment. *Personality and Individual Differences, 79*, 166–171. http://dx.doi.org/10.1016/j.paid.2015.01.029

Laumann, E. O., Gagnon, J. H., Michael, R. T., & Michaels, S. (1994). *The social organization of sexuality: Sexual practices in the United States*. Chicago, IL: University of Chicago Press.

Leak, G., & Cooney, R. (2001). Self-determination, attachment styles and well-being in adult romantic relationships. *Representative Research in Social Psychology, 25*, 55–62.

Leiblum, S. R., & Rosen, R. C. (1988). Changing perspectives on sexual desire. In S. Leiblum & R. Rosen (Eds.), *Sexual desire disorders* (pp. 1–20). New York, NY: Guilford Press.

Lenton, A. P., Bruder, M., Slabu, L., & Sedikides, C. (2013). How does "being real" feel? The experience of state authenticity. *Journal of Personality, 81*, 276–289. http://dx.doi.org/10.1111/j.1467-6494.2012.00805.x

Lerner, M. J. (1980). *The belief in a just world: A fundamental delusion*. New York, NY: Plenum Press.

Levins, R. (1968). *Evolution in changing environments*. Princeton, NJ: Princeton University Press.

Levy, K. N., Kelly, K. M., & Jack, E. L. (2006). Sex differences in jealousy: A matter of evolution or attachment history? In M. Mikulincer & G. S. Goodman (Eds.), *Dynamics of romantic love: Attachment, caregiving, and sex* (pp. 128–145). New York, NY: Guilford Press.

Levy, K. N., Meehan, K. B., Kelly, K. M., Reynoso, J. S., Weber, M., Clarkin, J. F., & Kernberg, O. F. (2006). Change in attachment patterns and reflective function in a randomized control trial of transference-focused psychotherapy for borderline personality disorder. *Journal of Consulting and Clinical Psychology, 74*, 1027–1040. http://dx.doi.org/10.1037/0022-006X.74.6.1027

Li, N. P., Bailey, J. M., Kenrick, D. T., & Linsenmeier, J. A. (2002). The necessities and luxuries of mate preferences: Testing the tradeoffs. *Journal of Personality and Social Psychology, 82*, 947–955. http://dx.doi.org/10.1037/0022-3514.82.6.947

Li, N. P., & Kenrick, D. T. (2006). Sex similarities and differences in preferences for short-term mates: What, whether, and why. *Journal of Personality and Social Psychology, 90*, 468–489. http://dx.doi.org/10.1037/0022-3514.90.3.468

Linardatos, L., & Lydon, J. E. (2011). Relationship-specific identification and spontaneous relationship maintenance processes. *Journal of Personality and Social Psychology, 101*, 737–753. http://dx.doi.org/10.1037/a0023647

Linden, M., Baumann, K., Lieberei, B., Lorenz, C., & Rotter, M. (2011). Treatment of posttraumatic embitterment disorder with cognitive behaviour therapy based on wisdom psychology and hedonia strategies. *Psychotherapy and Psychosomatics, 80*, 199–205. http://dx.doi.org/10.1159/000321580

Linehan, M. M. (1993). *Cognitive behavioral treatment of borderline personality disorder*. New York, NY: Guilford Press.

Liotti, G., & Gilbert, P. (2011). Mentalizing, motivation, and social mentalities: Theoretical considerations and implications for psychotherapy. *Psychology and Psychotherapy, 84*, 9–25.

Litwack, S. D., Aikins, J. W., & Cillessen, A. H. N. (2012). The distinct roles of sociometric and perceived popularity in friendship: Implications for adolescent depressive affect and self-esteem. *The Journal of Early Adolescence, 32*, 226–251. http://dx.doi.org/10.1177/0272431610387142

Lodge, A. C. (2015). Sexuality in long-term relationships. In J. DeLamater & R. F. Plante (Eds.), *Handbook of the sociology of sexualities* (pp. 243–259). Cham, Switzerland: Springer International.

Lohr, J. M., Olatunji, B. O., Baumeister, R. F., & Bushman, B. J. (2007). The psychology of anger venting and empirically supported alternatives that do no harm. *Scientific Review of Mental Health Practice, 5*, 53–64.

Lombardo, M. V., & Baron-Cohen, S. (2011). The role of the self in mindblindness in autism. *Consciousness and Cognition, 20*, 130–140. http://dx.doi.org/10.1016/j.concog.2010.09.006

Lopez, F. G., & Rice, K. G. (2006). Preliminary development and validation of a measure of relationship authenticity. *Journal of Counseling Psychology, 53*, 362–371. http://dx.doi.org/10.1037/0022-0167.53.3.362

Lormée, H., Jouventin, P., Chastel, O., & Mauget, R. (1999). Endocrine correlates of parental care in an Antarctic winter breeding seabird, the emperor penguin, *Aptenodytes forsteri*. *Hormones and Behavior, 35*, 9–17. http://dx.doi.org/10.1006/hbeh.1998.1491

Lowenstein, L. F. (2005). Causes and associated features of divorce as seen by recent research. *Journal of Divorce & Remarriage, 42*, 153–171. http://dx.doi.org/10.1300/J087v42n03_09

Luborsky, L., & Crits-Christoph, P. (1998). *Understanding transference: The Core Conflictual Relationship Theme method* (2nd ed.). Washington, DC: American Psychological Association. http://dx.doi.org/10.1037/10250-000

Lusterman, D. D. (2011). Marital infidelity: The effects of delayed traumatic reaction. In F. P. Piercy, K. M. Hertlein, & J. L. Wetchler (Eds.), *Handbook of the clinical treatment of infidelity* (pp. 71–81). New York, NY: Routledge.

Lydon, J. E., Meana, M., Sepinwall, D., Richards, N., & Mayman, S. (1999). The commitment calibration hypothesis: When do people devalue attractive alternatives? *Personality and Social Psychology Bulletin, 25*, 152–161. http://dx.doi.org/10.1177/0146167299025002002

Machiavelli, N. (1999). *The prince*. New York, NY: Penguin Classics.

Magai, C., Distel, N., & Liker, R. (1995). Emotion socialisation, attachment, and patterns of adult emotional traits. *Cognition and Emotion, 9*, 461–481. http://dx.doi.org/10.1080/02699939508408976

Main, M., & Hesse, E. (1990). Parents' unresolved traumatic experiences are related to infant disorganized attachment status: Is frightened and/or frightening parental behavior the linking mechanism? In M. T. Greenberg, D. Cicchetti, & E. M. Cummings (Eds.), *Attachment in the preschool years: Theory, research, and intervention* (pp. 161–182). Chicago, IL: University of Chicago Press.

Main, M., & Solomon, J. (1986). Discovery of a new, insecure-disorganized/disoriented attachment pattern. In M. Yogman & T. B. Brazelton (Eds.), *Affective development in infancy* (pp. 95–124). Norwood, NJ: Ablex.

Manning, W. D., Longmore, M. A., & Giordano, P. C. (2005). Adolescent's involvement in non-romantic sexual activity. *Social Science Research, 34*, 384–407. http://dx.doi.org/10.1016/j.ssresearch.2004.03.001

Marcus, D. K., & Norris, A. L. (2014). A new measure of attitudes toward sexually predatory tactics and its relation to the triarchic model of psychopathy. *Journal of Personality Disorders, 28*, 247–261. http://dx.doi.org/10.1521/pedi_2013_27_118

Marlowe, F. (2005). Hunter-gatherers and human evolution. *Evolutionary Anthropology, 14*, 54–67. http://dx.doi.org/10.1002/evan.20046

Marshall, L. (1998). Sharing, talking, and giving: Relief of social tension among the !Kung Bushmen. In R. B. Lee & I. DeVore (Eds.), *Kalahari hunter gatherers: Studies of the !Kung San and their neighbors* (pp. 350–372). Cambridge, MA: Harvard University Press.

Maslow, A. H. (1968). *Toward a psychology of being* (2nd ed.). Princeton, NJ: Van Nostrand.

Matsumoto, D., & Ekman, P. (2004). The relationship among expressions, labels, and descriptions of contempt. *Journal of Personality and Social Psychology, 87*, 529–540. http://dx.doi.org/10.1037/0022-3514.87.4.529

McAllister, H. A., Baker, J. D., Mannes, C., Stewart, H., & Sutherland, A. (2002). The optimal margin of illusion hypothesis: Evidence from the self-serving bias and personality disorders. *Journal of Social and Clinical Psychology, 21*, 414–426. http://dx.doi.org/10.1521/jscp.21.4.414.22593

McCullough, M. E., Bono, G., & Root, L. M. (2007). Rumination, emotion, and forgiveness: Three longitudinal studies. *Journal of Personality and Social Psychology, 92*, 490–505. http://dx.doi.org/10.1037/0022-3514.92.3.490

McCullough, M. E., Kurzban, R., & Tabak, B. A. (2011). Evolved mechanisms for revenge and forgiveness. In P. R. Shaver & M. Mikulincer (Eds.), *Human aggression and violence: Causes, manifestations, and consequences* (pp. 221–239). Washington, DC: American Psychological Association. http://dx.doi.org/10.1037/12346-012

McCullough, M. E., Pedersen, E. J., Tabak, B. A., & Carter, E. C. (2014). Conciliatory gestures promote forgiveness and reduce anger in humans. *PNAS Proceedings of the National Academy of Sciences of the United States of America, 111*, 11211–11216.

McDonald, M. M., Donnellan, M. B., & Navarrete, C. D. (2012). A life history approach to understanding the Dark Triad. *Personality and Individual Differences, 52*, 601–605. http://dx.doi.org/10.1016/j.paid.2011.12.003

McGregor, H. A., Lieberman, J. D., Greenberg, J., Solomon, S., Arndt, J., Simon, L., & Pyszczynski, T. (1998). Terror management and aggression: Evidence that mortality salience motivates aggression against worldview-threatening others.

Journal of Personality and Social Psychology, *74*, 590–605. http://dx.doi.org/10.1037/0022-3514.74.3.590

McHoskey, J. W. (2001). Machiavellianism and sexuality: On the moderating role of biological sex. *Personality and Individual Differences*, *31*, 779–789. http://dx.doi.org/10.1016/S0191-8869(00)00180-X

McNulty, J. K., Wenner, C. A., & Fisher, T. D. (2016). Longitudinal associations among relationship satisfaction, sexual satisfaction, and frequency of sex in early marriage. *Archives of Sexual Behavior*, *45*, 85–97.

McNulty, J. K., & Widman, L. (2014). Sexual narcissism and infidelity in early marriage. *Archives of Sexual Behavior*, *43*, 1315–1325. http://dx.doi.org/10.1007/s10508-014-0282-6

Meehan, C. L., & Hawks, S. (2014). Maternal and allomaternal responsiveness: The significance of cooperative caregiving in attachment theory. In H. Otto & H. Keller (Eds.), *Different faces of attachment: Cultural variations on a universal human need* (pp. 113–140). Cambridge, England: Cambridge University Press. http://dx.doi.org/10.1017/CBO9781139226684.008

Merola, I., Prato-Previde, E., Lazzaroni, M., & Marshall-Pescini, S. (2014). Dogs' comprehension of referential emotional expressions: Familiar people and familiar emotions are easier. *Animal Cognition*, *17*, 373–385. http://dx.doi.org/10.1007/s10071-013-0668-1

Meston, C. M., & Buss, D. M. (2007). Why humans have sex. *Archives of Sexual Behavior*, *36*, 477–507. http://dx.doi.org/10.1007/s10508-007-9175-2

Mikulincer, M. (1997). Adult attachment style and information processing: Individual differences in curiosity and cognitive closure. *Journal of Personality and Social Psychology*, *72*, 1217–1230. http://dx.doi.org/10.1037/0022-3514.72.5.1217

Mikulincer, M., & Goodman, G. S. (2006). *Dynamics of romantic love: Attachment, caregiving, and sex*. New York, NY: Guilford Press.

Mikulincer, M., & Shaver, P. (2010). *Attachment in adulthood: Structure dynamics, and change*. New York, NY: Guilford Press.

Miller, G. (2000). *The mating mind*. New York, NY: Anchor Books.

Miller, G. (2008). Mating intelligence: Frequently asked questions. In G. Geher & G. Miller (Eds.), *Mating intelligence: Sex, relationships, and the mind's reproductive system* (pp. 367–394). New York, NY: Erlbaum.

Milot, T., Lorent, A., St-Laurent, D., Bernier, A., Tarabulsy, G., Lemelin, J.-P., & Éthier, L. S. (2014). Hostile-Helpless state of mind as further evidence of adult disorganized states of mind in neglecting families. *Child Abuse & Neglect*, *38*, 1351–1357. http://dx.doi.org/10.1016/j.chiabu.2014.02.015

Miner, E. J., & Shackelford, T. K. (2010). Mate attraction, retention and expulsion. *Psicothema*, *22*, 9–14.

Mogilski, J. K., Memering, S. L., Welling, L. L. M., & Shackelford, T. K. (2017). Monogamy versus consensual non-monogamy: Alternative approaches to pursuing a strategically pluralistic mating strategy. *Archives of Sexual Behavior*, *46*, 407–417.

Mogilski, J. K., & Wade, T. J. (2013). Friendship as a relationship infiltration tactic during human mate poaching. *Evolutionary Psychology, 11*, 926–943. http://dx.doi.org/10.1177/147470491301100415

Money, J. (1986). *Love maps: Clinical concepts of sexual/erotic health and pathology, paraphilia, and gender transposition in childhood, adolescence, and maturity*. New York, NY: Prometheus Books.

Montgomery, H. (2009). *An introduction to childhood: Anthropological perspectives on children's lives*. New York, NY: Wiley-Blackwell.

Moors, A. C., Conley, T. D., Edelstein, R. S., & Chopik, W. J. (2015). Attached to monogamy? Avoidance predicts willingness to engage (but not actual engagement) in consensual non-monogamy. *Journal of Social and Personal Relationships, 32*, 222–240. http://dx.doi.org/10.1177/0265407514529065

Morrison, A. P. (2011). The psychodynamics of shame. In R. L. Dearing & J. P. Tangney (Eds.), *Shame in the therapy hour* (pp. 23–43). Washington, DC: American Psychological Association. http://dx.doi.org/10.1037/12326-001

Muller, R. T., Kraftcheck, E. R., & McLewin, L. A. (2004). Adult attachment and trauma. In D. R. Catherall (Ed.), *Handbook of stress, trauma, and the family* (pp. 203–229). New York, NY: Brunner-Routledge.

Napolitano, L. A., & McKay, D. (2007). Dichotomous thinking in borderline personality disorder. *Cognitive Therapy and Research, 31*, 717–726. http://dx.doi.org/10.1007/s10608-007-9123-4

Neff, K. D., & Suizzo, M. A. (2006). Culture, power, authenticity and psychological well-being within romantic relationships: A comparison of European American and Mexican Americans. *Cognitive Development, 21*, 441–457. http://dx.doi.org/10.1016/j.cogdev.2006.06.008

Negash, S., Cui, M., Fincham, F. D., & Pasley, K. (2014). Extradyadic involvement and relationship dissolution in heterosexual women university students. *Archives of Sexual Behavior, 43*, 531–539. http://dx.doi.org/10.1007/s10508-013-0213-y

Nelson, S. K., Kushlev, K., & Lyubomirsky, S. (2014). The pains and pleasures of parenting: When, why, and how is parenthood associated with more or less well-being? *Psychological Bulletin, 140*, 846–895. http://dx.doi.org/10.1037/a0035444

Newlin, D. (2007). Self-perceived survival and reproductive fitness theory: Substance use disorder, evolutionary game theory, and the brain. In S. Platek, J. Keenan, & T. Shackelford (Eds.), *Evolutionary cognitive neuroscience* (pp. 285–326). Cambridge, MA: The MIT Press.

Norcross, J. C., & Wampold, B. E. (2011). Evidence-based therapy relationships: Research conclusions and clinical practices. *Psychotherapy, 48*, 98–102. http://dx.doi.org/10.1037/a0022161

Oatley, K., Keltner, D., & Jenkins, J. M. (2006). *Understanding emotions*. Malden, MA: Blackwell.

Ogas, O., & Gaddam, S. (2011). *A billion wicked thoughts: What the Internet tells us about sexual relationships*. New York, NY: Plume.

Okumura, Y., Kanakogi, Y., Kanda, T., Ishiguro, H., & Itakura, S. (2013). Infants understand the referential nature of human gaze but not robot gaze. *Journal of Experimental Child Psychology, 116*, 86–95. http://dx.doi.org/10.1016/j.jecp.2013.02.007

Oliver, M. B., & Hyde, J. S. (1993). Gender differences in sexuality: A meta-analysis. *Psychological Bulletin, 114*, 29–51. http://dx.doi.org/10.1037/0033-2909.114.1.29

Onley, M., Veselka, L., Schermer, J. A., & Vernon, P. A. (2013). Survival of the scheming: A genetically informed link between the dark triad and mental toughness. *Twin Research and Human Genetics, 16*, 1087–1095. http://dx.doi.org/10.1017/thg.2013.66

Orford, J. (1978). Hypersexuality: Implications for a theory of dependence. *The British Journal of Addiction, 73*, 299–10. http://dx.doi.org/10.1111/j.1360-0443.1978.tb00157.x

Oshio, A. (2009). Development and validation of the Dichotomous Thinking Inventory. *Social Behavior and Personality, 37*, 729–742. http://dx.doi.org/10.2224/sbp.2009.37.6.729

Oshio, A. (2012). An all-or-nothing thinking turns into darkness: Relations between dichotomous thinking and personality disorders. *Japanese Psychological Research, 54*, 424–429. http://dx.doi.org/10.1111/j.1468-5884.2012.00515.x

O'Sullivan, L., & Byers, E. S. (1992). College students' incorporation of initiator and restrictor roles in sexual dating interactions. *Journal of Sex Research, 29*, 435–446. http://dx.doi.org/10.1080/00224499209551658

Oth Vilaythong, T., Lindner, N. M., & Nosek, B. A. (2010). Do unto others: Effects of priming the golden rule on Buddhists' and Christians' attitudes toward gay people. *Journal for the Scientific Study of Religion, 49*, 494–506. http://dx.doi.org/10.1111/j.1468-5906.2010.01524.x

Overall, N. C., Simpson, J. A., & Struthers, H. (2013). Buffering attachment-related avoidance: Softening emotional and behavioral defenses during conflict discussions. *Journal of Personality and Social Psychology, 104*, 854–871. http://dx.doi.org/10.1037/a0031798

Owen, J., & Hilsenroth, M. J. (2014). Treatment adherence: The importance of therapist flexibility in relation to therapy outcomes. *Journal of Counseling Psychology, 61*, 280–280. http://dx.doi.org/10.1037/a0035753

Owen, J., Rhoades, G. K., & Stanley, S. M. (2013). Sliding versus deciding in relationships: Associations with relationship quality, commitment, and infidelity. *Journal of Couple & Relationship Therapy, 12*, 135–149. http://dx.doi.org/10.1080/15332691.2013.779097

Pallotta-Chiarolli, M., Haydon, P., & Hunter, A. (2013). "These are our children": Polyamorous parenting. In A. E. Goldberg & K. R. Allen (Eds.), *LGBT-parent families: Innovations in research and implications for practice* (pp. 117–131). New York, NY: Springer. http://dx.doi.org/10.1007/978-1-4614-4556-2_8

Parker, J., & Burkley, M. (2009). Who's chasing whom? The impact of gender and relationship status on mate poaching. *Journal of Experimental Social Psychology, 45*, 1016–1019. http://dx.doi.org/10.1016/j.jesp.2009.04.022

Pascual-Leone, A., Gilles, P., Singh, T., & Andreescu, C. A. (2013). Problem anger in psychotherapy: An emotion-focused perspective on hate, rage, and rejecting anger. *Journal of Contemporary Psychotherapy, 43*, 83–92. http://dx.doi.org/10.1007/s10879-012-9214-8

Patten, S. B. (1991). The loss of a parent during childhood as a risk factor for depression. *The Canadian Journal of Psychiatry, 36*, 706–711.

Paul, P. (2005). *Pornified: How pornography is transforming our lives, our relationships, and our families*. New York, NY: Holt.

Paulhus, D. L., & Buckels, E. (2012). Classic self-deception revisited. In S. Vazire & T. D. Wilson (Eds.), *Handbook of self-knowledge* (pp. 363–378). New York, NY: Guilford Press.

Paulhus, D. L., & John, O. P. (1998). Egoistic and moralistic biases in self-perception: The interplay of self-deceptive styles with basic traits and motives. *Journal of Personality, 66*, 1025–1060. http://dx.doi.org/10.1111/1467-6494.00041

Paulhus, D. L., & Williams, K. M. (2002). The dark triad of personality: Narcissism, Machiavellianism, and psychopathy. *Journal of Research in Personality, 36*, 556–563. http://dx.doi.org/10.1016/S0092-6566(02)00505-6

Pavelka, M. S. M. (1995). Sexual nature: What can we learn from a cross-species perspective? In P. R. Abramson & S. D. Pinkerton (Eds.), *Sexual nature, sexual culture* (pp. 17–36). Chicago, IL: University of Chicago Press.

Pedersen, F. A. (1991). Secular trends in human sex ratios: Their influence on individual and family behavior. *Human Nature, 2*, 271–291. http://dx.doi.org/10.1007/BF02692189

Peluso, D. M., & Boster, J. S. (2002). Partible parentage and social networks among the Esa Eja. In S. Beckerman & P. Valentine (Eds.), *Cultures of multiple fathers: The theory and practice of partible paternity in lowland South America* (pp. 137–159). Gainesville: University of Florida Press.

Perner, J., Leekam, S. R., & Wimmer, H. (1987). Three-year-olds' difficulty with false belief: The case for a conceptual deficit. *British Journal of Developmental Psychology, 5*, 125–137. http://dx.doi.org/10.1111/j.2044-835X.1987.tb01048.x

Peters, J. R., & Geiger, P. J. (2016). Borderline personality disorder and self-conscious affect: Too much shame but not enough guilt? *Personality Disorders, 7*, 303–308.

Petersen, J. L., & Hyde, J. S. (2010). A meta-analytic review of research on gender differences in sexuality, 1993–2007. *Psychological Bulletin, 136*, 21–38. http://dx.doi.org/10.1037/a0017504

Philips, A. (2007, January). *Emotional reactions to infidelity: The influence of relative mate value on distress*. Presented at the 8th Annual Meeting of the Society of Personality and Social Psychology, Memphis, TN. http://dx.doi.org/10.1037/e514412014-210

Pierson, H., & Hayes, S. C. (2007). Using acceptance and commitment therapy to empower the therapeutic relationship. In P. Gilbert & R. L. Leahy (Eds.), *The therapeutic relationship in the cognitive behavioral psychotherapies* (pp. 205–228). New York, NY: Routledge/Taylor & Francis Group.

Pincus, A. L. (2013). The pathological narcissism inventory. In J. S. Ogrodniczuk (Ed.), *Understanding and treating pathological narcissism* (pp. 93–110). Washington, DC: American Psychological Association. http://dx.doi.org/10.1037/14041-006

Pincus, A. L., Ansell, E. B., Pimentel, C. A., Cain, N. M., Wright, A. G. C., & Levy, K. N. (2009). Initial construction and validation of the Pathological Narcissism Inventory. *Psychological Assessment, 21*, 365–379. http://dx.doi.org/10.1037/a0016530

Pincus, A. L., Cain, N. M., & Wright, A. G. C. (2014). Narcissistic grandiosity and narcissistic vulnerability in psychotherapy. *Personality Disorders, 5*, 439–443. http://dx.doi.org/10.1037/per0000031

Plant, D. (2014). A look at narcissism through Professor Higgins in *Pygmalion*. *British Journal of Psychotherapy, 28*, 50–65. http://dx.doi.org/10.1111/j.1752-0118.2011.01264.x

Pollard, S. E., Hook, J. N., Corley, M. D., & Schneider, J. P. (2014). Support utilization by partners of self-identified sex addicts. *Journal of Sex & Marital Therapy, 40*, 339–348. http://dx.doi.org/10.1080/0092623X.2012.751076

Pollock, D. (2002). Partible paternity and multiple paternity among the Kulina. In S. Beckerman & P. Valentine (Eds.), *Cultures of multiple fathers: The theory and practice of partible paternity in lowland South America* (pp. 42–61). Gainesville: University of Florida Press.

Previti, D., & Amato, P. R. (2004). Is infidelity a cause or a consequence of poor marital quality? *Journal of Social and Personal Relationships, 21*, 217–230. http://dx.doi.org/10.1177/0265407504041384

Pronk, T. M., Karremans, J. C., & Wigboldus, D. H. J. (2011). How can you resist? Executive control helps romantically involved individuals to stay faithful. *Journal of Personality and Social Psychology, 100*, 827–837. http://dx.doi.org/10.1037/a0021993

Rammstedt, B., & Schupp, J. (2008). Only the congruent survive—personality similarities in couples. *Personality and Individual Differences, 45*, 533–535. http://dx.doi.org/10.1016/j.paid.2008.06.007

Raskin, R., & Hall, C. S. (1981). The Narcissistic Personality Inventory: Alternative form reliability and further evidence of construct validity. *Journal of Personality Assessment, 45*, 159–162. http://dx.doi.org/10.1207/s15327752jpa4502_10

Raskin, R. N., & Hall, C. S. (1979). A narcissistic personality inventory. *Psychological Reports, 45*, 590. http://dx.doi.org/10.2466/pr0.1979.45.2.590

Regan, P. C. (1998). What if you can't get what you want? Willingness to compromise ideal mate selection standards as a function of sex, mate value, and relationship context. *Personality and Social Psychology Bulletin, 24*, 1294–1303. http://dx.doi.org/10.1177/01461672982412004

Regnerus, M., & Uecker, J. (2011). *Premarital sex in America: How young Americans meet, mate, and think about marrying*. New York, NY: Oxford University Press.

Rhoades, G. K., Stanley, S. M., Markman, H. J., & Ragan, E. P. (2012). Parents' marital status, conflict, and role modeling: Links with adult romantic relationship quality. *Journal of Divorce & Remarriage, 53*, 348–367. http://dx.doi.org/10.1080/10502556.2012.675838

Ritchie, A., & Barker, M. (2006). "There aren't words for what we do or how we feel so we have to make them up": Constructing polyamorous languages in a culture of compulsory monogamy. *Sexualities*, 9, 584–601. http://dx.doi.org/10.1177/1363460706069987

Robbins, N. K., Low, K. G., & Query, A. N. (2016). A qualitative exploration of the "coming out" process for asexual individuals. *Archives of Sexual Behavior, 45*, 741–760.

Robson, S. L., van Shaik, C. P., & Hawkes, K. (2006). The derived features of human life history. In K. Hawkes & R. Paine (Eds.), *The evolution of human life history* (pp. 17–44). Santa Fe, NM: SAR Press.

Rodriguez, J. R. (2000). Attachment styles, relationship satisfaction and the demand/withdraw interactional pattern. *Dissertation Abstracts International: Section B. The Sciences and Engineering, 61*(5-B), 2820. (UMI No. AAI9975607)

Rodriguez Mosquera, P. M., Manstead, A. S. R., & Fischer, A. H. (2000). The role of honor-related values in the elicitation, experience, and communication of pride, shame, and anger: Spain and the Netherlands compared. *Personality and Social Psychology Bulletin, 26*, 833–844. http://dx.doi.org/10.1177/0146167200269008

Rogers, C. R. (1961). *On becoming a person: A therapist's view of psychotherapy*. Boston, MA: Houghton Mifflin.

Ronningstam, E. (2009). Narcissistic personality disorder: Facing *DSM–V*. *Psychiatric Annals*, 39, 111–121. http://dx.doi.org/10.3928/00485713-20090301-09

Roscoe, B., Cavanaugh, L. E., & Kennedy, D. R. (1988). Dating infidelity: Behaviors, reasons and consequences. *Adolescence, 23*, 35–43.

Rosenberg, H., & Kraus, S. (2014). The relationship of "passionate attachment" for pornography with sexual compulsivity, frequency of use, and craving for pornography. *Addictive Behaviors*, 39, 1012–1017. http://dx.doi.org/10.1016/j.addbeh.2014.02.010

Rusbult, C. E. (1983). A longitudinal test of the investment model: The development (and deterioration) of satisfaction and commitment in heterosexual involvements. *Journal of Personality and Social Psychology*, 45, 101–117. http://dx.doi.org/10.1037/0022-3514.45.1.101

Rush, B. (1812). *Medical inquiries and observation upon the diseases of the mind*. Philadelphia, PA: Kimber & Richardson.

Rust, P. C. (2003). Monogamy and polyamory: Relationship issues for bisexuals. In L. D. Garnets & D. C. Kimmel (Eds.), *Psychological perspectives on lesbian, gay, and bisexual experiences* (2nd ed., pp. 475–496). New York, NY: Columbia University Press.

Ryan, R., & Jetha, C. (2011). *Sex before dawn: How we mate, why we stray, and what it means for modern relationships*. New York, NY: Harper Perennial.

Safran, J. D., & Muran, J. C. (2003). *Negotiating the therapeutic alliance: A relational treatment guide*. New York, NY: Guilford Press.

Schimel, J., Wohl, M. J. A., & Williams, T. (2006). Terror management and trait empathy: Evidence that mortality salience promotes reactions of forgiveness among people with high (vs. low) trait empathy. *Motivation and Emotion, 30*, 217–227. http://dx.doi.org/10.1007/s11031-006-9040-y

Schlager, D. (1995). Evolutionary perspectives on paranoid disorder. *Psychiatric Clinics of North America, 18*, 263–279.

Schlenker, B. R. (2008). Integrity and character: Implications of principled expedient ethical ideologies. *Journal of Social and Clinical Psychology, 27*, 1078–1125. http://dx.doi.org/10.1521/jscp.2008.27.10.1078

Schmidt, A. E., Green, M. S., & Prouty, A. M. (2016). Effects of parental infidelity and inter-parental conflict on relational ethics between adult children and parents: A contextual perspective. *Journal of Family Therapy, 38*, 386–408. http://dx.doi.org/10.1111/1467-6427.12091

Schmitt, D. P. (2004). The Big Five related to risky sexual behaviour across 10 world regions: Differential personality associations of sexual promiscuity and relationship infidelity. *European Journal of Personality, 18*, 301–319. http://dx.doi.org/10.1002/per.520

Schmitt, D. P., Alcalay, L., Allik, J., Angleitner, A., Ault, L., Austers, I., . . . International Sexuality Description Project. (2004). Patterns and universals of mate poaching across 53 nations: The effects of sex, culture, and personality on romantically attracting another person's partner. *Journal of Personality and Social Psychology, 86*, 560–584. http://dx.doi.org/10.1037/0022-3514.86.4.560

Schmitt, D. P., & Buss, D. M. (2001). Human mate poaching: Tactics and temptations for infiltrating existing mateships. *Journal of Personality and Social Psychology, 80*, 894–917. http://dx.doi.org/10.1037/0022-3514.80.6.894

Schmitt, D. P., Jonason, P. K., Byerley, G. J., Flores, S. D., Illbeck, B. E., O'Leary, K. N., & Qudrat, A. (2012). A reexamination of sex differences in sexuality: New studies reveal old truths. *Current Directions in Psychological Science, 21*, 135–139. http://dx.doi.org/10.1177/0963721412436808

Schmookler, T., & Bursik, K. (2007). The value of monogamy in emerging adulthood: A gendered perspective. *Journal of Social and Personal Relationships, 24*, 819–835. http://dx.doi.org/10.1177/0265407507084185

Schneiderman, I., Zagoory-Sharon, O., Leckman, J. F., & Feldman, R. (2012). Oxytocin during the initial stages of romantic attachment: Relations to couples' interactive reciprocity. *Psychoneuroendocrinology, 37*, 1277–1285. http://dx.doi.org/10.1016/j.psyneuen.2011.12.021

Schriber, R. A., Chung, J. M., Sorensen, K. S., & Robins, R. W. (2013, June). *A first look at the contempt-prone personality*. Presented at the 3rd Biennial Conference of the Association for Research in Personality, Charlotte, NC. http://dx.doi.org/10.1037/e571452013-166

Scuka, R. F. (2015). A clinician's guide to helping couples heal from the trauma of infidelity. *Journal of Couple & Relationship Therapy*, *14*, 141–168. http://dx.doi.org/10.1080/15332691.2014.953653

Sedgwick, D. (1994). *The wounded healer: Countertransference from a Jungian perspective*. Florence, KY: Taylor & Frances/Routledge. http://dx.doi.org/10.4324/9780203359921

Selterman, D. F., & Maier, M. A. (2013). Secure attachment and material reward both attenuate romantic jealousy. *Motivation and Emotion*, *37*, 765–775. http://dx.doi.org/10.1007/s11031-013-9340-y

Shaver, P. R., & Mikulincer, M. (2006). Attachment theory, individual psychodynamics, and relationship functioning. In A. L. Vangelisti & D. Perlman (Eds.), *The Cambridge handbook of personal relationships* (pp. 251–271). New York, NY: Cambridge University Press. http://dx.doi.org/10.1017/CBO9780511606632.015

Shedler, J. (2015). Where is the evidence for "evidence-based" therapies? *The Journal of Psychological Therapies in Primary Care*, *4*, 47–59.

Shimberg, J., Josephs, L., & Tittel, L. (2016). Empathy as a mediator of attitudes toward infidelity among college students. *Journal of Sex & Marital Therapy*, *42*, 353–368. http://dx.doi.org/10.1080/0092623X.2015.1053019

Shin, J., & Ariely, D. (2004). Keeping doors open: The effect of unavailability on incentives to keep options viable. *Management Science*, *50*, 575–586. http://dx.doi.org/10.1287/mnsc.1030.0148

Shostak, M. (1976). A !Kung woman's memories of childhood. In R. B. Lee & I. DeVore (Eds.), *Kalahari hunter-gatherers: Studies of the !Kung San and their neighbors* (pp. 246–277). Cambridge, MA: Harvard University Press.

Shostak, M. (1981). *Nisa: The life and words of a !Kung woman*. Cambridge, MA: Harvard University Press.

Simonton, D. K. (2013). If innate talent doesn't exist, where do the data disappear? In S. B. Kaufman (Ed.), *The complexity of greatness: Beyond talent or practice* (pp. 17–26). New York, NY: Oxford University Press. http://dx.doi.org/10.1093/acprof:oso/9780199794003.003.0002

Singh, D. (2002). Female mate value at a glance: Relationship of waist-to-hip ratio to health, fecundity and attractiveness. *Neuroendocrinology Letters*, *23*(Suppl. 4), 81–91.

Skjærvø, G. R., & Røskaft, E. (2015). Wealth and the opportunity for sexual selection in men and Women. *Behavioral Ecology*, *26*, 444–451. http://dx.doi.org/10.1093/beheco/aru213

Skolnick, A. J., Bascom, K. L., & Wilson, D. T. (2013). Gender role expectations of disgust: Men are low and women are high. *Sex Roles*, 69, 72–88. http://dx.doi.org/10.1007/s11199-013-0279-y

Slaughter, V., & McConnell, D. (2003). Emergence of joint attention: Relationships between gaze following, social referencing, imitation, and naming in infancy. *The Journal of Genetic Psychology: Research and Theory on Human Development, 164*, 54–71. http://dx.doi.org/10.1080/00221320309597503

Smith, C. V., Hadden, B. W., Webster, G. D., Jonason, P. K., Gesselman, A. N., & Crysel, L. C. (2014). Mutually attracted or repulsed? Actor–partner interdependence models of Dark Triad traits and relationship outcomes. *Personality and Individual Differences, 67*, 35–41. http://dx.doi.org/10.1016/j.paid.2014.01.044

Smith, H. J., Goode, C., Balzarini, R., Ryan, D., & Georges, M. (2014). The cost of forgiveness: Observers prefer victims who leave unfaithful romantic partners. *European Journal of Social Psychology, 44*, 758–773. http://dx.doi.org/10.1002/ejsp.2054

Smith, M. M., Sherry, S. B., Chen, S., Saklofske, D. H., Flett, G. L., & Hewitt, P. L. (2016). Perfectionism and narcissism: A meta-analytic review. *Journal of Research in Personality, 64*, 90–101. http://dx.doi.org/10.1016/j.jrp.2016.07.012

Spanier, G. P., & Margolis, R. L. (1983). Marital separation and extramarital sexual behavior. *Journal of Sex Research, 19*, 23–48. http://dx.doi.org/10.1080/00224498309551167

Sprecher, S., & Fehr, B. (2011). Dispositional attachment and relationship-specific attachment as predictors of compassionate love for a partner. *Journal of Social and Personal Relationships, 28*, 558–574. http://dx.doi.org/10.1177/0265407510386190

Staheli, L. (1998). *Affair-proof your marriage: Understanding, preventing, and surviving an affair*. New York, NY: Harper-Perennial.

Stikkelbroek, Y., Prinzie, P., de Graaf, R., ten Have, M., & Cuijpers, P. (2012). Parental death during childhood and psychopathology in adulthood. *Psychiatry Research, 198*, 516–520. http://dx.doi.org/10.1016/j.psychres.2011.10.024

Stinson, R. D. (2010). Hooking up in young adulthood: A review of factors influencing the sexual behavior of college students. *Journal of College Student Psychotherapy, 24*, 98–115. http://dx.doi.org/10.1080/87568220903558596

Stoeber, J., Sherry, S., & Nealis, L. (2015). Multidimensional perfectionism and narcissism: Grandiose or vulnerable? *Personality and Individual Differences, 80*, 85–90. http://dx.doi.org/10.1016/j.paid.2015.02.027

Stone, J., & Josephs, L. (2015, May). *Anxiously attracted: How attachment style and facial expression impact sexual attraction*. Poster presented at the annual conference of the American Psychological Society (Student Research Award), New York, NY.

Strelan, P., Weick, M., & Vasiljevic, M. (2014). Power and revenge. *British Journal of Social Psychology, 53*, 521–540. http://dx.doi.org/10.1111/bjso.12044

Stricker, G., & Trierweiler, S. J. (1995). The local clinical scientist. A bridge between science and practice. *American Psychologist, 50*, 995–1002. http://dx.doi.org/10.1037/0003-066X.50.12.995

Stuewig, J., Tangney, J. P., Heigel, C., Harty, L., & McCloskey, L. (2010). Shaming, blaming, and maiming: Functional links among the moral emotions, externalization of blame, and aggression. *Journal of Research in Personality, 44*, 91–102. http://dx.doi.org/10.1016/j.jrp.2009.12.005

Sugiyama, L. S. (2005). Physical attractiveness in adaptationist perspective. In D. M. Buss (Ed.), *The handbook of evolutionary psychology* (pp. 292–343). Hoboken, NJ: Wiley.

Sun, C., Bridges, A., Johnson, J. A., & Ezzell, M. B. (2016). Pornography and the male sexual script: An analysis of consumption and sexual relations. *Archives of Sexual Behavior, 45*, 983–994.

Sunderani, S., Arnocky, S., & Vaillancourt, T. (2013). Individual differences in mate poaching: An examination of hormonal, dispositional, and behavioral mate-value traits. *Archives of Sexual Behavior, 42*, 533–542. http://dx.doi.org/10.1007/s10508-012-9974-y

Surbey, M. K. (1998). Parent and offspring strategies in the transition at adolescence. *Human Nature, 9*, 67–94. http://dx.doi.org/10.1007/s12110-998-1012-3

Sussman, S. (2010). Love addiction: Definition, etiology, treatment. *Sexual Addiction & Compulsivity, 17*, 31–45. http://dx.doi.org/10.1080/10720161003604095

Symons, D. (1979). *The evolution of human sexuality*. New York, NY: Oxford University Press.

Symons, D. (1987). Can Darwin's view of life shed light on human sexuality? In J. H. Geer & W. T. O'Donohue (Eds.), *Theories of human sexuality* (pp. 91–125). New York, NY: Plenum Press.

Tafoya, M. A., & Spitzberg, B. H. (2007). The dark side of infidelity: Its nature, prevalence, and communicative functions. In B. H. Spitzberg & W. R. Cupach (Eds.), *The dark side of interpersonal communication* (pp. 201–242). Mahwah, NJ: Erlbaum.

Tepper, M. S., Owens, A. F., Coleman, E., & Carnes, P. (2007). Current controversies in sexual health: Sexual addiction and compulsion. In A. F. Owens & M. S. Tepper (Eds.), *Praeger perspectives: Sex, love, and psychology. Sexual health: Vol. 4. State-of-the-art treatments and research* (pp. 349–363). Westport, CT: Praeger/Greenwood.

Terrizzi, J. A., Jr. (2014). *On the origin of shame: Feelings of disgust toward the self* (Doctoral dissertation). Ann Arbor, MI: ProQuest Dissertations and Theses database. (Accession order no. 3571580)

Thibaut, J. W., & Kelley, H. H. (1959). *The social psychology of groups*. New York, NY: Wiley.

Thomas, A., Chess, S., & Birch, H. G. (1970). The origin of personality. *Scientific American, 223*, 102–109. http://dx.doi.org/10.1038/scientificamerican0870-102

Tomasello, M. (1999). *The cultural origins of human cognition*. Cambridge, MA: Harvard University Press.

Tomasello, M. (2014). The ultra-social animal. *European Journal of Social Psychology, 44*, 187–194. http://dx.doi.org/10.1002/ejsp.2015

Treas, J., & Giesen, D. (2000). Sexual infidelity among married and cohabiting Americans. *Journal of Marriage and the Family*, *62*, 48–60. http://dx.doi.org/10.1111/j.1741-3737.2000.00048.x

Trivers, R. (1971). The evolution of reciprocal altruism. *Quarterly Review of Biology*, *46*, 35–57.

Trivers, R. (1972). Parental investment and sexual selection. In B. Campbell (Ed.), *Sexual selection and the descent of man: 1871–1971* (pp. 136–179). Chicago, IL: Aldine.

Tronick, E., Als, H., Adamson, L., Wise, S., & Brazelton, T. B. (1978). The infant's response to entrapment between contradictory messages in face-to-face interaction. *Journal of the American Academy of Child Psychiatry*, *17*, 1–13. http://dx.doi.org/10.1016/S0002-7138(09)62273-1

Trudel, G., Turgeon, L., & Piché, L. (2010). Marital and sexual aspects of old age. *Sexual and Relationship Therapy*, *25*, 316–341. http://dx.doi.org/10.1080/14681991003750467

Tuch, R. (2000). *The single woman–married man syndrome*. Lanham, MD: Aronson.

Tull, M. T., Weiss, N. H., Adams, C. E., & Gratz, K. L. (2012). The contribution of emotion regulation difficulties to risky sexual behavior within a sample of patients in residential substance abuse treatment. *Addictive Behaviors*, *37*, 1084–1092. http://dx.doi.org/10.1016/j.addbeh.2012.05.001

Turan, B., Guo, J., Boggiano, M. M., & Bedgood, D. (2014). Dominant, cold, avoidant, and lonely: Basal testosterone as a biological marker for an interpersonal style. *Journal of Research in Personality*, *50*, 84–89. http://dx.doi.org/10.1016/j.jrp.2014.03.008

Tversky, A., & Kahneman, D. (1981). The framing of decisions and the psychology of choice. *Science*, *211*, 453–458. http://dx.doi.org/10.1126/science.7455683

Twenge, J. M., Konrath, S., Foster, J. D., Campbell, W. K., & Bushman, B. J. (2008). Egos inflating over time: A cross-temporal meta-analysis of the Narcissistic Personality Inventory. *Journal of Personality*, *76*, 875–902. http://dx.doi.org/10.1111/j.1467-6494.2008.00507.x

Vail-Smith, K., Whetstone, L. M., & Knox, D. (2010). The illusion of safety in "monogamous" undergraduate relationships. *American Journal of Health Behavior*, *34*, 12–20. http://dx.doi.org/10.5993/AJHB.34.1.2

van den Broek, N., Deutz, M. H. F., Schoneveld, E. A., Burk, W. J., & Cillessen, A. H. N. (2016). Behavioral correlates of prioritizing popularity in adolescence. *Journal of Youth and Adolescence*, *45*, 2444–2454. http://dx.doi.org/10.1007/s10964-015-0352-7

Vazire, S., Naumann, L. P., Rentfrow, P. J., & Gosling, S. D. (2008). Portrait of a narcissist: Manifestations of narcissism in physical appearance. *Journal of Research in Personality*, *42*, 1439–1447. http://dx.doi.org/10.1016/j.jrp.2008.06.007

Vecchione, M., & Alessandri, G. (2013). Disentangling trait from state components in the assessment of egoistic and moralistic self-enhancement. *Personality and Individual Differences*, *54*, 884–889. http://dx.doi.org/10.1016/j.paid.2012.12.027

Visser, B. A., DeBow, V., Pozzebon, J. A., Bogaert, A. F., & Book, A. (2015). Psychopathic sexuality: The thin line between fantasy and reality. *Journal of Personality, 83*, 376–388. http://dx.doi.org/10.1111/jopy.12110

Volling, B. L., Yu, T., Gonzalez, R., Kennedy, D. E., Rosenberg, L., & Oh, W. (2014). Children's responses to mother-infant and father-infant interaction with a baby sibling: Jealousy or joy? *Journal of Family Psychology, 28*, 634–644. http://dx.doi.org/10.1037/a0037811

von Krafft-Ebing, R. (1965). *Psychopathia sexualis*. New York, NY: G. P. Putnam's Sons. (Original work published 1886)

Wachtel, P. L. (2010). Beyond "ESTs": Problematic assumptions in the pursuit of evidence-based practice. *Psychoanalytic Psychology, 27*, 251–272. http://dx.doi.org/10.1037/a0020532

Wachtel, P. L. (2014). *Cyclical psychodynamics and the contextual self: The inner world, the intimate world, and the world of culture and society*. (Relational perspectives series.) New York, NY: Routledge/Taylor & Francis Group.

Wallace, B. A. (2001). *Buddhism with attitude*. Ithaca, NY: Snow Lion.

Walz, T. (2002). Crones, dirty old men, sexy seniors: Representations of sexuality of older persons. *Journal of Aging & Identity, 7*, 99–112. http://dx.doi.org/10.1023/A:1015487101438

Wampold, B. E. (2001). *The great psychotherapy debate: Models, methods, and findings*. Mahwah, NJ: Erlbaum.

Wampold, B. E., & Imel, Z. E. (2015). *The great psychotherapy debate: The evidence for what makes psychotherapy work*. New York, NY: Routledge.

Watson, M. W., & Getz, K. (1990a). Developmental shifts in Oedipal behaviors related to family role understanding. *New Directions for Child Development, 48*, 29–45. http://dx.doi.org/10.1002/cd.23219904804

Watson, M. W., & Getz, K. (1990b). The relationship between oedipal behaviors and children's family role concepts. *Merrill-Palmer Quarterly, 36*, 487–505.

Weaver, J. M., & Schofield, T. J. (2015). Mediation and moderation of divorce effects on children's behavior problems. *Journal of Family Psychology, 29*, 39–48. http://dx.doi.org/10.1037/fam0000043

Weeks, G. R., Gambescia, N., & Jenkins, R. E. (2003). *Treating infidelity: Therapeutic dilemmas and effective strategies*. New York, NY: Norton.

Weinberg, K., & Josephs, L. (2014, August). *Hiding your true self: Gender, playing hard to get, and the false self*. Poster presented at the annual conference of the American Psychological Association, Division of Psychoanalysis, Washington, DC.

Weisman, O., Zagoory-Sharon, O., Schneiderman, I., Gordon, I., & Feldman, R. (2013). Plasma oxytocin distributions in a large cohort of women and men and their gender-specific associations with anxiety. *Psychoneuroendocrinology, 38*, 694–701. http://dx.doi.org/10.1016/j.psyneuen.2012.08.011

Weiss, J. (1995). Empirical studies of the psychoanalytic process. In T. Shapiro & R. N. Emde (Eds.), *Research in psychoanalysis: Process, development, outcome* (pp. 7–29). Madison, CT: International Universities Press.

Weiss, J. (1998). Patients' unconscious plans for solving their problems. *Psychoanalytic Dialogues*, *8*, 411–428. http://dx.doi.org/10.1080/10481889809539259

West-Eberhard, M. J. (2014). Darwin's forgotten idea: The social essence of sexual selection. *Neuroscience and Biobehavioral Reviews*, *46*, 501–508. http://dx.doi.org/10.1016/j.neubiorev.2014.06.015

Wickham, R. E., Reed, D. E., & Williamson, R. E. (2015). Establishing the psychometric properties of the Self and Perceived-Partner Authenticity in Relationships Scale—Short Form (AIRS–SF): Measurement invariance, reliability, and incremental validity. *Personality and Individual Differences*, *77*, 62–67. http://dx.doi.org/10.1016/j.paid.2014.12.049

Wiederman, M. W. (1997). Extramarital sex: Prevalence and correlates in a national survey. *Journal of Sex Research*, *34*, 167–174. http://dx.doi.org/10.1080/00224499709551881

Wilkins, A. C., & Dalessandro, C. (2013). Monogamy lite: Cheating, college, and women. *Gender & Society*, *27*, 728–751. http://dx.doi.org/10.1177/0891243213483878

Williams, G. C. (1992). *Natural selection*. New York, NY: Oxford University Press.

Winnicott, D. W. (1956). On transference. *The International Journal of Psychoanalysis*, *37*, 386–388.

World Health Organization. (1992). *The ICD–10 classification of mental and behavioural disorders: Clinical descriptions and diagnostic guidelines*. Geneva, Switzerland: World Health Organization.

Wu, C. H., & Yang, C.-T. (2012). Attachment and exploration in adulthood: The mediating effect of social support. *International Journal of Psychology*, *47*, 346–354. http://dx.doi.org/10.1080/00207594.2012.658402

Yeomans, F., Clarkin, J., & Kernberg, O. (2015). *Transference-focused psychotherapy for the borderline personality disorder: A clinical guide*. Washington, DC: American Psychiatric Association Press.

Yule, M. A., Brotto, L. A., & Gorzalka, B. B. (2015). A validated measure of no sexual attraction: The Asexuality Identification Scale. *Psychological Assessment*, *27*, 148–160. http://dx.doi.org/10.1037/a0038196

Zapf, J. L., Greiner, J., & Carroll, J. (2008). Attachment styles and male sex addiction. *Sexual Addiction & Compulsivity*, *15*, 158–175. http://dx.doi.org/10.1080/10720160802035832

Zetterberg, H. L. (1966). The secret ranking. *Journal of Marriage and the Family*, *28*, 134–142. http://dx.doi.org/10.2307/349268

Zitzman, S. T., & Butler, M. H. (2009). Wives' experience of husbands' pornography use and concomitant deception as an attachment threat in the adult pair-bond relationship. *Sexual Addiction & Compulsivity*, *16*, 210–240. http://dx.doi.org/10.1080/10720160903202679

INDEX

ABOUT THE AUTHOR

Lawrence Josephs, PhD, is a professor of psychology at the Gordon F. Derner Institute of Advanced Psychological Studies of Adelphi University. Dr. Josephs has been an editor for the *International Journal of Psychoanalysis*, book reviewer for *Psychoanalytic Psychology*, and a manuscript reviewer for *Clinical Psychology and Psychotherapy*. He has published articles in *Archives of Sexual Behavior*, *Journal of Sex and Marital Therapy*, *Self and Identity*, *International Journal of Psychoanalysis*, *Psychoanalytic Psychology*, *Psychoanalytic Dialogues*, *Contemporary Psychoanalysis*, *Journal of the American Psychoanalytic Association*, and *Psychodynamic Psychiatry*. In 2015 *The New York Times* published an op-ed piece written by Dr. Josephs called "When the Best Sex is Extra-Marital." Dr. Josephs has a private practice of individual and couples psychotherapy in New York City.